Horizons

Preschool

Teacher's Guide
Part 1
Lessons 1-90

Authors
Alan L. Christopherson, M.S.
Alpha Omega Publications

Original Interlock Curriculum by
Rebecca L. Avery

Adaptation/Revision for Horizons Preschool by
Marilyn Zent Schlitz
Alpha Omega Publications

Editor
Jeannie Burrus, B.S.

Illustrations & Layout
Jennifer Davis

 AOP

804 N. 2nd Ave. E.   Rock Rapids, IA 51246-1759   800-622-3070   www.aop.com

Horizons Preschool Teacher's Guide, Part 1
Copyright © MMVII

Alpha Omega Publications, Inc.®
804 N. 2nd Ave. E.
Rock Rapids, IA 51246-1759
All rights reserved.

A Horizons Preschool Student Book should be purchased for each student, whether in the Christian School classroom or in the Homeschool. In the classroom setting, always order one extra for the teacher so that you have copies of everything to reference. Students will take home the pages of the Student Book throughout the year.

You may use whatever Bible version your family studies. Horizons Preschool uses the KJV King James Version and the NIV New International Version of the Bible. Scripture is taken from the HOLY BIBLE, NEW INTERNATIONAL VERSION® Copyright © 1973, 1978, 1984 by International Bible Society. Used by permission of Zondervan. All Rights Reserved.

Original Weaver Interlock Copyright© 1987; Revised 1991, 1992, 1996, 2000

Printed in the United States of America

ISBN 978-0-7403-1449-0

Table of Contents

Scope & Sequence 2

Introduction 4

    Understanding the Young Child 4

    The Environment of the School 5

    The Classroom 6

    Determining Your Type of Program 7

    Components of the Horizons Preschool Program 8

    Lesson Structure of the Horizons Preschool Program 10

    Things to do Before School Begins 13

    Scheduling Suggestions 14

Media Resources 15

    Multimedia 15

    Internet Links 25

    Optional Reading Resources 25

    Optional Story Time Reading List 25

Supplies 28

    Student, Room, and General Supplies 28

    Weekly Supplies (Lessons 1-180) 31

Memory Verses 39

Days of Creation Numbers 40

Horizons Preschool Music CD Lyrics 41

Lessons 45

Horizons Preschool Scope and Sequence

The following list gives a breakdown by lesson groupings of the concepts that are covered in the preschool program. This list is certainly not exhaustive and primarily serves to illustrate the depth and progression of concepts as they are presented.

Lessons 1-30

- Day 1 – Day 3 of Creation
- God, Jesus, Holy Spirit, light, darkness, air, clouds, dry land, rocks
- Finger and action activities, spatial concepts, lists, names, sort, compare, rhyme, describe, classify
- Letter recognition Aa-Ii
- Numerals 1-6
- Oral counting 1-10
- Recognize red, green, blue, black, white, yellow
- Identify triangle, circle, and square
- Recognize first name, read an illustrated schedule
- Trace first two letters of first name
- Color, glue, stamp, draw, shape, fold, trace, cut, paint
- Self space, general space, ball activities, ribbon sticks, rhythm, run, skip, jump

Lessons 31-60

- Day 3 – Day 4 of Creation
- Soil, plants, grasses, seeds, trees, fruits, vegetables, sun, weather, day, night, seasons, hour
- Sort, solve puzzles, finger activities, label, vocabulary development
- Letter recognition Jj-Ss
- Numerals 7-10, 0
- Oral counting 0-10
- Recognize purple, orange, gray
- Identify rectangle, star
- Trace letters of first name
- Write the first letter of first name
- Glue, shape, paint, draw, solve puzzles, construct, color, stamp
- Jump, crawl, ribbon sticks, hopscotch, stretch, exercise

Lessons 61-90

- Day 4 of Creation
- Seasons, Earth's rotation, Earth's tilt, Moon, stars, constellations, astronomy, planets, comets, meteors
- Action rhymes, stories, finish stories, complete sentences, verbalize concepts, answer questions, rhyme, naming, comparing, vocabulary development, grouping
- Letter recognition Ss-Zz
- Letter sounds Aa-Bb
- Numerals 10-12
- Oral counting 0-20
- Tell time to the hour
- Addition 1 + 1

- Identify star, heart, oval
- Review colors
- Write first name with a guide
- Cut, shape, glue, draw, interpret, cut, assemble, trace
- Walk, skip, hop, balance beam, launch board, ballet
- Fire safety

Lessons 91-120

- Day 5 – Day 6 of Creation
- Fish, climate, ocean creatures, amphibians, eggs, birds, animals, mammals
- Comparison, action rhymes, role play, imitate, describe, finger play, rhyme, classify, vocabulary development, alphabetical order
- Letter sounds Cc-Ii
- Blend letter sounds Aa-Hh
- Write first name without a guide
- Addition 2 + 1, 3 + 1, 4 + 1
- Identify diamond, pictograph
- Shape, color, cut, glue, label, draw
- Catch, jump, ribbon dance, throw, fine motor skills

Lessons 121-150

- Day 6 of Creation
- Reptiles, insects, man, cells, senses, bones, digestion, breathing, muscles
- Size relationships, comparison, guessing, role play, describe, alphabetize, chart, vocabulary development, classify, sort
- Letter sounds Jj-Rr
- Blend letter sounds Aa-Rr
- Write home address and phone number
- Addition 5 + 1
- Subtraction 2 – 1, 3 – 1
- Review shapes
- Type one's name
- Mold, string, shape, paint, draw, stamp, cut, glue, trace
- Crawl, walk, jumping jacks, bowling, crouch & jump, ride tricycles, ring toss

Lessons 151-180

- Day 6 – Day 7 of Creation, Noah's flood
- Blood, circulation, brain, body parts, occupations, health & safety, music, work, rules, helpers, friends, family, promises, flood
- Letter sounds Ss-Zz
- Blend letter sounds Aa-Zz
- Write home address and phone number
- Initial sound of shape words
- Subtract 4 - 1, 5 – 1, 6 – 1
- Cut glue, shape, draw, color, paint, decorate
- Ring toss, swinging, bowling, dribble, kick, throw, rhythm sticks, ball rolling, tag, tumbling

Introduction

A preschool program is now a part of the Horizons product line. This program will serve as both a complement and an introduction to the other fine Horizons products. Give your preschoolers a foundation that will help them to be successful in kindergarten with this flexible and comprehensive curriculum choice from the Horizons series.

Our goal in early childhood education is to develop the best style of education, the optimum learning environment and to establish within the child the correct foundation emotionally, intellectually, socially, and spiritually.

Horizons Preschool is based upon the most perfect source available, the Bible. You and your students will be studying the world around you from the viewpoint of the Creator. Lessons begin with a Bible concept and flow into activities and academic subjects including social studies, language arts, math, phonics and science. Arts and crafts, music, story times, outdoor excursions, and other exciting learning activities enhance the student lessons. The Teacher's Guides contain daily lesson plans making learning and teaching fun and easy. *Horizons Preschool* helps students gain the important knowledge that God is the beginning of all things. It gives them a perspective of the world which can be gained in no other way.

The *Horizons Preschool* program is adaptable to many school situations, the home school, a day care setting or the traditional school classroom. Five days a week are provided, with the understanding that any number of days per week may be used successfully. New concepts are introduced on days 1, 3, and 5 of the week. Days 2 and 4 have activities that expand and further practice those concepts. You will be given a variety of learning experiences from which to choose in the material. Students coming into this program with preschool exposure will be more successful with the fine motor skills required to complete some of the worksheets. Students with less background may need more time writing letters in corn meal, sand or whipped cream. The great thing is that you will have lots of ideas to choose from in running a program that fits your situation.

Understanding the Young Child

As teachers and parents, we desire the best for our students. We go to great lengths to assure that they receive a good education. We want an environment where a child can freely explore the world using the five senses, feelings, and intellect to encompass the world. This type of a learning environment is rarely found in any school. What then, are the factors that give a special quality to the learning that will take place?

A young child is not at a mental distance from the world. A child will put his or her hand flat on the summer turf, feel it, and give a little shiver of private glee at the elastic firmness of the globe. They are not thinking how well it will do for some game, or to feed the sheep upon, they have an ecstatic sense of the thing's inherent characteristics. The image in the mind, and the actual object, are not clearly differentiated for the young child. The almost obsessive concern of some adults with reason and intellectualizing is not present in the young child. It isn't there to act as a barrier to the process of feeling deeply and gaining pleasure from sensual experience. A young child takes an element of our world and makes it their own. It is this personal relationship, this intermingling of self and experience that is characteristic of the development of understanding in young children. The knowledge is always acquired with personal sensual experience and it is in this way that a child gets close to the "inherent characteristics" of things.

An observant teacher will note that there is a world of difference between the learning experience in which the child is personally involved and one in which they are "going through the motions" with a task regarded as "school learning." We desire for the child to be personally involved. This can only occur through real-life, hands-on, manipulative experiences; i.e., through the use of as many of the five senses as possible. What the child feels, they internalize. And what they have internalized, they have learned, for learning is internalization.

We must also come to the realization that to the child there is no separation between the experience of the object at hand and themselves. Knowing this, the teacher understands that while we may separate subjects in our mind and call them Social Studies and Science, they are not so to the child. Nor should they be presented as such. These subjects are simply another part of the student's world, and rightly so, for in the integration of an experience into self true learning is achieved.

If we can grasp this understanding of a young child, we will save ourselves a tremendous amount of time and energy. The normal sequence of teaching involves the teaching of separation of subjects, and then, when the child has learned that, an attempt to integrate the subjects again. The resulting confusion is not necessary.

The *Horizons Preschool* has integrated the subject materials for you throughout the lessons. Although we have listed them in categories, you will want to flow between the lessons without notifying your students of a change in what you are teaching. Each lesson is formulated to flow smoothly, discussing the same subject throughout, and giving the child opportunities to explore, through various senses, the world about him or her. We do not desire to begin with a list of subjects, but rather with the child's relationship with the world. We desire to teach the child HOW to think rather than WHAT to think.

Following the teaching period, the child will also require a time period for internalizing what has been taught. An indication of internalization of teaching will occur when the child begins to play the subject that has been taught. The allowance for a play period is, therefore, very important to the school, as this is how the child learns. The concept is that the teacher should allow for a play period, and not expect the child to have internalized the materials presented before an adequate time span has passed.

In understanding and evaluating your student, you must decide when to make them a "student." How old should a "preschooler" be? All students are different at different ages so it makes sense that there is no hard and fast age to consider your child a preschooler. The usual age for starting *Horizons Preschool* is four years old. But there are three year olds that are more than ready, anxious to do school. And there are five year olds that simply aren't ready yet. This is a decision totally up to the parents and their observation of the child. If you just can't decide, try it. The child will let you know by complaint and disinterest if they aren't ready. The most important rule is "Don't Push." Let the child's actions and desires guide your decision, not their age.

The Environment of the School

The first step to successful education in early childhood is discipline. You need to discipline your students with a Godly perspective. Your students need to obey your voice command. They need to know the limits you have set. This gives them a sense of security, a sense of being loved.

There are many wonderful Christian books on the market about discipline. We suggest you read the books by Dr. James Dobson, Dr. Raymond Moore's writings on the subject, and *The Hurried Child* by David Elkind. Charles Stanley's book *How To Keep Your Children On Your Team* is also excellent. These books will give you an overall view of Godly discipline and how our society interacts with children. Godly discipline should be a priority in the home before formal education is begun.

The second step (but more important than the first) in successful education is the teacher's and/or parent's relationship with God. You cannot teach your students about someone whom you do not know. Throughout this course you will be using the Word of God in depth to teach about the world around us. You need to know the Creator on a personal level. When you do, you then have access to the wisest Teacher on earth from whom to learn.

The third step is the routine of your school. Students need to have a set routine which guides their days and nights. Without this, they lose their sense of judgment as to the time and the occurrence of things. A routine gives the child the security needed to expand their world. This is true for the home school and for the traditional school.

We suggest that the preschool student have no more than two hours of actual school. By interspersing action activities and meaningful play between the quieter academic sessions you will fill the time that is available. Morning time usually works better as the child is refreshed. Planning a schedule will benefit the teacher more than the child. Even though you retain a routine for school, let the teaching time be natural and flexible.

Knowing that the young child learns best by doing, you will want to plan the day to include times when everyone is working together at a task. In this way the child learns how to do a variety of things. Encourage the children to learn to do some of the jobs around the house and/or classroom. A four year old is quite capable of dusting, straightening books, or cleaning up toys. Give sufficient work so that the student realizes that they are a productive part of the society of your classroom or home. This type of scheduling alone will greatly improve his or her self-esteem.

As noted previously, internalization of what you have taught and what the child has experienced will only take place through play. The child needs to have sufficient unstructured time to play. It is only through play that the child relives, rethinks, and clarifies what they have seen and done. Following field trips and time spent "studying," give students the opportunity to verbalize and recreate their experience. Knowing this, the wise teacher not only allows for play time, but encourages it. If you will listen to your students while they play, it will give you an insight into what they have understood of the materials you have presented.

The Classroom

The environment at school needs to be clean and safe. Make it a school habit that everything is back in its place at the end of every day. Develop a routine of basic cleaning. Regularly spray and wipe any toys or manipulatives with disinfectant.

Consistency is the key to a smoothly running school. Make sure there is a big clock with large easy-to-read hands at the front of the room. Print out your basic schedule and post it in two or three places around the room. This said, remember that the schedule is your guide, not your task master.

We have scheduled the teaching lessons to cover five days a week. We suggest that if you want to do a three day school, that you chose Days 1, 3, and 5. If you are running a half day program you will want to select activities that can be completed in the time that is available. There are 180 lessons in this guide, so in some situations where a three day school is in session on a year long basis most of the lessons in this guide can be covered.

Set aside a special area where school supplies are kept. The child needs to know where supplies needed for creativity are kept and that they can reach them without your help. Include in this area glue, children's scissors, pencils, paper, color crayons, and colored markers. As the year progresses, add pets, plants, bulletin boards, and other items that will add to the educational environment. A supply list is included in this guide.

Younger children in the home may often distract you in the homeschool. Keep special toys for them to play with during your schooling time. This should be the only time they are allowed to play with these toys. Should the younger child be closer to the age of the preschool age child, you may use some of the preschool level with them. We caution you not to push the young child into work above their own level. Rather, let him exist along with your teaching, gaining what he will. As the younger child grows, they can be trained to sit still by gradually increasing the time they spend with you in a required quiet time. The homeschool works best if a special room is set aside as a classroom. At the least, have a bookcase set aside for school supplies, notebooks, and school work.

There are many wonderful books available for the Preschool age student. Try to provide good books in the classroom at all times. Purchase those that you can, then use the library regularly.

In the traditional school, make sure to provide a special cubby, drawer or cubicle for each student. Stacking plastic drawers work very well. Any personal items may be kept in the cubby. Notes for the parents have a better chance of success for reaching them if put in the cubby. Each student needs a small pillow or blanket for rest times.

Determining Your Type of Program

The *Horizons Preschool* program has been designed to meet the needs of two different types of pre-school programs. We will call them an *activity*-centered program and an *academically*-centered program. What's the difference? An *activity*-centered program places a stronger focus on meaningful play. Students form letter shapes with their bodies, write letters in pans of sand and/or cornmeal, trace the shapes of large felt letters. They build letters out of sticks, toys or items glued onto paper. Oral counting is practiced by counting objects as they encounter them in their surroundings. In this setting you see more emphasis on social skills, speaking skills, large motor development and discovery.

An *academically* centered program places more emphasis on a structured classroom setting. Students not only learn to recognize letters of the alphabet, they also learn to write them and learn introductory phonics skills that teaches them to sound out and read words. In addition to counting objects, they learn to recognize and write numbers, and begin to practice addition and subtraction skills. These students are talking about stories that the teacher reads, acting them out and creating new endings. Fine motor skills of cutting, pasting, coloring, and writing are used to complete worksheets and projects. The teacher spends a short portion of each day "teaching" with lecture, demonstration, review, and group practice of the concepts.

What does this mean to you? Basically, it means that there is far more material presented in this teacher's guide than what some classes of students can cover. You as the teacher or school administrator must first decide the overall goals and objectives for your school. From there you can use this teacher's guide to pick out the specific activities that support your philosophy of education. If the emphasis of the school is focused on meaningful play, you will choose activities from the guide that support that focus. If the emphasis is academic, you will select activities that include the worksheets and a deeper study of the concepts. For either program this guide provides a basic structure and sequence of activities.

We have also tried to accommodate the various schedules of the typical preschool programs. Some are half-day programs, some are three-day programs and some are all-day programs. Obviously, if the guide contains enough material for an all-day program the others must pick and choose activities based upon their school's goals and objectives. Because some of the three-day and half-day programs may be either activity or academically focused, this guide makes no attempt to make the decision for you as to which activities are recommended for the various programs.

Another factor that will determine the selection of activities is the previous experience of your students. During the school year you will have to take the students from where they currently are with their skills and abilities to where your school has determined they should be by the end of the year. As the instructor you must bridge whatever gap exists between the student's previous "school" experience and the goals and objectives of your school. If your students come from a play centered three year-old preschool program and you wish to be more academically focused, the gap to bridge will be greater and the activities you choose from the guide will be different than those one would choose if their students came from an experience with more academic focus.

It has been necessary to assume in designing this teacher's guide that the preschool teachers who will be using it have experience, training or knowledge of how to run a preschool program. We have not gone into detail about learning center layout, schedules, procedures, strategies or methods. There is enough here in the guide to give you direction but not enough to dictate what is done every minute of the preschool day. The guide suggests the concept to teach. For example, if you are to teach the letter M, whether you do board work, air writing, writing in sand/cornmeal, flashcards, felt shapes, body shapes or whatever to teach the concept has been left up to you. Through experience and practice a teacher "finds" her own methods of instruction that fit both her own personality and the needs of her students. Methods are a variable that each teacher must learn and develop on her own. If you are apprehensive about this issue there are plenty of methods resources available either from print resources or on the internet. You will be amazed at the volume of preschool information available on the internet. For some reason this group of people loves to share and display what they have learned about their preschool experience.

Components of the Horizons Preschool Program

This product has several distinctive components.

1. **Horizons Preschool Student Workbooks** contain the consumable student materials. Consumables are items that a student uses once either for arts and crafts or for practice in math, phonics or other academic topics.

   The 180 student lessons have been separated into two books. **Student Book 1** has lessons 1-90 and **Student Book 2** has lessons 91-180. These are 4-color; perfect-bound books with perforated pages for easy tear out. Most pages are front and back but some are 1-sided to be cut out for crafts.

2. **Horizons Preschool Teacher's Guide** is a detailed daily lesson planner that includes sufficient activities for a normal school day. The daily lesson planner includes an integrated selection of activities that as naturally as is possible flow from one to the other. All topic areas relate in some way to the themes examined in the Bible lesson for the day.

   The Horizons Preschool Teacher's Guide has 180 lessons. The 180 teacher lessons have been separated into two books. **Teacher's Guide Book 1** has the course introduction and lessons 1-90. **Teacher's Guide Book 2** has the course introduction and lessons 91-180. These are black and white books with a coil binding.

3. **Horizons Preschool Resource Packet** includes full-color **Teaching Aids** and **Black Line Masters** for reproducibles. The **Black Line Masters** include the **Memory Verse** cards, the **Alphabet Puzzle**, and other reproducible items for art and crafts. The **Teaching Aids** pages consist of **Flashcards** and colored pictures of animals, body systems, and other items found in nature that are used to demonstrate and illustrate lesson concepts. There are approximately 300 pages in this packet, of full-color loose sheets, that are shrink wrapped for shipping.

a. **Memory Verse** cards are send-home reproducibles for the memory verses learned in the program. The teacher has the option of choosing either KJV or NIV to reproduce for the memory verses.

b. **Alphabet Puzzle** is a manipulative to aid in teaching letters. The needed puzzle pieces are reproduced and cut out for the students.

c. **Flashcards** are used as manipulatives for teaching concepts. These include **Numbers** (1-12); **Letters** (Aa-Zz); **Colors** (red, green, blue, black, white, yellow, brown, pink, purple, orange, gray); **Shapes** (triangle, circle, square, rectangle, star, heart, oval, diamond); **Time** (analog clocks, digital clocks, and o'clock time to the hour); **Seasons** (Fall, Winter, Spring, Summer); and **Months** (January-December).

The **Numbers** cards have items on them for counting. The **Letters** cards have an animal or item that illustrate the sound that the letter makes. The **Colors** cards have a picture of a fruit or item that normally has the color. The **Shapes** cards are large geometric shapes, colored with the colors being taught in the program. The **Time** cards are very simple with both analog and digital clocks. The **Seasons** cards have illustrations that depict typical events for the season. The **Months** cards have illustrations that depict typical events for the month.

The **Flashcards** include both a handi-size for individual or small class instruction and a display-size which is a full page for large class instruction or wall display. All of the flashcards are two sided. The front side of the card includes a picture clue with the letter or word for the concept. The back side has either the letter or a picture clue for drilling the concept.

4. Several **Multimedia** items are included in the curriculum package. These include:

a. **Horizons Preschool Music CD** of the songs taught to the students that reinforce key topic areas. This has been recorded using some children's voices and serves as a sing-along instructional aid.

b. **Horizons Preschool Multimedia Package** consists of Videos, CDs, and Software that fit the lesson themes from the AOP library of titles. These can be purchased as a package or by individual titles from AOP.

c. **Suggested multimedia that is NOT part of the Package.** There are several recommended items that can be purchased or obtained from other sources.

The Lesson Structure of the Horizons Preschool Program

Each *Horizons Preschool* lesson is divided (for teacher purposes only) into subdivisions of Bible Reference, Bible Concept to Present, Bible Lesson, Social Studies, Science, Language Arts, Phonics, Reading, Writing, Memory Verse, Math, Shapes, Color, Story Time, Music, Health & Safety, Arts & Crafts, Outdoor Activity, Homework, and Physical Education. These divisions will be examined in the paragraphs that follow.

- **Bible Reference** is given for the purpose of going directly to the Scripture and researching any reference previous to teaching. We desire that you understand directly from the Bible what is being taught.

- **Bible Concept to Present** will give you an overall view of what we consider to be the objective of the lesson. This is presented from a nondenominational viewpoint.

- **Bible Lesson** is a format giving you the information that should be presented to the students. We suggest you do not read this directly from the book, but rather interpret it into your own terminology. Any illustration that can be used will supplement and reinforce your teaching.

- **Social Studies** is concerned with how the materials being studied affects the student's lives. Discussed under this subject will be items that have an impact on the child's lifestyle, those people around them, and how we use the Creation of God. Many of the suggestions are activity oriented.

- **Science** is concerned with the details of God's Creation. These are activity oriented ideas with specific subjects discussed. You will want to generally introduce the materials.

- **Language Arts** consists of the verbalization (expression) of ideas and preparatory materials for the teaching of reading. Language Arts in the *Horizons Preschool* includes word exercises, poems, verbalization, games, etc. **Note:** Reading should be taught only when the students are individually ready. Many of the action rhymes do not have specific actions given. This provides an excellent opportunity for you and the students to "create" actions to go along with the rhymes. Do them in an echo, response format, teacher says the verse, students repeat the verse. Some of these will become favorites of the students so repeat them more often than what is suggested in the lesson plan. They also can be dramatized as one group of students says the rhyme and another "acts" it out.

- **Phonics** initially focuses on letter recognition and alphabet order. Associating, differentiating, and blending the letters sounds comprise the remainder of the program. When the student reaches the Kindergarten level, we suggest *LIFEPAC Kindergarten Language Arts* or *Horizons Kindergarten Phonics and Reading*, both available from Alpha Omega Publications.

- **Reading** is an extremely important aspect to the entire program. One of the primary goals for the year is to increase the verbal skills of the students. This is a time when stories are read to the students and they work on listening and comprehension skills. After a story has been read, reviewed, and discussed it can be acted out by one or more students. This will help them learn and remember how to sequence events into a logical order.

- **Writing** is a section that contains general suggestions for building the skills a young child will need to be able to write. A developmental progression of activities is presented with the goal of enabling the student to independently write their first name.

- **Memory Verses** are suggested with ideas to illustrate them. The young child is very capable of memorizing verses of Scripture with the help of the teacher and repetition. The planting of the seeds of the Word of God now will aid the child greatly in the future. As it is common with young children to easily memorize, you will be surprised at the rapid rate with which they can learn the verses. Have them learn the verse, then the reference. Always insist that they add the reference to the end of their recitation. We give you the verses from the both the New International Version and the King James Version of the Bible. However, you may use whichever version your school prefers. There are reproducibles in the *Horizons Preschool Resource Packet* for both KJV and NIV. Make copies of the version that you wish to use for sending home with the students. We give you new verses almost every week, but the choice of how many to do is up to the teacher.

- **Math** lessons are planned to teach the fundamentals of number sense. They are multi-sensory experiences to aid the child in the acquisition of skills. Counting and number recognition are the initial focus with simple addition and subtraction concepts closing out the year. When the student reaches the Kindergarten level, we suggest *LIFEPAC Kindergarten Math* or *Horizons Kindergarten Math*, both available from Alpha Omega Publications.

- **Shapes** lessons will introduce and provide practice in identifying the basic geometric shapes that a student will need to be able to recognize in kindergarten. A new shape to study is introduced about every two weeks. Through the year the students will learn to recognize the circle, triangle, rectangle, square, star, heart, oval, and diamond shapes.

- **Colors** lessons will introduce and provide practice in identifying the basic colors that a student will need to be able to recognize in kindergarten. A new color to study is introduced about every two weeks. Through the year the students will learn to recognize the red, green, blue, black, white, yellow, brown, pink, purple, orange, and gray colors.

- **Story Time** is a wonderful time to generate an excitement for reading. In a very short time the preschoolers will begin to see letters as words, words as sentences, and sentences as stories. Stories create a visual image of an object or an event. Storybook reading is an effective means of helping the preschool child improve their vocabulary. With strong vocabulary skills a young child is better prepared to begin reading on their own. They then can focus on gaining skill in decoding words that already have meaning for them.

Story Time for the *Horizons Preschool* program has been left very open. We have provided a list of possible books to use but often do not give a specific book in the lesson plan. This gives you, the teacher, the opportunity to pick books from our list or use others that you like or have found work well with your students. We have included the list only to get you started in selecting the books that you will use with your program. There are many different opinions about what books are appropriate for preschool children. We have attempted to provide a balanced list that includes conservative, modern, classic, and traditional titles. We would recommend that you begin by borrowing books from a local library before you develop a list of titles that you would like to purchase and add to your classroom collection of resources. Any of the poems in this guide can be read again at a later time as part of the story time.

The books that you read during story time should be read several times. Each time you are helping the students to deepen their vocabulary skills. Spend time talking about and retelling the stories. Work on both listening and speaking skills during story time. Talk about the setting, the characters, and the sequence of events in the story. Stop at strategic times in the story to ask the students to predict what might happen next. Give the students an opportunity to use their imaginations to create a story based on the pictures or in creating a new ending for the story. Discuss the book format with title pages, illustrations, and story lines. Review the problem, conflict or question raised by the story, and how it is resolved in the sequence of events.

One day of the week could be used for story favorites. Allow the students to select books that have already been read or to bring books from home for this special day. Seeing what books are brought from home will give you an insight into what recommendations need to be given to parents. Encourage the parents to read to their preschooler on a regular basis. This will reinforce what they are learning in the classroom.

- **Music** is suggested for each lesson. You will find the tune to the songs suggested listed for you. Should they not be familiar tunes, the "Horizons Preschool Music" CD will have many of the songs for you. The songs are either character building songs or teaching songs that help to reinforce concepts. There is nothing wrong with making up a new melody for any of the teaching songs. Each new song appears in the lesson plan for seven lessons. This doesn't mean that you cannot use them any more, in fact some will become favorites of the students and they will ask to sing them very often. A few of the lessons do not specify any songs for the music time, on these days do any of the teaching songs that the students need or let them sing any of their favorites.

- **Arts & Crafts** are the process by which children create. We have given you the suggestion of the medium; the child will add the ideas. Note what the creates and praise them highly for work accomplished. Provide time for this activity to occur. Arts & Crafts are designed for sharpening the skills of observation in the child and for familiarizing them with various art tools. Do not expect perfect performance in these projects. The action involved will be of more value to the child than a perfect project.

- **Physical Education** is designed to not only be subject oriented when possible, but to develop the motor coordination needed in the child previous to the teaching of reading. Be certain your student is in good health prior to any exercise period. The physical education time should be used to develop the large muscle motor skills so the student can move with gracefulness and rhythm.

- **Outdoor Activities** are a time to observe the wonders of Creation and the responsibility for caring for it.

- **Creative Cooking** is the fun part to learning. It is a way to involve more of the senses in the learning process.

- **Health & Safety** is learning habits of hygiene and everyday safety skills.

- **Field Trips** are another way for the students to experience first hand what they have been learning. Suggestions are given for possible field trips. It is not necessary that the trip occur on the day that it is mentioned in a lesson. Look ahead so that you can be prepared. These do not need to be complicated or elaborate. Simply walking down the street and around the corner to visit a grocery store can serve as an excellent field trip.

Make arrangements to have some parents help with the supervision of the students. As an alternative have an "expert" come in and to give a simple demonstration to the students. Use the ideas that are given in the lessons as a springboard to come up with your own plans for a field trip.

- **Homework** pages are provided in the *Horizons Preschool Student Books*. Traditional school teachers may send the pages home with students as directed. Homeschool teachers may use the pages as they choose. These pages might be done with dad in the evenings. The main goal of the homework pages is to involve parents in what the student is learning.

- **Catch Up** time is listed every six to eight weeks. When you don't have time to do a lesson, make a note to save it for a Catch Up day.

Things to do Before School Begins

Make *Name Plates* for each student. Several will be needed for each student. Themed or seasonal ones will add color and interest to the classroom and can be either made or purchased. One name plate for each child should be taped to the top of the table where you want him/her to sit. Another set of name plates should hang on a bulletin board as a class roster. Another set can be used for flashcards in helping the students learn to read the names of their classmates.

Make a simplified, illustrated *Daily Schedule* of activities. This can be a poster or section of a bulletin board. If the activities are put on individual cards the schedule can be easily rearranged. If you plan to vary the schedule for each day of the week a weekly schedule may be needed.

Purchase or make a *Monthly Calendar*. This should be a blank template where the name of the month and the numbers for the dates can be changed each month. Themed artwork for the month will make this colorful and interesting for the students.

Plan to have the *visuals* constructed well ahead of the time that they are needed. There may be ways in which you can involve the students in making some of these.

Scheduling Suggestions

The difficult thing about scheduling is that each day is different. Science might take ten minutes on Monday and forty minutes on Thursday. Wednesday might include music while Friday has no music. These schedule plans are merely to be guidelines or suggestions. Use them with much flexibility.

HALF-DAY SCHEDULE

9:00	Bible Time
9:20	Social Studies/Science/Language Arts
10:00	Snack
10:15	Recess/Play break
10:30	Phonics/Memory Verse
10:45	Music/Physical Education/Health & Safety
11:00	Math
11:30	Arts & Crafts/Outdoor activity
12:00	Dismiss

ALL-DAY SCHEDULE

9:00	Bible Time
9:20	Social Studies/Science/Language Arts
10:00	Snack
10:15	Recess/Play break
10:30	Phonics/Memory Verse
11:00	Music/Physical Education
11:30	Math
12:00	Lunch break
12:20	Recess/Play break
12:50	Reading
1:20	Arts & Crafts
1:40	Health & Safety/Outdoor activity
2:00	Dismiss

Preparing Ahead: *Horizons Preschool* helps you prepare ahead by *ITALICIZING* things that need to be done ahead of school time.

Naptime: Many preschool children will need a time to rest if they are involved in an all-day program. This is an excellent time to read a story to the children. You can also review the shapes of figures, letters or numbers by drawing them on the ceiling with a flashlight while the room is dark. Each student should have a rug, mat or blanket on which to lie down on the floor.

Cubbies: Each student should have their own cubby or box in which to store their crayons, scissors, counters, shapes, flashcards, etc. Students may need both a cubby and a pencil box. If the cubbies are large enough they can store sleeping mats, jackets, etc. in them.

Media Resources

The following resources will need to be obtained in advance of when they are needed for the Lessons. They can be used several times if desired.

Lesson 1:
"Love" from the *Character Builders* video series
"The Amazing Book" CD

Lesson 2:
"Music Machine: The Majesty of God" CD
"The Amazing Book" CD

Lesson 3:
"Bullfrogs and Butterflies: God Loves Fun" CD
"The Amazing Book" CD

Lesson 4:
"The Amazing Book" CD

Lesson 5:
"Music Machine" video
"The Amazing Book" CD

Lesson 6:
"Music Machine: The Majesty of God" CD
"Rev-Up for Learning: Reading, Writing, & Arithmetic" DVD
"Bullfrogs and Butterflies: God is Great" CD
"Horizons Preschool Music" CD

Lesson 7:
"Bullfrogs and Butterflies: God is Great" CD

Lesson 8:
"Music Machine: The Majesty of God" CD
"Sir Oliver's Song" CD
"Politeness" from the *Character Builders* video series
"Bullfrogs and Butterflies: God is Great" CD

Lesson 9:
"Joy" from the *Character Builders* video series
"Bullfrogs and Butterflies: God is Great" CD

Lesson 10:
"Bullfrogs and Butterflies: God Loves Fun" CD
"Sharing" from the *Character Builders* video series
"Bullfrogs and Butterflies: God is Great" CD

Lesson 11:
"The Amazing Miracles" CD
"Rev-Up for Learning: Reading, Writing, & Arithmetic" DVD
"Music Machine: The Majesty of God" CD
Where Does Electricity Come From?, Usborne Publishers

Lesson 12:
"Bullfrogs and Butterflies: I've Been Born Again" CD
"Music Machine: The Majesty of God" CD
A simple biography of Helen Keller

Lesson 13:
"Music Machine: The Majesty of God" CD
A simple biography of Helen Keller
"Horizons Preschool Music" CD

Lesson 14:
"Music Machine: The Majesty of God" CD
A simple biography of Helen Keller

Lesson 15:
"Music Machine: The Majesty of God" CD
A simple biography of Helen Keller

Lesson 16:
"Rev-Up for Learning: Reading, Writing, & Arithmetic" DVD
"Bullfrogs and Butterflies: God is My Friend" CD
"Horizons Preschool Music" CD

Lesson 17:
"Faith" from the *Character Builders* video series
"Bullfrogs and Butterflies: God is My Friend" CD

Lesson 18:
"Horizons Preschool Music" CD
"Bullfrogs and Butterflies: God is My Friend" CD

Lesson 19:
  "Bullfrogs and Butterflies: God is My Friend" CD

Lesson 20:
  "Bullfrogs and Butterflies: God Loves Fun" CD
  "Bullfrogs and Butterflies: God is My Friend" CD

Lesson 21:
  "Self Control" from the *Character Builders* video series
  "The Amazing Children" CD
  "Rev-Up for Learning: Reading, Writing, & Arithmetic" DVD

Lesson 22:
  "The Amazing Children" CD

Lesson 23:
  "Bullfrogs and Butterflies: God is Great" CD
  "Music Machine: The Fruit of the Spirit" CD
  "Horizons Preschool Music" CD
  "The Amazing Children" CD

Lesson 24:
  "The Amazing Children" CD

Lesson 25:
  "Music Machine: The Majesty of God" CD
  "The Amazing Children" CD

Lesson 26:
  "The Amazing Miracles" CD
  "Nathaniel the Grublet" CD
  "Rev-Up for Learning: Reading, Writing, & Arithmetic" DVD

Lesson 27:
  "Bullfrogs and Butterflies: God Loves Fun" CD
  "Nathaniel the Grublet" CD

Lesson 28:
  "Nathaniel the Grublet" CD

Lesson 29:
  "Nathaniel the Grublet" CD

Lesson 30:
  "Bullfrogs and Butterflies: God Loves Fun" CD
  "The Amazing Children" CD
  "Nathaniel the Grublet" CD

Lesson 31:
  "The Amazing Miracles" CD
  "Rev-Up for Learning: Reading, Writing, & Arithmetic" DVD
  "Horizons Preschool Music" CD

Lesson 32:
  "The Amazing Miracles" CD

Lesson 33:
  "Patience" from the *Character Builders* video series
  "The Amazing Miracles" CD

Lesson 34:
  "The Amazing Miracles" CD

Lesson 35:
  "Horizons Preschool Music" CD
  "The Amazing Miracles" CD

Lesson 36:
  "Bullfrogs and Butterflies: I've Been Born Again" CD
  "Rev-Up for Learning: Reading, Writing, & Arithmetic" DVD

Lesson 37:
  "Bullfrogs and Butterflies: I've Been Born Again" CD

Lesson 38:
  "Bullfrogs and Butterflies: I've Been Born Again" CD

Lesson 39:
  "Bullfrogs and Butterflies: I've Been Born Again" CD

Lesson 40:
  "Bullfrogs and Butterflies: I've Been Born Again" CD

Lesson 41:
  "Bullfrogs and Butterflies: God Loves Fun" CD
  "Music Machine: The Fruit Of The Spirit" CD
  "Rev-Up for Learning: Reading, Writing, & Arithmetic" DVD

Lesson 42:
  "Music Machine: The Fruit Of The Spirit" CD

Lesson 43:
"Music Machine: The Fruit Of The Spirit" CD
First Book of Nature, Usborne Publishers

Lesson 44:
"Music Machine: The Fruit Of The Spirit" CD
Planting a Rainbow, by Lois Ehlert

Lesson 45:
"Music Machine: The Fruit Of The Spirit" CD

Lesson 46:
"Sir Oliver's Song" CD
"Rev-Up for Learning: Reading, Writing, & Arithmetic" DVD
First Book of Nature, Usborne Publishers

Lesson 47:
"The Amazing Miracles" CD
"Sir Oliver's Song" CD

Lesson 48:
"Sir Oliver's Song" CD

Lesson 49:
"Horizons Preschool Music" CD
"Sir Oliver's Song" CD

Lesson 50:
"Sir Oliver's Song" CD

Lesson 51:
"Music Machine: All About Love" CD
"Rev-Up for Learning: Reading, Writing, & Arithmetic" DVD
"Horizons Preschool Music" CD

Lesson 52:
"Music Machine: All About Love" CD

Lesson 53:
"Music Machine: All About Love" CD

Lesson 54:
"Music Machine: All About Love" CD
Eating the Alphabet, by Lois Ehlert

Lesson 55:
"Music Machine: Benny's Biggest Battle" video
"Music Machine: All About Love" CD

Lesson 56:
"Bullfrogs and Butterflies: God is Great" CD
"Sir Oliver's Song" CD
"Bullfrogs and Butterflies: God Loves Fun" CD
"Rev-Up for Learning: Reading, Writing, & Arithmetic" DVD
"Horizons Preschool Music" CD
Rockets and Space Flight, Usborne Publishers

Lesson 57:
"Music Machine: The Majesty of God" CD
"Bullfrogs and Butterflies: God Loves Fun" CD

Lesson 58:
"The Amazing Miracles" CD
"Bullfrogs and Butterflies: God Loves Fun" CD

Lesson 59:
"Bullfrogs and Butterflies: God is Great" CD
"Bullfrogs and Butterflies: God Loves Fun" CD
"The Amazing Miracles" CD

Lesson 60:
"Horizons Preschool Music" CD
"Bullfrogs and Butterflies: God Loves Fun" CD

Lesson 61:
"The Birthday Party" CD
"The Gift" from the *Kingdom Under the Sea* adventure video series
"Rev-Up for Learning: Reading, Writing, & Arithmetic" DVD

Lesson 62:
"Thankfulness" from the *Character Builders* video series
"The Birthday Party" CD
"The Gift" from the *Kingdom Under the Sea* adventure video series

Lesson 63:
"The Birthday Party" CD
"The Gift" from the *Kingdom Under the Sea* adventure video series

Lesson 64:
"The Birthday Party" CD
"The Gift" from the *Kingdom Under the Sea* adventure video series

Lesson 65:

"The Birthday Party" CD
"The Gift" from the *Kingdom Under the Sea* adventure video series

Lesson 66:

"Once Upon A Christmas" CD
"The Gift" from the *Kingdom Under the Sea* adventure video series
"Rev-Up for Learning: Reading, Writing, & Arithmetic" DVD

Lesson 67:

"Joy" from the *Character Builders* video series
"Nathaniel the Grublet" CD
"The Amazing Children" CD
"Once Upon A Christmas" CD
"The Gift" from the *Kingdom Under the Sea* adventure video series

Lesson 68:

"Once Upon A Christmas" CD
"The Gift" from the *Kingdom Under the Sea* adventure video series

Lesson 69:

"Once Upon A Christmas" CD
"The Gift" from the *Kingdom Under the Sea* adventure video series

Lesson 70:

"Once Upon A Christmas" CD
"The Gift" from the *Kingdom Under the Sea* adventure video series

Lesson 71:

"The Birthday Party" CD
"The Gift" from the *Kingdom Under the Sea* adventure video series
"Rev-Up for Learning: Reading, Writing, & Arithmetic" DVD

Lesson 72:

"Peace" from the *Character Builders* video series
"Horizons Preschool Music" CD
"The Birthday Party" CD
"The Gift" from the *Kingdom Under the Sea* adventure video series

Lesson 73:

"Bullfrogs and Butterflies: I've Been Born Again" CD
"The Birthday Party" CD
"The Gift" from the *Kingdom Under the Sea* adventure video series
Rockets and Space Flight, Usborne Publishers

Lesson 74:

"The Birthday Party" CD
"The Gift" from the *Kingdom Under the Sea* adventure video series

Lesson 75:

"The Birthday Party" CD
"The Gift" from the *Kingdom Under the Sea* adventure video series

Lesson 76:

"Music Machine: The Majesty of God" CD
"Once Upon A Christmas" CD
"The Gift" from the *Kingdom Under the Sea* adventure video series
"Rev-Up for Learning: Reading, Writing, & Arithmetic" DVD
The Christian Mother Goose Book of Nursery Rhymes, by Marjorie Ainsborough Decker

Lesson 77:

"Once Upon A Christmas" CD
"The Gift" from the *Kingdom Under the Sea* adventure video series

Lesson 78:

"Once Upon A Christmas" CD
"The Gift" from the *Kingdom Under the Sea* adventure video series

Lesson 79:

"Once Upon A Christmas" CD
"The Gift" from the *Kingdom Under the Sea* adventure video series

Lesson 80:

"Once Upon A Christmas" CD
"The Gift" from the *Kingdom Under the Sea* adventure video series

Lesson 81:

"Rev-Up for Learning: Reading, Writing, & Arithmetic" DVD
"Music Machine: Benny's Biggest Battle" video

Lesson 82:

"Music Machine: Benny's Biggest Battle" video

Lesson 83:
"Music Machine: Benny's Biggest Battle" video

Lesson 84:
"Music Machine: Benny's Biggest Battle" video

Lesson 85:
"Bullfrogs and Butterflies: God Loves Fun" CD
"Music Machine: Benny's Biggest Battle" video

Lesson 86:
"The Amazing Book" CD
"Rev-Up for Learning: Reading, Writing, & Arithmetic" DVD
"Horizons Preschool Music" CD

Lesson 87:
"The Amazing Book" CD

Lesson 88:
"The Amazing Book" CD

Lesson 89:
"The Amazing Book" CD

Lesson 90:
"The Amazing Book" CD

Lesson 91:
"Bullfrogs and Butterflies: God is Great" CD
"The Red Tide" from the *Kingdom Under the Sea* adventure video series
"Rev-Up for Learning: Reading, Writing, & Arithmetic" DVD
"Horizons Preschool Music" CD
First Book of Nature, Usborne Publishers

Lesson 92:
"The Amazing Miracles" CD
"Bullfrogs and Butterflies: God is Great" CD
"The Red Tide" from the *Kingdom Under the Sea* adventure video series

Lesson 93:
"Bullfrogs and Butterflies: God is Great" CD
"The Red Tide" from the *Kingdom Under the Sea* adventure video series

Lesson 94:
"Bullfrogs and Butterflies: God is Great" CD
"The Red Tide" from the *Kingdom Under the Sea* adventure video series

Lesson 95:
"Bullfrogs and Butterflies: God is Great" CD
"The Red Tide" from the *Kingdom Under the Sea* adventure video series

Lesson 96:
"Bullfrogs and Butterflies: God is Great" CD
"Bullfrogs and Butterflies: God is My Friend" CD
"Music Machine: The Majesty of God" CD
"Rev-Up for Learning: Reading, Writing, & Arithmetic" DVD

Lesson 97:
"Sharing" from the *Character Builders* video series
"Music Machine: The Majesty of God" CD
The Rainbow Fish, by Marcus Pfister and J. Alison James

Lesson 98:
"Music Machine: The Majesty of God" CD

Lesson 99:
"Music Machine: The Majesty of God" CD
One Fish, Two Fish, Red Fish, Blue Fish, by Dr. Seuss

Lesson 100:
"Music Machine: The Majesty of God" CD

Lesson 101:
"Bullfrogs and Butterflies: God is Great" CD
"Music Machine: The Fruit of the Spirit" CD
"Bullfrogs and Butterflies: God is My Friend" CD
"Rev-Up for Learning: Reading, Writing, & Arithmetic" DVD
"Horizons Preschool Music" CD
First Book of Nature, Usborne Publishers

Lesson 102:
"Bullfrogs and Butterflies: God is My Friend" CD

Lesson 103:
"Bullfrogs and Butterflies: God is My Friend" CD

Lesson 104:
"Bullfrogs and Butterflies: God is My Friend" CD

Feathers for Lunch, by Lois Ehlert

Lesson 105:
"Bullfrogs and Butterflies: God is My Friend" CD

Lesson 106:
"The Amazing Children" CD
"Rev-Up for Learning: Reading, Writing, & Arithmetic" DVD

Lesson 107:
"The Amazing Children" CD

Lesson 108:
"The Amazing Children" CD

Lesson 109:
"The Amazing Children" CD

Lesson 110:
"The Amazing Children" CD

Lesson 111:
"Nathaniel the Grublet" CD
"Rev-Up for Learning: Reading, Writing, & Arithmetic" DVD
First Book of Nature, Usborne Publishers

Lesson 112:
"Nathaniel the Grublet" CD

Lesson 113:
"Nathaniel the Grublet" CD

Lesson 114:
"Nathaniel the Grublet" CD
Stellaluna, by Janell Cannon

Lesson 115:
"Nathaniel the Grublet" CD

Lesson 116:
"Gentleness" from the *Character Builders* video series
"The Amazing Miracles" CD
"Rev-Up for Learning: Reading, Writing, & Arithmetic" DVD

Lesson 117:
"Bullfrogs and Butterflies: God is Great" CD
"Bullfrogs and Butterflies: God Loves Fun" CD
"The Amazing Miracles" CD
Millions of Cats, by Wanda Gag

Lesson 118:
"The Amazing Miracles" CD

Lesson 119:
"Responsibility" from the *Character Builders* video series
"The Amazing Miracles" CD
"Babe" a Universal Studios video

Lesson 120:
"The Amazing Miracles" CD

Lesson 121:
"Bullfrogs and Butterflies: God is Great" CD
"Bullfrogs and Butterflies: I've Been Born Again" CD
"Rev-Up for Learning: Reading, Writing, & Arithmetic" DVD

Lesson 122:
"Bullfrogs and Butterflies: I've Been Born Again" CD
A, You're Adorable, by Buddy Kaye, Fred Wise and Sidney Lippman, illustrated by Martha G. Alexander

Lesson 123:
"Bullfrogs and Butterflies: I've Been Born Again" CD

Lesson 124:
"Bullfrogs and Butterflies: I've Been Born Again" CD

Lesson 125:
"Bullfrogs and Butterflies: I've Been Born Again" CD

Lesson 126:

"Music Machine: The Majesty of God" CD

"Goodness" from the *Character Builders* video series

"Music Machine: The Fruit Of The Spirit" CD

"Rev-Up for Learning: Reading, Writing, & Arithmetic" DVD

"Horizons Preschool Music" CD

First Book of Nature, Usborne Publishers

Lesson 127:

"Music Machine: The Fruit Of The Spirit" CD

Five of the following Eric Carle books: *The Very Hungry Caterpillar, The Grouchy Ladybug, The Honeybee and the Robber, The Very Busy Spider, The Very Quiet Cricket,* or *The Very Lonely Firefly*

Lesson 128:

"Bullfrogs and Butterflies: God is Great" CD

"Bullfrogs and Butterflies: God is My Friend" CD

"Music Machine: The Fruit Of The Spirit" CD

Five of the following Eric Carle books: *The Very Hungry Caterpillar, The Grouchy Ladybug, The Honeybee and the Robber, The Very Busy Spider, The Very Quiet Cricket,* or *The Very Lonely Firefly*

Lesson 129:

"Music Machine: The Fruit Of The Spirit" CD

Five of the following Eric Carle books: *The Very Hungry Caterpillar, The Grouchy Ladybug, The Honeybee and the Robber, The Very Busy Spider, The Very Quiet Cricket,* or *The Very Lonely Firefly*

Lesson 130:

"Bullfrogs and Butterflies: God is Great" CD

"Music Machine: The Fruit Of The Spirit" CD

Five of the following Eric Carle books: *The Very Hungry Caterpillar, The Grouchy Ladybug, The Honeybee and the Robber, The Very Busy Spider, The Very Quiet Cricket,* or *The Very Lonely Firefly*

Lesson 131:

"The Amazing Children" CD

"Sir Oliver's Song" CD

"Rev-Up for Learning: Reading, Writing, & Arithmetic" DVD

Five of the following Eric Carle books: *The Very Hungry Caterpillar, The Grouchy Ladybug, The Honeybee and the Robber, The Very Busy Spider, The Very Quiet Cricket,* or *The Very Lonely Firefly*

Lesson 132:

"Bullfrogs and Butterflies: I've Been Born Again" CD

"Bullfrogs and Butterflies: God Loves Fun" CD

"Sir Oliver's Song" CD

Five of the following Eric Carle books: *The Very Hungry Caterpillar, The Grouchy Ladybug, The Honeybee and the Robber, The Very Busy Spider, The Very Quiet Cricket,* or *The Very Lonely Firefly*

Lesson 133:

"Sir Oliver's Song" CD

The Little Engine That Could, by Watty Piper

Lesson 134:

"Music Machine: The Fruit of the Spirit" CD

"Sir Oliver's Song" CD

Lesson 135:

"Music Machine: The Majesty of God" CD

"Love" from the *Character Builders* video series

"Bullfrogs and Butterflies: God is My Friend" CD

"Sir Oliver's Song" CD

Lesson 136:

"The Story of Little Tree" CD

"Return of the King" from the *Kingdom Under the Sea* adventure video series

"Rev-Up for Learning: Reading, Writing, & Arithmetic" DVD

Lesson 137:

"The Story of Little Tree" CD

"Return of the King" from the *Kingdom Under the Sea* adventure video series

Lesson 138:
"The Story of Little Tree" CD
"Return of the King" from the *Kingdom Under the Sea* adventure video series

Lesson 139:
"The Story of Little Tree" CD
"Return of the King" from the *Kingdom Under the Sea* adventure video series
My Five Senses, by Aliki

Lesson 140:
"The Story of Little Tree" CD
"Return of the King" from the *Kingdom Under the Sea* adventure video series

Lesson 141:
"Bullfrogs and Butterflies: God Loves Fun" CD
"The Story of Little Tree" CD
"Return of the King" from the *Kingdom Under the Sea* adventure video series
"Rev-Up for Learning: Reading, Writing, & Arithmetic" DVD

Lesson 142:
"Music Machine: The Fruit of the Spirit" CD
"Bullfrogs and Butterflies: God is Great" CD
"Rack, Shack, and Benny," a Veggie Tales® movie by Big Idea. Or "Obedience" from the *Character Builders* video series
"The Amazing Miracles" CD
"The Story of Little Tree" CD
"Return of the King" from the *Kingdom Under the Sea* adventure video series

Lesson 143:
"Music Machine: The Fruit of the Spirit" CD
"Horizons Preschool Music" CD
"The Story of Little Tree" CD
"Return of the King" from the *Kingdom Under the Sea* adventure video series
Bread and Jam for Frances, by Russell Hoban (1993)
Gregory, the Terrible Eater, by Mitchell Sharmat
Oliver's Fruit Salad, by Vivian French

Lesson 144:
"Bullfrogs and Butterflies: God is My Friend" CD
"The Story of Little Tree" CD
"Return of the King" from the *Kingdom Under the Sea* adventure video series

Lesson 145:
"The Story of Little Tree" CD
"Return of the King" from the *Kingdom Under the Sea* adventure video series

Lesson 146:
"Music Machine: All About Love" CD
"Rev-Up for Learning: Reading, Writing, & Arithmetic" DVD

Lesson 147:
"Honesty" from the *Character Builders* video series
"Music Machine: All About Love" CD
Dem Bones, by Bob Barner, 1996

Lesson 148:
"Music Machine: All About Love" CD
Oliver's Milk Shake, by Vivian French, 2000

Lesson 149:
"Music Machine: All About Love" CD
Junie B. First Grader: Toothless Wonder, by Barbara Park

Lesson 150:
"Music Machine: All About Love" CD

Lesson 151:
"Bullfrogs and Butterflies: God Loves Fun" CD
"Rev-Up for Learning: Reading, Writing, & Arithmetic" DVD

Lesson 152:
"Music Machine: The Majesty of God" CD
"Bullfrogs and Butterflies: God Loves Fun" CD

Lesson 153:
"Horizons Preschool Music" CD
"Bullfrogs and Butterflies: God Loves Fun" CD

Lesson 154:
"The Amazing Children" CD
"Bullfrogs and Butterflies: God Loves Fun" CD
"Where's God When I'm Scared," a Veggie Tales® video from Big Idea

Lesson 155:
"Love" from the *Character Builders* video series
"The Amazing Book" CD
"Bullfrogs and Butterflies: God Loves Fun" CD

Lesson 156:
"Music Machine: Benny's Biggest Battle" video
"Rev-Up for Learning: Reading, Writing, & Arithmetic" DVD

Lesson 157:
"Kindness" from the *Character Builders* video series
"Music Machine: Benny's Biggest Battle" video
The Berenstain Bears and Too Much Junk Food, by Jan and Stan Berenstain

Lesson 158:
"The Amazing Book" CD
"The Amazing Children" CD
"Music Machine: Benny's Biggest Battle" video
Mike Mulligan and His Steam Shovel, by Virginia Lee Burton. Written in 1939

Lesson 159:
"Music Machine: Benny's Biggest Battle" video

Lesson 160:
"Music Machine: Benny's Biggest Battle" video

Lesson 161:
"Music Machine: The Majesty of God" CD
"Rev-Up for Learning: Reading, Writing, & Arithmetic" DVD
"Horizons Preschool Music" CD
Any one of the following: *The Tale of Peter Rabbit* by Beatrix Potter, *Frog and Toad Are Friends* by Arnold Lobel, *A Bear Called Paddington* by Michael Bond, *Winnie the Pooh* by A. A. Milne, *The Boxcar Children* by Gertrude Chandler Warner, any of the *Little House on the Prairie* books by Laura Ingalls Wilder, *Mr. Popper's Penguins* by Richard Atwater, *Sarah Plain & Tall* & its sequel, *Skylark*, by Patricia MacLachlan, or *Black Beauty* by Anna Sewell

Lesson 162:
"Sir Oliver's Song" CD

Lesson 163:
"Joy" from the *Character Builders* video series
"Horizons Preschool Music" CD
"The Hallelujah Chorus," by George Frideric Handel from *The Messiah* audio CD

Lesson 164:
"Bullfrogs and Butterflies: God Loves Fun" CD
"Faith" from the *Character Builders* video series
"Dave and the Giant Pickle," a Veggie Tales® video from Big Idea

Lesson 165:
"Music Machine: The Majesty of God" CD

Lesson 166:
"Confidence" from the *Character Builders* video series
"Rev-Up for Learning: Reading, Writing, & Arithmetic" DVD

Lesson 167:
"Horizons Preschool Music" CD

Lesson 168:
a baby name book

Lesson 169:
"Bullfrogs and Butterflies: God is My Friend" CD
Stone Soup, by Marcia Brown

Lesson 170:
"Sir Oliver's Song" CD

Lesson 171:
"Kindness" from the *Character Builders* video series
"Rev-Up for Learning: Reading, Writing, & Arithmetic" DVD

Lesson 172:
"Nathaniel the Grublet" CD
"Obedience" from the *Character Builders* video series

Lesson 173:
"Nathaniel the Grublet" CD
"Josh and the Big Wall," a Veggie Tales® video by Big Idea

Lesson 174:
"Sharing" from the *Character Builders* video series
"The Amazing Book" CD
"The Amazing Children" CD

Lesson 175:
"Bullfrogs and Butterflies: God Loves Fun" CD

Lesson 176:
"Faith" from the *Character Builders* video series
"Bullfrogs and Butterflies: God is My Friend" CD
"The Amazing Book" CD or "The Amazing Sing Along" DVD
"The Amazing Miracles" CD or "The Amazing Sing Along" DVD
"Rev-Up for Learning: Reading, Writing, & Arithmetic" DVD

Lesson 177:
"Bullfrogs and Butterflies: God is My Friend" CD
"The Amazing Book" CD or "The Amazing Sing Along" DVD
"The Amazing Miracles" CD or "The Amazing Sing Along" DVD

Lesson 178:
"Bullfrogs and Butterflies: God is My Friend" CD
"The Amazing Book" CD or "The Amazing Sing Along" DVD
"The Amazing Miracles" CD or "The Amazing Sing Along" DVD
"Peace" from the *Character Builders* video series
"Horizons Preschool Music" CD

Lesson 179:
"Bullfrogs and Butterflies: God is My Friend" CD
"The Amazing Book" CD or "The Amazing Sing Along" DVD
"The Amazing Miracles" CD or "The Amazing Sing Along" DVD
"Fantasia 2000" a Disney video
The Honey Makers, by Gail Gibbons (1997)

Internet Links

Occasionally there are some suggested internet links in the lessons. As with all materials found on the internet, these materials need to be used with care and caution. The links were current when this material went to press but since web content is very dynamic the links may no longer point to the correct location. If a link is broken then do a search for keywords that fit the topic. You will find many other sites with good content that can be used to supplement the lesson material.

Reading Resources: Totally optional but very helpful.

The Big Book of Books and Activities: An Illustrated Guide for Teacher, Parents, and Anyone Who Works With Kids!, by Dinah Zike, Dinah-Might Activities, Inc., 1996
Creation Crafts, by Darlene Hoffa, Concordia, 1993
Nature Crafts for Kids, by Diehn and Krautwurst, Sterling Publishers Co., Inc., New York, 1997
Play and Find Out About Science: Easy Experiments for Young Children, by Janice VanCleave, John Wiley & Sons, 1996
Preschool Readiness, by Mary Ellen Quint, Alpha Omega Publications, 800.622.3070
Six-Minute Science Experiments, by Faith Hickman Brynie, Sterling Publishers Co., Inc., 1996
What is Inside You?, Usborne Publishers
What Makes It Rain?, Usborne Publishers
Why Do People Eat?, Usborne Publishers
The Usborne Big Book of Experiments, Usborne Publishers

Story Time Reading List: Optional but very helpful.

A Child's Garden of Verses, by Robert Louis Stevenson (illustrated by Tasha Tudor)
"A Hunting We Will Go," (Traditional Rhyme)
A Rainbow All Around Me, by Sandra L. Pinkney
A Story for Bear, by Dennis Haseley
Aesop's Fables
Agapanthus Hum and Major Bark, by Jennifer Plecas
Alfie Gives a Hand, by Shirley Hughes
Aloha, Dolores, by Barbara Samuels
Alphabet Under Construction, by Denise Fleming
America's Champion Swimmer: Gertrude Ederle, by David A. Adler
"An Old Person From Ware," by Edward Lear (Poem)
Apple Pie 4th of July, by Janet S. Wong
At the Edge of the Woods: A Counting Book, by Cynthia Cotten
"At the Seaside," by Robert Louis Stevenson (Poem)
"Bat, Bat," (Traditional Rhyme)
Beatrix Potter: The Complete Tales, by Beatrix Potter (Peter Rabbit, etc.)
Bedtime for Frances, by Russell Hoban, 1960 (Harper)
Blessings Every Day, by Carla Barnhill, Tyndale House Publishers, Inc.
"Bobby Shafto," (Traditional Rhyme)
Bonaparte, by Marsha Wilson Chall
Boundless Grace, by Mary Hoffman
Brown Bear, Brown Bear, What Do You See? by Bill Martin, Jr.
Cam Jansen and the Birthday Mystery, by David A. Adler
Caps for Sale, by Esphyr Solbodkina
Cinderella, Anonymous. Fairy tales, folk tales, and nursery rhymes
Clifford, the Big Red Dog, by Norman Bridwell
Corduroy at the Zoo, by Don Freeman

Corduroy, by Don Freeman, 1968 (Viking Press)
Curious George, by H. A. Rey
"Diddle, Diddle Dumpling, My Son John," (Traditional Rhyme)
"Doctor Foster," (Traditional Rhyme)
Dog Food, by Saxton Freymann
Dream Carver, by Diana Cohn
Duck on a Bike, by David Shannon
Eaglet's World, by Evelyn Minshull
Emily's First 100 Days of School, by Rosemary Wells
Everything to Spend the Night: From A to Z, by Ann Whitford Paul
Faraway Home, by Jane Kurtz
Farmer Brown Shears His Sheep: A Yarn About Wool, by Teri Sloat
Flower Garden, by Eve Bunting
Frog's Best Friend, by Marion Dane Bauer
Giant Steps for Little People, by Kenneth N. Taylor, 1985 (Tyndale House Publishers)
Go, Dog, Go, by Philip D. Eastman, 1961 (Beginner Books)
"Goldilocks and the Three Bears," Anonymous. Fairy tales, folk tales, and nursery rhymes
Goodnight Moon, by Margaret Wise Brown
Hamster Chase, by Anastasia Suen
Harry, the Dirty Dog, by Gene Zion
Henry Hikes to Fitchburg, by D. B. Johnson
"Here We Go Round the Mulberry Bush," (Traditional Rhyme)
"Hickety, Pickety, My Black Hen," (Traditional Rhyme)
"Higglety, Pigglety, Pop!" by Samuel Goodrich (Poem)
How Many? How Much? by Rosemary Wells
How to Catch an Elephant, by Amy Schwartz
Hunter's Best Friend at School, by Elliott, Laura Malone.
I Stink! by Kate McMullan
Ira Sleeps Over, by Bernard Waber, 1972 (Houghton Mifflin)
It's Just in Time, Amber Brown, by Paula Danziger
"Jack-o-Lantern," by Aileen Fisher (Poem)
"January," by Maurice Sendak (Poem)
"Jump or Jiggle," by Evelyn Beyer (Poem)
Just in Case You Ever Wonder, by Max Lucado, 1992 (Word Publishers)
King of the Stable, by Melody Carlson, Crossway Books/Good News Publishers
Letters and Sounds, by Rosemary Wells
"Little Red Riding Hood," Anonymous. Fairy tales, folk tales, and nursery rhymes
"Lucy Locket," (Traditional Rhyme)
Mad Maddie Maxwell, Zonderkidz, The Children's Group of Zondervan Stacie Maslyn
Madeline, by Ludwig Bemelmans, 1963 (Viking Press)
Make Way for the Ducklings, by Robert McCloskey, 1941 (The Viking Press)
Max and Jax in Second Grade, by Jerdine Nolen
Measuring Penny, by Loreen Leedy
Millions of Cats, by Wanda Gág, 1928 (Coward, McCann & Geoghengan)
Miss Nelson Is Missing! by Harry Allard
Mother Goose rhymes.
Mouse in King Solomon's House, by Mack Thomas, Questar Publishers, Inc.
Nicholas Pipe, by Robert D. San Souci
Noah's Ark, by Peter Spier, 1977 (Doubleday)
Old Thunder and Miss Raney, by Sharon Darrow
Oliver Finds His Way, by Phyllis Root
On My Way, by Tomie De Paola
"Once I Saw a Little Bird," (Traditional Rhyme)

"One for the Money," (Traditional Rhyme)
One Lighthouse, One Moon, by Anita Lobel
"One Misty, Moisty Morning," (Traditional Rhyme)
"Pat-a-Cake," (Traditional Rhyme)
"Pease Porridge Hot," (Traditional Rhyme)
Peekaboo Morning, by Rachel Isadora
"Peter, Peter Pumpkin Eater," (Traditional Rhyme)
Peter's Chair, by Ezra Jack Keats, 1967 (Harper & Row)
"Polly Put the Kettle On," (Traditional Rhyme)
Praise And Worship, by Ken & Angela Abraham, Tommy Nelson
"Pussy Cat, Pussy Cat," (Traditional Rhyme)
"Rain, Rain Go Away," (Traditional Rhyme)
Rainbow Fish to the Rescue, by Marcus Pfister
"Raindrops," by Aileen Fischer (Poem)
"Ride a Cock Horse," (Traditional Rhyme)
"Ring Around the Rosey," (Traditional Rhyme)
Ring! Yo? by Chris Raschka
"Rock-a-bye, Baby," (Traditional Rhyme)
"Singing Time," by Rose Fyleman (Poem)
Sixteen Cows, by Lisa Wheeler
Song of Night: It's Time to Go to Bed, by Katherine Riley Nakamura
Spaghetti Eddie, by Ryan SanAngelo
Stone Soup, by Ann McGovern, 1986 (Scholastic)
Stories Jesus Told, by Nick Butterworth and Mick Inkpen, Questar Publishers, Inc.
Tanya and the Red Shoes, by Patricia Lee Gauch
The Berenstain Bears, by Stan & Jan Berenstain
The Bravest Cat: The True Story of Scarlett, by Laura Driscoll
The Cat in the Hat, by Dr. Seuss, 1957 (Houghton Mifflin)
The First Thing My Mama Told Me, by Susan Marie Swanson
"The Gingerbread Man," Anonymous. Fairy tales, folk tales, and nursery rhymes
The Girl Who Spun Gold, by Virginia Hamilton
The Honest to Goodness Truth, by Pat McKissack
The Hosanna Bible, by Ken and Angela Abraham, Word, Inc.
The Kidderminster Kingdom Series - King Leonard's Celebration, by Christopher Lane, Victor Books
The Lion and the Mouse and Other Aesop Fables, by Doris Orgel
The Little Engine That Could, by Watty Piper, 1976 (Platt & Munk)
The Little House, by Virginia Lee Burton
The Little Red Hen, various authors since 1942
The Lorax, by Dr. Seuss
The Moffats, by Eleanor Estes
The New Bible in Pictures for Little Eyes, by Ken Taylor, Moody Publishers
"The Old Woman Must Stand at the Tub,Tub,Tub," (Traditional Rhyme)
"The Pancake," by Christine Rossetti (Poem)
The Parable Series (Set of 4), by Liz Curtis Higgs, Tommy Nelson
The Puppy Who Wanted a Boy, by Jane Thayer, 1958 (Morrow)
The Rhyme Bible Storybook for Toddlers, by Linda Sattgast, Zondervan Publishing House
"The Snowy Day," by Ezra Jack Keats
The Story About Ping, by Marjorie Flack
The Story of Babar, the Little Elephant, by Jean De Brunhoff
The Tale of Peter Rabbit, by Beatrix Potter (Public Domain, online versions available)
"The Three Little Pigs," Anonymous. Fairy tales, folk tales, and nursery rhymes (Public domain)
The Velveteen Rabbit, by Margery Williams (Public domain)
The Very Hungry Caterpillar, by Eric Carle

"The Worm," by Ralph Bergengren (Poem)
"There was a Crooked Man," (Traditional Rhyme)
"There Was a Fat Pig," by Arnold Lobel (Poem)
"This Is the Way the Ladies Ride," (Traditional Rhyme)
"This Little Piggy Went to Market," (Traditional Rhyme)
Three Cheers for Catherine the Great! by Cari Best
"To Market, To Market," (Traditional Rhyme)
"Tom, Tom, the Piper's Son," (Traditional Rhyme)
"Two Little Blackbirds," (Traditional Rhyme)
"Wee Willie Winkie," (Traditional Rhyme)
What's Up, What's Down? by Lola M. Schaefer
Where the Wild Things Are, by Maurice Sendak, 1963 (Harper & Row)
Willie's Birthday, by Anastasia Sue
Winnie-the-Pooh Series, by A.A. Milne
Yoshi's Feast, by Kimiko Kajikawa
Young Classics: Alice in Wonderland, by Julie Fior

Supply List

Though supplies are listed for each week, you will only need supplies for the activities you choose to do. We include this supply list to help you prepare in advance. Please plan your week at one time so you will know which activities you are doing and which supplies you need.

Student Supplies:
Each student should be responsible for bringing some basic supplies.
Develop a list prior to the school year that can be communicated as early as possible to the parents.
Each student should bring an old shirt for Arts & Crafts time.

Room Supplies:

Abacus or a set of 20 beads on a wire, clothesline or dowel (for counting and addition/subtraction practice)
Alphabet blocks
Banner paper for the Creation Mural (the larger this can be the better)
Bulletin boards
Calendar (perpetual monthly, see instructions)
CD player

Chore list:
   clean white board
   change week of the year card
   empty trash
   turn off lights
   turn on lights
   hold door, etc.

Clock (analog, moveable hands)
Clock (digital, wipe off or one with changeable numbers)
Clock hour flashcards (o'clock time on top, clock face in center, digital time on bottom, analog clock
   only on back side)
Color dice (one color on each side)
Color flashcards: red, green, blue, black, white, yellow, brown, pink, purple, orange, gray
Color spinners (pointer points to color and number)
Computer for word processing
Counters (coins, seeds, sticks, tokens)
Counting Train (see the instructions)
Daily schedule
Days of the week chart (Sunday-Saturday, numbered 1-7)
Days of the week flashcards
Letter flashcards Aa-Zz
Months of the year chart (January-December)
Months of the year flashcards
Name plates
Number blocks
Number flashcards 1-20
Pop Beads
Rope
Shape flashcards: triangle, circle, square, rectangle, star, heart, oval, diamond
Recording device (phone or computer)
Television or computer with DVD player
Week of the school year cards to hang on a peg, numbered 1-36. One of the classroom chores
   can be to have a student hang a new card each week of the school year.
White board
Wooden blocks of a variety of shapes and sizes

General Supplies: Always have on hand
Aluminum foil
Cardstock, all colors including white
Cellophane tape
Cotton balls
Craft sticks
Crayons (Keep the crayons nice. Nothing is more depressing than a big box of broken crayons.
   BUT keep the pieces for crafts.)
Construction paper, 8.5 x 11 and 11 x 17, all colors including white
Magnifying Glass: It would be beneficial if each student had a magnifying glass.
   But also have at least one high quality magnifying glass.

Masking tape
Markers (Test the markers occasionally to be sure they still have ink)
Paint brushes
Paint: Tempura washable
Pencils
Plain, white paper
Play-doh®
Poster board
Ribbon
Scissors (children's)
Stickers, a variety of shapes, characters, and sizes
Tacky Glue, glue sticks
Waxed paper

It is recommended that you purchase a roll of white freezer paper (butcher paper or banner paper), especially if you have more than one or two students. Paper with a plastic backing will be ideal for some of the activities.

Many usable supplies are thrown away in our trash each day. As a teacher, it is a good habit to save certain items through the year. If you have a large class, enlist parents to help you. Send a list home of item for them to save and send to school. Also keep cardboard boxes labeled "Paper scraps" and "Craft scraps." There will be many art and craft lessons that use bits and pieces of paper, yarn, chenille wire, pipe cleaners, etc.

Here is a brief list of usable items to save:

cardboard egg cartons	pieces of thin cardboard
clear lids, like coffee can	scraps of foil
film canisters	shoe boxes
foam deli food trays	small jars with lids
frozen dinner containers	toilet paper rolls
magazines	yarn scraps
old sponges	wrapping paper rolls
paper towel rolls	plastic berry baskets
fabric scraps	

Other Resources:
The Picture Rulebook of Kids' Games, by Roxanne Henderson and Michael Brown, McGraw-
    Hill/Contemporary Books; April 1, 1996
Hopscotch, Hangman, Hot Potato, & Ha Ha Ha: A Rulebook of Children's Games, by Jack Macguire,
    Fireside, August 1, 1990

Weekly Supplies:

Supplies for Week 1, Lesson 1-5

box of inexpensive small envelopes
world globe
lunch bags, the brown kind
old magazines and catalogs to cut pictures from
craft sticks
carpet squares (samples)
recording device (phone or computer)
11 x 17 colored construction paper
freezer paper (from a grocer or a food service supply)

narrow sponges
clothespins
tempera paint
liquid dish soap
puppet
glitter
cotton balls
contact paper

Supplies for Week 2, Lessons 6-10

pencil
peanut butter
honey
dry milk
rolling pin
cardboard
dull knife
contact paper or wallpaper
empty film canisters, one each, a small plastic water
    bottle will also work

stickers
various sizes of pom-poms
small wiggly eyes
fresh eggs, one each
little disposable bowls
large weed
rice
graham crackers

Supplies for Week 3, Lessons 11-15

alphabet cereal
magnetic alphabet letters
flashlight
candle and matches
lamp
9 x 13 pan
cornmeal
rice
science book on the workings of the eye
abacus or a simple set of 20 beads on a wire or string
    that can slide back and forth for counting exercises

stickers
number line
blindfolds
piece of board
flour, salt, oil: clay recipe
tissue paper
alarm clock
colored blocks
magazines

Supplies for Week 4, Lessons 16-20

yard stick
blackboard or poster board
flashlight
blocks
computer
number line
raisins or beans or dominoes
bright light
cut out numbers 1-9
sand paper
foil cookie sheets

large ball
shaving cream
prism
tempera paint-yellow, blue and red
classical music
any other music
lamp or large flashlight
long piece of string
several flowering plants
gardening tools
water colors

Supplies for Week 5, Lessons 21-25
bicycle pump
colored blocks
music tape
balloons, round and long
water colors with brush
drinking straw
blow dryer
two wet rags
paper triangle, circles and squares
ribbon sticks or ribbons glued to a plastic shower ring

cotton balls
stickers
ribbon
hula hoops
a fan
long skinny balloons, one each
a helium filled balloon
small glider airplanes

Supplies for Week 6, Lessons 26-30
globe
tub of dirt
magnifying glass
tweezers
9 x 13 pan
cornmeal
rice
room freshener
breathing mask
rolling pin
sand ball
celery

peanut butter
plastic spoons
raisins
heavy cardboard
masking tape
Fruit Loops® or Cheerios®
string
empty 2-liter soda bottle
paper towels
small amount of sand
charcoal

Supplies for Week 7, Lesson 31-35
large magnet
rolled cookie recipe
raisins
frosting
stapler
blocks
two planters or jars
several small plants, one each
ribbon sticks or ribbons glued to a plastic shower ring

sand
soil
dirt
bucket or pan
ground cover to plant in yard
clay
small planters, one each

Supplies for Week 8, Lessons 36-40
blocks
grass seed
waterproof glue
shoe box
garden seeds
3 x 5 cards

sponges, one for each
magnifying glass
high fiber wheat bread
margarine
plastic knives, one each
small paper plates

Supplies for Week 9, Lessons 41-45

number line
tomato
blackberry
potting soil
two pots
shapes previously cut from construction paper
seed catalog
seeds or pictures of fruit and seeds
gardening book
tray
baskets

blocks
whole cloves
orange
ribbon
vegetables
peanut butter
loaf of bread
ribbon pieces
plastic knives
zippered sandwich bags

Supplies for Week 10, Lessons 46-50

electric clothes iron
crayon shavings
stapler
raisins
colored pencils
dry beans
glass bottle
fruit patterns from week 9 day 3
basket
number line

pine cones
serrated knife or saw
mixed bird seed
a set of Lincoln Logs™
evergreen branch
dry corn or wheat kernels
small round rock
large flat rock
a variety of noodles

Supplies for Week 11, Lessons 51-55

vitamins found in fruits and vegetables
gardening magazines to cut up
old magazines with pictures of food
sidewalk chalk for marking hopscotch
sticks
grass
clay
encyclopedia
globe

digital recording device (phone or computer)
veggies
white foam meat trays
garment made of 100% cotton
blunt tip large embroidery needles
several colors of yarn
woven linen material

Supplies for Week 12, Lessons 56-60

oatmeal boxes
paper bags
yellow clay
breakfast bars
globe
flashlight
old magazines
sidewalk chalk
gold glitter
pieces of 4 x 4 wood

bananas
large wooden frame
cheesecloth
staples
artist's blade
brads
kitchen timer
shallow metal pan
shallow glass pan

Supplies for Week 13, Lessons 61-65
butcher paper
glitter
supplies for marshmallow topping
umbrella on a toothpick
small, green leaves from a tree
fall colored leaves from real trees or magazines
twig from a tree in the shape of a rake
old December, January, and February magazines

sand
popcorn
yellow tennis ball
candy corn
pipe cleaner
piece of terry cloth
plastic cling wrap
tape

Supplies for Week 14, Lessons 66-70
yellow and black pipe cleaners
short pencil
wiggly eyes
number line

house plant
glitter glue
pictures of heat sources
yellow and/or gold yarn

Supplies for Week 15, Lessons 71-75
globe
flashlight
small ball
blocks
cheese slices
9 x 13 pan

cornmeal
rice
laundry baskets
cardboard
chairs

Supplies for Week 16, Lessons 76-80
poems about stars
number line
cardboard
star stickers
yellow clay
cement blocks
rock
binoculars
2 x 4 that is 6 feet long with a brick for
    each end for a balance beam

cookie dough to roll out
cornmeal/rice box
hanger, one each
yarn
glitter
foil pie pan, one each
nails
string
chicken & stars soup

Supplies for Week 17, Lessons 81-85
poster or map of stars
cardboard tube
number line
glitter
musical instrument or pan lids

lively music
quiet music
calm music for ballet
gold star stickers
toilet paper tubes, one for each

Supplies for Week 18, Lessons 86-90
foam balls:
   1 - 10 inches in diameter
   1 - 8 inches
   1 - 6 inches
   3 - 1 1/2 inches
   2 - 7/8 inches
straight pin with a bright colored head
white or silver glitter glue

string and thumbtacks
masking tape
ball
tempera paint

Supplies for Week 19, Lessons 91-95
large map of U.S.
dowel rod
string
magnet
long piece of ribbon

classical music
globe
book on sea life
a whole fish
crab legs or a whole crab

Supplies for Week 20, Lessons 96-100
big plastic bag
chalkboard
chalk
multi-colored sequins
frog hatchery kit (optional)
fish eggs from a bait shop

sardines
small plates
plastic knives
craft clear varnish
small paint brushes

Supplies for Week 21, Lessons 101-105
active music
gliding, serene music
disinfecting solution, Lysol®
dark paint
string
adding machine tape

egg recipe for family
eggs for boiling
markers to use on eggs
library book on birds
real bird nest

Supplies for Week 22, Lessons 106-110
pine cone
bird seed
fat
globe
four pencils
chocolate chips

Chinese noodles
jelly beans and/or M&Ms®
balloons, one for each
flour
whisk
string and/or yarn

Supplies for Week 23, Lessons 111-115
magazine with animals in it
small carton of milk, one for each
plastic animals

a bathroom scale
a mammal pet

Supplies for Week 24, Lessons 116-120

book with pictures of mammals
straws
yarn

animal coloring books
baby animal video

Supplies for Week 25, Lessons 121-125

music
book with snakes
colored beads
string
fake fur
leather
piece of fish with skin
feathers (these may need to be purchased due to recent
    health problems associated with birds)

baby doll
glitter
fake eyes
a reptile pet
flour and salt
computer or old typewriter

Supplies for Week 26, Lessons 126-130

bug jar
cardboard or foam with pins
small jars, like baby food jars
small, lightweight rug
large tea jar
smaller jar
sand or soil
ants
the game Cootie®
spray paint
Chinese noodles
cream cheese
crackers
paper plates
plastic knives
sugar cookies, round or oval (vanilla wafers will work)

piece of real silk
magnifying glasses
tweezers
stamp pads with colored ink
paper towel rolls
bug eyes
small foam balls
pipe cleaners
magnifying glasses
lids or trays
red and/or black frosting
black licorice
black jelly beans
sliced black and green olives
computer or old typewriter

Supplies for Week 27, Lessons 131-135

mirror
paper plates
magazines
stamp pad
soapy sponge
clay recipe

computer
box of gingerbread mix
gingerbread cookie cutters
canned frosting
fine dirt

Supplies for Week 28, Lessons 136-140

two clear plastic 8 oz glasses
sugar
yeast
two liter bottle
a big deflated balloon
a dozen eggs
zippered sandwich bags
two pieces of bread

cinnamon
applesauce
wire
paper towel tube, one for each
pair of glasses
contact lenses
chicken skin

Supplies for Week 29, Lessons 141-145

8 oz foam cups
a hearing aid
all different scents
cinnamon
paper plates
ribbon
apples

onion
sugar free Jell-O®
gingerbread man cookie cutter
cheese
plastic knives
big bone

Supplies for Week 30, Lessons 146-150

large rubber bands
English muffins, cut in half and toasted
American or jack cheese
various fruits, cut into chunks
skeleton kit
food from the food groups or plastic food
instant pudding
milk

a set of dentures
toothbrush, one for each
poster on tooth brushing
clay recipe
vanilla or peppermint flavoring
balloons, one for each
small bottle
sponges, one piece for each

Supplies for Week 31, Lessons 151-155

stethoscope
cow heart
teddy bear shaped cookies or grahams

camera and film
large butcher paper

Supplies for Week 32, Lessons 156-160

cardboard egg cartons
bug eyes
pipe cleaners
string or ribbon
occupational accessories

detergent
medicine
some kind of good food
waffles
toaster

Supplies for Week 33, Lessons 161-165

a chapter book
dry noodles, several kinds
Handel's Messiah, or similar work
a set of eight glasses
teaspoons
musical instruments
whale songs CD
candy sprinkles/coconut/chopped nuts
envelopes

pretzels
candy melts
paper towels
pipe cleaners
wooden clip clothespins
compass, one for each would be great
magnet, one for each would be great
carrots
bottle of blow bubbles, one for each

Supplies for Week 34, Lessons 166-170

straws or toothpicks
cookie sheet
soil or dirt
toilet paper tubes
fake jewels
coloring book

cardboard egg cartons
clay recipe
green food coloring
a cake mix
egg
soil

Optional: chocolate chips, coarsely chopped semi-sweet chocolate, white chocolate chips, peanut butter chips, butterscotch chips, raisins, coconut, toasted-coarsely chopped nuts
cookie sheets

Supplies for Week 35, Lessons 171-175

paper plates
large brown grocery bags, one for each
plastic animals from Week 23
paper towel rolls, one for each
real or play phone

computer
ceramic praying hands, one for each
silver or gold ceramic paint
magnetic strip
foam board

Supplies for Week 36, Lessons 176-180

wood pieces, variety
a family tree
Noah's ark set
long piece of white butcher paper
Noah's Trail mix: popcorn, pretzels, raisins, sunflower
    seeds, almonds, walnuts, pecans, or coconut

rainbow party goods
rainbow rewards
party food and punch
glitter

Memory Verses

Week	Verse
Weeks 1 and 2	Genesis 1:1
Weeks 3 and 4	Genesis 1:3
Week 5	Genesis 1:6
Weeks 6 and 7	Genesis 1:10
Week 8	I Peter 1:24-25
Weeks 9 and 10	Genesis 8:22
Week 11	Review
Week 12	Genesis 1:16a
Week 13	Psalm 90:12
Week 14	Psalm 89:1
Week 15	Genesis 1:16 a and b
Week 16	Genesis 1:16 all
Week 17	Revelation 22:16
Week 18	Psalm 148:13
Week 19	Genesis 1:26
Week 20	Psalm 48:1
Weeks 21 and 22	Matthew 6:26a
Weeks 23 and 24	Genesis 1:24a
Weeks 25 and 26	Review
Weeks 27 – 30	Psalm 139:14-16
Week 31	Review
Weeks 32 – 33	Genesis 2:2
Week 34	Proverbs 17:17a
Week 35	Romans 3:23
Week 36	Review

Days of Creation Numbers

Many of the Bible Lessons use a set of the Days of Creation Numbers as a visual aid. These numbers have two functions:

A.   They aid in number recognition.

B.   They provide a visual summary of what God created on that day of the Creation week.

We suggest that the days of Creation be illustrated by making the numbers one through seven from cardboard, foam core, or poster board. A set of numbers that can be used as patterns is provided on the back pages of this Teacher's Guide. The size of the pattern numbers can be increased or reduced using a scanner or copier depending on your needs. To these numbers add:

#1.   Foil overlay for Day One

#2.   Blue paper with cotton ball clouds for Day Two

#3.   Rocks and various seeds for Day Three

#4.   Sun, Moon, stars, comets, and planets for Day Four

#5.   Fish and bird stickers for Day Five

#6.   Mammal and people stickers for Day Six

#7.   Make Day Seven look like a bed, with a coverlet of material and a cotton ball for a pillow.

Use these numbers to both teach and review what God did on each of the seven days. Size the numbers appropriate for the number of students that you will be teaching.

During the Bible Lesson a number will be held by the teacher as they discuss the Creation events that occurred on that day. Eventually, all seven numbers will be posted on a bulletin board or on the wall for review.

Lyrics to The "Horizons Preschool Music" CD

I Know He Loves Me Too (# 1)

I love   (student's name)   .
I love   (student's name)   .
I love   (student's name)   .
And I know she (he) loves me too.

Note: Continue through the group, singing each student's name. Include the teacher's name. The last verse is:

We love Jesus.
We love Jesus.
We love Jesus,
And we know He loves us too.

I Have a Shadow (# 2)

Frank Hernandez / Copyright 2007 His & Hernandez
    Music

I have a shadow, (I have a shadow)
That follows me, (That follows me)
(Everywhere I go.)

I have a shadow, (I have a shadow)
If I go fast, (If I go fast)
If I go slow, (If I go slow)
It follows me, (It follows me)
(Wherever I go.)

I'm A Little Candle (# 3)

Frank Hernandez / Copyright 2007 His & Hernandez
    Music

I'm a little candle shining in the dark,
It's the light of Jesus shining in my heart,
I will shine,
I will shine,
Like a candle in the dark,
I will shine.

We are little candles shining in the dark,
It's the light of Jesus shining in our hearts,
We will shine,
We will shine,
Like little candles in the dark,
We will shine.

God Made You, God Made Me (# 4)

Frank Hernandez / Copyright 2007 His & Hernandez
    Music

God made you, God made me
God made us how we should be
Birdies fly
Fishes swim
God made you and me to love like Him

(Additional verses)
God made you, God made me
God made us how we should be
Bunnies hop
Fishes swim
God made you and me to love like Him

God made you, God made me
God made us how we should be
Horses prance
Fishes swim
God made you and me to love like Him

Heaven Is A Happy Place (# 5)

Frank Hernandez / Copyright 2007 His & Hernandez
    Music

Heaven is a happy place,
Heaven is a happy place,
Hallelujah, Hallelujah,
We will smile and see God's face,
That's why Heaven is a happy,
It's a happy place.

Heaven is a happy place,
Heaven is a happy place,
Hallelujah, Hallelujah,
We will smile and see God's face,
That's why Heaven is a happy,
It's a happy place.

My God Is So Big (# 6)
Karen Mitzo Hilderbrand & Kim Mitzo Thompson,
    1999 Twin Sisters IP, LLC

My God is so big, so strong and so mighty.
There's nothing my God cannot do. (clap, clap)

My God is so big, so strong and so mighty.
There's nothing my God cannot do. (clap, clap)

The mountains are His. The valleys are His.
The trees are His handiwork, too. (clap, clap)

My God is so big, so strong and so mighty.
There's nothing my God cannot do. (clap, clap)

He Plants Me Like A Seed (# 7)
Dave Huntsinger & Dottie Rambo, 1978
    HeartWarming Music (Admin. by Brentwood-
    Benson Music Publishing Inc.

He plants me like a seed,
And watches as I grow.
He waters me with love
And shields me from the cold.
My tender leaves may bend
Beneath the storms and wind.
But comes the morning sun
I'm growing strong again.

He plants me like a seed
Beneath the fertile land.
My roots grow strong and deep
While tended by His land.
And soon the plants will bear
The harvest sweet and fair.
The Master smiles to see
The fruit from one small seed.

Countdown (# 8)
Dorothy Montgomery, 1966 by Dorothy G.
    Montgomery

Somewhere in outer space,
God has prepared a place,
For those who trust Him and obey.
Jesus will come again,
And though we don't know when,
The countdown's getting lower everyday.

Ten and nine,
Eight and seven,
Six and five and four,
Call upon the Savior while you may.
Three and two,
Coming through the clouds in bright array.
The countdown's getting lower everyday.

Great Is Thy Faithfulness (# 9)
Thomas Obediah Chisholm & William Marion
    Runyan, 1923. Renewed 1951 Hope Publishing
    Company

Summer and winter and springtime and har-
vest,
Sun, Moon and stars in their courses above
Join with all nature in manifold witness
To Thy great faithfulness, mercy and love.

Great is Thy faithfulness.
Great is Thy faithfulness.
Morning by morning new mercies I see.
All I have needed Thy hand has provided.
Great is Thy faithfulness, Lord unto me.

He's Still Working On Me (# 10)
Joel Hemphill, 1980 Family & Friends Music (Admin.
    by Brentwood-Benson Music Publishing, Inc.

He's still working on me
To make me what I ought to be.
It took Him just a week to make the Moon and
stars
The Sun and the Earth and Jupiter and Mars.
How loving and patient He must be
He's still working on me.

Peter, James, and John In A Sailboat (# 11)

Peter, James and John in a sailboat.
Peter, James and John in a sailboat.
Peter, James and John in a sailboat,
Out on the deep, deep sea.

We are fishers of men for Jesus.
We are fishers of men for Jesus.
We are fishers of men for Jesus,
Out on life's big sea.

The Birds Upon The Treetop (# 12)

Hal Wright, Karen Hilderbrand & Kim Thompson,
2002 Twin Sisters IP,LLC

The birds upon the treetops sing their song.
The angels chant their chorus all day long.
The flowers in the garden blend their hue.
So why shouldn't I, why shouldn't you
Praise Him too?

Skeeters And The Bed Bugs (# 13)

(Sometimes called "The Whipper Whopper" song or
"Eener Meener" song)

I woke up Saturday morning
And looked up on the wall.
The skeeters and the bed bugs
Were playin' a game of ball.
The score was six to nothin'
The skeeters were ahead.
The bed bugs hit a home run
And knocked me out of bed, I'm singing ...

Eenie, meenie and a miny-mo
Catch a wiffle-waffle by his toe.
And if he hollers, hollers, hollers
Let him go, singing
Eenie, meenie and a miny-mo

The Wake-up Song (# 14)

Frank Hernandez / Copyright 2007 His & Hernandez
Music

Wake up, wake up,
Wake up you sleepy head.
It's time, It's time,
It's time to get out of that bed.

There's lots of work and things to do,
There's lots of play and fun things, too.
Wake up, wake up,
Wake up you sleepy head!

(repeat)

God Put A Rain Cloud In The Sky (# 15)

God put a rain cloud in the sky.
And Noah was safe in the ark.
God put a rain cloud in the sky.
And Noah was safe in the ark.
Lions, tigers, and kangaroos,
Monkeys, zebras, and people too.
God put a rain cloud in the sky.
But Noah was safe in the ark.

God put a rainbow in the sky.
And Noah knew it was safe.
God put a rainbow in the sky.
And Noah knew it was safe.
He freed the animals, big and small.
And thanked God for saving them all.
God put a rainbow in the sky.
And Noah knew it was safe.

Head And Shoulders, Knees and Toes (# 16)

Head and shoulders, knees and toes
Knees and toes,
Knees and toes.
Head and shoulders, knees and toes.
Clap your hands and praise Him.

(repeat)

Say To The Lord I Love You (# 17)

Debby Kemer Rettino & Ernie Rettino, 1981
Rettino/Kerner Publishing (Admin. by Word Music
Group, Inc.)

Touch your finger to your nose,
Bend from the waist way down and touch your
toes,
And when you come up slowly,
Start to sing,
And say to the Lord, I love You.

I love You, I love You
Say to the Lord, I love You
I love You, I love You
Say to the Lord, I love You.

Activities in this Lesson: Bible Lesson, Social Studies, Language Arts, Phonics, Reading, Writing, Math, Color, Story Time, Music, Arts & Crafts, Physical Education, Homework, Additional Bible Lesson

Bible Reference: Genesis 1:1.

Bible Concept to Present: God is our Father who always was, is now, and always will be.

Bible Lesson: Before time began, God was alive. God has always been alive. God does not have a Mommy or a Daddy or a birthday. God has always been. God is alive right now. This very minute, even as we talk, God is alive. God knows everything. He knows what you are doing now. He knows your name is _____ (have students say their name). He knows all about you. God even knows what you had for breakfast this morning. God loves you very much. He cares about what you think and do.

Did you know that God never goes on vacation? He never goes to sleep. He is always there to take care of us and help us. I am happy to have a God who takes such good care of me and is so loving and kind. God is my Heavenly Father, just like your Dad who takes care of you and loves you like my dad who loves me. God is our Father. (Be sensitive in your comments to any children who have lost their father or who live in single parent homes.)

Fathers do very special things for their children. Do you remember a time when your dad bought you a present? Or fixed your lunch? Or helped you get dressed? Our Heavenly Father (God) has done something very nice for us, too. He has given us a very special gift. Do you know what that very special gift is? God gave us our world, every little bug, our beautiful trees and flowers, the ocean and the beautiful sky. God gave all these things to us. He made all of them for us.

I am happy to have God for my Heavenly Father, and to have Him make such a nice gift for me. Let's thank God now for the world He made for us and for being such a nice Father to us. Pray here, thanking God for our earthly Dad who gives us good things and then our Heavenly Father who gives us a beautiful world.

Illustration: *Prepare ahead – Make copies of the Lesson 1 Resource page on white cardstock. Make enough copies so that each student can have a small picture of the world. Address one small envelope to each student personally. Put a picture of the world inside the envelope.* Pass out the envelopes to the students, explaining that just as it is special to receive a gift from Dad, so it is special to receive the gift of our world from our Heavenly Father, God. Let the students color their world pictures and take them home. **Note:** If your students have not been acquainted with the concept of the globe representing our world, you will need to introduce that thought previous to the unwrapping of the globe picture. The children should be introduced to the fact that the globe is like a picture of our world.

Social Studies: Discuss with your students the relationship of a father to his child. Talk about how special your father, or a grandfather, is to you. Ask questions that will require more than a yes or no answer. The following are types of questions you may ask:

1. Why do you love your Daddy?
2. What do you like to do best with your Daddy?
3. How does your dad let you know he loves you?
4. When do you like to spend special time with your dad?

After your students have answered these questions, have them draw a picture of themselves and their Daddy. Use a half sheet of paper that is folded in half to make the card. Make this a special card to take home to the student's fathers. Write FATHER or DAD on the cards for the students. Have a Praise Yell for fathers. Let the students shout, "I love my daddy because..." or "I love my grandpa because..." Allow them to call out things for as long as they will participate.

Multimedia Resources: Watch "Love" from the *Character Builders Video Series*.

Language Arts: *Use old magazines and catalogs to cut out pictures to represent Daddy. Glue onto a craft stick. Cut out other pictures of men that could represent the father of a friend.* Try to find a variety of hair colors on the models. Discuss how fathers may look different and have different names, but they still are someone's daddy.

Do the following action activity with your students. Your goal is for the students to imitate your actions, and say as many of the words after you as possible.

Three Little Ducks

Three little ducks went out to play (Hold up three fingers)
Over the hill and far away (Make a waving motion with fingers)
When the Mommy says "Quack, Quack" (Children repeat quack sound)
Two little ducks come waddling back (Hold up two fingers as your body waddles as a duck)

Two little ducks went out to play (Hold up two fingers)
Over the hill and far away (Make a waving motion with fingers)
When the Mommy says "Quack, Quack" (Children repeat quack sound)
One little duck comes waddling back (Repeat as above)

One little duck went out to play (Hold up one finger)
Over the hill and far away (Make a waving motion with finger)
When the Mommy says "Quack, Quack" (Children repeats quack sound)
No little ducks come waddling back (Clench fist, and waddle body)

No little ducks went out to play (Clench fist to represent 0)
Over the hill and far away (Waving motion)
When the Daddy says "Quack, Quack" (BIG quack sound)
Three little ducks come waddling back (Hold up three fingers)

Note: The above poem is not intended to teach disobedience to a mother figure, but rather to emphasize obedience to the father. You may discuss the actions of the ducks in relationship to the mother.

Phonics: Teach the letter Aa. The first step to learning to read is to be able to consistently recognize the alphabet. You may find that your students already know the order of the alphabet, having learned it from the traditional "ABC Song" or by other means. If so, all you need to do at this point is to be certain that your students know each letter of the alphabet when it is shown to them. It is vital that consistency is apparent, that they can name the letters every time and name them correctly.

If your students can not yet recognize all the letters of the alphabet, or can only recognize some of them consistently, then you must teach them. This can be done very simply provided you are not in a rush to do so. Begin by using the alphabet letter flashcards that are provided in the Resource Packet. These can be displayed to the students as you drill the letter recognition. You can also make letter patterns from felt cloth or contact paper for the students to recognize or trace with their fingers. If you use contact paper (like the sticky kind you use to line your shelves), trace the outline of the letter on the contact paper. Then cut it out, leaving the back on the contact paper. Have the children repeat the name of the letter after you, while tracing the letter with their fingers.

We will be learning the letters in alphabetical order. This will lead to skills in dictionary usage as well as reinforce the concepts like before, after, and between. Initially you will be focusing on learning the letter names, letter sounds will come later.

Point out any student's name beginning with the letter *A*. Write some words beginning with the letter *A* on the board. Include any student names from the class that begin with letter *A*. Underline the capital *A* that begins the words. Read through the words and point out the shape of letter *A*. Have the students trace the A in the air as you trace the letter *A* beginning each name.

> Boys: Aaron, Abel, Abraham, Adam, Adrian, Alan, Albert, Alberto, Alec, Alejandro, Alex, Alexander, Alexis, Allen, Andre, Andres, Andrew, Angel, Anthony, Antonio, Armando, Arthur, Austin
> Girls: Abby, Abigail, Adriana, Adrianna, Alejandra, Alexa, Alexandra, Alexandria, Alexis, Alicia, Alisha, Alison, Allison, Allyson, Alyssa, Amanda, Amber, Amelia, Amy, Ana, Andrea, Angel, Angela, Angelica, Anna, Anne, April, Ariana, Ariel, Ashlee, Ashleigh, Ashley, Asia, Audrey, Autumn
> Vocabulary words: April, August

Note: The names used for capital letter recognition have been taken from lists of common names that parents have given to their children in recent years. You should also add the name of your city and state when it becomes appropriate.

Do the Lesson 1 Phonics worksheet. Complete the letter Aa worksheet. Have the students trace the letters Aa with their fingers. They should trace the letters with their fingers and say the names of the letters. Demonstrate the proper strokes for them on the board. Say the words for each of the pictures and look at the Aa letters that begin them.

Reading: Recognize written first name. If you have posted a Name Plate for each student have them find their Name Plate on the bulletin board. Point out any of the first names that begin with the letter *A*.

Writing: For the first two weeks focus on having the students recognize their own first name. During this time, write the students' names on all worksheets and papers.

Other writing practice will take place in the Phonics and Math subject areas. These activities will not be listed under the Writing category. This is a good example of the holistic approach that each lesson takes.

Writing Skill Builders: These objectives are listed in each lesson for you to keep in mind as you direct the class. They are things to watch for and to incorporate into work and play in all areas. Include small muscle control activities: tear, fold, and paste whenever possible. Give instructions and reminders to hold a writing instrument correctly. Incorporate writing strokes: horizontal, vertical lines, spiral, and circle into arts and crafts.

Note: For those children who have difficulty holding a pencil correctly, rubber pencil grips can be used to teach the proper tripod grip.

Math: Teach number recognition of 1. For this week we will be studying the concept of one with your students. As a teacher, you need to be aware of the "one" concept in all that you do. We will be doing some patterning with the number one, learning about the number one around us, etc. Look for "ones" in everything that you do with the students to facilitate their acquisition of the concept of one.

Show the students the 1 flashcard. Ask them how many objects or animals are on the card. Talk about the shape of the number 1 and ask them what it reminds them of. Have them draw the number 1 in the sand or with chalk on the sidewalk.

Purchase or make a perpetual monthly calendar for one of the bulletin boards of the classroom. Make 12 monthly banners and 31 calendar pieces. You will need a row for the days of the week and 6 rows of 7 squares on which to hang or pin the calendar cards.

Point to your beginning school date on the calendar, this is day 1 of the school year. Point to the week that begins the school year, this is week 1 of school. If you have hung cards for the week of the school year point out the Week 1 card. You can point out the number 1 on the calendar. Explain that the days of the month are numbered. One (1) is used to count the first day of the month. Find other ways to illustrate the concept of 1. The line leader will be person number 1 in our line. Have the line leader carry a 1 flashcard as you move from place to place in lines. The Bible reference is Genesis 1:1.

Do the Lesson 1 Math worksheet. Identify the pictures and count the number in each group. Example: 1 tree, 1 house, 1 car, etc. Draw the lines to match the ones that are the same. Remember that all pages should be removed from the student workbook to promote good penmanship.

Color: Introduce the colors red, green, and blue. Point out the red and blue colors in the American flag. Talk about grass being the color green. Ask the student's to find things in the classroom that are red. What things do they see that are green? What things can they find that are blue? Show them the red, green, and blue flashcards. Associate the items on the cards with the colors. If this is too many colors to cover at one time focus on one color for 2-3 days and then add another for 2-3 days until all 3 can be recognized by the students. These three colors will be reviewed for about two weeks and then one new color will be introduced at a time.

Throughout the curriculum, you will find notes referring to a color to teach your students. We suggest you teach the colors by utilizing a natural, relaxed teaching style. We also suggest you concentrate on one color at a time. For example, when teaching the color red, you may choose to serve students a red apple, commenting on the fact that the apple is red. The children may wear a red blouse or shirt. Every time you see red, comment on the color. When describing an object, name its color. You may also have a color day where everything eaten is the color you are learning and you and the students wear that color.

Story Time: Read one short story to the students.

Music: Teach students this little song, to the tune of "Twinkle, Twinkle Little Star"

Daddy We Love You

Daddy, Daddy, we love you
And we know you love us, too.
You are very big and strong
You work for us all day long.
Daddy, Daddy we love you
And we know you love us, too.

Teach the "ABC Song." If the students do not already know it, work on one line at a time until all lines are mastered. This will help to develop an awareness of the entire alphabet. The students can sing along even though they cannot recognize the individual letters.

A B C Song
Tune of Twinkle, Twinkle, Little Star

A B C D E F G
H I J K L M N O P
Q R S T U and V
W X Y and Z.
Now I've learned my ABCs.
Next time won't you sing with me!

Multimedia Resources: This week, listen and sing along to selections from "The Amazing Book" CD.

Arts & Crafts: Use Lesson 1 Resource page to make a "World" card.

Physical Education: Self Space. Children need to know the difference between self space and general space. Some space is shared like a sidewalk or a hallway. Other space is self space and only one person can be there at a time. Give each student a carpet square (hula hoops could also be used) and then ask them to arrange the squares into a circle and sit down on them. Dots or taped X's in a circle pattern on the floor will help them with this. Explain to them that the square on which they are sitting is their space and that no one else can get into that space. Illustrate this by trying to sit down on a carpet square where a student is sitting. What happens? You would have to sit down on top of them and they would get hurt. Have the students close their eyes and think about the movements that they could do in this space. Can they wiggle their fingers? Can they breathe in and out? Can they smile? The concepts of self space and general space are critical so that the students can move safely in physical education and also in the classroom environment throughout the school year. Have each student stand up and put their carpet square away.

Homework: Take the "World" card home and share it with dad or grandfather. Tell them what you learned today.

Additional Bible Lesson: If you choose to teach an additional Bible Lesson to your students, the story of Abraham and Isaac makes a wonderful lesson to present. Place emphasis on the idea that Abraham really wanted Isaac and was happy when God sent Isaac to Abraham and Sarah. The story is found in Genesis 21:1-8.

NOTES:

Activities in this Lesson: Bible Lesson, Social Studies, Homework Review, Language Arts, Phonics, Reading, Writing, Memory Verse, Math, Shapes, Color, Story Time, Music, Arts & Crafts, Outside Activity, Physical Education, Optional Math/Language Arts/Bible/Arts & Crafts Activity

Bible Reference: Genesis 1:1.

Bible Concept to Present: God is ever present, always there for us.

Bible Lesson: Review yesterday's Bible lesson. Repeat the lesson, letting the students share in the telling, filling in important words. Ask them questions about the lesson: What does God know about us? Does God ever go on vacation? Does God ever go to sleep? He is always watching over us. He is always there, just like our police officers and fire fighters are always there.

Multimedia Resources: Listen to the songs "The Majesty Of God" and "Here, There, Everywhere" from "Music Machine: The Majesty of God" CD.

Social Studies: Does anyone know a police officer or fire fighter? These city helpers work in shifts so that some of them are always on duty. Many of them work through the night, while we are sleeping. What are some of the things they do? Ask students that want to participate, to stand up and act out one of the things that these helpers do for us. Let the students that want to participate take a turn. Examples: They protect us. They keep people from doing crimes. They help at accidents. They put out fires. They help us cross the street. They direct traffic, even when it is raining or storming. They help us in emergencies. Let us thank God for our police officers and fire fighters. (Share a brief prayer. Let children pray that want to.)

Note: This would be a good day for a visit from a police officer or fire fighter. This would be a good time to talk about the 911 emergency phone number. Remind the students that it should be dialed only when there is a real emergency. Many young children have saved the life of a parent or adult by calling 911. Ask some of the questions that the 911 operator will ask when 911 is called.

Homework Review: Ask the children to share about taking the card to their dads or grandfathers. Use the globe to show students the world. Show them where they live on the globe. Explain that there are dads and granddads all over the world, loving their children and families. And there are police officers and fire fighters all over the world, helping to take care of people.

Language Arts: Repeat the Three Little Ducks action activity from yesterday with students.

Phonics: Review the letter Aa. With an Aa letter flashcard and at least one other letter flashcard hold one card in each hand and have the students tell you where the Aa card is located. (left/right, top/bottom, over/under, etc.) Review some of the *A* words from Lesson 1.

We will be learning the letters in alphabetical order. This will lead to skills in dictionary usage as well as reinforce the concepts like before, after, and between.

Provide a classroom setting that is rich in printed materials. Letter shapes and word posters can be made by the students and displayed for constant review.

Point out any student's name beginning with the letter *A*.

Reading: Recognize written first name. Change the order of the Name Plates that you have posted and have each student find their Name Plate on the bulletin board. Point out any of the first names that have a small letter *a* in them.

Writing: Continue to focus on having the students recognize their own first name. During this time, write the students' names on all worksheets and papers.

Writing Skill Builders: Keep these objectives in mind as you direct the class. Include small muscle control activities: tear, fold, and paste whenever possible. Give instructions and reminders to hold a writing instrument correctly. Incorporate writing strokes: horizontal, vertical lines, spiral, and circle into arts and crafts.

Memory Verse: Share with your students that God likes us to memorize or learn His Word. Remember that some students might not know what a Memory Verse is. Read Genesis 1:1 from a Bible.

> In the beginning, God created the heavens and the earth. Genesis 1:1 NIV

> In the beginning, God created the heaven and the earth. Genesis 1:1 KJV

Write the verse on the board or on poster board, whether all of the students can read or not. Point to each word as you say it again. Let the students try to say it with you. Be sure to hand out a prepared copy of the Memory Verse for the students to take home, Memory Verse Card 1. Duplication masters are provided for both NIV and KJV cards in the *Horizons Preschool Resource Packet*. Duplicate the version that you plan to use. Cut the cards out and send home only one card at a time. Instruct the students to show the memory verse to their parents and to take the Memory Verse Card to their room, perhaps keeping it on their nightstand or posting it on a bulletin board.

Math: Review number recognition of 1. Ask the students questions about items of 1 regarding their bodies. Ask the students, "How many noses do you have?" "How many heads do you have?" "How many mouths do you have?" "How many chins do you have?" "How many necks do you have?" "How many hearts do you have?" "How many stomachs do you have?" "How many backs do you have?" Have them draw the number 1 in the air or on the board. If your students form a line to go outside or to the restroom point out the students that are standing tall and straight by saying, "I see a 1 here; I see another 1 here, as you move your arm to trace a 1 over how they are standing.

Do the Lesson 2 Math worksheet. Cut out the numbers from the strip. Help the students as is needed with cutting out the numbers. Count each group of objects and paste the correct number in the box.

Shapes: Students will learn how to use scissors. Provide children's scissors for each student. Give each student a piece of construction paper, using all different colors. Show them some examples of triangles. Pass out several samples that can be traced and cut out or draw the shapes on light colored construction paper for the students. Ask them to cut out triangles of all sizes and colors. See how many they can cut out of one piece of paper. If there is more than one student, let them trade triangles with other students, collecting lots of colors. Share with the children how thankful we are that God gave us so many beautiful colors in our world. Make sure that there is time for cleaning up, placing all of the trash in the trash can.

Color: Review the colors red, green, and blue.

Story Time: Read a story or stories of your choice.

Music: Review "Daddy We Love You." Teach the "ABC Song." If the students do not already know it, work on one line at a time until all lines are mastered. This will help to develop an awareness of the entire alphabet. The students can sing along even though they cannot recognize the individual letters.

A B C Song
Tune of Twinkle, Twinkle, Little Star

A B C D E F G
H I J K L M N O P
Q R S T U and V
W X Y and Z.
Now I've learned my ABCs.
Next time won't you sing with me!

Multimedia Resources: This week, listen and sing along to selections from "The Amazing Book" CD.

Arts & Crafts: Do the Lesson 2 Arts & Crafts worksheet. The letter Aa maze. Draw some simple mazes on the board to demonstrate how to do them. The students can also make a maze out of objects or toys on the table or floor.

Outside Activity: Take a nature walk. Ask, How many things can you see that are green? Red? Blue? Emphasize the goodness of God and the beauty He made for us.

If possible, this would be a good day to make a visit to a firehouse or police station. The focus of the visit should be on how these workers help us. How do they keep us safe? What are they doing to help protect our homes? How can the students help them back?

Physical Education: *Self Space.* Children need to know the difference between self space and general space. Give each student a carpet square and then ask them to arrange the squares into a circle and sit down on them. Dots or taped X's in a circle pattern on the floor will help them with this. They may need assistance getting into position. Greet each student now that they are in their self space. This is a good time to complement them on something good that they have done. Ask the students for movements that they can do while sitting on the squares. Have them perform the movements as they say them. End the time by having them close their eyes and spend some time resting quietly. Have each student stand up and put their carpet square away.

Optional Math/Language Arts/Bible/Arts & Crafts Activity: Throughout this year, the students will be learning the numbers 0 - 12. In the student worksheet booklet you will find patterns and illustrations for Bible Numbers. You may either use these to reinforce the teaching of the number at the time you teach that number, or use them for a review later in the year. They may also be used as an additional Language Arts project as you tell the stories. This activity will be given on Day 2 of the weekly schedule but it can be spread over several days or moved to other days of your yearly schedule.

1 Lost Coin: Luke 15:8-10, read the Bible verses and tell the story.
Jesus told the story of a woman who lost one coin. She had nine other coins, but she hunted through her house until she found the one lost coin.

Do the Lesson 2 Bible Numbers worksheet. Give each student a sheet of white construction paper and the worksheet. Cut out the items on the worksheet and glue them to construction paper as illustrated in the drawing. Draw in the arms and face for the "1" lady. Glue glitter on the lamp flame. Glue toothpicks and yarn on the drawing to make the broom.

NOTES:

Activities in this Lesson: Bible Lesson, Social Studies, Language Arts, Phonics, Reading, Writing, Memory Verse, Math, Shapes, Color, Story Time, Music, Arts & Crafts, Physical Education, Homework

Bible Reference: John 14.

Bible Concept to Present: Jesus and God are one. They both helped to create the world.

Bible Lesson: Ask, Do you remember the Christmas story when Jesus was born to Mary and Joseph? You will recall that Jesus was God's son, too. And that He came to earth for us because He loved us. Well, today's story tells us about something that happened when Jesus was here on earth.

> One day, Jesus was with His special friends. These friends were men who loved Jesus and obeyed Him. Jesus had often told them about His Father, God. On this day, Jesus was telling them about His wonderful home in Heaven where God was making beautiful homes for each of them. Jesus told them that where He went, they would go, too. One of Jesus' friends became worried about where Jesus was taking them and how he would know the way to get there. Jesus told them that He knew the way to God's home because He had lived there before He came to earth.

Do you remember the story we had about how God made the world? Well, Jesus was with God when He made the world. Jesus helped God to make our world. And then later, Jesus came down to earth to be a little baby. I am happy that God and Jesus are together. I am happy that Jesus came down to earth, and that someday we, too, can go to live in the beautiful home God is making for us in Heaven. Let's thank God now for Jesus. Let's thank Jesus for making our world with God. Let's thank Jesus and God for the home they are making for us in Heaven.

Multimedia Resources: Listen to the song "A Great Big God" from the "Bullfrogs and Butterflies: God Loves Fun" CD.

Do the Lesson 3 Bible worksheet. Identify each of the items on the sheet and discuss that these are things that Jesus and God created. Have the students color the items, cut them out, and paste them on a piece of construction paper.

Social Studies: God is Jesus' Father too. Discuss more facts about fathers. You may wish to include a very special loving story about your own dad to illustrate how special daddies are. Discuss the home you live in and how your dad worked very hard to give you the home you had as a child. Then relate this to the home God is making for us now in Heaven.

Teach your students the address of their home. *Pass out cards with student's addresses on them.* To teach the address, use a puppet. Any puppet will be adequate. Manipulate the puppet to "say" the address, and then have your student repeat it. Students may make simple puppets out of paper lunch bags, and then make the puppets say their address.

Language Arts: Here's another option for an effective way to teach your students their home address. Use a digital recording device to record your students saying their address in a full sentence. Example: I live at _____. It is a _____ (color) house. Replay the recorded message. The objective is for your student to verbalize in complete sentences.

Read the following story.

The Country Mouse and the City Mouse

Once upon a time, a country mouse had a friend who lived in the city. He invited the city mouse to come and visit him for a peaceful and quiet vacation. He prepared all the best morsels that he had, even though they were plain and simple. He wanted the best for his friend. When the city mouse came to visit, he was not used to the simple fare, so he picked carefully at his food, all the while thinking of how much better his food was at home. After a time, he asked the country mouse, "How can you stand this simple and dull life when so many exciting things await you in the city? There are fine restaurants, luxurious hotels, fine cars, and shopping malls to visit. And you would meet the finest people in the city. In fact, I live with some very rich folks. You are wasting your life here in the country. Why don't you come with me now, and see the 'good life'?"

These words were too much for the country mouse, so he decided to pack his suitcase, and have a vacation in the city. It was midnight when the two mice reached the great house where the city mouse lived. The house was gorgeous inside. The furnishings showed great wealth. On the table, was a splendid uneaten meal. The city mouse ran all over trying to give the country mouse the best food. They ate tidbit after tidbit, when suddenly the door opened, and in came beautiful women and handsome men. The two mice ran for cover and breathing hard, looked for a hiding place and found one under the velvet drapes. Before they could begin to relax, a large cat came into the room, smelling and searching. The big cat came closer and closer and was about to discover their hiding place when the lady of the house called the cat to dinner. The two mice were terribly frightened! That cat had almost found them! The mice remained hidden until all was quiet. When they knew the household was asleep, they crept out of their hiding place. The country mouse whispered in the city mouse's ear, "This has been a nice visit, but I want to return to the peace and quiet of the country, where there is security and no fear of becoming a tasty morsel myself."

(Moral: It is better to live in peace and be safe, than to have the best and live in danger.)

Phonics: Review the letter Aa. Make a capital letter *A* on the floor with 5 students lying down. First make a triangle with 3 students and then have 2 students make the legs. Repeat with other groups of 5 students.

As each letter of the alphabet is taught be sure to include activities that enable the students to experience the letter through all of their senses.
>   **hear** the letter
>   **see** the letter
>   **say** the letter
>   **touch** the letter
>   **write** the letter
>   **read** the letter

Teach the small letter *a*. Write some words beginning with the letter *a* on the board. Include words from stories or activities that tie this lesson to other things that have already been done. Underline the small *a* that begins the words. Read through the words and point out the shape of the letter *a*. Have the students trace the *a* in the air as you trace the letter *a* beginning each word.

Common words: a, about, act, add, after, again, air, all, also, am, an, and, animal, answer, any, are, as, ask, at

Vocabulary words: above, addition, afternoon, against, alive, already, always, ankle, arm, around, away

Note: The lists of vocabulary words given for lowercase letter recognition include color, shape, and number words and other basic vocabulary words that a preschool student should know. The common words have been taken from lists of most common words of the English language and other resources.

Reading: Use a simplified, illustrated daily schedule of activities. Go over the activities on the Daily Schedule poster. Ask before and after questions about the schedule.

Writing: Continue to focus on having the students recognize their own first name. During this time, write the students' names on all worksheets and papers.

Writing Skill Builders: Keep these objectives in mind as you direct the class. Include small muscle control activities: tear, fold, and paste whenever possible. Give instructions and reminders to hold a writing instrument correctly. Incorporate writing strokes: horizontal, vertical lines, spiral, and circle into arts and crafts.

Memory Verse: Review Genesis 1:1. Say the verse together with the students several times.

Math: Review number recognition of 1. Ask the students questions about items of 1 regarding the classroom. Ask the students: "How many ceilings are in the room?" "How many clocks are on the walls of the room?" "How many floors are in the room?" "How many red cabinets are in the room?" "How many blue balls are in the room?" "How many green plants are in the room?" "How many trucks are on top of the book shelf?" Use any question that has 1 for an answer. Mix in a review of colors and position words if possible.

Do the Lesson 3 Math worksheet. Count each group of items and circle the correct number for the group.

Teach oral counting 1-10. Make a Counting Train with an engine, ten cars and a caboose. Patterns can be round in the *Horizons Preschool Resource Packet*. Plan to extend the train to include the numbers 11-20. This should be large enough to hang above the white board or over a bulletin board. You can make the train from construction paper or simply draw and color a train on banner paper. Color the boxcars with the colors that will be learned this year. 1 should be red, 2 green, 3 blue, 4 black, 5 white, 6 yellow, 7 brown, 8 pink, 9 purple, and 10 orange. Plan to extend the train to include the numbers 11-20 once the numbers 1-10 have been mastered.

Introduce the students to the Counting Train. Point out that there are 10 boxcars in the train to help learn counting 1-10 and that each boxcar is a different color that will be learned during the year. With a pointer or yardstick point to the numbered boxcars and have the students count after you. The students are not expected to recognize the numbers or to count objects to 10, they are simply memorizing how to say the number words in order 1-10.

Learn the "One, Two, Buckle My Shoe" rhyme/song to help learn counting 1-10. Use the 1-10 lines of either of the two versions below.

One, Two Buckle My Shoe

One, Two—buckle my shoe;
Three, Four—open the door;
Five, Six—pick up sticks;
Seven, Eight—lay them straight;
Nine, Ten—a good fat hen.

Eleven, Twelve—I hope you're well;
Thirteen, Fourteen—draw the curtain;
Fifteen, Sixteen—the maid's in the kitchen;
Seventeen, Eighteen—she's in waiting.
Nineteen, Twenty—my stomach's empty.

One, Two Buckle My Shoe

One two buckle my shoe
Three, four, knock at the door
Five, six, pick up sticks
Seven, eight, lay them straight
Nine, ten, a big fat hen

Eleven, twelve, dig and delve
Thirteen, fourteen, maids a-courting
Fifteen, sixteen, maids in the kitchen
Seventeen, eighteen, maids in waiting
Nineteen, twenty, my plates empty

Shapes: Introduce the shape of the triangle. Show your student what a triangle is and count the sides of the triangle. Look around the room, pointing out any triangle shapes. *Use a triangle you have made with wooden craft sticks as a visual aid. Also make a stick puppet for triangles. You will make one of these for each shape that is taught. To make the puppet, cut a triangle out of construction paper and glue it to a craft stick.* Allow students to make their own triangles with craft sticks. Repeat the poem below while holding up the triangles.

Timmy Triangle

I'm a triangle
Timmy's my name.
I have three sides
I play a little game.

I pretend to stand upon my head. (Turn triangle to a side)
I lay on my side (Turn triangle to another side)
I lay on my bed. (Continue to turn to 3rd side of triangle)

Some people don't see the difference in me.
They just see three sides; one, two, and three.
(Count sides as you say the number, tapping each side)

Note: The objective is for your student to recognize the shape of the triangle. He will, by practice, learn to count to three, but this is not the primary objective. Let your student manipulate the stick triangles. Allow adequate time for the child to internalize what he has just learned. He will do this by playing with the puppet.

Do the Lesson 3 Shapes worksheet. Have the students trace the triangle with a red, blue or green crayon.

Color: Review the colors red, green, and blue. Hold up colored sheets of construction paper. See if the students can correctly identify the color.

Story Time: Read a story or stories of your choice.

Music: Review "Daddy We Love You." Teach the song "Around the Circle We Will Go" to the tune of "London Bridge is Falling Down."

Around the Circle We Will Go
Tune of London Bridge is Falling Down
Author Unknown

Around the circle we will go
We will go
We will go
Around the circle we will go
Hallelujah!

Jesus is God's Son, I know
God's Son, I know
God's Son, I know
Jesus is God's Son, I know
Hallelujah!

Note: Transition music may be used any time you change activities. One suggestion is to use the tune "All Around The Mulberry Bush," such as, "This is the way we pick up our toys, pick up our toys, pick up our toys. This is the way we pick up our toys so early in the morning."

Multimedia Resources: This week, listen and sing along to selections from "The Amazing Book" CD.

Arts & Crafts: Use the Lesson 3 Arts & Crafts worksheet to illustrate what Heaven might be like. Add cotton for clouds and glitter for the city buildings to highlight them. You may label it "God's House." Although your students cannot read this, the labeling is great for visual preparation for reading, especially if you take the time to read it, and point out the words. You may even discuss the letters in the word "God."

Physical Education: Self Space. Have each student pick up a carpet square and then arrange themselves into a circle and sit down on the squares. Dots or taped X's in a circle pattern on the floor will help them with this. They may need assistance getting into position and will need enough space to do the Timmy Triangle activity that follows. Greet each student as they find their self space. This is a good time to complement each one on something good that he/she has done.

Ask your student to attempt to shape their body into the shape of a triangle. Can they look like Timmy Triangle? Add verbal directions such as: Sit on the floor with your legs straight out in front of you. Make your back as straight as you can, and then bend slightly forward to stretch your arms to your toes. Grab your toes. Do you look like a triangle?

Ask your students to tell you some movements that they cannot do while they are sitting on the carpet squares. Select a couple of students to follow-the-leader with you being the leader. Have them stand up and follow you as you walk around the circle and through open spaces in the circle of students. Lead them back to their squares where they can be seated again. Do this with several groups of students. Have all the students stand and put their carpet squares away.

Homework: Continue the discussion of the home that fathers have made for their families and the home that God is making for His children. Tell the students that they will be drawing a picture of their home on their homework sheet. Send home the Lesson 3 Homework worksheet where the students will draw a simple picture of their home. A parent may help them draw the place where they live. The worksheet is to be brought back tomorrow. Praise every student for their efforts.

NOTES:

Activities in this Lesson: Bible Lesson, Social Studies, Language Arts, Phonics, Reading, Writing, Memory Verse, Math, Shapes, Story Time, Color, Music, Arts & Crafts/Homework, Health & Safety/Arts & Crafts/Outdoor Activity, Physical Education

Bible Reference: John 14.

Bible Concept to Present: Jesus and God are one. Jesus is preparing Heaven for us.

Bible Lesson: Review yesterday's Bible lesson. Repeat the lesson, letting the students share in the telling, filling in important words. Ask questions about the lesson: Who was Jesus' mother and father? What did Jesus tell His friend about Heaven? (That He is preparing homes for us there; that one day we will be there with Jesus; that Jesus would know the way because He used to live there.)

Social Studies: Review addresses. Ask the students to repeat their addresses to one another or to the teacher. Wait until everyone has had several turns of saying their address. Talk to the children about sharing their address. Let them know it is OK to share in class, but that they should never tell a stranger their address, or tell anyone that they don't know who calls on the phone.

Review the discussion of the 911 emergency phone number. The 911 operator may ask for your address so knowing it is very important.

Language Arts: Review the Reading story from yesterday, Lesson 3. Be sure to review the information asked in the game below. Play "YES OR NO." Ask the students these questions and let them respond together:

Let's play "YES OR NO." You tell me if the sentence I say is TRUE = YES or FALSE = NO:
　　The city mouse visited the country mouse for a quiet vacation. YES
　　The city mouse *just loved* the simple food in the country. NO
　　The city mouse missed his rich friend and fancy house. YES
　　The country mouse went to visit the city mouse, arriving *at noon.* NO
　　Both mice had to hide under the velvet drapes when all the rich people came in to eat. YES
　　The mice were so scared when the huge *dog* came closer and closer. NO
　　The country mouse was very happy to return to his simple, quiet life. YES

Phonics: Review the letter Aa. Make a large letter *A* on the floor with colorful masking or plastic tape. One at a time, have the students hop, crawl, jump or walk along the lines of the letter. They can either walk backwards or turn around and retrace steps to stay on the line.

Do the Lesson 4 Phonics worksheet. Complete the letter Aa worksheet. Notice that all of the letters of the alphabet are displayed on the page and that the letters Aa are highlighted with a background. As the students get better at letter recognition you can call out a letter and ask the students to point it out with their finger. Trace the large letter and the small letter. The students can trace the letters between the guide lines. Review the pictures and the colored first letter of the words. The students can color the letters as desired.

Reading: Use a simplified, illustrated daily schedule of activities. Go over the activities on the Daily Schedule poster once again. Ask before and after questions about the schedule.

Writing: Continue to focus on having the students recognize their own first name. During this time, write the students' names on all worksheets and papers.

Writing Skill Builders: Keep these objectives in mind as you direct the class. Include small muscle control activities: tear, fold, and paste whenever possible. Give instructions and reminders to hold a writing instrument correctly. Incorporate writing strokes: horizontal, vertical lines, spiral, and circle into arts and crafts.

Memory Verse: Review Genesis 1:1. Say the verse, leaving out one word. Let the students repeat the verse, filling in the word. Repeat several times, leaving out a different word each time.

Math: Review number recognition of 1. Send your students on a scavenger hunt. Have them find one of the following items: one sock, one shoe, one teddy bear, one piece of candy (make sure there is enough candy for all students), one ruler, one pencil. Make sure these are around the room. Students may work together. Reward each student with one hug.

Do the Lesson 4 Math worksheet. Count each group of items and draw a line to the correct number.

Learn the "This Old Man, He Played One" song to help learn counting. Just work on verse one.

This Old Man, He Played One

Verse 1
This old man, he played one, He played nick-nack on my thumb;
with a nick-nack paddy whack, give a dog a bone. This old man came rolling home.

Teach oral counting 1-10 with the Counting Train. Review the "One, Two, Buckle My Shoe" rhyme/song to help learn counting 1-10.

Shapes: Do the Lesson 4 Shapes worksheet. Have the students color the triangles red and then cut them out. They will be making a set of red, blue, and green triangles over the next couple of days. The different sizes and colors can be used for sorting exercises.

Color: Review the colors red, green, and blue. Display 2 colors of construction paper at a time to the students. Hang them on a line, pin them to a bulletin board or stand them up on the tray of the board. Put one color of construction paper on the left and another on the right. Ask the student's to identify the color by telling you whether the color you ask for is on the right or on the left.

Story Time: Read a story or stories of your choice.

Music: Review "Daddy We Love You." Sing yesterday's song "Around the Circle We Will Go" to the tune of "London Bridge is Falling Down," using a digital recording device to record the students as they sing. Let the girls sing one verse then the boys sing the next. Then everyone sing together. Allow the students to listen to themselves singing the song. Children love to hear themselves on tape.

Multimedia Resources: This week, listen and sing along to selections from "The Amazing Book" CD.

Arts & Crafts/Homework: Ask, Did you complete your homework from yesterday? Tell us a little bit about what you drew. Everyone lives in a different kind of home. How is your home different from other homes around your town?

Health & Safety/Arts & Crafts/Outdoor Activity: First, talk to the students about a clean environment in our city. What is litter? Where does all the litter around the streets come from? What do we call someone who throws trash around the town? A LITTER BUG. Ask, If Gordon throws out a gum wrapper in the yard, how many gum wrappers are there? ONE. If everyone in our class or home throws a gum wrapper in the yard, how many gum wrappers would there be? (NUMBER OF STUDENTS) What if everyone in our neighborhood threw down a gum wrapper? Help the students understand that every piece of trash is litter and is important.

Give every student a paper lunch bag. Let them draw their version of a LITTER BUG on the bag. Give them complete creative freedom to draw their LITTER BUG. Then take a walk around the perimeter of your school or property. Have the children pick up litter, putting it in their bags. Bring it all back inside and dump it in a large trash can. Students can take their litter bags home to use in their cars, or pick up litter on their streets. Make sure to tell them to go with a sibling or parent. You may want to give each child a pair of plastic disposable gloves to use while picking up trash. Also, have the students wash hands thoroughly and/or use waterless hand sanitizer when finished.

Physical Education: Take a shape walk. As you walk around your neighborhood, look for various triangle shapes.

Self Space – Rise and Sink. Have each student pick up a carpet square and then arrange themselves into a circle and sit down on the squares. Greet each student as they find their self space. This is a good time to complement each one on something good that he/she has done. Ask them to close their eyes and relax. Have them wiggle their fingers, rock back and forth, wiggle their toes, move their heads back and forth, etc. Have them open their eyes and get onto their knees and make themselves as small as is possible on their carpet square. From this position do a Rise and Sink, by slowly rising into the largest shape they can make with their bodies, and then slowly sinking back into the smallest shape. Count to eight as they rise and back down to one again as they sink. Repeat this several times counting faster each time so that by the end they are rising and sinking very quickly. End the time with some relaxation activities while seated on the carpet square. Have the students stand and put their carpet squares away.

NOTES:

Lesson 5

Week 1: Day 5

Activities in this Lesson: Bible Lesson, Social Studies, Language Arts, Phonics, Reading, Writing, Memory Verse, Math, Shapes, Color, Story Time, Music, Arts & Crafts, Physical Education

Bible Reference: Genesis 1:2.

Bible Concept to Present: The Holy Spirit was with God when He made our world. God, Jesus, and the Holy Spirit all worked together in making our world.

Bible Lesson: This week in school we have been talking about how Jesus and God made the world in which we live. They made it so beautiful, didn't they? Tell me one thing you like about the world God made for us. (Students answer. You then relate one thing you particularly like.) God and Jesus did a wonderful job of making us a beautiful world. But did you know that there was someone else who helped them to make our world? That someone was the Holy Spirit. In the second verse of the Bible, God tells us that the Holy Spirit was with Him and helped Him to make our world. I am glad that the Holy Spirit was part of God and Jesus and helped to make our world, too. The Holy Spirit was a friend who helped God make the world, and He is a friend who helps us now. The Holy Spirit is a very special helper to people who believe in Jesus. The Holy Spirit helps people who believe in Jesus to love Jesus and to obey Him. I'm glad the Holy Spirit helps people like you and me to love Jesus and obey Him. Let's thank God now for the Holy Spirit and the world He made for us with Jesus and God. Let's tell God "Thank You" for giving us the Holy Spirit as a special friend to help us.

Illustration: Review with your students that God, Jesus, and the Holy Spirit made our world. To illustrate this, say the "In the Beginning" finger play poem. Have the students repeat each line after you say it first.

In the Beginning

A long time ago (wave arms in a circular motion)
Our world was made (form hands into circle)
God says it was so. (Hold hands like a Bible)

God made our world (Hold up one finger)
The Holy Spirit did too (Hold up two fingers)
Jesus was there (Hold up three fingers)
God says this is true. (Hold hands like a Bible)

Thank You Dear God (Hands formed for prayer)
For the world you made.
Thank You Jesus
For the help You gave.
Thank You Holy Spirit
For the work that You did.
Thanks to all Three (Hold up three fingers)
It is as God has said. (Hands held to form a Bible)

Social Studies: Discuss the concept that God tells the truth all the time. What God says is always true. Tell your student that God always tells the truth. If you need to explain what "Truth" is, explain that when someone is telling the truth and they say they will do something, they do it. For example, "If I am telling the truth and I say I will give you a big hug, I give you a big hug." God said that the Holy Spirit was with Him and Jesus when they made our world, so we know this is true.

Play a game similar to "Simon Says." Use the statement "God Said" prefacing the statement you make. The students will clap their hands if they hear you say "God Said." Use the following statements:

> God said, "Jesus helped me make the world." (Child claps)
> God said, "The Holy Spirit helped me make the world." (Child claps)
> God said, "I helped to make the world." (Child claps)
> We all made the world. (Child does not clap)
> (Continue with your own statements.)

Multimedia Resources: Watch the video "Music Machine" which teaches about the Fruit of the Spirit.

Language Arts: Do this activity with a tape recorder. Record a series of true statements about yourself repeating the previous statements each time. For example: "I am a lady." "I am a lady. I have brown hair." "I am a lady. I have brown hair. I am tall." "I am a lady. I have brown hair. I am tall. I have brown shoes." Play each statement, and then let the students repeat the information. See how far they can go with more and more information.

Phonics: Teach the letter Bb. Today teach capital *B*.

Show the students the Bb flashcard. Compare the shape of *B* to *A*. Point out any student's name beginning with the letter *B*. Write some words beginning with the letter *B* on the board. Include any student names from the class that begin with letter *B*. Underline the capital *B* that begins the words. Read through the words and point out the shape of letter *B*. Have the students trace the *B* in the air as you trace the letter *B* beginning each name.

> Boys: Ben, Boaz, Betty, Bob, Blake, Bobby, Bradley, Brady, Brandon, Brendan, Brent, Brett, Brian, Bryan, Bryce
> Girls: Bethany, Bianca, Brandi, Brandy, Breanna, Brenda, Briana, Brianna, Bridget, Britney, Brittany, Brittney, Brooke
> Vocabulary words: Boys (restroom), Bus Stop

Do the Lesson 5 Phonics worksheet. Complete the letter Bb worksheet. Have the students trace the letters Bb with their fingers. They should trace the letters with their fingers and say the names of the letters. Demonstrate the proper strokes for them on the board. Say the words for each of the pictures and look at the Bb letters that begin them.

Reading: Read the first names of classmates. See if students can recognize the names of their fellow students. Have each student find the Name Plate of someone who sits next to him or her on the Class Roster bulletin board.

Writing: Continue to focus on having the students recognize their own first name. During this time, write the students' names on all worksheets and papers.

Writing Skill Builders: Keep these objectives in mind as you direct the class. Include small muscle control activities: tear, fold, and paste whenever possible. Give instructions and reminders to hold a writing instrument correctly. Incorporate writing strokes: horizontal, vertical lines, spiral, and circle into arts and crafts.

Memory Verse: Review Genesis 1:1. Say phrases of the verse and have the students complete the rest.

Math: Review number recognition of 1. For today's lesson of the number one, trace your student's footprints onto construction paper. On the left footprint, place one dot - on the right, write the number one. Tell your student to count the dots on the left footprint. How many are there? One. Now show them the number one on the other footprint. Tell them this number (1) represents one. *Prepare a pan (9x13) which contains cornmeal and rice mixed together (covering the bottom of the pan well)* and have students practice writing the number one. Practice counting one item throughout the house or classroom.

Do the Lesson 5 Math worksheet. Notice that all of the numbers are displayed on the page and that the number 1 is highlighted with a background. As the students get better at number recognition you can call out a number and ask the students to point it out with their finger. Have the students trace the large number 1 with the proper stroke by following the arrow. Count each group of items and trace the number.

Review verse one of "This Old Man, He Played One."

Teach oral counting 1-10 with the Number Train.

Shapes: *Prepare ahead – Cut out some really large triangles from 11 x 17 colored paper.* Review again the "Timmy Triangle" poem found in Lesson 3. Discuss the concept of larger and smaller as you show students the triangles. You will want to encourage students to verbalize the relationship between the triangles.

Do the Lesson 5 Shapes worksheet. Have the students color the triangles blue and then cut them out. They will be making a set of red, blue, and green triangles. The different sizes and colors can be used for sorting exercises.

Color: Review the colors red, green, and blue. Drill with flashcards.

Story Time: Read a story or stories of your student's choice.

Music: Review "Daddy We Love You" and "Around the Circle We Will Go." Teach the "Three In One" song to the tune of "Three Blind Mice."

Three In One
Tune of Three Blind Mice

Three in one (Hold up three fingers, then one)
Three in one (Hold up three fingers, then one)
See how they work
See how they work
They all are working together to make

Our world which is so neat and great
Three in one (Hold up three fingers, then one)
Three in one. (Hold up three fingers, then one)

Multimedia Resources: This week, listen and sing along to selections from "The Amazing Book" CD.

Arts & Crafts: Obtain some narrow sponges from the grocery store. Cut them into the basic shapes of a circle, square, rectangle, and triangle. Place a clothespin on the back of them for ease in picking them up. Dip the shape sponges into thick finger paint and then place them onto paper.

Note: Thick paint can be mixed easily by purchasing the dry tempera paints. If you will add a few drops of liquid dish soap to the paint before you mix, it will more easily be removed from clothing. Freezer paper works the best for this type of painting, as it contains a wax on the back of it to stop leakage. This type of paper may be purchased from your grocer, a food service supply or businesses online.

Physical Education: Cut large triangles from contact paper. Place them on the floor of the room where you exercise. Can your student do these things while standing on the shape?

1. Touch your hand to your head?
2. Touch your finger to your nose?
3. Place your ear on your shoulder?
4. Bend down and touch your toes?
5. Hold your arms out straight and pretend to be an airplane?
6. Bend at the waist, putting your hands on top of your head?
7. Hop on one foot?
8. Hop on two feet?
9. Hold one leg while hopping?
10. Smile real big for the teacher?

Note: If your students do not know the parts of their body, illustrate them for them. If they cannot hop on one foot, or hold one leg while hopping, this is an indication that they may not be ready for the reading or writing skills in this program.

NOTES:

Lesson 6

Week 2: Day 1

Activities in this Lesson: Bible Lesson, Social Studies, Language Arts, Phonics, Reading, Writing, Memory Verse, Math, Shapes, Color, Story Time, Music, Arts & Crafts, Physical Education

Bible Reference: Genesis 1:26 uses a plural term when referring to the Creation. By this reference and others, we know there was more than one personage present in Creation. Colossians 1:13-16 states that Jesus created, with God, all things. Genesis 1:2 states that the Spirit was upon the face of the waters. Thus we have Three in One in the Creation of our world. This is referred to as the Trinity. Review the "Three In One" finger play song from Lesson 5.

Bible Concept to Present: God the Father, God the Holy Spirit, and God the Son are one.

Note: Your students will not fully understand this. It is not our intent that they do so. Rather, we are presenting this information as a "trail blazer" so as to have a path to follow later. This is one instance in which you as a teacher expect nothing more than the names of the Godhead and the fact that they interrelate in some manner, to be retained by your students. Refer back to this concept in normal conversation by personal reference to God as "The Father," "The Son - Jesus" or "The Holy Spirit."

Illustration: At tables, give each student a disposable bowl. Bring in one egg for each student. (If you have a small class, you may do this illustration with one egg, but it is more fun if each student has their own egg.) First, hold up an egg. Help each student to break the egg into the bowls. Ask, "What is inside the egg? We have an egg yolk, egg white, and egg shell. That is three things. Yet they are all one egg. Three in one." Clean up and wash hands then continue with the story below.

Bible Lesson: In the beginning God, Jesus, and the Holy Spirit created our world. God, Jesus, and the Holy Spirit are one. Can you tell me about the egg we just studied? How many eggs were there? (Students should answer: one.) But how many parts were there to the egg? (Three.) This is like our God. We use the name God when we are talking about God, the Father. We use the name God when we are talking about God, the Son (Jesus). We use the name God when we are talking about God, the Holy Spirit. All three have different names, but yet they are One. They each have special things that they do. I am happy that God, Jesus, and the Holy Spirit are one, aren't you?

Multimedia Resources: Listen to the song "God Is Forever" from the "Music Machine: The Majesty of God" CD.

Social Studies: You will be presenting the concept that although there are different members in a family, it is still one family. Ask students to share who the people are in their family. Let them list the names. Share the members of your family. Though there are several members, it is still one family. We have the same last name. (Be sensitive to the fact that some families have two or three last names represented.) This is the way it is with God, Jesus, and the Holy Spirit. They are individual, but one.

Language Arts: Call each child by their first and last name. Ask them to come and sit with you in a separate area (such as on the floor) of the room. Have them repeat the following, echoing you: "My name is _____ (First and Last Name)." Now, play a game using three things that are related (example: scissors, glue, pencil). Have your students look at them for one minute. Then remove one item as the children close their eyes. Have them open their eyes and guess which item is missing.

Phonics: Review the letter Bb. Make a capital letter *B* with your body. Have the students stand up straight and tall to make the straight side of capital *B*. Then have them hold their hands together and touch their foreheads. Now make a big circle motion down to their waists and from their waist down to their ankles. They will have to bend over to do this. Have them stand tall and straight again with arms at their sides. Can they "see" the big circles they made in front of themselves as a capital letter *B*?

Teach the small letter *b* today. Show the students the Bb flashcard. Compare the shape of small *b* to small *a*. Write some words beginning with the letter *b* on the board. Include words from stories or activities that tie this lesson to other things that have already been done. Underline the small *b* that begins the words. Read through the words and point out the shape of letter *b*. Have the students trace the *b* in the air as you trace the letter *b* beginning each word.

> Common words: back, be, been, before, between, big, boy, build, but, by
> Vocabulary words: behind, below, black, blood, blue, body, bottom, breathe, brown, bulb

Reading: Read the first names of classmates. See if students can recognize the names of their fellow students. Have each student find the Name Plate of someone who sits next to him or her on the Class Roster bulletin board.

Multimedia Resources: View the Aa-Bb segments of "Rev-Up for Reading" from the "Rev-Up for Learning" DVD to drill letter recognition and sound. The students should say each letter sound along with the presentation.

Writing: Continue to focus on having the students recognize their own first name. During this time, write the students' names on all worksheets and papers.

Writing Skill Builders: Keep these objectives in mind as you direct the class. Include small muscle control activities: tear, fold, and paste whenever possible. Give instructions and reminders to hold a writing instrument correctly. Incorporate writing strokes: horizontal, vertical lines, spiral, and circle into arts and crafts.

Multimedia Resources: View the Aa segments of "Rev-Up for Writing" from the "Rev-Up for Learning" DVD to review the writing of upper- and lowercase letters. The students should write each letter in the air along with the presentation. Since the first half of the presentation covers lowercase letters and the second half uppercase letters some navigation will be needed to skip to the letters that are covered in this lesson.

Memory Verse: Review Genesis 1:1. Recite the verse several times during the school day.

Math: Teach number recognition of 2. Introduce the number 2 by counting items. Show them the number 2 flashcard. Use the student's footprints again. On one footprint draw two circles or dots and on the other write the number 2. Have your students count two of items around your home or classroom then find two shoes, two eyes, two ears, two fingers, two feet, two teddy-bears, two dolls, two raisins, etc. If you have hung cards for the week of the school year point out the Week 2 card.

Compare the number 1 and number 2 flashcards. Count the items on each card.

Teach oral counting 1-10 with the Number Train. Review the "One, Two, Buckle My Shoe" rhyme/song.

Review the number 1 by learning the "One Little Puppy" finger play.

One Little Puppy
by Al Christopherson

One little puppy, one little flea, (Hold up one finger)
One puppy sitting, there by the tree, (Hold up one finger, point to a tree)
One puppy running, along with me, (Hold up one finger, wiggle fingers like running legs)
One is a number I love, you see. (Hold up one finger, cross arms over heart)

Do the Lesson 6 Math worksheet. Count each group and draw lines to match groups that have the same number.

Shapes: Look for everyday items that are triangular in shape. Items such as the hands on a clock, etc. can be pointed out to students. See if your students can observe other triangles around the room or home. Repeat the "Timmy Triangle" poem in the first day's lesson.

Do the Lesson 6 Shapes worksheet. Have the students color the triangles green and then cut them out. They now have a set of red, blue, and green triangles. The different sizes and colors can be used for sorting exercises.

Color: Review the colors red, green, and blue.

Story Time: Read a story or stories of your choice.

Music: Review "Daddy We Love You," "Around the Circle We Will Go," and "Three In One." Sing the following song, inserting the names of your students. Play the song "I Know He Loves Me Too" from the "Horizons Preschool Music" CD.

I Know He Loves Me Too

I Know He Loves Me Too
I love   (student's name)
I love   (student's name)
I love   (student's name)
And I know she (he) loves me too.

The song continues with each student's name inserted. The last verse is sung as "We love Jesus," and continued as above.

Multimedia Resources: This week, listen and sing along to selections from "Bullfrogs and Butterflies: God is Great" CD.

Arts & Crafts: Let each student draw their family, including every member. Be certain that each student knows their first and last name and their father's name.

Note: Be aware of how your students draw the people in their family. Do they have the arms coming out of the head? Does the person they have drawn have legs and arms? The way a child draws people is an indication of their readiness to teach reading.

"A Ripping Good Time." Have the students rip various shapes from red, green, and blue construction paper and put them into a bag. Make a collage by gluing the torn pieces of paper onto a sheet of white paper. Hang them around the room for all to enjoy before sending them home.

Physical Education: Do the following activity items in sets of three to go with the three in one theme of this lesson. Repeat the activity in sets of two to reinforce the study of the number 2.

1. Take three steps forward.
2. Take three steps backward.
3. Hop three times.
4. Jump on one foot three times.
5. Hop on the other foot three times.
6. Stretch your arms toward the sky three times.
7. Breathe deeply three times.
8. Touch your toes three times.
9. Sit down on the floor, relax your body like a rag doll, and count to three.

NOTES:

Lesson 7

Week 2: Day 2

Activities in this Lesson: Bible Lesson, Social Studies, Language Arts/Arts & Crafts, Phonics, Reading, Writing, Memory Verse/Music, Math, Shapes, Color, Story Time, Music, Health & Safety, Physical Education, Homework, Optional Math/Language Arts/Bible/Arts & Crafts Activity

Bible Reference: Genesis 1:26.

Bible Concept to Present: God has three names: God the Father, God the Son, and God the Holy Spirit

Bible Lesson: Review yesterday's story. Make sure students know the three names: God the Father, Jesus the Son, and Holy Spirit. Review the "Three In One" finger play song.

Illustration: *Find a large weed. Carefully pull it up including the roots. Wash off the roots. Spread it out on a piece of white construction paper, placed on a cookie sheet.* Show the weed, or plant, to the students. Ask, "What is this? This plant has three parts." Point to the roots and ask, "What are these?" Point to the leaves and ask, "What are these?" Point to the stem and ask, "What are these?" Your students probably won't know all three; tell them what the parts of the plant are, if necessary. Let them feel the plant. "So, we have leaves, stems, and roots. But these are all one plant. Three in one."

Social Studies: Talk about our families. What makes a family? The typical family is a dad, mom, and children. But there are many kinds of families. Let the students share about their families. Who has the biggest family? Who has the most sisters? The most brothers? Are pets part of a family? What kind of pets do you have? Who has the most pets? If you could be any pet, what would it be? Let the students have a little loud time, pretending to be their favorite pet. Have some students talk about their extended family. How many brothers and sisters does dad have? Does mom have?

Language Arts/Arts & Crafts: *Before class, write the students' names large and very clearly on white construction paper.* Give each student a piece of construction paper with their name on it. Have poster pens available. Ask them to decorate their names. You might use a dry erase board to show them how to make animals out of letters, by adding eyes or feet or wings. Encourage them to use their imaginations. Collect these for a follow-up exercise that will be done tomorrow.

Phonics: Review the letter Bb.

Do the Lesson 7 Phonics worksheet. Complete the letter Bb worksheet. Notice that all of the letters of the alphabet are displayed on the page and that the letters Bb are highlighted with a background. As the students get better at letter recognition you can call out a letter and ask the students to point it out with their finger. Trace the large letter and the small letter. The students can trace the letters between the guide lines. Review the pictures and the colored first letter of the words. The students can color the letters as desired.

Reading: Use a simplified, illustrated daily schedule of activities. Continue to review the schedule by asking before and after questions.

Writing: Continue to focus on having the students recognize their own first name. During this time, write the students' names on all worksheets and papers.

Writing Skill Builders: Keep these objectives in mind as you direct the class. Include small muscle control activities: tear, fold, and paste whenever possible. Give instructions and reminders to hold a writing instrument correctly. Incorporate writing strokes: horizontal, vertical lines, spiral, and circle into arts and crafts.

Memory Verse/Music: Review Genesis 1:1. Say the memory verse for the class. Remember, some students might have never done a memory verse before. Have a big bowl of rice available for the students. Give each child an empty film canister. Let them scoop up some rice into their canister and carefully snap on the lids. Make sure all lids are tightly closed. Lead a Memory Verse March. Let the children march around the room, or outside, chanting the memory verse and shaking their rice.

Math: Review number recognition of 2. Continue to teach your students to count to, and understand by counting items, the number 2. Give them various blocks and have them count two of each. Give them a stack of shapes (triangles and squares) and have them find two of each. Have them glue two of each on a piece of paper. Each two must be on a separate sheet glued side by side. Ask them with each activity to count the sets of two. How many are in each set?

Teach oral counting 1-10 with the Number Train.

Review the number 1 by reviewing the "One Little Puppy" finger play.

Do the Lesson 7 Math worksheet. Cut out the numbers from the strip. Assist the students as is needed with cutting out the numbers. Count each group of objects and paste the correct number in the box.

Shapes: Continue to look for everyday items that are triangular in shape.

Do the Lesson 7 Shapes worksheet. Have the students count the number of triangles on the sheet. They can color, cut, and paste the triangles to make the hats.

Color: Review the colors red, green, and blue. Play the game Red light/Green light by holding up red or green flashcards rather than saying the word. Large circles can also be cut from colored construction paper to play the game.

Red Light, Green Light is played with two lines at opposite ends of the playing area. One line is the goal line; the other is the starting line. One player is "It" and stands on the goal line. IT shuts their eyes and counts to 10 a number of times. At the end of a count to 10, he calls out, "Green light" or any other color light. While they are counting to 10 again, the players advance toward the goal line. When IT calls "Red light," he open their eyes and all of the players must stop moving. Any player who IT catches in motion must return to the starting line. Players can continue moving if any color other than "Red light" is called. The suspense of the game occurs as the players wonder what color will be called. The first player to reach the goal wins. The last one is IT for the next game.

Story Time: Read a story or stories of your choice.

Music: Review "Daddy We Love You," "Around the Circle We Will Go," "Three In One," and "I Know He Loves Me Too." Continue to teach the "ABC Song." If the students do not already know it, work on one line at a time until all lines are mastered. This will help to develop an awareness of the entire alphabet. The students can sing along even though they cannot recognize the individual letters.

A B C Song
Tune of Twinkle, Twinkle, Little Star

A B C D E F G
H I J K L M N O P
Q R S T U and V
W X Y and Z.
Now I've learned my ABCs.
Next time won't you sing with me!

Multimedia Resources: This week, listen and sing along to selections from "Bullfrogs and Butterflies: God is Great" CD.

Health & Safety: Bring the weed from the Bible illustration back to the class. Talk about different kinds of "weeds." There are some weeds that we shouldn't touch. Mention some weeds or plants in your area of the country that are poisonous. Explain to the students that they should never touch weeds or plants unless they are sure that they are OK. Examples of plants poisonous to humans: foxglove, irises, lily of the valley, mushrooms, oleander, poison ivy, poison oak, poison sumac, wisteria.* Did you ever get a rash from touching a plant? A rash is little red bumps on your skin. And it is very itchy. If you get a rash anywhere on your body, be sure and tell your parents.

Physical Education: Self Space and General Space. Have each student pick up a carpet square and then arrange themselves into a circle and sit down on the squares. Start by asking the students to look around the room and name some of the things that they can see. Explain to the students that what they have seen and mentioned is their space. Within this space we can explore both self space and general space. Show them an example of self space by standing in one spot and moving your arms and legs. Say, Within this space I can make these kinds of movements. Then move all around the room using the whole body which is general space. Say, In the rest of the room I can make these kinds of movements. Have the students do some movements in their self space on the carpet squares and then do some movements in the general space of the room. After moving around the room, have them return to their carpet square and do some more movements while standing on the square. Have the students pick up the squares and put them away.

Homework: Say, Tomorrow, we will be talking about work. Take the Lesson 7 Homework worksheet, home and help your parents with a chore tonight. Bring your homework sheet back tomorrow.

Optional Math/Language Arts/Bible/Arts & Crafts Activity: Throughout this year, the students will be learning the numbers 0-12. In the student worksheet booklet you will find patterns and illustrations for Bible Numbers. You may either use these to reinforce the teaching of the number at the time you teach that number, or use them for a review later in the year. They may also be used as an additional Language Arts project as you tell the stories. This activity will be given on Day 2 of the weekly schedule but it can be spread over several days or moved to other days of your yearly schedule.

2 Boys: Genesis 25:24-28, read the Bible verses and tell the story.

Isaac and Rebekah had two baby boys. They were twins.
Their names were Jacob and Esau.
A tent was their home as they were growing up.

Do the Lesson 7 Bible Numbers worksheet. Give each student a sheet of white construction paper and the worksheet. Cut out the items on the worksheet and glue them to construction paper as illustrated in the drawing. Draw in the arms and faces for the "2" boys. Draw a tent in the background and sand under the numbers.

NOTES:

*Cornell University Poisonous Plants Database from the internet

Lesson 8

Week 2: Day 3

Activities in this Lesson: Bible Lesson, Social Studies, Language Arts, Phonics, Reading, Writing, Memory Verse, Math, Shapes, Color, Story Time, Music, Arts & Crafts, Physical Education, Homework

Bible Reference: Genesis 1:26.

Bible Concept to Present: Jesus, God, and the Holy Spirit all created our world.

Bible Lesson: On our last school day, we talked about how God is really three persons. Can you remember the special names we have for God? There is God the Father, God the Son, and God the Holy Spirit. Did you know that when God created our world, God the Father, God the Son, and God the Holy Spirit all had a special job they did? That's right. All three of them worked together to make our world for us. We are not told in the Bible what each of them did, but we are told that they all had very special things they did and that they all worked together to make our world very beautiful for us. I am happy God the Father, God the Son, and God the Holy Spirit worked together to make our world. They did such a nice job for us. Let's thank God now for the work He, Jesus, and the Holy Spirit did to make our world for us.

Multimedia Resource: Listen to the song "God Cares" from the "Music Machine: The Majesty of God" CD and the song "Only Elohim" from "Sir Oliver's Song" CD.

Illustration: Tell your students how important it is for people to work together. "God, Jesus, and the Holy Spirit worked together to create our world. God wants us to do things together, too. Let's clean our classroom together. You will help to get the work done." As you work, explain to your students how much faster the work goes when we have help. Hand out damp paper towels for students to use. Relate how the work you are doing together is similar to the work the Trinity did when they created our world, in the relationship that they worked together.

Social Studies: Working together is important. Discuss things we do in our family every day working together. Ask students to share any chores they already do. Talk about what is too hard and what is doable. Explain that students will be making a Chore Chart to help them start doing helpful chores for their family. Everyone needs to learn how to work and help one another.

Multimedia Resources: Watch "Politeness" from the *Character Builders Video Series*.

Language Arts: Do the "Left, Right Finger Play" finger activity:

Left, Right Finger Play

This little hand is left (Hold up left hand)
This little hand is right (Hold up right hand)
Both little hands will work for *Teacher* (*Mommy, Daddy, Jesus, etc.*)
Every day and night.

Make a "Touch 'n' Say" box by covering a small box with contact paper or wallpaper. Cut a hole in the lid. Put several items into the box, at least as many items as you have students: pencils, eraser, fork, spoon, balloon, quarter, wash cloth, small ball, paper cup, etc. Have each student guess what each item is before he pulls it from the box. Ask, How does your object feel? Is it soft? Is it heavy?

Phonics: Teach the letter Cc.

Show them the letter Cc flashcard. Point out any student's name beginning with the letter *C*. Write some words beginning with the letter *C* on the board. Include any student names from the class that begin with letter *C*. Underline the capital *C* that begins the words. Read through the words and point out the shape of letter *C*. Have the students trace the *C* in the air as you trace the letter *C* beginning each name.

> Boys: Cain, Carmen, Chris, Caleb, Calvin, Cameron, Carl, Carlos, Casey, Cesar, Chad, Chance, Charles, Chase, Christian, Christopher, Clayton, Cody, Colby, Cole, Colin, Collin, Colton, Conner, Connor, Corey, Cory, Craig, Cristian, Curtis

> Girls: Caitlin, Caitlyn, Candace, Carly, Caroline, Carolyn, Casey, Cassandra, Cassidy, Catherine, Chelsea, Chelsey, Cheyenne, Chloe, Christina, Christine, Ciara, Cierra, Cindy, Claire, Claudia, Colleen, Courtney, Cristina, Crystal, Cynthia

Do the Lesson 8 Phonics worksheet. Complete the letter Cc worksheet. Have the students trace the letters Cc with their fingers. They should trace the letters with their fingers and say the names of the letters. Demonstrate the proper strokes for them on the board. Say the words for each of the pictures and look at the Cc letters that begin them.

The Alphabet Puzzles from the Resource Packet can be used to reinforce letter recognition. Follow the given instructions for duplicating and using the puzzles.

Reading: Read the first names of the classmates. Use the Language Arts/Arts & Crafts activity from yesterday to review first names. Point out at least one good thing about each person's artwork. Ask a few of the students to describe their artwork to the class. (If you are on a three day schedule you can do both the artwork and the discussion today.)

Writing: Continue to focus on having the students recognize their own first name. During this time, write the students' names on all worksheets and papers.

Writing Skill Builders: Keep these objectives in mind as you direct the class. Include small muscle control activities: tear, fold, and paste whenever possible. Give instructions and reminders to hold a writing instrument correctly. Incorporate writing strokes: horizontal, vertical lines, spiral, and circle into arts and crafts.

Memory Verse: Review Genesis 1:1. Make up some actions for the verse.

Math: Review number recognition of 2. Show your students what a number 2 looks like. When we count to two we are counting (write this out...) 1 and 2. In writing, it looks like this. Let's make our own counting book. Make a simple book from a folded 1/2 sheet of paper that has an outline of the number one on the front. On that page the student colors the one, and places one sticker beside it. On the next page write an outline of the number 2. Have students color it, and place two stickers on that page. Praise good work. You will want students to stay inside the lines when they color, and they will need to count out the number of stickers to place beside each number.

Review the number 1 by reviewing the "One Little Puppy" finger play.

Do the Lesson 8 Math worksheet. Demonstrate how to do this on the board. Have several students come up and draw the lines that match the number of objects to the number. Go through the objects on the worksheet together recognizing the item and counting how many there are of each thing. Have the students count again to themselves and draw the line to the number.

Start learning the second verse to "This Old Man, He Played One."

This Old Man, He Played One

Verse 1
This old man, he played one, He played nick-nack on my thumb;
with a nick-nack paddy whack, give a dog a bone. This old man came rolling home.

Verse 2
This old man, he played two, He played nick-nack on my shoe;
with a nick-nack paddy whack, give a dog a bone. This old man came rolling home.

Teach oral counting 1-10 with the "Counting Train."

Additional Math: Ask your students to line up in size sequence. Who is the tallest? Who is next? Who is the shortest or smallest? Emphasize that people come in all sizes and God made each one special and loves them just as they are.

Shapes: Make some triangle-shaped cookies.*Use the recipe below to make cookie dough.* Then using a plastic knife, outline the shape of a triangle on the dough several times and have students cut the cookies. You may also cut a shape from cardboard and have students cut around it. Teach safety as you do this exercise.

Peanut Butter Playdough

1 part peanut butter
1 part honey
2 parts dry milk

Mix together and roll into a flat circle. Cut out shapes. If dough is sticky, add more dry milk.

Do the Lesson 8 Shapes worksheet. Have the students count, trace, and color the triangles. They can color the rest of the picture.

Color: Review the colors red, green, and blue.

Start a growth chart either on banner paper or a chart that has been purchased. Measure your students regularly, naming and dating the notation.

Story Time: Read a story or stories of your choice.

Music: Review "I Know He Loves Me Too," "Three In One," "Around the Circle We Will Go," and "Daddy We Love You."

Teach this little song to the tune of "The More We Get Together."

For Here We are Together
Tune of The More We Get Together

For here we are together, together, together
For here we are together
Helping teacher work (add Mommy, Daddy, etc.)

Use the "Hokey Pokey" song to help teach the concept of right and left.

Hokey Pokey

You put your left foot in
You take your left foot out,
You put your left foot in,
And you shake it all about.
You do the Hokey Pokey and you turn yourself around.
And that's what it's all about.
Hey! (clap)

(Continue using various body parts and left and right.)

Multimedia Resources: This week, listen and sing along to selections from "Bullfrogs and Butterflies: God is Great" CD.

Arts & Crafts: Ask your students to make large items and small items with playdough. Then ask them to make an item we would use in work with someone else (rolling pins, knives, plates, outdoor tools, etc.). Give students plenty of time to create. Accept their interpretation of a subject without criticism from you in any form.

Physical Education: Explore ways to make yourselves very small and very large similar to the Rise and Sink activity done in Lesson 4. Can you make yourself very small? How? Make yourself to be the smallest you can be. Now how can you make yourself to be the largest you can be? Discuss the ways, and then try it. (For small, roll into a tight ball. For large, stretch out as tall as you can.) This activity can be done on the carpet squares or outside in a grassy area. The students can demonstrate for each other how they make themselves small and large.

Homework: Talk about the chores the students did last night. Are chores sometimes fun? Do they need to be done even if they are hard? Send the Lesson 8 Homework worksheet Making Chore Hands home with the students. Make sure that they understand that these will not be returned to class.

NOTES:

Lesson 9

Week 2: Day 4

Activities in this Lesson: Bible Lesson, Outdoor Activity, Music, Social Studies, Phonics, Reading, Writing, Memory Verse, Math, Shapes, Color, Story Time, Arts & Crafts, Health & Safety/Creative Cooking, Physical Education, Homework

Bible Reference: Genesis 1:26.

Bible Concept to Present: God, Jesus, and the Holy Spirit created with joy.

Bible Lesson: Review yesterday's story. Emphasize that God, Jesus and the Holy Spirit joyfully did their work.

Outdoor Activity: Say, Everyone learns how to work. When we work hard, it makes our play time more special. Today, we are going to work outside. Take the students outside to clear the grounds of sticks, leaves, twigs, and trash. As they did trash last week, look more for sticks, leaves, and twigs. You may provide plastic bags or lunch bags for each student. Explain that if they work for fifteen minutes, then they can play for fifteen minutes.

Multimedia Resources: Watch "Joy" from the *Character Builders Video Series*.

Music: While clearing the grounds, sing this song with the students to the tune of "The Mulberry Bush." Review "For Here We are Together," "Hokey Pokey," and "I Know He Loves Me Too."

This is the Way We Do Our Work
Tune of The Mulberry Bush

This is the way we do our work, do our work, do our work.
This is the way we do our work, so early in the morning.
This the way we pick up leaves...
This the way we help our school...
This is the way do our part...

Multimedia Resources: This week, listen and sing along to selections from "Bullfrogs and Butterflies: God is Great" CD.

Social Studies: *Bring tools or pictures of tools: a broom, a hammer, a phone, gardening tools, a sewing machine, a ruler, a watering can, a computer,* anything that can be used for work. Say, Look at this hammer. This is a tool. We use tools to do work. What kind of work can we do with this hammer? Let children respond. Repeat with all of the tools you have brought.

Phonics: Review the letter Cc.

Do the Lesson 9 Phonics worksheet. Complete the letter Cc worksheet. Notice that all of the letters of the alphabet are displayed on the page and that the letters Cc are highlighted with a background. As the students get better at letter recognition you can call out a letter and ask the students to point it out with their finger. Trace the large letter and the small letter. The students can trace the letters between the guide lines. Review the pictures and the colored first letter of the words. The students can color the letters as desired.

The Alphabet Puzzles from the Resource Packet can be used to reinforce letter recognition. Follow the given instructions for duplicating and using the puzzles.

Reading: Use a simplified, illustrated daily schedule of activities. Read the first names of classmates.

Writing: Continue to focus on having the students recognize their own first name. During this time, write the students' names on all worksheets and papers.

Writing Skill Builders: Keep these objectives in mind as you direct the class. Include small muscle control activities: tear, fold, and paste whenever possible. Give instructions and reminders to hold a writing instrument correctly. Incorporate writing strokes: horizontal, vertical lines, spiral, and circle into arts and crafts.

Memory Verse: Finish work on Genesis 1:1 today. Let the students recite if they are willing.

Math: Review number recognition of 2. Use the Lesson 9 Resource sheet, Counting Pennies chart to count the group of 1 penny and the group of 2 pennies. Say the number 1 and then count one penny. Say the number 2 and then count one, two pennies, point to each penny as you count.

Teach oral counting 1-10 with the Counting Train.

Review the number 1 by reviewing the "One Little Puppy" finger play.

Do the Lesson 9 Math worksheet. Count each group of items and circle the correct number for the group.

Shapes: Continue to look for everyday items that are triangular in shape. Create some shape songs to sing to your favorite tunes. They can be very simple and funny. Something like "Old MacDonald had a Triangle" is all they need to have some fun. Combine the song with some actions whenever possible.

Do the Lesson 9 Shapes worksheet. Trace the triangles, color the biggest triangle blue, color the smallest triangle red, and draw lines to complete the triangle ice cream cone.

Color: Review the colors red, green, and blue.

Story Time: Read a story or stories of your choice.

Arts & Crafts: *Gather some old newspapers. Cut the full newspaper sheets in half.* Make hats with the students, folding them in the same way you fold to make a boat. Say, We are all going to be workers today, workers that wear hats. What kind of worker are you? Put on your hat and tell us who you are. Examples: crossing guard, construction worker, fast food salesperson, police officer, fire fighter; baker, baseball player, nurse, doctor, butcher, etc.

Health & Safety/Creative Cooking: Make cookies. As you make the cookies together, explain how important clean hands are to everyone. Everything we touch has germs so we wash our hands several times throughout the day. Measuring is very important. Each ingredient has to be measured. Let the students help measure and mix. When the cookies are done, talk about size. Use the terms "large, larger, largest, small, smaller, smallest" for the cookies.

Pumpkin Chocolate Chip Cookies

INGREDIENTS:

1 can of pumpkin	1 teaspoon cinnamon
1 egg	1 1/2 teaspoons salt
1/2 c. oil	1 teaspoon baking soda
1 c. sugar	1 teaspoon milk
2 teaspoons Baking Powder	1 teaspoon vanilla
2 c. Flour	1 - 12 oz. bag Chocolate chips

Pre-heat the oven to 350 degrees. Mix ingredients together as listed. Let the students stir by turns between each addition. Drop by spoonfuls on an un-greased cookie sheet. Bake for 12-15 minutes. Let cool on waxed paper.

Physical Education: Continue to explore Self Space and General Space. Sing the song "Hokey, Pokey" while standing on the carpet squares.

Homework: Let the students share who have completed their homework. Did they make their hand card? What chores are they doing?

NOTES:

Activities in this Lesson: Bible Lesson, Social Studies, Language Arts, Phonics, Reading, Writing, Memory Verse, Math, Shapes, Color, Story Time, Music, Arts & Crafts, Physical Education

Bible Reference: The Bible references on this concept are scattered throughout Scripture. John 10:30, Colossians 2:8 & 9, Romans 1:20, Matthew 3:16-17, Deuteronomy 6:4. We, as adults, understand that the work that is done by each personage of the Godhead differs somewhat. In this lesson we will be presenting the basic concept of each Personage's work.

Bible Concept to Present: God, Jesus, and the Holy Spirit are very special friends to us.

Bible Lesson: God, Jesus, and the Holy Spirit are three very special friends of ours. God is our Father. He cares for us very much and knows how to do very nice things for us. God loved us so much He made our beautiful world for us, and then gave us His own Son. (Refer to whatever facts your students already know about Jesus.) Jesus came to live on earth. He came as a little baby, and He loves us so much that He is now busy making a home for us in Heaven. The Holy Spirit is with us now. He helps us to love Jesus and to obey what Jesus and God have said for us to do. He helps us everyday to do good things. He cares about us very much and gives us special help when we need it. God, Jesus, and the Holy Spirit are good friends of ours. I am very happy to have God, Jesus, and the Holy Spirit for my friends.

Illustration: Use the Lesson 10 Resource page to illustrate this lesson.

Social Studies: Say, We have friends here on earth that we enjoy. Who are your friends? We are all friends here. What do you like about one another? Have older students make a card for each friend that says "Thank You for being such a good friend." The drawing on the front of the card can be of your student and a friend doing something together that is very special to each.

Multimedia Resources: Listen to the song "Friends Forever" from the "Bullfrogs and Butterflies: God Loves Fun" CD.

Language Arts: Sharing Project: Give every other student a whole graham cracker. Have him or her share it with the teacher or another student. Talk about sharing. *Prepare ahead of time a box with two things that go together*, for example, a sock and a shoe, hammer and nail, fork and spoon, salt and pepper. Mix them up and let the students sort and put the items together. The more items you have, the more challenging the game will be.

Multimedia Resources: Watch "Sharing" from the *Character Builders Video Series*.

Complete the Lesson 10 Language Arts worksheet. Use a crayon or pencil to draw straight and wavy lines to connect the items that go together.

Phonics: Review the letter Cc.

Teach the small letter *c*. Write some words beginning with the letter *c* on the board. Include words from stories or activities that tie this lesson to other things that have already been done. Underline the small *c* that begins the words. Read through the words and point out the shape of letter *c*. Have the students trace the *c* in the air as you trace the letter *c* beginning each word.

> Common words: call, came, can, cause, change, city, close, come, could, country, cover, cross
> Vocabulary words: calendar, catch, cheek, chest, chin, circle, climb, clock, cold, countryside

Do the Lesson 10 Phonics worksheet. Have the students put a red X on the Aa and Cc letters and a blue triangle around the Bb letters. Give them one direction at a time so they can focus on finding the correct letter shape. Begin with capital *A*, then lower case *a*, etc. Show them examples with flash-cards or letters written on the board.

Reading: Use a simplified, illustrated daily schedule of activities. Read the first names of classmates.

Writing: Continue to focus on having the students recognize their own first name. During this time, write the students' names on all worksheets and papers.

Writing Skill Builders: Keep these objectives in mind as you direct the class. Include small muscle control activities: tear, fold, and paste whenever possible. Give instructions and reminders to hold a writing instrument correctly. Incorporate writing strokes: horizontal, vertical lines, spiral, and circle into arts and crafts.

Memory Verse: Finish work on Genesis 1:1. Let the students recite if they are willing.

Math: Review number recognition of 2. Orally drill number recognition of 1 and 2 with flashcards. Give the students 3 counters and place them at the top of their desks or tables. Hold up a 1 or 2 flashcard and have the students move that number of counters from the top of their desk to the bottom. Do this several times.

Teach oral counting 1-10 with the number train.

Review the number 1 by reviewing the "One Little Puppy" finger play.

Do the Lesson 10 Math worksheet. Notice that all of the numbers are displayed on the page and that the number 2 is highlighted with a background. As the students get better at number recognition you can call out a number and ask the students to point it out with their finger. Have the students trace the large number 2 with the proper strokes by following the arrows. Count each group of items and trace the number.

Size Relationships: Reinforce the concept of big and little. We will do this by *cutting out two sizes of triangles (one noticeably larger than the other), and several of each size* or use the triangles made in Lessons 4-6. Mix the two sizes of triangles together and then let the students take turns sorting the various triangles into their two respective piles. Tell students over and over again: "This one is larger" or "This one is smaller." Toward the end of the sorting period, ask students to verbalize which is larger and which is smaller. Intersperse terms such as big, little, smaller, and larger in your daily conversation.

Shapes: This will be the last day to review the shape of the triangle. We recommend that on this day you give your students various sizes of triangles and have them make a picture, drawing on faces, etc. You may also take a large triangle and cut it into three smaller triangles. Reinforce the idea that there are three Personages in one in the Godhead. Although your students may not fully understand this idea, they will see how to cut smaller triangles from a larger one and make three pieces from one.

Color: Teach the color black. Show them the black color flashcard. Teach the color black as in the "black night." Review the colors red, green, and blue.

Story Time: Read a story or stories of your student's choice or ones they have brought from home.

Music: Review "This is the Way We Do Our Work," "For Here We are Together," "Hokey Pokey," "I Know He Loves Me Too," and "Three In One." Teach the following song to the tune of "Frère Jacques" (Are You Sleeping, Brother John).

Be a Friend
Tune of Frère Jacques

Be a friend
Be a friend
All the time
All the time
Working together
Loving together
Be a friend
Be a friend

Multimedia Resources: This week, listen and sing along to selections from "Bullfrogs and Butterflies: God is Great" CD.

Arts & Crafts: From a craft store, obtain various sizes of pom-poms. You may also obtain small wiggly eyes. Have students glue the pom-poms together to make "people." Smaller sizes of pom-poms may serve for arms. If you do not have the eyes available, use small beads. Remember to tell students not to place anything in their mouths. They may make their entire family, friends of the family or special pets.

For added fun, encourage your students to invite a friend over to create with them. When a child has a friend over, it is a good opportunity to teach the child how to share, how to treat company and how to cooperate with others. You need to give your students clear direction as to what friendship is about and how to keep friends. Be alert enough to notice when your students are being selfish, and correct them appropriately.

Physical Education:
Walk to a friend's house for a visit. If you do not live in an area near your child's friend, make friends with a neighbor by paying a friendly call. This is a good time to enforce "visiting manners."

NOTES:

Activities in this Lesson: Bible Lesson, Social Studies, Science, Language Arts, Phonics, Reading, Writing, Memory Verse, Math, Shapes, Color, Story Time, Music, Arts & Crafts, Physical Education

Bible Reference: Genesis 1:3-5.

Bible Concept to Present: God made light.

Bible Lesson: In the very beginning of time God was. You will remember last week and the week before that we talked about how God, Jesus, and the Holy Spirit helped to create our world. Now we are going to begin to study how our world was created. In the very, very beginning, everything was dark. There were no birds, or flowers, or fish. There was only darkness, water, and God, Jesus, and the Holy Spirit.

On the very first day of Creation, God said "Let there be light." Hold up the #1 Days of Creation Number. (See the Table of Contents for the location of the instructions.) The foil overlay represents the light that was created. And guess what? The dark, dark, world became light. Let's pretend for a minute. First, close your eyes. It is very, very dark, isn't it? When God made light, the world was even darker than it seemed to be when you closed your eyes. It was even darker than nighttime. It was very, very dark. God is so powerful. He only had to say "Let there be light," and light appeared. Now open your eyes. Isn't the light wonderful? I'm thankful God made light. God was happy He made light, too, because He looked at it after He had made it and said it was good. Let's thank God for the light He made.

Multimedia Resources: Listen to the song "Keep on Praying" from "The Amazing Miracles" CD.

Illustration: Find a room in your school or home that is dark like a closet. *Clear the floor ahead of time* so that there is room to stand inside. Talk about how dark it is and that this is how our world would have been (only darker) when God decided to create it. Now switch on a light or open the shades and discuss light and how wonderful it is. *Where Does Electricity Come From?,* an Usborne book, has an illustration and explanation of a light bulb. Praise God for making light.

Social Studies: There are many things for which we use light. Tell your students how pioneer people (our great-grandparents) did not have lights like we do today. They had to use either a candle or an oil lamp to see and often it did not give very much light. Walk through your house or school and look at all the areas from which we receive light.

Science: Light is very important to us. All light comes from God. Light comes in waves. Do you know what a wave is? A wave is a squiggly line that weaves in and out. (Draw a wave line on the board or on paper.) Light comes from God to us by a lot of squiggly lines. We call those squiggly lines light waves. I am happy God made light waves.

Note: As already mentioned, we do not expect students to fully understanding some of this material. We mention it to them to "hang a hook" of information; to form a beginning area of information. The child will not master this information for several years to come, but it does give you, as a teacher, a starting place when describing light.

Language Arts: *Bring a flashlight, candle and lamp to the lesson.* Go into a darkened room. Turn on each light separately. Discuss which light is the brightest. Introduce the following finger play poem.

Just for You

I have one nose (Hold up one finger)
See what I can do (Point to your nose)
Sniff, sniff (Sniff nose)
Just for you (Point to someone else)

I have two eyes (Hold up two fingers)
See what they can do (Point to eyes)
Blink, blink (Blink eyes)
Just for you (Point to someone else)

I have two ears (Hold up two fingers)
See what they can do (Point to ears)
Wiggle, wiggle (Wiggle ears with fingers)
Just for you (Point to someone else)

I have two hands (Hold up two fingers)
See what they can do (Point to hands)
Clap, clap (Clap hands)
Just for you (Point to someone else)

I have two feet (Hold up two fingers)
See what they can do (Point to feet)
Stamp, stamp (Stamp feet)
Just for you (Point to someone else)

Phonics: Teach the letter Dd.

Show them the letter Dd flashcard. Point out any student's name beginning with the letter *D*. Write some words beginning with the letter *D* on the board. Include any student names from the class that begin with letter *D*. Underline the capital *D* that begins the words. Read through the words and point out the shape of letter *D*. Have the students trace the *D* in the air as you trace the letter *D* beginning each name.

Boys: David, Dakota, Dalton, Damian, Daniel, Danny, Darius, Darren, David, Dennis, Derek, Derrick, Devin, Devon, Diego, Dillon, Dominic, Dominique, Donald, Douglas, Drew, Dustin, Dylan
Girls: Donna, Deborah, Daisy, Dana, Daniela, Danielle, Deanna, Denise, Desiree, Destiny, Diamond, Diana, Dominique
Vocabulary words: December, DON'T WALK

Do the Lesson 11 Phonics worksheet. Complete the letter Dd worksheet. Have the students trace the letters Dd with their fingers. They should trace the letters with their fingers and say the names of the letters. Demonstrate the proper strokes for them on the board. Say the words for each of the pictures and look at the Dd letters that begin them.

Reading: Use a simplified, illustrated daily schedule of activities. Read the first names of classmates.

Multimedia Resources: View the Aa-Dd segments of "Rev-Up for Reading" from the "Rev-Up for Learning" DVD to drill letter recognition and sound. The students should say each letter sound along with the presentation.

Writing: For these two weeks focus on having the students trace the first letter of their first name. During this time, write the students' names on all worksheets and papers making the first letter dotted or something that can be traced.

Writing Skill Builders: Keep these objectives in mind as you direct the class. Paste stickers on horizontal, vertical lines, and spirals. Hold a writing instrument correctly. Incorporate writing strokes: horizontal, vertical lines, spiral, and circle into arts and crafts.

Multimedia Resources: View the Aa-Dd segments of "Rev-Up for Writing" from the "Rev-Up for Learning" DVD to review the writing of upper- and lowercase letters. The students should write each letter in the air along with the presentation. Since the first half of the presentation covers lowercase letters and the second half uppercase letters some navigation will be needed to skip to the letters that are covered in this lesson.

Memory Verse: Genesis 1:3.

>   And God said, "Let there be light" and there was light. Genesis 1:3 NIV

>   And God said, Let there be light and there was light. Genesis 1:3 KJV

The students will be taking home Memory Verse Card 2 tonight. It is their memory verse. Duplication masters are provided for both NIV and KJV cards in the *Horizons Preschool Resource Packet*. Give the students the Lesson 11 Memory Verse worksheet. Let them color and then cut out the candle pieces. Instruct students to glue the candle and the candle holder to a piece of construction paper. Save the flame. You might paper clip it to each one's paper. As students memorize their verse, allow them to glue the flame to the candle.

Math: Teach number recognition of 3. Begin to teach the concept of the number 3 by counting items. Show them the number 3 flashcard. Place three of an item on the table. Help students to count to three. Move each item as you count l, 2, 3. Help them to count several other items to three. Look for items of three around the classroom or home. You may continue to use the foot pattern if you desire. On one foot, add three dots; on the other, the number 3. Try to familiarize students with the number 3 itself. Have them describe its shape and what it reminds them of. Draw 1, 2, and 3 numerals in the air. If you have hung cards for the week of the school year point out the Week 3 card.

Start learning the song "Baa, Baa, Black Sheep" to reinforce the concept of 3.

Baa, Baa, Black Sheep

Baa, baa, black sheep
Have you any wool?
Yes sir, yes sir, three bags full.
One for my master,
One for my dame,
And one for the little boy
Who lives down the lane.

Teach oral counting 1-10 with the Counting Train.

Do the Lesson 11 Math worksheet. Go through the objects on the worksheet together recognizing the item and counting how many there are of each thing. Have the students count again to themselves and trace the line to the group that matches.

Multimedia Resources: View "Rev-Up for Arithmetic" from the "Rev-Up for Learning" DVD to practice number recognition and counting 1-9.

Shapes: Introduce the circle shape. Show examples and look for circle shapes around the room. The Arts & Crafts activity will also help to teach this concept.

Do the Lesson 11 Shapes worksheet. Have the students trace the circle.

Color: Teach the colors black and white. Show them the white and black flashcards. Review the colors red, green, and blue.

Story Time: Read a story or stories of your choice.

Music: Review "Be a Friend," "This is the Way We Do Our Work," "For Here We are Together," "Hokey Pokey," "I Know He Loves Me Too," and "Three In One." Teach the following song to the tune of "I'm A Little Teapot."

I'm a Little Candle
Tune of I'm A Little Teapot

I'm a little candle in the dark
Here is my holder, here is my spark (Make a fist for holder, and stick up thumb on same hand
    for spark)
When I get so very hot, then I shout
Move me over, but don't blow me out.

Teach this song to the tune of "Where is Thumbkin?"

I Am One
Tune of Where is Thumbkin?

I am one
I am one
We are two
We are two
One and one make two
One and one make two
Now we're through
Now we're through

Multimedia Resources: This week, listen and sing along to selections from the "Music Machine: The Majesty of God" CD.

Arts & Crafts: *Prepare ahead – Using a plate as a pattern, cut out black and white circles, about 6" wide, from construction paper. Cut each circle in half. Cut out enough white and black circles so that each student has a half of a white circle and a half of a black circle.* Give students their circle halves and a piece of pale blue construction paper. Let them glue the half circles on their paper, making a circle to represent the Earth, daylight and nighttime. You may also *copy and cut out the memory verse for each student.* You have permission to duplicate additional copies of Memory Verse Card 2. Have students glue the verse to the bottom of their Earth picture.

Physical Education: Review the concept of one in Physical Education. Concentrate on one during the following exercises. Run one block. Skip by one house. Hop by one house. Walk one block. Count as you walk the next block, emphasizing each right step with the count of one. Now jog again one block. You should have gone about 1/4 of a mile. Your student will be ready now for a quieter activity.

Repeat the sets of three activity from Lesson 6.

NOTES:

Activities in this Lesson: Bible Lesson, Science, Social Studies, Language Arts, Phonics, Reading, Writing, Memory Verse, Math, Shapes, Color, Story Time, Music, Outdoor Activity, Physical Education, Homework, Optional Math/Language Arts/Bible/Arts & Crafts Activity

Bible Reference: Genesis 1:3-5.

Bible Concept to Present: God created light alone on the first day.

Bible Lesson: Review yesterday's story. When we learn about the other days of Creation, we will understand that light was very, very important. God created light alone on the first day.

Multimedia Resources: Listen to the song "Come To The Light" from the "Bullfrogs and Butterflies: I've Been Born Again" CD.

Science: Allow the students to draw a picture of their favorite form of light. They can chose illustrations from yesterday (flashlight, candle light, or lamp) or chose something different. Instruct the students to draw light waves beaming out from their light source. These light waves will be what they *think* light waves look like.

Social Studies: Before class, set an alarm clock to go off right at the end of Social Studies time. Talk about living by the light. Some families don't have alarm clocks. They live by the light outside. They wake up early and go to bed late. These are often families that live in very poor countries. Do the animals have alarm clocks? How do the animals know when to wake up? When to go to sleep? When to eat? When the alarm clock goes off, tell the students it is time to go for a walk.

Language Arts: Repeat the "Just for You" finger play poem from yesterday with students.

Phonics: Review the letters Aa-Dd. Use letter flashcards to review all of the letters covered so far. Make a spinner with the letters Aa-Dd. Let one student at a time spin the spinner and name the letter.

Reading: Use a simplified, illustrated daily schedule of activities. Read the first names of classmates.

Writing: Continue to focus on having the students trace the first letter of their first name. During this time, write the students' names on all worksheets and papers making the first letter dotted or something that can be traced.

Writing Skill Builders: Keep these objectives in mind as you direct the class. Paste stickers on horizontal, vertical lines, and spirals. Hold a writing instrument correctly. Incorporate writing strokes: horizontal, vertical lines, spiral, and circle into arts and crafts.

Give each student some alphabet cereal. Have them find as many letters as is possible in their name. They should have their Name Plates to look at while doing this. Can they spell their name with the cereal? Glue the letters in the correct order onto a card and eat the leftovers.

Memory Verse: Review Genesis 1:3. Practice saying the memory verse. If any students know their verse, let them glue the flame on their candle. Hang their artwork on the wall.

Math: Review number recognition of 3. Use the counting pennies chart to practice recognizing and counting to 3. Ask them to name a toy with 3 wheels, tricycle. How many sides does it take to make a triangle? How many children make up a set of triplets? Can they think of anything else that always has 3? Many buildings use structural components that are made from triangles. If a nearby building is under construction take a discovery walk and look for 3 sided features of the building.

Do the Lesson 12a Math worksheet. Instruct the students to count each group and draw a line to the number.

Do the Lesson 12b Math worksheet. Use different triangle shapes to teach drawing dot-to-dot on the board before the students do this worksheet.

Teach oral counting 1-10 with the Counting Train.

Shapes: Do the Lesson 12 Shapes worksheet. Count, color, cut, and paste the circles to make the flowers. Review the concept of large and small with the circles after the students have cut them out. Ask them to hold up the large circle, and then ask them to hold up the small circle.

Color: Continue to teach the colors black and white. Review the colors red, green, and blue.

Story Time: Obtain a simple biography of Helen Keller from the juvenile section of the library. Read it to your class. You will be reading for several days, so choose a book with 3-5 chapters. Explain any words that your students don't understand.

Music: Review "I'm a Little Candle," "I Am One," "Be a Friend," "This is the Way We Do Our Work," "For Here We are Together," "Hokey Pokey," and "I Know He Loves Me Too." Continue to teach the "ABC Song." If the students do not already know it, work on one line at a time until all lines are mastered. This will help to develop an awareness of the entire alphabet. The students can sing along even though they cannot recognize the individual letters.

> **A B C Song**
> Tune of Twinkle, Twinkle, Little Star
>
> A B C D E F G
> H I J K L M N O P
> Q R S T U and V
> W X Y and Z.
> Now I've learned my ABCs.
> Next time won't you sing with me!

Multimedia Resources: This week, listen and sing along to selections from the "Music Machine: The Majesty of God" CD.

Outdoor Activity: Take a texture walk. Let the students take several sheets of tissue and pencils along. Show them how to do rubbings. Lay the tissue on stucco, bark or concrete and rub with the pencil to get a "rubbing." Remind them that they have to rub gently. Back in the classroom, talk about textures and the sense of feeling. Does tree bark feel different than concrete? Does grass feel different than water?

Physical Education: Self Space and General Space. Have each student pick up a carpet square and then arrange themselves into a circle and sit down on the squares. Discuss how words can be used to suggest movement. Ask them for some movement words. Some sample words are: leaping, galloping, skipping, running, jumping, hopping, walking, grinning, giggling, shouting, wiggling, waving, standing, sitting, praying, kneeling, etc. As students give you the words ask them if they can do the motion on their carpet square or if they need more space. Do one motion and have them return to the carpet squares before doing another.

Homework: Let the students have Lesson 12 Homework worksheet Draw Differences at Night to take home and do tonight. Be sure the students know that they are to return the page tomorrow.

Optional Math/Language Arts/Bible/Arts & Crafts Activity: Throughout this year, the students will be learning the numbers 0 - 12. In the student worksheet booklet you will find patterns and illustrations for Bible Numbers. You may either use these to reinforce the teaching of the number at the time you teach that number, or use them for a review later in the year. They may also be used as an additional Language Arts project as you tell the stories. This activity will be given on Day 2 of the weekly schedule but it can be spread over several days or moved to other days of your yearly schedule.

3 Gifts: Matthew 2:1-11, read the Bible verses and tell the story.

Wise-men from the East came to worship the baby Jesus. They brought three gifts to Him. The gifts were gold, frankincense, and myrrh.

Do the Lesson 12 Bible Numbers worksheet. Give each student a sheet of white construction paper and the worksheet. Cut out the items on the worksheet and glue them to construction paper as illustrated in the drawing. Draw in the arms and legs for the "3" king. Glue glitter to section 1 of the number 3. Drop some perfume on section 2 of the number 3. Glue spice to the section 3 of the number 3.

NOTES:

Lesson 13

Week 3: Day 3

Activities in this Lesson: Bible Lesson, Social Studies, Science, Homework Review, Language Arts, Phonics, Reading, Writing, Memory Verse, Math, Shapes, Color, Story Time, Music, Arts & Crafts, Physical Education

Bible Reference: Genesis 1:3-5.

Bible Concept to Present: The opposite of light is darkness.

Bible Lesson: Yesterday we had the story about how the world was so very dark and then God made the light. Let's go look out our window now. Is it light or dark outside? That's right. It is light outside. Our Sun gives us our light. But long ago, there was no Sun because God had not made it. It was very dark. Come with me now into a dark room. Let's shut the shades so it will be very dark in here. Now it is dark, isn't it? Now I will turn on a flashlight. It is light, isn't it? Do you see that everywhere there is light, it is not dark any longer? Where there is light there cannot be darkness. God made the light so that it would not be dark. I'm happy God did away with the darkness. Let's thank God for light.

Illustration: The illustration is explained in the story. You do need access to a flashlight to do the suggested illustration.

Social Studies: Things that are opposite from one another are things that are very different from one another. Find things in your home or classroom that are opposites and show them to your students. Emphasize that we call items that are very different from each other opposites. Now take a walk through the room, pointing to things that are opposite. After doing this, create a situation of dark and then light again. Ask your students questions so that they tell you that light is the opposite of darkness.

Illustration: Do this illustration to teach opposites. *Taking a square of poster board, cut out a door shape, cutting only three sides of the door. Make poster board picture panels of opposites to place behind the door, for example: black/white, a glass that is empty/a glass that is full. The pictures for the panels may be drawn on paper or cut out of magazines.* Shut the door. Put one opposite picture behind the door. Show one opposite picture to students, and then have them guess what is behind the door. Be sure the right opposites are paired. This can be used to teach categories such as shapes and colors, etc.

Science: It is a scientific fact that where there is light there cannot be darkness. You have illustrated this in your lesson. Refer to the lesson again and tell your students that God made it a fact that where there is light, there cannot be darkness. God never changes. So today, long after God first made light, it is still true that where there is light, there cannot be darkness. We know that light will always chase away the darkness because God made it to be so and HE NEVER CHANGES. Turn off the lights and make the room as dark as is possible. Point out how difficult it is to see things in the dark. Turn the lights back on again. Ask if there are anymore dark places in the room. Look in a bookshelf, under a table, behind a door and other places where there is light but no darkness. Hold up a closed box. Inside the box it is dark. From playing inside a large cardboard box the students should know that it is dark inside the box. What happens when we open the box? Light enters the box and the darkness is gone. Where there is light there cannot be any darkness.

Homework Review: Ask students to share their homework page. What did they observe by going out at night?

Language Arts: Finger Activity - "Open Them, Shut Them"

Open Them, Shut Them

Open them, shut them (Open both hands in front of you to show palms)
Open them, shut them (Close hands into a fist)
Give a little clap (Clap)

Open them, shut them (Open both hands in front of you to show palms)
Open them, shut them (Close hands into a fist)
Now put them for a nap (Place hands folded in lap)

Phonics: Review the letter Dd.

Teach the small letter *d*. Write some words beginning with the letter *d* on the board. Include words from stories or activities that tie this lesson to other things that have already been done. Underline the small *d* that begins the words. Read through the words and point out the shape of letter *d*. Have the students trace the *d* in the air as you trace the letter *d* beginning each word.
Common words: day, did, differ, do, does, don't, down, draw
Vocabulary words: dance, diamond, different, dime, dollar, during

If your class has a nap time you can shine a flashlight on the ceiling while the room is dark in letter and number patterns. See if your students can correctly identify the letter or number that you have drawn. For variation allow a student to draw the letters or numbers.

Reading: Use a simplified, illustrated daily schedule of activities. Read the first names of classmates.

Writing: Continue to focus on having the students trace the first letter of their first name. During this time, write the students' names on all worksheets and papers making the first letter dotted or something that can be traced.

Writing Skill Builders: Keep these objectives in mind as you direct the class. Paste stickers on horizontal, vertical lines, and spirals. Hold a writing instrument correctly. Incorporate writing strokes: horizontal, vertical lines, spiral, and circle into arts and crafts.

Memory Verse: Review Genesis 1:3. Repeat the verse several times together.

Math: Review number recognition of 3. Do the Lesson 13a Math worksheet counting to 3. Let the students color and then cut out the 3 flowers. Glue them on the stems. Trace the number 3 on the pot.

Teach oral counting 1-10 with the Counting Train.

Do the Lesson 13b Math worksheet. Demonstrate how to do these on the board for the students. Count the number in each group and then circle the correct numeral that tells how many are in the group.

Do the Lesson 13c Math worksheet. Begin by displaying 3 same objects and 1 different object. Ask the students to identify the object that is different. Have some of the students create their own groups from objects that you have available. Do the worksheet together as a class.

Shapes: Review the circle. We are discussing the Earth, which is shaped like a circle. Trace your student's fingers around the shape of a circle. Place cornmeal with a little rice (rice keeps the moisture out of the cornmeal) into a 9x13 pan. Let the children trace the shape of a circle all over the bottom of the pan.

Do the Lesson 13 Shapes worksheet. count, trace, and color the 3 circles.

Color: Review the colors red, green, blue, black, and white.

Story Time: Continue reading the Helen Keller Story.

Music: Review "I'm a Little Candle," "I Am One," "Be a Friend," "This is the Way We Do Our Work," "For Here We are Together," and "Hokey Pokey." Teach "Head and Shoulders, Knees and Toes from the "Horizons Preschool Music" CD to the tune of "London Bridge is Falling Down."

Head and Shoulders, Knees and Toes
Tune of London Bridge is Falling Down

Head and shoulders, knees and toes
Knees and toes
Knees and toes

Head and shoulders, knees and toes
Hallelujah!
(Touch head, shoulders, knees, and toes at appropriate time.)
(Repeat)

Multimedia Resources: This week, listen and sing along to selections from the "Music Machine: The Majesty of God" CD.

Arts & Crafts: *Prepare ahead – Draw a large number one on white paper, then copy to have one per student.* Have lots of colors of crayons or poster pens available. Let the students color only one line at a time of each color on the number one, continuing to repeat the colors until the number one is completely colored.

Prepare ahead – Cut out large squares of several different textures of paper for each student: paper towel, tissue paper, freezer paper, typing paper, construction paper, cardboard. Let the students write their name on each square. Talk about textures.

Physical Education: Do one each of the following: jumping jack, frog hop, kangaroo jump, stand on one foot, place one elbow on one knee, kneel on one knee, take one step forward, take one step backward, sit down quietly with no noises or wiggles for one minute.

Note: Do not illustrate these activities to your students. Your goal is to train them to listen.

NOTES:

AOP's Commitment to Quality—Tell us how we are doing

As a publisher dedicated to providing high quality educational materials we invite you to tell us how we are doing. Please visit our website at www.aop.com to give us your comments, concerns, and/or compliments concerning Horizons Preschool. Contact information can be found in the support area for Horizons at the AOP website.

Lesson 14

Week 3: Day 4

Activities in this Lesson: Bible Lesson, Science, Language Arts, Phonics, Reading, Writing, Memory Verse, Math, Color, Music, Story Time, Arts & Crafts, Physical Education, Homework

Bible Reference: Genesis 1:3-5.

Bible Concept to Present: Without light, there is only darkness.

Bible Lesson: Review the Bible lesson from Lesson 13.

Illustration: If possible, purchase small flashlights for each student. Talk about the light replacing or taking away the darkness. Let the students lie on the floor and direct their lights to whatever object in the room you name.

Science: Read this history of Braille. Share the story with your students. Then tell them that they will be seeing the Braille alphabet tomorrow.

> Many, many years ago, a man named Barbier made alphabet letters in a code, using dots and dashes. He made this code so that the French army could send messages in the dark. Barbier visited a school for blind children around this time, and showed his code to them. His code was named Sonography.
>
> A blind student, Louis Braille, "was thunderstruck when he first touched the dots of the sonography samples. He had often played around with tactile writing at home on summer vacation in Coupvray. Neighbors later recalled that as a child Louis had tried leather in various shapes and even arranged upholstery pins in patterns, hoping to find a workable tactile communication method, but with no success. Once he touched the dots, he knew he had found his medium...." *
>
> Louis worked at night to try to perfect a system of dots for letters. In 1824, when Louis was only 15, he introduced his Braille Alphabet to the other blind students. Students and teachers were amazed and excited at this wonderful invention that would let the blind read.

Language Arts: *Prepare ahead – Use a digital recording device. Spend some time recording different sounds, indoors and outdoor. This might take several days. Try to record an assortment of common sounds. Leave a blank space between each sound.* (dog barking; water running in tub; door slamming; phone ringing; coughing; walking; wind blowing in trees; traffic) Ask the students to put their heads down and close their eyes. Play the sounds, one at a time, and let the students guess what the sound is.

Phonics: Review the letter Dd. Complete the Lesson 14 Phonics worksheet. Notice that all of the letters of the alphabet are displayed on the page and that the letters Dd are highlighted with a background. As the students get better at letter recognition you can call out a letter and ask the students to point it out with their finger. Trace the large letter and the small letter. The students can trace the letters between the guide lines. Review the pictures and the colored first letter of the words. The students can color the letters as desired. With the flashlights used in the Bible lesson have the students trace the letters Aa-Dd on the ceiling or a wall. Always follow the correct strokes for forming the letters and expect the students to do the same.

Reading: Use a simplified, illustrated daily schedule of activities. Read the first names of classmates.

Writing: Continue to focus on having the students trace the first letter of their first name. During this time, write the students' names on all worksheets and papers making the first letter dotted or something that can be traced.

Writing Skill Builders: Keep these objectives in mind as you direct the class. Paste stickers on horizontal, vertical lines, and spirals. Hold a writing instrument correctly. Incorporate writing strokes: horizontal, vertical lines, spiral, and circle into arts and crafts.

Use magnetic alphabet letters and have the students spell their names by placing the letters in the correct order. They will need their Name Plates for this activity.

Memory Verse: Review Genesis 1:3. Prepare ahead – *Write the words for the memory verse on individual pieces of construction paper, putting the Bible book on one page and the reference on another.* Let the students have the words and try putting them together correctly on the floor. Some students will be able to read the words, some will need help.

Math: Review number recognition of 3. Use the Counting Pennies chart to count the groups of pennies to 3. Say the number 1 and then count one penny. Say the number 2 and then count one, two pennies. Say the number 3 and then count one, two, three pennies while pointing to each penny as you count.

Teach oral counting 1-10 with the counting train.

Do the Lesson 14a Math worksheet. Instruct the students to count each group and draw a line to the number.

Do the Lesson 14b Math worksheet. Use different triangle shapes to teach drawing dot-to-dot on the board before the students do this worksheet. Instruct the students to connect the dots to complete the picture. The students can color the picture.

Learn another verse of "This Old Man, He Played One."

This Old Man, He Played One

Verse 1
This old man, he played one, He played nick-nack on my thumb;
with a nick-nack paddy whack, give a dog a bone. This old man came rolling home.

Verse 2
This old man, he played two, He played nick-nack on my shoe;
with a nick-nack paddy whack, give a dog a bone. This old man came rolling home.

Verse 3
This old man, he played three, He played nick-nack on my on my knee;
with a nick-nack paddy whack, give a dog a bone. This old man came rolling home.

Color: Review the colors red, green, blue, black, and white.

Story Time: Continue reading the Helen Keller Story.

Music: Review "Head and Shoulders, Knees and Toes," "I'm a Little Candle," "I Am One," "Be a Friend," "This is the Way We Do Our Work," "For Here We are Together," and "Hokey Pokey." Continue to teach the "ABC Song." If the students do not already know it, work on one line at a time until all lines are mastered. This will help to develop an awareness of the entire alphabet. The students can sing along even though they cannot recognize the individual letters.

A B C Song
Tune of Twinkle, Twinkle, Little Star

A B C D E F G
H I J K L M N O P
Q R S T U and V
W X Y and Z.
Now I've learned my ABCs.
Next time won't you sing with me!

Multimedia Resources: This week, listen and sing along to selections from the "Music Machine: The Majesty of God" CD.

Arts & Crafts: Make clay together. Let the students get involved. Dump the following ingredients together in a big bowl or tub. The size of your class will determine the amount of ingredients.

Flour	2 Cups	3 Cups	5 Cups
Table Salt	3/4 Cup	1 Cup	1 3/4 Cup
Water	3/4 Cup	1 Cup	1 3/4 Cup
Oil	6 Drops	10 Drops	15 Drops

Students may take turns mixing. The clay needs to be mixed and mixed, then kneaded. When it is very, very smooth, it is ready. (You may use Play-Doh® if you don't want to make the clay.) Give each student about half a cup of clay, the size of his fist. Instruct them that they need to make six small balls, just like marbles or dots. When they make the six balls, then have them press each ball down just a little bit, making a slightly flat side. Let the students set their clay "dots" aside on a piece of paper to dry until tomorrow. They will be used to demonstrate Braille. (Let the students play with any left over clay, making whatever they chose.)

Physical Education: Self Space and General Space. Have each student pick up a carpet square and then arrange themselves into a circle and sit down on the squares. Today have the students pretend that they are blind. Turning off the lights may help with this activity. Allow the students to do any motion that they would like to do so long as they stay on the home base of their carpet square. Suggest doing pushups, sit ups, waving, jumping jacks, shaking, lie on back and kick legs, stretching, etc. After they have done their movements ask them why they would feel comfortable doing these if they were blind. Look for an answer like knowing that they had enough space or room between themselves so no one would be hurt. When finished have the students put the carpet squares away.

Homework: Send Lesson 14 Homework worksheet home with the student. You will use it tomorrow in class.

NOTES:

* http://www.brailler.com/braillehx.htm

Lesson 15

Week 3: Day 5

Activities in this Lesson: Bible Lesson, Social Studies, Social Studies/Homework Review, Science, Language Arts, Phonics, Reading, Writing, Memory Verse, Math, Shapes, Color, Story Time, Music, Arts & Crafts, Health & Safety, Safety, Physical Education

Bible Reference: Genesis 1:3-5.

Bible Concept to Present: Light is important for all living things.

Bible Lesson: Our God is very smart. He is much wiser or smarter than we are. God made light on the very first day of Creation. He knew that everything He was going to make after the first day of Creation would need light. Plants need light to grow. Animals need light to see and grow. People need light, too. Do you know that we could not see at all if there were no light. It is necessary for light to be present for us to see. I'm thankful God made the light first.

Read the following poem as a prayer.

Thank You God for Light
Author Unknown

Thank You God for the light You gave.
The light You knew we would need.
It helps the plants to grow so tall,
From a tiny, tiny seed.

Animals need the light You made
To see where they are going.
And we, as people, need it too,
So that our eyes keep showing
All the wonderful things You made
And put within our world.
The mountain tall, the ladybug small,
Daddy's and my fingers curled
Around a flower that smells so grand,
And that I can hold within my hand.

So Thank You God for the light You gave
I'm glad that I can see.
I'm thankful for these eyes of mine.
I'm thankful to be me.

Social Studies: Discuss all things around you that you can see. We can see because God gave us light and because God made our eyes so that they use the light to see. There are many people who cannot see at all. They are blind. They do not see light. They only see darkness. There have been some blind people who have done wonderful things for all people. One person who was blind and who helped people was a girl named Helen Keller. She was a very special person. Although all she could see was darkness, she helped others. Ask, What have you learned so far about Helen Keller? Finish the story about Helen Keller today.

Social Studies/Homework Review: (Teachers with many students will need help with this lesson.) Have the students take out their homework sheets, Lesson 14a and 14b Homework worksheets. Parents hopefully have helped in the traditional class by drawing their student's names in Braille. Students will use the six dots they made yesterday to form the letters of their name, one letter at a time. You may copy Lesson 15b Resource page to help students place their dots correctly.

Science: We see because light comes into our eyes. Show the child how light comes into the eye and makes a picture for our mind with the Lesson 15a Resource page. When our mind sees the picture, it tells us what we have seen. Discuss the eyes of various animals and how they are different from our eyes. A mole, for example, has eyes that see very well for underground use. The owl's eyes are very sharp for the darkness so it can catch its food. A cat has eyes that see up and down to see the mice it needs for its dinner. A horse sees from side to side to tell where it is going. God made each eye different for the work it would need to do. Use the eye diagram on Lesson 15a Resource page to show students how the eye works, remembering that you are only introducing the subject. The Usborne book *What's Inside You?* has an illustration of an eye.

Language Arts: Play the game "Guess the Sound." Say, Today let's make our own sounds. Close your eyes and listen to the sounds I'm making. Include some sounds from indoors, outdoors, familiar objects, etc. If you are teaching more than one child, let each child take a turn making a noise and have the other child or children guess the sounds. You are teaching listening skills.

Phonics: Teach the letter Ee.

Show the students the letter Ee flashcard. Point out any student's name beginning with the letter *E*. Write some words beginning with the letter *E* on the board. Include any student names from the class that begin with letter *E*. Underline the capital *E* that begins the words. Read through the words and point out the shape of letter *E*. Have the students trace the *E* in the air as you trace the letter *E* beginning each name.

> Boys: Edgar, Eduardo, Edward, Edwin, Elijah, Emmanuel, Enrique, Eric, Erick, Erik, Ethan, Evan
> Girls: Elizabeth, Ellen, Emily, Emma, Erica, Erika, Erin, Eve, Evelyn
> Vocabulary words: EXIT

Do the Lesson 15 Phonics worksheet. Complete the letter Ee worksheet. Have the students trace the letters Ee with their fingers. They should trace the letters with their fingers and say the names of the letters. Demonstrate the proper strokes for them on the board. Say the words for each of the pictures and look at the Ee letters that begin them.

Reading: Use a simplified, illustrated daily schedule of activities. Read the first names of classmates.

Writing: Continue to focus on having the students trace the first letter of their first name. During this time, write the students' names on all worksheets and papers making the first letter dotted or something that can be traced.

Writing Skill Builders: Keep these objectives in mind as you direct the class. Paste stickers on horizontal, vertical lines, and spirals. Hold a writing instrument correctly. Incorporate writing strokes: horizontal, vertical lines, spiral, and circle into arts and crafts.

Memory Verse: Review Genesis 1:3. Alternate saying phrases with the students.

Lesson 15
(Cont.)

Math: Review number recognition of 3. Orally drill number recognition of 1, 2, and 3 with flashcards. Give the students 5 counters and place them on the left side of their desk or table. Hold up a 1, 2, or 3 flashcard and have the each student move that number of counters from the left side of their desk to the right. Do this several times.

Teach oral counting 1-10 with the Counting Train.

Do the Lesson 15 Math worksheet. Notice that all of the numbers are displayed on the page and that the number 3 is highlighted with a background. As the students get better at number recognition you can call out a number and ask the students to point it out with their finger. Have the students trace the large number 3 with the proper strokes by following the arrows. Instruct the students to count each group of items and then trace the number.

Practice writing the number one. Write it several times, but do not exceed 15 times. Give your students verbal instructions: Draw one triangle (all drawing is to take place in the cornmeal and rice pan). Place number one inside the triangle. Now place one sticker on the back of your hand for the good work you have done.

Review verses 1-3 of "This Old Man, He Played One."

Shapes: Continue to teach circles. Make a stick puppet as you did for triangles by cutting a circle from construction paper and gluing it to a craft stick. Use the following poem:

I Have No Beginning

I have no beginning (Make circles in the air as you say the poem.)
I have no start
I keep on going
I'm very smart

I do not stop
I have no end
I keep on going
I don't pretend

I go round and round
Cindy Circle's my name
I don't start or stop
That is my game

Color: Teach the color yellow. Show them the yellow color flashcard. Teach the color yellow as in the "yellow sun."

Review the colors red, green, blue, black, and white.

Story Time: Finish reading the Helen Keller Story.

Music: Review "I am One." Review "Head and Shoulders, Knees and Toes," "I'm a Little Candle," "I Am One," "Be a Friend," and "This is the Way We Do Our Work." Teach the "ABC Song." If the students do not already know it, work on one line at a time until all lines are mastered. This will help to develop an awareness of the entire alphabet. The students can sing along even though they cannot recognize the individual letters.

A B C Song
Tune of Twinkle, Twinkle, Little Star

A B C D E F G
H I J K L M N O P
Q R S T U and V
W X Y and Z.
Now I've learned my ABCs.
Next time won't you sing with me!

Teach the "Traffic Light" song.

Traffic Light
Tune of Twinkle, Twinkle Little Star

Twinkle, Twinkle, traffic light,
Standing on the corner bright,
When it's green, it's time to go,
When it's red, it's stop, you know.
Twinkle, twinkle, traffic light,
Standing on the corner bright.

Multimedia Resources: This week, listen and sing along to selections from the "Music Machine: The Majesty of God" CD.

Arts & Crafts: Make Traffic Lights. Coat a graham cracker with white frosting and place red, yellow and green M&M's' on it to make a traffic light. You can review the concepts of circles with the round candy. Reinforce counting to three by counting how many candies they have placed on their cracker. Check each student's cracker to make sure the colors were placed in the proper order. Then they may eat the cracker while you hold up red, green and yellow circles to demonstrate what to do at a traffic light. Green means go ahead and take a bite, yellow means chew and move slowly, red means to stop.

Health & Safety: Stress the need to care for our eyes. We do not poke anything in our eyes or anyone else's. We hold pencils and scissors and knives down when we walk so that they will not get in our eyes if we fall. We never look directly at the Sun or a bright light. God gave us only one set of eyes. Each one is important to us to see. We need to care for what God has given us. Say a prayer together, thanking God for our eyes.

To reinforce the concepts of red, green and yellow and the concept of circles make a traffic light visual to post in the classroom out of poster board. Cut a piece of black poster board into a rectangle. Glue red, yellow, and green circles made from colored construction paper on the poster board to make the lights. Instruct the students in the meaning of red, green, and yellow and how they should respond. Stress the importance of stopping for a red light. Also make some WALK and DON'T WALK signs to post in the classroom and explain what they mean.

Make a WALK and DON'T WALK sign for the line leader to hold up as you move the class from place to place. Either make two separate signs or one two-sided sign. Glue them onto a paint stir stick for the line leader to hold.

Physical Education: Take your students on an obstacle course with their eyes blindfolded. Go under a tree. Require that they step over a piece of board. You will want to guide them so that they do not fall. See if they can walk to a certain point by themselves in an area of the yard where they will not get hurt. Did they get there? Why not? This is how it would be if they were blind. Guide each child in expressing their feelings about the walk.

NOTES:

Activities in this Lesson: Bible Lesson, Social Studies, Science, Language Arts, Phonics, Reading, Writing, Memory Verse, Math, Shapes, Shapes/Arts & Crafts, Color, Story Time, Music, Arts & Crafts, Physical Education

Bible Reference: Genesis 1:3-5.

Bible Concept to Present: Light causes shadows.

Bible Lesson: Can you recall what subject we have been talking about in school? That's right. We have been talking about light. Hold up the #1 Days of Creation Number. Can you recall some of the things you know about light? Who made light? God did. Do you remember what the opposite of light is? The opposite of light is dark. Do all living things need light? Light is necessary for all living things. God made light to be very special. I am thankful that He did. Do you know there are some very special things light does? For instance, when light is shining on a tree, the tree will make a shadow. Let's go outdoors now and look to see if this is true. Take students outdoors and continue to talk about how shadows are made and how each shadow is different. You will want to discuss how we can make shadows, too. Further discussion on shadows will occur during the Social Studies and Science sessions. Close your Bible Lesson with prayer to God, thanking Him for the shadows that are made.

Social Studies: Shadows are very important to us. A shadow of a tree, for example, provides shade for us and protection from the hot sun. Discuss how nice and cool the shade of a tree feels when it is a hot day. If it is hot at your house now, walk out into the sun and let your student feel how much warmer it is in the direct sun than it is in the shade. If it is not warm enough, recall a story about a summer picnic you have had under a shady tree or read the following story to your student.

Note: Un-illustrated stories are very beneficial, if spaced appropriately. Our world is so programmed to visual stimulation, that we fail to give our children enough time for creativity and imagery.

Thank You, God, For Shade

Joey and his parents were going on a picnic. Joey was so happy to be going. "Oh, please hurry, Mommy," he said. "I can't wait to play in the park." Mommy hurried to pack the lunch and Daddy got the blanket to sit on at the park. They packed the car and got ready to leave. Fluffy, Joey's cat would have to stay home where it was cool. It would be too hot for Fluffy at the park, and she might run away. Joey told Fluffy good-bye and the family left their home for the park. At the park, Joey played on the swings and slid down the slide. The sun felt hotter and hotter. Joey soon found he was very hungry, thirsty and hot. Joey's Mommy called him over to the blanket to rest. The blanket had been laid under a nice shady tree. It was cool under the tree. Joey and his family ate their lunch and then lay down to rest a bit. Before long, Joey was fast asleep. When Joey awoke, he looked up into the tree. "Why did God make the tree so big?" Joey asked. "Because He knew we would need it to be big, Joey," answered Daddy. "When trees are little, they do not give very much shade. But a big tree gives us lots and lots of shade. It is cooler in the shade than in the hot sun. God made the shadows of the tree to provide a shelter for us from the hot sun." Joey looked again into the branches of the tree. "Oh, I am so glad God cared enough for me to make the shadows of the tree to keep me cool. God really loves me." said Joey. "Yes, He does." Daddy said.

Science: Discuss with your students how shadows change. Although your students still cannot fully comprehend the process in change, they can note that the shadow of a tree gets longer during certain times of the day. This is dependent upon the position of the Sun. To illustrate this, measure the shadow of a tree at noon. Use a yard stick to do this. On the ground at the end of the shadow make a marker, such as the placement of a row of rocks. Measure the tree again at 2 p.m. Did the tree shadow change? Why? Now mark this measurement with a row of markers. Discuss the changes in the shadow and explain that the shadows get longer because of the way the sun shines on them

Language Arts: Draw a shape such as a circle or square on a blackboard or poster board. Have your student shine a flashlight beam beside the shape, under the shape, in the center of the shape, and other positions words. Let the students use their little individual flashlights.

Phonics: Review the letter Ee.

Teach the small letter *e*. Write some words beginning with the letter *e* on the board. Include words from stories or activities that tie this lesson to other things that have already been done. Underline the small *e* that begins the words. Read through the words and point out the shape of letter *e*. Have the students trace the *e* in the air as you trace the letter *e* beginning each word.

    Common words: each, earth, end, even, every, eye
    Vocabulary words: ear, eight, eighteen, eighth, elbow, eleven, empty, equal, evening, excuse me, eyebrow, eyelash

Reading: Identify examples of print such as door and wall signs, cereal boxes, billboards, etc. Collect objects using an illustrated list. Use a simplified, illustrated daily schedule of activities. Read the first names of classmates.

Multimedia Resources: View the Aa-Ee segments of "Rev-Up for Reading" from the "Rev-Up for Learning" DVD to drill letter recognition and sound. The students should say each letter sound along with the presentation.

Writing: Continue to focus on having the students trace the first letter of their first name. During this time, write the students' names on all worksheets and papers making the first letter dotted or something that can be traced.

Writing Skill Builders: Keep these objectives in mind as you direct the class. Paste stickers on horizontal, vertical lines, and spirals. Hold a writing instrument correctly. Incorporate writing strokes: horizontal, vertical lines, spiral, and circle into arts and crafts.

Multimedia Resources: View the Aa-Ee segments of "Rev-Up for Writing" from the "Rev-Up for Learning" DVD to review the writing of upper- and lowercase letters. The students should write each letter in the air along with the presentation. Since the first half of the presentation covers lowercase letters and the second half uppercase letters some navigation will be needed to skip to the letters that are covered in this lesson.

Memory Verse: Review Genesis 1:3. Get out the film canisters filled with rice. Let the students walk around the room, chanting the verse.

Math: Teach number recognition of 4. Show them the number 4 flashcard. Teach the number 4 by counting items. Show the students what 4 of an item is. Show them the number 4. As you count 4 of an item, continually show them the number 4, so that they understand that the number 4 represents 4 of an item. Count out 4 blocks, 4 shoes, 4 eggs, 4 crackers. If there are 4 in the family, have the child set the table for the evening meal for 4, counting each place. If you have hung cards for the week of the school year point out the Week 4 card.

Teach oral counting 1-10 with the Counting Train.

Do the Lesson 16 Math worksheet. Go through the objects on the worksheet together recognizing the item and counting how many there are of each thing. Have the students count again to themselves and trace the line to the group that matches.

Multimedia Resources: View "Rev-Up for Arithmetic" from the "Rev-Up for Learning" DVD to practice number recognition and counting 1-9.

Shapes: Do the Lesson 16 Shapes worksheet. Count and color the number of triangles in the pinwheel. Color each of the triangles a different color. Use four of the colors studied so far: red, green, blue, black, white or yellow. Circle the number on the bottom of the page.

Shapes/Arts & Crafts: *Bring a box of Fruit Loops or Cheerios and some string.* Let the students string the cereal and make a necklace. Explain that these are circles. Then they can eat it!

Color: Continue to teach the color yellow. Review the colors red, green, blue, black, and white.

Story Time: Read a story or stories of your choice.

Music: Review "I Am One," "Head and Shoulders, Knees and Toes," "I'm a Little Candle," "I Am One," and "Be a Friend." Learn the song, "I Have A Shadow," from the "Horizons Preschool Music" CD.

Continue to teach the "ABC Song." If the students do not already know it, work on one line at a time until all lines are mastered. This will help to develop an awareness of the entire alphabet. The students can sing along even though they cannot recognize the individual letters.

A B C Song
Tune of Twinkle, Twinkle, Little Star

A B C D E F G
H I J K L M N O P
Q R S T U and V
W X Y and Z.
Now I've learned my ABCs.
Next time won't you sing with me!

Multimedia Resources: This week, listen and sing along to selections from the "Bullfrogs and Butterflies: God is My Friend" CD.

Arts & Crafts: Make a silhouette of each student. Place a bright light behind the child in a darkened room. Have your child sit so that the profile of their face is seen in the shadow. Now trace around the shadow onto white paper. Mount onto a light background. These make wonderful pictures for gifts for grandparents, or a family portfolio. It may be saved for years to come and will bring great joy as the years pass. This project will need some helpers if you have several students. You may copy and cut out the memory verse to put on the bottom of the silhouette. You have permission to copy Memory Verse Card 2.

Give your students construction paper and scissors and allow them the time to create.

Physical Education: Go out into the sunlight and have your students make various shadows by doing different dance movements or routines. Can they catch their shadow? Why not? (Their opinion.) Try to make shadows to look like a rabbit, a frog, a kangaroo, etc.

NOTES:

Activities in this Lesson: Bible Lesson, Science, Language Arts, Phonics, Reading, Writing, Memory Verse, Math, Shapes, Color, Story Time, Music, Arts & Crafts, Outdoor Activity, Health & Safety, Physical Education, Optional Math/Language Arts/Bible/Arts & Crafts Activity

Bible Reference: Genesis 1:3-5.

Bible Concept to Present: Shadows can be useful to us.

Bible Lesson: Review yesterday's story. Remember that light causes shadows. Shadows can be very useful to us.

Do the Lesson 17 Bible worksheet. Have the students draw a line from the farm animal to its shadow.

Science: Did you know that early clocks were made using shadows? As light moved, the shadow moved and helped people know that time had passed. Remember how the shadow moved from our rock markers yesterday? Let's go outside and see where the shadow is right now. Go outside and check the rock markers. Show students that the shadow is in the same place today as it was yesterday. This is how faithful God is. He is the same every day, day after day, always loving us and taking care of us. Show the students a picture or an example of a sundial.

Multimedia Resources: Watch "Faith" from the *Character Builders Video Series*.

Illustration: Set a lamp on a table, or use a big flashlight. Shine the light on a blank wall. Let each student make a funny shadow. Have other students try to guess what the student is making in shadow.

Talk some more about light. Light can't go around corners. Light waves move in a straight line. Turn the lights out in the room, so that a shadow can be made. Use a large flashlight and a piece of poster board or box to make a shadow. Show the students that the shadow is made because the light goes in a straight line. Tie a long piece of string to the flashlight. Have a student move the end of the string to the end of the shadow, to show students the straight line of light. Shine the light on different objects, allowing different students to stretch the string along the line of light.

Language Arts: Introduce students to rhyme. Tell them that some words have the same sound. Write the word LIGHT on the board. Ask, can anyone tell me a word that rhymes with light? Let the students continue sharing words, writing them on the board. (No, they probably can't read them yet, but they need to constantly see words.) Bite, daylight, fight, fright, height, kite, might, mite, night, right, sight, tight. Explain that "sight" is dependent upon "light." Explain that the word "light" also can mean something that isn't heavy, or a color that isn't very dark. Words are very interesting. Students will learn more and more about words as they grow older.

Phonics: Review the letter Ee. Complete the Lesson 17 Phonics worksheet. Notice that all of the letters of the alphabet are displayed on the page and that the letters Ee are highlighted with a background. As the students get better at letter recognition you can call out a letter and ask the students to point it out with their finger. Trace the large letter and the small letter. The students can trace the letters between the guide lines. Review the pictures and the colored first letter of the words. The students can color the letters as desired.

Lesson 17
(Cont.)

Reading: Identify examples of print such as door and wall signs, cereal boxes, billboards, etc. Collect objects using an illustrated list. Use a simplified, illustrated daily schedule of activities. Read the first names of classmates.

Writing: Continue to focus on having the students trace the first letter of their first name. During this time, write the students' names on all worksheets and papers making the first letter dotted or something that can be traced.

Writing Skill Builders: Keep these objectives in mind as you direct the class. Paste stickers on horizontal, vertical lines, and spirals. Hold a writing instrument correctly. Incorporate writing strokes: horizontal, vertical lines, spiral, and circle into arts and crafts.

Memory Verse: Review Genesis 1:3. Let the students have their little flashlights. Tell them to flash their lights whenever it fits into the memory verse. Say the verse aloud and pause for their flash when the word "light" is said.

Then God said, "Let there be *FLASH*" and there was *FLASH* Genesis 1:3

Let the class recite the verse with you several times.

Math: Review number recognition of 4. Give 2 or more students each a set of 1-4 flashcards. Place a 1-4 group of counters, crayons, etc., in front of them to see if they can select the correct flashcard for the group. Do this several times with each group of students.

Teach oral counting 1-10.

Do the Lesson 17a Math worksheet. Say the "Baa, Baa, Black Sheep" rhyme and have the students trace the missing numbers in each row as they count 1, 2, 3.

Do the Lesson 17b Math worksheet. Instruct the students to count each group. Trace the numbers and draw a line from the group to the number.

Shapes: Have a circle hunt. Let the students roam the room, looking for circles. Write the name of each object on the board, familiarizing students with the written words.

Do the Lesson 17 Shapes worksheet. Give instructions to color the large circles blue and the small circles red. They can use the other colors studied so far, green, black, white, and yellow to color the rest of the picture.

Color: Review the colors red, green, blue, black, white, and yellow.

Story Time: Read a story or stories of your choice.

Music: Review "I Have A Shadow," "I Am One," "Head and Shoulders, Knees and Toes," "I'm a Little Candle," and "I Am One." There is a wonderful old song about light that students might have heard in church. Sing it together.

This Little Light of Mine

This little light of mine, I'm gonna' let it shine, (hold up one finger as a light)
This little light of mine, I'm gonna' let it shine,
Let it shine, let it shine, let it shine.
Hide it under a bushel, NO! (clap hands), I'm gonna' let it shine,
Hide it under a bushel, NO! (clap hands), I'm gonna' let it shine,
Let it shine, let it shine, let it shine.

Won't let Satan "whoosh" it out, (blow on the finger) I'm gonna' let it shine,
Won't let Satan "whoosh" it out, I'm gonna' let it shine,
Let it shine, let it shine, let it shine.

Let it shine till Jesus comes, (hold finger up high) I'm gonna' let it shine,
Let it shine till Jesus comes, I'm gonna' let it shine,
Let it shine, let it shine, let it shine.

Multimedia Resources: This week, listen and sing along to selections from the "Bullfrogs and Butterflies: God is My Friend" CD.

Arts & Crafts: Give students playdough. Let them make their light from "This Little Light of Mine," imagining what their light looks like.

Outdoor Activity: *Purchase several outdoor flowering plants. The smallest size will do fine. Bring small gardening tools.* Spend time outdoors, planting the plants. Let every student dig at least one hole. Plant half of the plants in a sunny spot, a spot that gets full sun for at least part of the day. Plant the other half of the plants in full shade, in a spot that gets absolutely no sun. Explain to the students that this is an experiment. We are going to find out what full shade, or "shadow," does to plants. Is light important to plants? Will the plants have shadow all day long? Don't talk about sunshine or sunlight yet, as that will be covered in future lessons. Concentrate on the shadow aspect of the lesson.

Health & Safety: Spend time cleaning the area around the plants. Wash the tools. Dry the tools and put them away. Talk about taking care of what God has provided for us. Have each student carefully wash their hands. Explain how important hand washing is to everyone. Show students how to clean under their nails, where dirt can hide.

Review traffic lights with the song "Twinkle, Twinkle Traffic Lights."

Twinkle, Twinkle Traffic Light
Tune of Twinkle Twinkle Little Star

Twinkle, twinkle traffic light
Standing on the corner bright
Green means GO, we all know
Yellow means WAIT, even if you're late
Red means STOP......   (Pause before going on.)
Twinkle, twinkle traffic light
Standing on the corner bright

Physical Education: Play Shadow Tag. Do this activity outside where there is plenty of sunshine and everyone makes a shadow with their body. Select an open area without hiding places but give them some boundaries to keep everyone somewhat together. Pair the students up and designate one child as the walker and the other as the tagger. When you say GO the tagger will try to tag the walker by stepping on their shadow. When this happens they will switch places and continue playing. Tagging can only be done by stepping on the shadow and no touching should be allowed. When the tagger tags the walker they should say the word "light" so that the walker knows that they have been tagged. Play for awhile and then switch partners and play some more.

Optional Math/Language Arts/Bible/Arts & Crafts Activity: Throughout this year, the students will be learning the numbers 0 - 12. In the student worksheet booklet you will find patterns and illustrations for Bible Numbers. You may either use these to reinforce the teaching of the number at the time you teach that number, or use them for a review later in the year. They may also be used as an additional Language Arts project as you tell the stories. This activity will be given on Day 2 of the weekly schedule but it can be spread over several days or moved to other days of your yearly schedule.

4 Fishermen: Matthew 4:18-22, read the Bible verses and tell the story.

Jesus called four fishermen to become "fishers of men." Two of them were casting a net into the sea and the other two were mending their nets. The men's names were Peter, Andrew, James, and John.

Do the Lesson 17 Bible Numbers worksheet. Give each student a sheet of white construction paper and the worksheet. Cut out the items on the worksheet and glue them to construction paper as illustrated in the drawing. Draw in the arms, legs, and face for the "4" fisherman. Draw in the rest of the picture.

NOTES:

Activities in this Lesson: Bible Lesson, Social Studies, Science, Language Arts, Phonics, Reading, Memory Verse, Math, Shapes, Color, Story Time, Music, Arts & Crafts, Arts & Crafts/Outdoor Activity, Outdoor Activity, Physical Education

Bible Reference: Genesis 1:3-5.

Bible Concept to Present: When God made light, He made it so that it would reflect from certain objects.

Bible Lesson: You will need a mirror. Also, have a picture of a lighthouse to show the students. Say, We learned that light can cause shadows. I'm thankful God made the light to cause shadows. The shade is so nice in the summer time. God made the light to do another very special thing. God made the light to reflect. Do you know what the word reflect means? The word *reflect* means to bounce back from, to show the same picture back. When light shines in a mirror, it bounces back off the mirror and we see a reflection of the light. Let's look in a mirror now. The light is bouncing off the back of the mirror and reflecting what is seen - us! Our eyes reflect light. When light reflects, often it makes the light seem brighter. Long ago, when lighthouses were put by the ocean to guide ships, they would put big reflectors in the back of the light. It made the light seem bigger and brighter and could then be seen from miles away. (Show students the picture of a lighthouse and tell them about lighthouses.) I'm thankful God made light to reflect.

Social Studies: Find items around your home or classroom that reflect light. Discuss their purpose. Don't forget solar reflectors, if you have those. Discuss too, that God made the light that reflects on Day One. Use the #1 Days of Creation Number which has a foil covering to represent light as a reminder of what God made on Day One. Place the large #1 Days of Creation Number on a wall where you can refer to it at all times. From this point on, it will serve as a review when you request the child to repeat what God made on Day One.

Science: If possible, give every student a small mirror or use the ones made in the Arts & Crafts that follows. Go outside, take it into the sun and see how the light bounces from it. Bounce the light onto the dark side of a building or into a shaded area under a tree. How many patterns can be made with the light that is reflected from the mirror? Teach the students not to shine the light from the mirror in anyone's eyes.

Language Arts: Do the following action activity with your student:

I Have a Mirror

I have a mirror (Pretend to hold a mirror)
In the mirror, me I see (Point to self)
I can touch the mirror (Pretend to be touching the mirror)
But in the mirror
I can't touch me (Point to self again)

Lesson 18
(Cont.)

Phonics: Teach the letter Ff.

Show the students the letter Ff flashcard. Point out any student's name beginning with the letter *F*. Write some words beginning with the letter *F* on the board. Include any student names from the class that begin with letter *F*. Underline the capital *F* that begins the words. Read through the words and point out the shape of letter *F*. Have the students trace the *F* in the air as you trace the letter *F* beginning each name.

> Boys: Fernando, Francisco, Frank
> Girls: Faith, Felicia
> Vocabulary words: February

Do the Lesson 18 Phonics worksheet. Complete the letter Ff worksheet. Have the students trace the letters Ff with their fingers. They should trace the letters with their fingers and say the names of the letters. Demonstrate the proper strokes for them on the board. Say the words for each of the pictures and look at the Ff letters that begin them.

Reading: Identify examples of print such as door and wall signs, cereal boxes, billboards, etc. Collect objects using an illustrated list. Use a simplified, illustrated daily schedule of activities. Read the first names of classmates.

Writing: Continue to focus on having the students trace the first letter of their first name. During this time, write the students' names on all worksheets and papers making the first letter dotted or something that can be traced.

Writing Skill Builders: Keep these objectives in mind as you direct the class. Paste stickers on horizontal, vertical lines, and spirals. Hold a writing instrument correctly. Incorporate writing strokes: horizontal, vertical lines, spiral, and circle into arts and crafts.

Memory Verse: Review Genesis 1:3. Practice the verse several times during the school day.

Math: Review number recognition of 4. Continue to teach the number 4 by counting items. Have your students count out 4 circles and 4 triangles from shapes you have cut from construction paper. Then give students 4 pieces of paper to make 4 different pictures.

Teach oral counting 1-10 with the Counting Train.

Do the Lesson 18 Math worksheet. Instruct the students to count each group and draw a line to groups with the same number.

Shapes: Continue to teach the concept of circles. Discuss circles as you eat, finding circles in everything you eat. Include all kinds of circular objects; disks, spheres, cylinders etc. For lunch today have a circle lunch. Make your sandwiches into circles; eat an apple, raisins, cheese balls, bologna, etc.

Do the Lesson 18 Shapes worksheet. The Beach Ball worksheet. Color the triangles brown and the circles yellow. The rest of the beach ball can be colored red, green, blue, black or white.

Color: Teach the color brown. Show the students the brown flashcard. Review the colors red, green, blue, black, white, and yellow.

Story Time: Read a story or stories of your choice.

Music: Review "I Have A Shadow," "I Am One," "Head and Shoulders, Knees and Toes" and "I'm a Little Candle." Sing the song "I'm A Little Candle" from the "Horizons Preschool Music" CD.

I'm A Little Candle
Frank Hernandez
Copyright 2007, His & Hernandez Music

I'm a little candle shining in the dark,
It's the light of Jesus shining in my heart,
I will shine,
I will shine,
Like a candle in the dark,
I will shine.

Multimedia Resources: This week, listen and sing along to selections from the "Bullfrogs and Butterflies: God is My Friend" CD.

Arts & Crafts: *Prepare ahead – Cut enough pieces of cardboard squares for each student to have one. Also cut squares of foil, larger than the cardboard squares.* Let the students put a spot of glue on the cardboard, lay the foil on it, then wrap the foil around the edges of the square. Turn out the light. Get the big flashlight and shine it around the room at the student's foil squares. Show them how the light is reflected off the foil and onto the walls.

Arts & Crafts/Outdoor Activity: *Purchase foil cookie sheets, enough for each student to have one. Bring enough whipped cream so that each student may have a large dollop.* Let the students sit on the grass outside. Give each one a cookie sheet and a big dollop of whipped cream. Let the students practice their letters or numbers or draw pictures. Licking fingers is allowed.

Outdoor Activity: Water the flowering plants that were planted in Lesson 17.

Physical Education: Light bounces back. Give a student a ball (preferably a larger one). Your goal is for the student to be able to throw the ball at the target (you) with both hands. Some students may be able to throw the ball on target with one hand. Practice bouncing the ball between you. Sit down on the ground (concrete helps) and roll the ball back and forth between you and the student. Next give it one bounce between you, then two, etc. Try to bounce the ball from a wall and catch it on two bounces, then one. All of these will take practice. They are skills which will serve as a sign of readiness for reading and writing.

NOTES:

Lesson 19

Week 4: Day 4

Activities in this Lesson: Bible Lesson, Language Arts, Phonics, Reading, Writing, Memory Verse, Math, Shapes, Color, Story Time, Music, Arts & Crafts, Outdoor Activity, Physical Education, Homework, Catch Up

Bible Reference: Genesis 1:3-5.

Bible Concept to Present: Light is beautiful and God said that it was good.

Bible Lesson: Read the three verses to the children. Say, God saw the light and said that it was good. God was happy with the light He had made. God saw all the things light could do. How many things have we learned about light? Light helps us see. Light makes shadows. Light helps us tell time. Light replaces darkness. Light reflects.

Illustration: Light is beautiful, and God said it was good. How do we look when we feel good? How do we look when we feel bad? Sad? Angry? Excited? Happy? Our face looks so much better when we are happy, doesn't it? God loves us so much, so we can be happy all the time.

Do the Lesson 19 Bible worksheet. Have the students draw a line from each animal to its shadow.

Language Arts: Today, review the poem from yesterday, but let the students hold their little mirrors. Ask them to then look in the mirrors and share what they see. Who has blonde hair? Who has brown eyes? Who has freckles? Ask, how did we get our hair? Our eyes? Only God could have done it. Thank God for making everyone different and wonderful.

Do Lesson 19 Language Arts worksheet. Find the item in each row that is different. Have the students circle the different item in each row.

Phonics: Review the letter Ff.

Do the Lesson 19 Phonics worksheet. Complete the letter Ff worksheet. Notice that all of the letters of the alphabet are displayed on the page and that the letters Ff are highlighted with a background. As the students get better at letter recognition you can call out a letter and ask the students to point it out with their finger. Trace the large letter and the small letter. The students can trace the letters between the guide lines. Review the pictures and the colored first letter of the words. The students can color the letters as desired.

Reading: Identify examples of print such as door and wall signs, cereal boxes, billboards, etc. Collect objects using an illustrated list. Use a simplified, illustrated daily schedule of activities. Read the first names of classmates.

Writing: Continue to focus on having the students trace the first letter of their first name. During this time, write the students' names on all worksheets and papers making the first letter dotted or something that can be traced.

Writing Skill Builders: Keep these objectives in mind as you direct the class. Paste stickers on horizontal, vertical lines, and spirals. Hold a writing instrument correctly. Incorporate writing strokes: horizontal, vertical lines, spiral, and circle into arts and crafts.

Memory Verse: Review Genesis 1:3. Students should know the verse by now. Use your own judgment about having each student say the verse to the class. Say, God loves us to read and memorize His Word. There is a long chapter in the Bible, Psalm 119 that tells us how precious God's Word is. Read Psalm 119:11a; 42b; 161b; 172a. We are to treasure God's Word, trust God's Word, be in awe of God's Word, and SING God's Word!

Math: Review number recognition of 4. Place a large number 4 on the floor of the room. Have each student collect a group of 4 objects from the room and bring them to the 4 on the floor. You can have them sit around the 4 on the floor and hold their objects in their laps. Pick up the 4 and put down another number 1-3. The students should then put that same number of objects on the floor. End with 4 on the floor.

Teach oral counting 1-10 with the Counting Train.

Do the Lesson 19 Math worksheet. Notice that all of the numbers are displayed on the page and that the number 4 is highlighted with a background. As the students get better at number recognition you can call out a number and ask the students to point it out with their finger. Have the students trace the large number 4 with the proper strokes by following the arrows. Instruct the students to count each group of items and then trace the number.

Learn another verse of "This Old Man, He Played One."

This Old Man, He Played One

Verse 1
This old man, he played one, He played nick-nack on my thumb;
with a nick-nack paddy whack, give a dog a bone. This old man came rolling home.

Verse 2
This old man, he played two, He played nick-nack on my shoe;
with a nick-nack paddy whack, give a dog a bone. This old man came rolling home.

Verse 3
This old man, he played three, He played nick-nack on my on my knee;
with a nick-nack paddy whack, give a dog a bone. This old man came rolling home.

Verse 4
This old man, he played four, He played nick-nack on my door;
with a nick-nack paddy whack, give a dog a bone. This old man came rolling home.

Shapes: Continue to look for everyday items that are circles in shape.

Do the Lesson 19 Shapes worksheet. Trace the circles, color the biggest circle yellow, color the smallest circle brown and draw lines to complete the happy/mad faces.

Color: Continue to teach the color brown. Review the colors red, green, blue, black, white, and yellow.

Story Time: Read a story or stories of your choice.

Music: Review "This Little Light of Mine," "I Have A Shadow," "I Am One," and "Head and Shoulders, Knees and Toes." Review the song "I'm A Little Candle" from the "Horizons Preschool Music" CD. Continue to teach the "ABC Song." If the students do not already know it, work on one line at a time until all lines are mastered. This will help to develop an awareness of the entire alphabet. The students can sing along even though they cannot recognize the individual letters.

A B C Song
Tune of Twinkle, Twinkle, Little Star

A B C D E F G
H I J K L M N O P
Q R S T U and V
W X Y and Z.
Now I've learned my ABCs.
Next time won't you sing with me!

Teach the "Wheels on the Bus" song to help reinforce the concept of circles.

Wheels On the Bus

Wheels on the bus go round and round,
Round and round, round and round.
Wheels on the bus go round and round,
All through the town.
Horn on the bus goes beep, beep, beep.
Beep, beep, beep.
Beep, beep, beep.
Horn on the bus goes beep, beep, beep.
All through the town.

Repeat using different lyrics:

People .... go up and down
Babies .... go 'waa, waa, waa'
Mommies .... go 'shh, shh, shh.'
Daddies .... read their paper.
Money .... goes clink, clink, clink.
Lights .... go blink, blink, blink.
Windows .... go up and down.
Door .... goes open and shut.
Seats .... go squeak, squeak, squeak.
Wipers .... go swish, swish, swish

Multimedia Resources: This week, listen and sing along to selections from the "Bullfrogs and Butterflies: God is My Friend" CD.

Arts & Crafts: *Cut freezer paper into circles, one for each student.* Provide water colors and a cup of water for each student. Play a classical music selection. Let the students paint as desired with water colors, listening to the music for inspiration. If necessary, tape the freezer paper to the tables or desks.

Outdoor Activity: Go outside and water the plants. See if there is any difference in them yet. It might take awhile for the difference in the light to be obvious.

Physical Education: Repeat this activity from Lessons 18. Light bounces back. Give students a ball (preferably a larger one). Your goal is for the student to be able to throw the ball at the target (you) with both hands. Some students may be able to throw the ball on target with one hand. Practice bouncing the ball between you. Sit down on the ground (concrete helps) and roll the ball back and forth between you and the student. Next give it one bounce between you, then two, etc. Try to bounce the ball from a wall and catch it on two bounces, then one. All of these will take practice.

Homework: Send Lesson 19 Homework worksheet Home Circle Hunt home with the students. Ask them to bring their homework back tomorrow.

Catch Up: Do any assignment that you didn't have time for earlier in the month.

Note: Make sure there is a shelf or ledge somewhere that doesn't get dusted. You will use this dust for Lesson 24.

NOTES:

Lesson 20
Week 4: Day 5

Activities in this Lesson: Bible Lesson, Social Studies, Science, Phonics, Reading, Writing, Memory Verse, Math, Shapes, Color, Story Time, Music, Arts & Crafts, Health & Safety, Outdoor Activity, Physical Education, Additional Bible Lessons

Bible Reference: Genesis 1:3-5.

Bible Concept to Present: The light that God made on the first day is necessary for colors.

Bible Lesson/Outdoor Activity: You will be presenting your Bible Lesson as you take a walk in the morning. Tell students this will be a story walk, and it will be necessary for them to listen to you. As you walk, point out all the colors around you. Each color is able to be seen because of light. If God had not given us light, no colors would exist. Could you imagine a world all dark? Colors are found in order. If you could obtain a prism you would be able to see the colors as God made them in light. (If you can obtain a prism, do so, and let your students view the colors.) Use Resource Page Lesson 20b to illustrate this concept. God did not just make one color, He made many colors. As you walk, see how many different colors you can find.

Multimedia Resources: Listen to the song "I Love You Lord" from the "Bullfrogs and Butterflies: God Loves Fun" CD.

Social Studies: All people like color. Some of us like one color better than another. What is your favorite color? What is your Mommy's? Your Daddy's? How about Grandma and Grandpa? Make a color book with each page representing someone's favorite color. Have the students draw a picture of that person on the color page of the person's choice. Use a 1/2 or 1/4 sheet of paper for each page of the book. Staple the top corner or hole punch and tie the pages together with yarn to make a book.

Science: Some colors mix together to form other colors. For example: blue and yellow make green, red and yellow make orange, and red and blue make purple. Red, blue and yellow are called primary colors. Mix these colors as you speak. Try mixing all colors and see what happens. Dry tempera paint works best for this. After your students have mixed various colors, let them paint with them.

Note: Not all of these colors have been taught at this point. Use Lesson 20 Resource page to help illustrate this concept.

Phonics: Review the letters Aa-Ff. Use the flashcards or any other letter visuals.

Teach the small letter *f*. Write some words beginning with the letter *f* on the board. Include words from stories or activities that tie this lesson to other things that have already been done. Underline the small *f* that begins the words. Read through the words and point out the shape of letter *f*. Have the students trace the *f* in the air as you trace the letter *f* beginning each word.

Common words: far, farm, father, few, find, first, follow, food, for, form, found, from

Vocabulary words: face, face-to-face, fast, feet, fewer, fifteen, fifth, finally, finger, first, five, flower, foot, forehead, forest, four, fourteen, fourth, front, fruit, full

Do the Lesson 20 Phonics worksheet. Have the students put a black circle around the Dd letters, a yellow X on the Ee letters, and a brown triangle around the Ff letters. Give them one direction at a time so they can focus on finding the correct letter shape. Begin with capital D, then lower case *d*, etc. Show them examples with flashcards or letters written on the board.

Reading: Identify examples of print such as door and wall signs, cereal boxes, billboards, etc. Collect objects using an illustrated list. Use a simplified, illustrated daily schedule of activities. Read the first names of classmates.

Writing: Continue to focus on having the students trace the first letter of their first name. During this time, write the students' names on all worksheets and papers making the first letter dotted or something that can be traced.

Writing Skill Builders: Keep these objectives in mind as you direct the class. Paste stickers on horizontal, vertical lines, and spirals. Hold a writing instrument correctly. Incorporate writing strokes: horizontal, vertical lines, spiral, and circle into arts and crafts.

Memory Verse: Review Genesis 1:3.

Math: Review number recognition of 4. Have your students build block towers using sets of 4 blocks. See how creative they are within the boundaries of the 4 concept. Can they make the shape of a large 4 on the floor with their block towers of 4?

Teach oral counting 1-10 with the Counting Train.

Do the Lesson 20 Math worksheet. Instruct the students to count each group and then trace the number for the group.

Shapes: Continue to teach the circle concept. Today, plan to make a rolled cookie and cut it into circles. Or if you desire, use the peanut butter playdough recipe given previously. Decorate with other circular items such as raisins or frosting placed into circles for eyes, etc.

In addition, make a circle book. To do so, cut out several pieces of paper in the shape of a large circle. Staple the book together. On the cover write "Student's Name Circle Book." Include pictures on the inside of the book of things that are circles, for example, balls, cookies, etc. The pictures can be cut from old magazines and pasted onto the pages.

Do Lesson 20 Shapes worksheet. The Sailboat worksheet. Ask the students to tell where they see triangles in the picture. There are triangles on the sails, at the front and back of the boat, the front sail and the back sail and the sails together. Ask the students to tell where they see circles in the picture. Color the large triangles green and the small triangles brown. Color the circles yellow and the rest of the picture any color they desire.

Homework Review: Let's share your homework page with the class. Did you find lots of circles around your house? Who found the most unusual circle?

Story Time: Read a story or stories of your student's choice or ones they have brought from home.

Color: Review the colors red, green, blue, black, white, yellow, and brown.

Music: Review "Wheels On the Bus," "This Little Light of Mine," "I Have A Shadow," and "I Am One." Review the song "I'm A Little Candle" from the "Horizons Preschool Music" CD. Continue to teach the "ABC Song." If the students do not already know it, work on one line at a time until all lines are mastered. This will help to develop an awareness of the entire alphabet. The students can sing along even though they cannot recognize the individual letters.

A B C Song
Tune of Twinkle, Twinkle, Little Star

A B C D E F G
H I J K L M N O P
Q R S T U and V
W X Y and Z.
Now I've learned my ABCs.
Next time won't you sing with me!

Multimedia Resources: This week, listen and sing along to selections from the "Bullfrogs and Butterflies: God is My Friend" CD.

Arts & Crafts: Make a rainbow of colors. Although there is a definite order for the colors, you do not need to follow it at this time. We will be making the rainbow correctly at the end of the year. Your goal now is to acquaint students with the colors only, and that there are many different colors. Using the paint you mixed previously for science, paint a rainbow on a piece of paper. If you wish to explain a rainbow, do so. Students will be able to see colors of the rainbow if you will spray a hose outside with the sun at your back.

Health & Safety: Review the traffic light. Review left and right. Say the following finger play poem "Traffic Light Poem."

Traffic Light Poem
Original Author Unknown

Red says stop (hold up left hand in "stop" gesture)
Green says go. (right arm motioning)
Yellow says wait. (hold up index finger)
You'd better go slow.
When I reach a crossing place (cross arms at wrist)
To the left and right I turn my face. (look to left and right)
I walk, not run across the street. (use fingers)
And use my head to guide my feet. (point to head and feet)

Outdoor Activity: Water the flowering plants that were planted in Lesson 17.

Physical Education: Prepare two types of music for listening. Let your body follow the motions of how the music makes you feel. Now, describe a color, and let your student display how that color makes them feel. The child may interpret something that is the color to which you refer, for example, when we gave the color red to our preschooler to express, he pretended to be fire (it was winter and a fire was in the fireplace); for black he pretended to be ashes; for blue, the ocean.

Additional Bible Lessons: Joseph's Coat of Many Colors, found in Genesis 37; Saul's Conversion and the Bright Light, found in Acts 8:1-3 and Acts 9.

NOTES:

Lesson 21

Week 5: Day 1

Activities in this Lesson: Bible Lesson, Social Studies, Science, Language Arts, Phonics, Reading, Writing, Memory Verse, Math, Color, Story Time, Music, Arts & Crafts, Outdoor Activity, Physical Education

Bible Reference: Genesis 1:6-8.

Bible Concept to Present: God made the air on the second day of Creation.

Bible Lesson: For the past two weeks we have studied about light that God made for us. Hold up the #1 Days of Creation Number. (See the Table of Contents for the location of the instructions.) We learned that 1) God made the light; 2) Light is the opposite of dark and light dispels darkness; 3) Light is important for all living things; 4) We need light to see; 5) Light causes shadows; 6) Light reflects; 7) Colors come from light.

All of this happened on the first day of Creation. On the second day of Creation, God made air. Hold up the #2 Days of Creation Number where the blue paper represents the sky that is filled with air. Air is all around us. We don't see air, we don't really feel air (because our skin adjusts to the pressure automatically), and we don't hear air unless it is moving. Can you taste air? But air is there. Air is very important to us. God made the air to separate the waters that were above and below the earth. God made the air for us so that we can breathe. We could not live without air. I am thankful God made the air for us.

Social Studies: *Bring some old magazines to class.* We need air to live. God made us so that if there were no air, we would not be able to live. Animals need air too. So do fish. Everything around us needs air. Pass out the magazines. Let the students cut out pictures of things that need air. Glue them onto a piece of construction paper. Label the paper "Things that God made that need air" or "Thank you God for air."

Science: Air contains very special things. Air contains gases which we call oxygen and nitrogen. Without oxygen, nothing could live. Oxygen is a gas our bodies need to live. Air also contains water. Show students how water evaporates into the air in the form of steam. Take students into a kitchen for an experiment. Place a pan of water on the heat and bring it to a hard boil. While it is heating, talk to students about always being very careful around stoves or anything hot. Pan handles are always turned in so the pan can't be knocked off the stove. When the water is boiling, notice the steam. Be sure students know to keep hands away from the steam. Where does the steam go? Into the air. Do we see the steam in the air now, after the heat has been shut off? No. Yet the steam is there. Steam is water that is evaporating. Our air contains water too, but we don't always see the water.

Multimedia Resources: Watch "Self-Control" from the *Character Builders Video Series*.

Additional Idea: Using the air from a bicycle pump, blow up an inner-tube. Ask your students questions concerning how the tube gets larger and how air plays a part in this. This can also be illustrated by blowing up a balloon.

Horizons Preschool

Language Arts: Do this finger activity with your students:

The Wind is Full of Tricks Today

The wind is full of tricks today (Make sweeping motion with hand for wind)
He blew my Mommy's hat away (Pretend to sweep hat off head)
He chased our paper down the street (One hand chases the other around)
He almost blew me off my feet (Pretend to almost fall down)
He makes the trees and bushes dance (Make dancing motions with arms)
Just listen to him howl and prance (Cup hand to ear)
... Author Unknown

Phonics: Teach the letter Gg.

Show the students the letter Gg flashcard. Point out any student's name beginning with the letter *G*. Write some words beginning with the letter *G* on the board. Include any student names from the class that begin with letter *G*. Underline the capital *G* that begins the words. Read through the words and point out the shape of letter *G*. Have the students trace the *G* in the air as you trace the letter *G* beginning each name.

Boys: Gabriel, Gage, Garrett, Gary, Gavin, George, Gerardo, Giovanni, Grant, Gregory
Girls: Gabriela, Gabriella, Gabrielle, Genesis, Gina, Grace, Guadalupe
Vocabulary words: Girls

Do the Lesson 21 Phonics worksheet. Complete the letter Gg worksheet. Have the students trace the letters Gg with their fingers. They should trace the letters with their fingers and say the names of the letters. Demonstrate the proper strokes for them on the board. Say the words for each of the pictures and look at the Gg letters that begin them.

Reading: Dictate a simple letter, invitation, or thank you note.

Multimedia Resources: View the Aa-Gg segments of "Rev-Up for Reading" from the "Rev-Up for Learning" DVD to drill letter recognition and sound. The students should say each letter sound along with the presentation.

Writing: For these two weeks focus on having the students trace the first two letters of their first name. During this time, write the students' names on all worksheets and papers making the first two letters dotted or something that can be traced.

Writing Skill Builders: Keep these objectives in mind as you direct the class. Coloring a simple drawing. Incorporate writing strokes horizontal and vertical lines, point, moon, and cross. Trace and then independently draw the outlines of geometric shapes and irregular forms.

Give the students some time to locate the letters found in their names in the old magazines used in the Social Studies activity. They will cut out the letters and paste them on a sheet of paper in the correct order to form their names. They will need their Name Plates for this activity.

Multimedia Resources: View the Aa-Gg segments of "Rev-Up for Writing" from the "Rev-Up for Learning" DVD to review the writing of upper- and lowercase letters. The students should write each letter in the air along with the presentation. Since the first half of the presentation covers lowercase letters and the second half uppercase letters some navigation will be needed to skip to the letters that are covered in this lesson.

Memory Verse: Genesis 1:6.

> And God said, "Let there be [air] between the waters to separate water from water." Genesis 1:6 NIV

> Then God said, "Let there be [air] in the midst of the waters and let it separate the waters from the waters." Genesis 1:6 NASB

> And God said, Let there be a firmament in the midst of the waters, and let it divide the waters from the waters. Genesis 1:6 KJV

(We are translating "an expanse" into "air.") Begin to teach Genesis 1:6. Put the verse to a tune you know or make up a tune to go with it. Let the students take home Memory Verse Card 3, their memory verse.

Math: Teach number recognition of 5. Show the students the number 5 flashcard. Teach your students the concept of 5. Count 5 spoons, 5 raisins, 5 plates, etc. Show your child the number 5 and tell them that this associates with 5 in counting. You may continue to make the footprints if you desire. If you have hung cards for the week of the school year point out the Week 5 card.

Teach oral counting 1-10. Use the Counting Shapes Lesson 21 Resource sheet which counts the shapes you will cover this year or make a large poster of shapes to hang on the wall.

Do the Lesson 21 Math worksheet. Notice that all of the numbers are displayed on the page and that the number 5 is highlighted with a background. As the students get better at number recognition you can call out a number and ask the students to point it out with their finger. Have the students trace the large number 5 with the proper strokes by following the arrows. Instruct the students to count each group of items and then trace the number. Draw dots on the hats to match the number. The students can color the clown hats.

Multimedia Resources: View "Rev-Up for Arithmetic" from the "Rev-Up for Learning" DVD to practice number recognition and counting 1-9.

Color: Review the colors red, green, blue, black, white, yellow, and brown.

Story Time: Read a story or stories of your choice.

Music: Review "Wheels On the Bus," "This Little Light of Mine," "I Have A Shadow," and "I Am One." Review the song "I'm A Little Candle" from the "Horizons Preschool Music" CD. *Blow up enough balloons so that each student can have one.* Play some lively music. Instruct students to keep the balloons in the air until you stop the music. For added interest have students keep the balloons in the air by blowing on them.

Multimedia Resources: This week, listen and sing along to selections from "The Amazing Children" CD.

Arts & Crafts: Paint a picture of the sky. Using blue tones, teach students to go from a darker blue at the top of the sky to a lighter one at the bottom of the sky. Water colors work well with this. Paint the blue on the top of the paper, and simply add water to your brush to smear it down the page. Save this paper, because in Lesson 25 we will be adding clouds.

Outdoor Activity: Water the flowering plants that were planted in Lesson 17.

Physical Education: Air is important for our breathing. We will be doing some exercises so that we will need to breathe deeply.

Note: If a student has a heart condition - do not have them do these exercises.

Begin by bending down to touch your toes. Then stretch up to the ceiling.

Stretch to your right three times, and to your left three times.

Now jump in place for five counts, jump forward for five counts, jump backward for five counts, and in place again for five counts.

Run in place for five counts, backward five counts, and forward five counts.

How hard are you breathing now? Do you need lots of air?

Now begin to slow down. Walk slowly around the room, but do not stop. Pretend to be on a lion hunt, look under and around furniture for the lion. Walk slower and slower until your breathing is back to normal. Now how hard are you breathing? Does your body still need air?

NOTES:

Lesson 22

Week 5: Day 2

Activities in this Lesson: Bible Lesson, Science, Language Arts, Phonics, Reading, Writing, Memory Verse, Math, Color, Story Time, Music, Arts & Crafts, Health & Safety, Outdoor Activity, Physical Education, Optional Math/Language Arts/Bible/Arts & Crafts Activity

Bible Reference: Genesis 1:6-8.

Bible Concept to Present: The air God made can be different temperatures.

Bible Lesson: Review yesterday's introduction of Genesis 1:6-8. Remind students that we are now studying Day 2 of Creation. We thank God for air. The air around us can be different temperatures. If the air is cold, we are cold. If the air is hot, we are hot. How does the air feel today? What is it like outside today? Thank you, God, for keeping the air around us comfortable.

Science: *Bring a fan in to class.* There is a lot of air around our Earth. When we look up into the sky, we can't see the top of the air. We can't even see the air itself. But birds use the air to fly on. Airplanes fly on the air. When can we see air? When there is smoke in it. Or fog. When the wind is blowing, we can see how the air moves by watching the leaves and dust. What do we do when the air is cold? We wear coats and hats, and maybe mittens, to stay warm. Often, we have to stay inside because the air outside is so cold. What happens if we leave a window open? The cold air comes inside. What happens to our breath when it is cold outside? We can see the air coming out of our mouths. When it is hot, we try to move the air to make us feel cooler. We might use a fan to move the air. Let's turn the fan on and see how it feels. Is it cold? In summer time, it feels really good. Summer is the time of year when it is hot.

Language Arts: Ask the students if they have ever had something blow away. Have them describe the item that blew away and how the wind moved the item. Did the item slide along the ground? Did the item float up in the air? Did the item tumble over and over? Did the item move back and forth? Was the item pulled out of their hand? What was it like trying to catch the item? Work on their oral skills in describing the item.

Phonics: Review the letter Gg.

Reading: Dictate a simple letter, invitation, or thank you note.

Writing: For these two weeks focus on having the students trace the first two letters of their first name. During this time, write the students' names on all worksheets and papers making the first two letters dotted or something that can be traced.

Writing Skill Builders: Keep these objectives in mind as you direct the class. Coloring a simple drawing. Incorporate writing strokes horizontal and vertical lines, point, moon, and cross. Trace and then independently draw the outlines of geometric shapes and irregular forms.

Memory Verse: Review Genesis 1:6. Say the verse together several times.

Math: Review number recognition of 5.

Teach oral counting 1-10. Use the Counting Train, Counting Pennies, or Counting Shapes visuals.

Do the Lesson 22 Math worksheet. Count the items in each box. Draw a line to match the number with the group of objects.

Color: Review the colors red, green, blue, black, white, yellow, and brown.

Do the Lesson 22 Color worksheet. Have the students color one animal red and one of them brown. The third animal can be colored any color of their choice.

Story Time: Read a story or stories of your choice.

Music: Review "Wheels On the Bus," "This Little Light of Mine," and "I Have A Shadow." Review the song "I'm A Little Candle" from the "Horizons Preschool Music" CD. Continue to teach the "ABC Song." If the students do not already know it, work on one line at a time until all lines are mastered. This will help to develop an awareness of the entire alphabet. The students can sing along even though they cannot recognize the individual letters.

> **A B C Song**
> Tune of Twinkle, Twinkle, Little Star
>
> A B C D E F G
> H I J K L M N O P
> Q R S T U and V
> W X Y and Z.
> Now I've learned my ABCs.
> Next time won't you sing with me!

Multimedia Resources: This week, listen and sing along to selections from "The Amazing Children" CD.

Arts & Crafts: *Prepare ahead - blow up long skinny balloons, about six inches long, for each student.* Hand out Lesson 22a and 22b Arts & Crafts worksheets. Let the students color the butterfly wings with markers. Classes with several students will need helpers. Help the students to cut out the butterfly wings, MAKING SURE THEY DO NOT CUT OFF THE TAB, and attach them to their balloons with tape. Talk about the beautiful colors that God gave to butterflies.

Give students playdough. Encourage them to make something that flies on the air.

Health & Safety: Yesterday, we did some fun exercises. Was it hard? Did you breathe hard? Breathing draws air from around us into our body. Our body has to have the air to live. Our body uses the oxygen in the air as a fuel. Take a big deep breath. Stop. Now let it out. Didn't that feel good? Some people have difficulty breathing. They can't do a lot of work or exercise. It isn't their fault. A friend of mine, Karen, has to sit and watch other children play. We should be kind to Karen, because she really would like to play. How could we be kind to Karen?

Outdoor Activity: Go outside and check on the plants again. You should be able to see the difference that the light makes. Be sure to call it "the light" and not "the sun." Share the fact that things don't grow as well in shadow. But sometimes, we need to have a shadow to help us stay cool. Trees planted by buildings help keep the buildings cool.

Physical Education: Continue walking around the buildings and playground areas looking for places that are cool or hot. You will need a warm sunny day to do this. Perhaps the wind can be a factor in whether an area is warm or cold. Go inside and outside if needed to find warm and cold areas. Discuss what you have learned about warm and cold places. After some areas have been found have the students run to an area that is hot and then run to an area that is cold when you shout the words "hot" or "cold."

Optional Math/Language Arts/Bible/Arts & Crafts Activity: Throughout this year, the students will be learning the numbers 0 - 12. In the student worksheet booklet you will find patterns and illustrations for Bible Numbers. You may either use these to reinforce the teaching of the number at the time you teach that number, or use them for a review later in the year. They may also be used as an additional Language Arts project as you tell the stories. This activity will be given on Day 2 of the weekly schedule but it can be spread over several days or moved to other days of your yearly schedule.

> **5 Stones:** I Samuel 17:32-54, read the Bible verses and tell the story.
>
> David took five stones from a brook with him when he went to fight Goliath.
> He knocked Goliath down with the very first stone.

Do the Lesson 22 Bible Numbers worksheet. Give each student a sheet of white construction paper and the worksheet. Cut out the items on the worksheet and glue them to construction paper as illustrated in the drawing. Draw in the arms, legs, and face for the "5" David. Draw in the rest of the picture.

NOTES:

Activities in this Lesson: Bible Lesson, Social Studies, Science, Language Arts, Phonics, Reading, Writing, Memory Verse, Math, Shapes, Color, Story Time, Music, Arts & Crafts, Outdoor Activity, Physical Education

Bible Reference: Genesis 1:6-8.

Bible Concept to Present: God made air so that it had weight, to contain dust, and to move about.

Bible Lesson: We learned that God made air for us on the second day of Creation. Air is very important for us to breathe, isn't it? We also learned that air contains gases and water. Did you know that when God made the air, He made it to have weight? Just like you weigh a certain amount, air has weight also. Some air is heavier than others. Helium balloons can go up in the sky because the helium air inside of them weighs less than the normal air outside. Let's go out now and see if we can make a balloon go up into the air. I am thankful God made the air to have weight. (Go outside and bat a balloon around.) It would be fun to bring helium balloons to class. Let the students play, observing the way they float.

The air also contains dust particles. Did you ever wonder why, when we get done dusting the house, it gets dusty again? That is because the air carries some dirt in it. Little hairs in our nose help keep the dirt outside our bodies.

The wind sometimes carries dirt around. The wind is air that is moving very fast from one place to another. The wind will sometimes carry dirt and little seeds with it. The wind is very important to us. It helps to keep our air clean.

Can you see if the wind is blowing now? How do you know the wind is blowing? Will the balloon we release tell us if the wind is blowing? Why? I'm thankful God made the wind. It helps us in so many ways.

Multimedia Resources: Listen to the song "Jesus Gave Me Wings" from the "Bullfrogs and Butterflies: God is Great" CD.

Social Studies: Discuss how we use the wind. One way we use the wind is to dry our clothes. The wind blows the air around the clothes and makes the clothes dry. You may want to illustrate how the wind dries our clothes by placing a wet article in a place where the wind can reach it easily. Tell students how this was once the only way the clothes could be dried. Discuss how the electric dryer uses air.

The wind keeps our air clean too. In large cities the air gets dirty from dust, fires, fumes and engine exhaust. The wind can blow this dirty air away and replace it with cleaner air.

Science: We use the pressure (weight) of air when we suck a straw. Discuss how the straw has air in it. When we suck the air out of the straw, we suck up the liquid. Use the air in the straw to air paint to illustrate this. Place the bottom of the straw in paint, and place your finger over the end of it. Then lift your finger off the straw over the paper and let the paint go. For added interest, blow on the straw end where your finger was. Do not let the child suck on the straw.

Language Arts: Take a hair dryer or blow dryer. Blow dry two wet rags. Discuss what happens when the wind blows. How do we know the wind is blowing? Trees move, dust blows, things on the ground blow, signs wiggle, our hair blows, windows rattle, and the wind makes a noise. Everyone make a sound like the wind blowing. You may allow students to straw paint. Put a little bit of liquid paint in small cups. Let the students stick a straw into the paint and then blow it out onto white paper. Be sure to tell them not to suck on the straws!

Multimedia Resources: Listen to the song "The Whistle Song" from the "Music Machine: The Fruit of the Spirit" CD.

Phonics: Review the letters Aa-Gg.

Teach the small letter g. Write some words beginning with the letter g on the board. Include words from stories or activities that tie this lesson to other things that have already been done. Underline the small g that begins the words. Read through the words and point out the shape of letter g. Have the students trace the g in the air as you trace the letter g beginning each word.

    Common words: get, give, go, good, great, grow
    Vocabulary words: globe, good morning, good-bye, good evening, good night, gray, green

Reading: Dictate a simple letter, invitation, or thank you note.

Writing: For these two weeks focus on having the students trace the first two letters of their first name. During this time, write the students' names on all worksheets and papers making the first two letters dotted or something that can be traced.

Writing Skill Builders: Keep these objectives in mind as you direct the class. Coloring a simple drawing. Incorporate writing strokes horizontal and vertical lines, point, moon, and cross. Trace and then independently draw the outlines of geometric shapes and irregular forms. Do the Lesson 23 Writing worksheet to practice horizontal and vertical lines.

Memory Verse: Review Genesis 1:6. Repeat the music that you made up to the memory verse from Lesson 21.

Math: Review number recognition of 5. Continue to teach the concept of 5 by counting items. Today, if your students can count out 5 items, let them take a fun test. Give them several raisins. If they can count to 5 and only 5, let them eat the raisins they counted. Have each student separate items into 5 of each item at lunch, such as 5 small pieces of cheese, 5 chips, 5 slices of apple, etc.

Do this Finger Activity.

Five Little Firefighters

Five little firefighters sit very still. (hold up five fingers)
Until they see a fire on the top of the hill;
Number one rings the bell, ding-dong; (bend down thumb)
Number two pulls his big boots on; (bend down pointer finger)
Number three jumps on the fire engine red; (bend down middle finger)
Number four puts a red fire hat on his head; (bend down ring finger)
Number five drives the red fire truck to the fire, (bend down little finger)

As the big, yellow flames go higher and higher. (spread arms)
'Whooooo-ooooo! Whooooo-ooooo! Hear the fire truck say. (imitate siren)
All of the cars get out of the way.
Shhhhhh! goes the water from the fire hose spout, (rub palms together)
And quicker than a wink the fire is out. (clap hands)

Teach oral counting 1-10. Use the Counting Pennies or the Counting Shapes Resource sheets.

Do the Lesson 23 Math worksheet. Count each row of items and then have the students draw a line from the number to the row of items.

Shapes: Do the Lesson 23 Shapes worksheet. Have the students name the shape of the balls, count the number of circles and then color the circles.

Color: Review the colors red, green, blue, black, white, yellow, and brown.

Story Time: Read a story or stories of your choice.

Music: Review "Wheels On the Bus" and "This Little Light of Mine." Learn the song "God Made You, God Made Me" from the "Horizons Preschool Music" CD.

Multimedia Resources: This week, listen and sing along to selections from "The Amazing Children" CD.

Arts & Crafts: Splatter paint with tempera paint and straws. Cover the tables with newspaper. Give each student a sheet of paper and a straw. Make sure the students have their craft shirts on. Dab some watered down tempera paint onto each student's paper and have them blow the paint around with the straw to make drawings.

Outdoor Activity: Water the flowering plants that were planted in Lesson 17.

Physical Education: Have your students act out how the wind would feel when it is blowing.

NOTES:

Lesson 24

Week 5: Day 4

Activities in this Lesson: Bible Lesson, Science, Language Arts, Phonics, Reading, Writing, Memory Verse, Math, Color, Story Time, Music, Arts & Crafts, Health & Safety, Outdoor Activity, Physical Education, Homework

Bible Reference: Genesis 1:6-8.

Bible Concept to Present: Air helps us in many ways.

Bible Lesson: Review yesterday's lesson. Air is very important to our lives. Air helps us. Air can be pressed together to be stronger. Air in tires is pressed together. When divers go down deep into the ocean, they wear tanks filled with air. Airplanes pump air into the plane so people can breathe far up in the sky.

Illustration: Man has learned how to use the air God gave us. When we heat our homes, cold air is brought into a heater, heated up and then blown back out into our houses. The same is true of cooling our homes. Except in this case the hot air is cooled. Our bodies need a certain temperature around them. It can't be too hot or too cold in our homes for our bodies to be comfortable.

Science: *Bring in a can of room freshener or perfume.* Say, Remember, we talked about dust in the air? What do you think dust is? Dust is little pieces of our clothes, of dirt and of our skin, that float around and land on furniture. Let's look at a dusty shelf. See, all of that dust was floating in the air. Write the word "dust" in the dust. Explain that we have tiny, tiny hairs in our nose that catch the dust in the air so it won't go down into our lungs. When there is smoke in the air, it can go through the hairs and into our body. This isn't good for us. Spray a can of room freshener. Ask, how is the smell getting from the can to your nose? It is being carried on the air. You might let the students get out their little flashlights. Turn off the light in the room. Tell students to turn on their lights and point them at the room freshener can. Now spray the freshener. They should be able to see the spray going out into the air.

Language Arts: Play a rhyme game. Say the sentence, leaving the last word blank. Let the students fill in the blank with words that rhyme with "air."

I use a brush to comb my _____ . HAIR
There are rides and cotton candy at the _____ . FAIR
He lives in the forest and has brown fur. He sleeps in the winter and is a
_____ . BEAR
When I have two socks, they are called a _____ . PAIR
James fell and ripped his pants. That's called a _____ . TEAR
When I tell someone I love them, and hug them, and help them, it shows that I _____ .
CARE
A shape that has four equal sides is called a _____ . SQUARE

Phonics: Review the letters Aa-Gg.

Do the Lesson 24 Phonics worksheet. Complete the letter Gg worksheet. Notice that all of the letters of the alphabet are displayed on the page and that the letters Gg are highlighted with a background. As the students get better at letter recognition you can call out a letter and ask the students to point it out with their finger. Trace the large letter and the small letter. The students can trace the letters between the guide lines. Review the pictures and the colored first letter of the words. The students can color the letters as desired.

Reading: Dictate a simple letter, invitation, or thank you note.

Writing: For these two weeks focus on having the students trace the first two letters of their first name. During this time, write the students' names on all worksheets and papers making the first two letters dotted or something that can be traced.

Writing Skill Builders: Keep these objectives in mind as you direct the class. Coloring a simple drawing. Incorporate writing strokes horizontal and vertical lines, point, moon, and cross. Trace and then independently draw the outlines of geometric shapes and irregular forms. Do the Lesson 24 Writing worksheet to practice horizontal and vertical lines.

Memory Verse: Review Genesis 1:6. Let the students lie on the floor. Turn out the lights. Have a quiet time reciting the memory verse together several times.

Math: Review number recognition of 5.

Teach oral counting 1-10. Use the Counting Train, Counting Pennies, or Counting Shapes visuals.

Do the Lesson 24 Math worksheet. Use a red crayon to connect the dots to make the umbrella.

Learn another verse of "This Old Man, He Played One."

This Old Man, He Played One

Verse 1
This old man, he played one, He played nick-nack on my thumb;
with a nick-nack paddy whack, give a dog a bone. This old man came rolling home.

Verse 2
This old man, he played two, He played nick-nack on my shoe;
with a nick-nack paddy whack, give a dog a bone. This old man came rolling home.

Verse 3
This old man, he played three, He played nick-nack on my on my knee;
with a nick-nack paddy whack, give a dog a bone. This old man came rolling home.

Verse 4
This old man, he played four, He played nick-nack on my door;
with a nick-nack paddy whack, give a dog a bone. This old man came rolling home.

Verse 5
This old man, he played five, He played nick-nack on my hive;
with a nick-nack paddy whack, give a dog a bone. This old man came rolling home.

Color: Review the colors red, green, blue, black, white, yellow, and brown.

Story Time: Read a story or stories of your choice.

Music: Review "God Made You, God Made Me" and "Wheels On the Bus."

Multimedia Resources: This week, listen and sing along to selections from "The Amazing Children" CD.

Arts & Crafts: Let the students draw a picture of their favorite way that man uses air.

Health & Safety: *Try to obtain an inexpensive breathing mask. Most pharmacies carry them. If possible, get one for each student.* Say, Some cities have problems with dirty air. It is called smog. Smog is caused by cars, trucks, and factories. The air also gets dirty if there is a fire, especially a forest fire. Have you seen pictures of fire fighters wearing masks? That is to keep the junk in the air out of their bodies. Sometimes, germs can float in the air. (Put on the mask.) Doctors and nurses wear a mask so that they don't give their patients a sickness or so that patients don't give THEM a sickness. Sickness can travel from one person to another. Even when we sneeze, germs can travel in the air. That is why we cover our noses when we sneeze or our mouths when we cough. That is also why we need to wash our hands often, to keep the germs off our body.

Outdoor Activity: Take one more look at the flowers outside, talking about shadow and light. Are the plants looking different? Mention that plants also need air. Tell students that the leaves on the plants "breathe." They take in oxygen.

Physical Education: Cloud Hopping. The air helps to make things float. Clouds seem to float through the air. Spread out carpet squares or hula hoops that are far enough apart so that the students will need to jump to get from one to another. Give each student a ribbon stick which can be made by attaching two or three 36 inch strips of 1 1/2 to 2 inch wide ribbon to a plastic shower ring. Use a hot glue gun to attach the ribbons to the ring and fold the free end of the ribbon over twice and glue to keep it from fraying. Explain to the students that they are going to be the wind blowing across the sky. To do this they will jump across the clouds and wave their ribbons. Watch as the ribbons float on the air.

Homework: Pass out Lesson 24 Homework worksheet, Dust Around the House, for the students to take home. Tell the students to bring it back tomorrow.

NOTES:

Activities in this Lesson: Bible Lesson, Science, Homework Review, Social Studies, Language Arts, Phonics, Reading, Writing, Memory Verse, Math, Color, Story Time, Music, Arts & Crafts, Physical Education

Bible Reference: Genesis 1:6-8.

Bible Concept to Present: God made the air to contain clouds. Hold up the #2 Days of Creation Number where the cotton balls represent the clouds in the sky. Clouds are particles of dirt and water. God planned it so that the air would separate the waters above and below the earth.

Bible Lesson: When God made the air He made it for a very special reason. Not only did God know that we would need it to breathe, but God made it to separate the waters that were above the earth from the waters below the earth. In a way He made a sandwich of water and air. God gathered little pieces of dust and little pieces of water together and called them clouds. There are different kinds of clouds in our sky. But they all look fluffy and like cotton, don't they? Let's go out now and look at the clouds God made. **Note:** As you go outdoors, teach the Science lesson below.

Science: There are basically three types of clouds. Cumulus clouds look like fluffy bits of cotton. They look so soft and almost like you could bounce on them. Stratus clouds look like a blanket has been spread out over our Earth. They look sort of thin sometimes. Cirrus clouds look like little wisps of cotton floating in the sky. Can you look at the sky now and identify some of the clouds? Help your students with this. Now it is time to go indoors.

Multimedia Resources: Listen to the song "Some Invisible Things Are Real" from the "Music Machine: The Majesty of God" CD.

Homework Review: Ask students to share their homework page. Did anyone find anything interesting in the dust? How does a magnifying glass help us discover facts?

Social Studies: Some people like to look at the clouds to find shapes or patterns. Our minds like to find shapes that we can identify. That is why, when we write letters or numbers, we try to make them look the same every time that we write them. If the letters or numbers are written correctly other people can identify and read them. It is important that everyone learns the same way of writing and speaking so that we can understand each other. Think of how confusing it is to try to speak to someone who speaks a different language. The clouds in the sky are living artwork because they are always moving. It is fun to look for animal, letter or number shapes in the clouds.

Language Arts: Clouds not only have different shapes but they also have many colors. Ask the students to describe a rain cloud. How do they know from looking at the cloud that it may rain? What colors have they seen in a sunrise or a sunset? The sun shining through the clouds makes these colors. Say the old weather proverb.
> *Red sky at night, sailor's delight...*
> *Red sky in the morning, sailors take warning.*

Phonics: Teach the letter Hh.

Show the students the letter Hh flashcard. Point out any student's name beginning with the letter *H*.

Write some words beginning with the letter *H* on the board. Include any student names from the class that begin with letter *H*. Underline the capital *H* that begins the words. Read through the words and point out the shape of letter *H*. Have the students trace the *H* in the air as you trace the letter *H* beginning each name.

Boys: Harrison, Hayden, Hector, Henry, Hunter
Girls: Hailey, Haley, Hanna, Hannah, Hayley, Heather, Holly, Hope

Do the Lesson 25 Phonics worksheet. Complete the letter Hh worksheet. Have the students trace the letters Hh with their fingers. They should trace the letters with their fingers and say the names of the letters. Demonstrate the proper strokes for them on the board. Say the words for each of the pictures and look at the Hh letters that begin them.

Reading: Dictate a simple letter, invitation, or thank you note.

Writing: For these two weeks focus on having the students trace the first two letters of their first name. During this time, write the students' names on all worksheets and papers making the first two letters dotted or something that can be traced.

Writing Skill Builders: Keep these objectives in mind as you direct the class. Coloring a simple drawing. Incorporate writing strokes horizontal and vertical lines, point, moon, and cross. Trace and then independently draw the outlines of geometric shapes and irregular forms.

Memory Verse: Review Genesis 1:6. Cut cloud shapes out of white paper. If your student can say the memory verse by today have them glue cotton to the clouds and place it on a ribbon. For every day in the following week that the student can recite the memory verse, have them place more cotton on the clouds and glue them on a ribbon. The number of clouds they have at the end of the week will represent the number of days they haves been able to say the verse on their own. Praise students for their work on their memory verse.

Math: Review number recognition of 5. Review the concept of the number 5 by counting items. Be certain that your students understand that the number 5 is the symbol for 5 of an item. You may review 5 with the following finger play.

Five Little Monkeys

Five little monkeys jumping on the bed (Fingers jump in palm)
One fell off and hurt his head (point to head)
Mamma called the doctor (Pretend to dial on phone)
And the doctor said (Shake finger)
No more monkeys jumping on the bed. (Shake head 'No')

(Continue this counting down to one monkey.)

Teach oral counting 1-10. Use the Counting Pennies or the Counting Shapes Resource pages. Do the Lesson 25 Math worksheet. Instruct the students to count each group and then trace the number for the group. Read and trace the numbers at the bottom of the page.

Color: Teach the color pink. Show the students the pink flashcard. Look for pink things in the room. Look for pink clothing items that the students might be wearing. Teach the color pink as in pink flowers. Legend has it that pink has been associated with baby girls since the Middle Ages. It was thought that baby girls were born inside pink roses. Baby boys have been clothed in blue because blue was a color of heavenly spirits who could combat the evil spirits that hung around in a baby's room. Review the colors red, green, blue, black, white, yellow, and brown. Review the color blue as in the sky is blue.

Story Time: Read a story or stories of your student's choice or ones they have brought from home.

Music: Review "God Made You, God Made Me" and "Wheels On the Bus."

Multimedia Resources: This week, listen and sing along to selections from "The Amazing Children" CD.

Arts & Crafts: Give the students several pieces of cotton, some paper and some glue. Have them glue the clouds on their paper to look like the clouds in the sky. Make all three types of clouds mentioned in the Science lesson. Let the students cut around their cotton clouds. Bring them to the blue sky background you painted for Lesson 21. Use tacky glue or a stapler to attach the clouds to the blue sky.

An alternative procedure would be to have the students make the clouds directly on the blue sky background that was painted in Lesson 21. Give each of the students their blue sky painting and 4-5 cottons balls. Go around the room and put 4-5 drops of glue in a cluster pattern on each students painting. Have them put one of the cotton balls on each of the drops of glue. These should represent cumulus clouds discussed in the science lesson. Next give each student a scrap of white cloth or white construction paper that has been cut into a cloud shape to represent a stratus cloud. Smear a spot of glue on each students painting where they can glue on the stratus cloud. Finally, give each student one more cotton ball. Have them pull the cotton ball into long thin strips to represent cirrus clouds. Do one more smear of glue on each students painting and have them glue on their cirrus cloud.

Another alternate is to make clouds from foam packing peanuts and toothpicks.

Praise the students for their hard work on this project.

Physical Education: The air helps to make things float. Clouds seem to float through the air. Ask students to interpret for you how a floating cloud would feel. You may wish to put on some peaceful music to help them with this. After you are done, go out and lie on the grass and look at the clouds. What do you see? Any animal shapes?

NOTES:

Lesson 26

Week 6: Day 1

Activities in this Lesson: Bible Lesson, Social Studies, Science, Language Arts, Phonics, Reading, Writing, Memory Verse, Math, Shapes, Color, Story Time, Music, Arts & Crafts, Science Activity, Creative Cooking, Physical Education

Bible Reference: Genesis 1:9-10.

Bible Concept to Present: God gathered the waters together to make dry land on Day 3 of Creation. (See the Table of Contents for the location of the instructions.) Hold up the #3 Days of Creation Number where the rocks represent the dry land. He called the dry land Earth, and the waters He called sea.

Bible Lesson: When God made our world, thousands of years ago, He said "Let there be light" and there was light. That was the first day of Creation. The second day of Creation, God made the air to separate the waters above and below the earth. God was happy with everything that He had made. But God's work was not done yet. The earth was covered with water. It did not have any dry land yet. So on day three, God made the dry land to appear. He also made the waters to be gathered into one place and He called them seas. The dry land He made He called Earth. Remind the students of the earth card that they took home that was copied from the Lesson 1 Resource page.

I am very glad God made the dry land. I would not like to have to live in water, would you? But God did make the seas to be very special. It is fun to go to the seashore and play, isn't it? God is a very good God to carefully make these things for us. Let's thank Him for them.

Social Studies: Where you live right now is dry land. If you did not live on dry land you would have to live in water. Do you think you would get along very well living in water? I don't think I would. God did not make us to live in water. He made us to live on the dry land which He made for us. Look on a globe and find all the areas of dry land. Find the specific area of dry land on which you live. Now point out where the seas are. You may wish to tell your students some of the names of the bodies of water. Most of our world is water. God made it this way. He made the water because it is important for us. He made the dry land because it is important for us to live on dry land.

Science: Our Earth is round. God made it the shape of a circle. It is round like a circle, but it is solid and round, so we call it a sphere. Can you say that word? A sphere is like a ball. Our Earth is the shape of a ball. Our Earth has air all around it, water above it and water below it. It has dry ground on it and water on it. Our Earth spins around and around (spin globe). God keeps our Earth in just the right place at the right time. I am happy that God made our Earth for us to live in and that He takes care of it. Hand out Lesson 26 Science worksheet to each student. Point out the areas that are water and those that are land. Have the students color the land areas brown and the water areas blue.

Multimedia Resources: Listen to the song "Water, Water" from "The Amazing Miracles" CD.

Language Arts: Finger Activity, "So Big." Review the size and position words used in the poem.

So Big

How big is God's World?
So Big (Stretch arms wide)
How high is God's sky?
So High (Stretch arms up)
Where is God's child?
So Near (Cross arms over chest)
    ... Author Unknown

Phonics: Review the letter Hh.

Teach the small letter *h*. Write some words beginning with the letter *h* on the board. Include words from stories or activities that tie this lesson to other things that have already been done. Underline the small *h* that begins the words. Read through the words and point out the shape of letter *h*. Have the students trace the *h* in the air as you trace the letter *h* beginning each word.

    Common words: had, hand, hard, has, have, he, head, help, her, here, high, him, his, home, hot, house, how

    Vocabulary words: hair, hearing, heart, heavy, heel, hello, hi, hip

Reading: Dictate a simple letter, invitation, or thank you note.

Multimedia Resources: View the Aa-Hh segments of "Rev-Up for Reading" from the "Rev-Up for Learning" DVD to drill letter recognition and sound. The students should say each letter sound along with the presentation.

Writing: For these two weeks focus on having the students trace the first two letters of their first name. During this time, write the students' names on all worksheets and papers making the first two letters dotted or something that can be traced.

Writing Skill Builders: Keep these objectives in mind as you direct the class. Dictate a caption for a photo or drawing. Incorporate writing strokes spiral, moon, and cross. Trace and then independently draw the outlines of geometric shapes and irregular forms.

Multimedia Resources: View the Aa-Hh segments of "Rev-Up for Writing" from the "Rev-Up for Learning" DVD to review the writing of upper- and lowercase letters. The students should write each letter in the air along with the presentation. Since the first half of the presentation covers lowercase letters and the second half uppercase letters some navigation will be needed to skip to the letters that are covered in this lesson.

Memory Verse: Genesis 1:10.
God called the dry ground "land," and the gathered waters He called "seas." And God saw that it was good. Genesis 1:10 NIV

And God called the dry land Earth; and the gathering together of the waters called he Seas: and God saw that it was good. Genesis 1:10 KJV

Go over the memory verse with your students. Repeat it as they do the following project: From construction paper, draw a circle and cut it out. On the circle, place blue bodies of water and brown shapes of land. Glue the pieces on the "earth" you have made. Write the memory verse underneath it. Repeat the verse again. Ask this question: Did God like what He had made? (Yes) Do you like what you made? Pass out Memory Verse Card 4 for students to take home.

Math: Teach number recognition of 6. Show the students the number 6 flashcard. Begin by showing your students a number 6 and having them count out 6 of an item. Practice with various items. Count groups of six at every opportunity. If you have hung cards for the week of the school year point out the Week 6 card.

Teach oral counting 1-10. Use the Counting Train, Counting Pennies, or Counting Shapes visuals.

Do the Lesson 26 Math worksheet. Instruct the students to draw a line between the groups that have the same number.

Multimedia Resources: View "Rev-Up for Arithmetic" from the "Rev-Up for Learning" DVD to practice number recognition and counting 1-9.

Shapes: Review the circle. We are discussing the Earth, which is shaped like a circle. Trace your student's fingers around the shape of a circle. Place cornmeal with a little rice (rice keeps the moisture out of the cornmeal) into a 9x13 pan. Let the children trace the shape of a circle all over the bottom of the pan.

Color: Continue to teach the color pink. Review the colors red, green, blue, black, white, yellow, and brown.

Story Time: Read a story or stories of your choice.

Music: Review "God Made You, God Made Me." Teach the following song to the tune of "Three Blind Mice."

Let's Make a Garden
Tune of Three Blind Mice

Let's make a garden
Let's make a garden
And watch things grow
And watch things grow

First we dig and rake the ground (Pretend to dig and rake)
Then we plant, but not too deep (Pretend to plant a seed)
Now our seed must go to sleep (Hands folded by head)
So tuck them in (Place right fingers into left cupped hand)
Tuck them in (Place right fingers into left cupped hand)

Multimedia Resources: This week, listen and sing along to selections from the "Nathaniel the Grublet" CD.

Arts & Crafts: Roll playdough flat to about an inch in thickness. Have the students make a flat map of the Earth. This will be very simple. They may wish to add a mountain on it or an indent for an ocean. You may need to show them how to do this. Next roll playdough into a ball shape. This is how our earth looks. Let the students practice making Earth.

Science Activity: *Prepare ahead – Bring enough paper plates so that each child has one. Fill one or several tubs with dirt, depending on the number of students. It would be nice if every student had a magnifying glass and tweezers, but bring as many as you have.* Set one tub of dirt before one or several students. Let them use the tweezers to separate the parts of the dirt such as sand, gravel, etc. You may then examine them under the magnifying glass. After observing the content of the dirt, you may add water to the dirt and examine the result.

Creative Cooking: *Bring paper plates and celery, washed and cut into three inch pieces. Bring peanut butter and plastic spoons. Be sure to check for peanut allergies.* Give each student a piece of celery on a plate. Then give each one a big spoonful of peanut butter. Tell students to spread the "soil" on the celery. Raisins may be added to represent "bugs" on the "dirt." You may discuss how celery grows, and how the earth's soil is important to the celery for nutrients to grow.

Physical Education: We will be doing activities with balls all this week. Teach each student to roll the ball to you or to another child. If they can roll the ball in the general vicinity of where it should be, good. If they cannot, keep up the practice. Next, teach each child to bounce the ball to you. It does not have to be a certain number of bounces to you, just so it gets to you. When they can do this, have them throw the ball to you. If the student has trouble with this, begin working with a larger ball, going gradually to a smaller ball over a period of time. Have the student practice throwing the ball to you and then catching it. This larger muscle coordination must be developed before the child should be taught to do finer muscle coordination skills such as writing. If your student can do these things, play a game with him such as "Foursquare" where the bouncing must be done in certain confines. Continue this the entire week.

NOTES:

Lesson 27

Week 6: Day 2

Activities in this Lesson: Bible Lesson, Science, Language Arts, Phonics, Reading, Writing, Memory Verse, Math, Shapes, Color, Story Time, Music, Arts & Crafts, Outdoor Activity, Physical Education, Optional Math/Language Arts/Bible/Arts & Crafts Activity

Bible Reference: Genesis 1:9-10.

Bible Concept to Present: God made everything in and on the land on Day 3.

Bible Lesson: Review yesterday's story. God was amazing when He made the land. How many different things did He make when He made the land? Talk about mountains and valleys, rocks and sand, dirt and gravel. He made the precious stones in the ground: diamonds, emeralds, gold, and silver.

Illustration: If you have samples of any of these precious metals, show them to your students. If you have access to a rock collection, the students would love to see it.

Multimedia Resources: Listen to the song "Shout Hallelujah" from the "Bullfrogs and Butterflies: God Loves Fun" CD.

Science/Language Arts: Children love to gather rocks. Take a walk outside and look for "special" rocks. Only allow students to gather their favorite two or three so that you don't get too many. Come back inside and have students describe the rocks that they collected. Have them tell why they picked those rocks. They should speak in complete sentences. For example: I found this rock by the..., I like this rock because it is..., My rock is..., I would like to give my special rock to... These rocks can be saved for an Arts & Crafts activity in Lesson 28.

Language Arts: Do the finger activity again, from yesterday, "So Big."

Phonics: Review the letters Aa-Hh.

Do the Lesson 27 Phonics worksheet. Complete the letter Hh worksheet. Notice that all of the letters of the alphabet are displayed on the page and that the letters Hh are highlighted with a background. As the students get better at letter recognition you can call out a letter and ask the students to point it out with their finger. Trace the large letter and the small letter. The students can trace the letters between the guide lines. Review the pictures and the colored first letter of the words. The students can color the letters as desired.

Reading: Dictate a simple letter, invitation, or thank you note.

Writing: For these two weeks focus on having the students trace the first two letters of their first name. During this time, write the students' names on all worksheets and papers making the first two letters dotted or something that can be traced.

Writing Skill Builders: Keep these objectives in mind as you direct the class. Dictate a caption for a photo or drawing. Incorporate writing strokes spiral, moon, and cross. Trace and then independently draw the outlines of geometric shapes and irregular forms. Do the Lesson 27 Writing worksheet to practice spiral, cross and horizontal lines.

Memory Verse: Review Genesis 1:10. The verse assigned is kind of long. You might divide it into three sections, learning one section at a time.

ONE	God called the dry ground "land,"
TWO	and the gathered waters He called "seas."
THREE	And God saw that it was good. Genesis 1:10

Math: Review number recognition of 6.

Teach oral counting 1-10. Use the Counting Train, Counting Pennies, or Counting Shapes visuals.

Do the Lesson 27 Math worksheet. Cut out the numbers from the strip. Count each group of objects and paste the correct number in the box.

Shapes: Do the Lesson 27 Shapes worksheet. Review shapes with the Over and Under worksheet. Color and cut out the shapes and put the circles over the line and the triangles below the line.

Color: Continue to teach the color pink. Review the colors red, green, blue, black, white, yellow, and brown.

Story Time: Read a story or stories of your choice.

Music: Review "Let's Make a Garden" and "God Made You, God Made Me." Continue to teach the "ABC Song." If the students do not already know it, work on one line at a time until all lines are mastered. This will help to develop an awareness of the entire alphabet. The students can sing along even though they cannot recognize the individual letters.

> **A B C Song**
> Tune of Twinkle, Twinkle, Little Star
>
> A B C D E F G
> H I J K L M N O P
> Q R S T U and V
> W X Y and Z.
> Now I've learned my ABCs.
> Next time won't you sing with me!

Multimedia Resources: This week, listen and sing along to selections from the "Nathaniel the Grublet" CD.

Arts & Crafts: Give each student a piece of construction paper, tacky glue, and a paper cup of sand. Let the students first "draw" with the glue on their paper, then carefully pour sand over the glue. After the sand 'sets' a bit, shake it off into the trash. Talk about sand being dirt or earth. Let the artwork dry overnight before letting the students take it home to hang it on the refrigerator. This would make a nice outdoor activity in good weather.

Outdoor Activity: Check the plants outside. Time has passed. Are there major differences in the plants? We do hope so! Bring the students back into the classroom and have them draw the plants and the differences they saw in them.

Physical Education: We will be doing activities with balls all this week. Teach each student to roll the ball to you or to another child. If the student can roll the ball in the general vicinity of where it should be, good. If they cannot, keep up the practice. Next, teach each child to bounce the ball to you. It does not have to be a certain number of bounces to you, just so it gets to you. When they can do this, have them throw the ball to you. If they have trouble with this, begin working with a larger ball, going gradually to a smaller ball over a period of time. Have the student practice throwing the ball to you and then catching it. This larger muscle coordination must be developed before the child should be taught to do finer muscle coordination skills such as writing. If your student can do these things, play a game with him such as "Foursquare" where the bouncing must be done in certain confines. Continue this the entire week.

Optional Math/Language Arts/Bible/Arts & Crafts Activity:

6 Days: Genesis 1:1-31, read the Bible verses and tell the story.

God made the earth and everything in it in six days. The animals were made on the sixth day. Adam and Eve were also made on the sixth day.

Do the Lesson 27 Bible Numbers worksheet. Give each student a sheet of white construction paper and the worksheet. Cut out the items on the worksheet and glue them to construction paper as illustrated in the drawing. Draw in the arms, legs, and face for the "6" Creation man. Draw in the rest of the picture.

NOTES:

Activities in this Lesson: Bible Lesson, Social Studies, Science/Outdoor Activity, Language Arts, Phonics, Reading, Writing, Memory Verse, Math, Shapes, Color, Story Time, Music, Arts & Crafts, Physical Education

Bible Reference: Genesis 1:9-10.

Bible Concept to Present: When God made the earth, He made rocks with it. Rocks are part of the land God made. Hold up the #3 Days of Creation Number. There are many kinds of rocks which God made.

Bible Lesson: God made the dry land to appear from the water. He gave the dry land a name. He named the dry land earth. When God made the dry land, He made some of it to be rocks. Rocks are very hard. Not all rocks are the same. Rocks are very different from each other. Some rocks were made from the earth being very hot. Some rocks were made by sand and dirt settling into piles and becoming hard. Rocks are necessary for us. I am happy God made the rocks for us when He made the earth.

Social Studies: We use rocks for many things. It is on rocks that we build our houses. Under the ground of your house is a solid base of rock. The rock helps to keep our house safe. We use rocks in the building of houses and buildings too. Some of the rocks are to make the building look pretty. Some of the rocks make the walls stay up.

Science/Outdoor Activity: Take a walk outside to find various kinds of rocks. Look for mica and various colors in the rocks. Identify the rocks that you can. Have the students identify what they can. Collect various sizes of rocks. You may want to make a rock garden using rocks as ornamentation.

Language Arts: In Science, you have already collected rocks. Sort the rocks into categories. Encourage students to verbalize as you compare hardness, size and weight of rocks.

Phonics: Teach the letter Ii.

Show the students the letter Ii flashcard. Point out any student's name beginning with the letter *I*. Write some words beginning with the letter *I* on the board. Include any student names from the class that begin with letter *I*. Underline the capital *I* that begins the words. Read through the words and point out the shape of letter *I*. Have the students trace the *I* in the air as you trace the letter *I* beginning each name.

> Boys: Ian, Isaac, Isaiah, Ivan
> Girls: Isabel, Isabella

Do the Lesson 28 Phonics worksheet. Complete the letter Ii worksheet. Have the students trace the letters Ii with their fingers. They should trace the letters with their fingers and say the names of the letters. Demonstrate the proper strokes for them on the board. Say the words for each of the pictures and look at the Ii letters that begin them.

Reading: Dictate a simple letter, invitation, or thank you note.

Writing: For these two weeks focus on having the students trace the first two letters of their first name. During this time, write the students' names on all worksheets and papers making the first two letters dotted or something that can be traced.

Writing Skill Builders: Keep these objectives in mind as you direct the class. Dictate a caption for a photo or drawing. Incorporate writing strokes spiral, moon, and cross. Trace and then independently draw the outlines of geometric shapes and irregular forms. Do the Lesson 27 Writing worksheet to practice spiral, cross, moon, vertical, and horizontal lines.

Memory Verse: Review Genesis 1:10. Have the students repeat phrase after phrase after you. For added interest you may place three circles on the wall. Write part of the Memory Verse on each circle. When the children can say that part of the memory verse, place a sticker on the circle. At the end of the two-week period, your students should be able to say the verse completely and have stickers on all of the circles.

Math: Review number recognition of 6. Teach your students the symbol for the number 6. For each group of 6 items they count, place the number 6 beside it. Have the students find the number 6 in their environment.

Teach oral counting 1-10. Use the Counting Train, Counting Pennies, or Counting Shapes visuals.

Do the Lesson 28 Math worksheet. Notice that all of the numbers are displayed on the page and that the number 6 is highlighted with a background. As the students get better at number recognition you can call out a number and ask the students to point it out with their finger. Have the students trace the large number 6 with the proper stroke by following the arrow. Instruct the students to count each group of items and then trace the number.

Shapes: *Previous to this lesson cut out a square from construction paper and place it on a craft stick, as you did when you taught triangles and circles.* Introduce the shape of a square. Show your student what a square is. Show the students the square flashcard. Use the square stick puppet with the following finger play poem:

Sammy Square

My name is Sammy
I'm a square.
Count my sides
If you dare.

I have one side (point to one side)
I have two (point to another side)
I have three sides (point to third side)
Four is for you. (point to last side)

I'm the same
Wherever you look.
Watch with care,
I'm Sammy Square.

Do the Lesson 28 Shapes worksheet. Have the students trace and color the square.

Color: Continue to teach the color pink. Review the colors red, green, blue, black, white, yellow, and brown.

Story Time: Read a story or stories of your choice.

Music: Review "Let's Make a Garden" and "God Made You, God Made Me." Teach the following song to the tune of "The Mulberry Bush."

Here We All Go Around the Rock
Tune of The Mulberry Bush

Here we all go around the rock
Around the rock
Around the rock
Here we all go around the rock
And then we all sit down

(Other verses)
Here we all run around the rock
Here we all skip around the rock
Here we all jump over the rock.

(You may pretend to actually have a rock, and do the exercises.)

Multimedia Resources: This week, listen and sing along to selections from the "Nathaniel the Grublet" CD.

Arts & Crafts: Do the Lesson 28 Arts & Crafts worksheet. Make the Square Train. Count, color, cut, and paste the squares to make the train. Count the wheels (circles) on the train.

Gather various small rocks. Make rock pictures or paint faces on the rocks. You may glue them on a heavy piece of cardboard for a rock family.

Physical Education: Continue the ball exercises.

NOTES:

Lesson 29

Week 6: Day 4

Activities in this Lesson: Bible Lesson, Social Studies, Science, Language Arts/Shapes, Phonics, Reading, Writing, Math, Color, Music, Story Time, Arts & Crafts, Physical Education, Homework

Bible Reference: Genesis 1:9-10.

Bible Concept to Present: Some rocks that God made are huge. They are famous with famous names.

Bible Lesson: Review yesterday's story. Go on the nternet and print out some pictures of some famous rocks that God made to show your students. Find just a few: Morro Rock, Morro Bay, California; Pike's Peak, Colorado Springs, Colorado; The Rosetta Stone, British Museum, London; Stonehenge, England (actually, a collection of rocks); Rock of Gibraltar, Spain; Plymouth Rock, Plymouth, Massachusetts; the Hope Diamond, Smithsonian, Washington D.C. Find a picture of Mount Rushmore, South Dakota. Ask your students if God made this rock. Explain that God made it and then man carved it.

Social Studies: God made many parts of our earth to be used by man. Some rocks are used in building and carving. Coal is used for heat. In order to get the rocks and coal out of the ground, we have to mine it. There are many kinds of mines. Miners are people that work in mines. Mines can be above ground or underground. There are three basic kinds of underground mines: slope, shaft and drift. Slope: the tunnel goes into a hillside at an angle; shaft: a tunnel goes straight down into the earth; drift: a tunnel goes straight into the middle of a hill. Would you like to work in a mine? Why would it be hard? Miners have to use flashlights like ours, but much bigger. Sometimes, their flashlight is on their hard hat. They also have to use a breathing mask because the air gets full of dust and fumes.

Science: *Prepare ahead: a 2 liter soda bottle, cut in half; paper towels; sand; small pieces of charcoal; cotton balls; dirty water – made by stirring dirt clods into water.* Set the top half of the soda bottle down in the bottom, like a funnel. Let the students help you layer filtering materials in the funnel. Talk about each material, especially the sand and the charcoal, parts of the earth God made. Isn't it interesting that sand and charcoal can actually CLEAN water? Layer the filtering materials in this order, from the bottom: cotton balls, paper towel folded, sand, charcoal. Ask, what do you think each of these will filter out? Slowly pour the dirty water through your filter. Do this at a sink or table where all of the students can see. After the water filters through, take the filter apart and look at each filter material to see what it stopped. How could we make the filter better? You might do the experiment several times to see what order of filtering works best.

Language Arts/Shapes: Have a square hunt. Let the students roam the room, looking for squares. Write the name of each object on the board, familiarizing students with the written words.

Phonics: Review the letter Ii.

Do the Lesson 29 Phonics worksheet. Complete the letter Ii worksheet. Notice that all of the letters of the alphabet are displayed on the page and that the letters Aa are highlighted with a background. As the students get better at letter recognition you can call out a letter and ask the students to point it out with their finger. Trace the large letter and the small letter. The students can trace the letters between the guide lines. Review the pictures and the colored first letter of the words. The students can color the letters as desired.

Reading: Dictate a simple letter, invitation, or thank you note.

Writing: For these two weeks focus on having the students trace the first two letters of their first name. During this time, write the students' names on all worksheets and papers making the first two letters dotted or something that can be traced.

Writing Skill Builders: Keep these objectives in mind as you direct the class. Dictate a caption for a photo or drawing. Incorporate writing strokes spiral, moon, and cross. Trace and then independently draw the outlines of geometric shapes and irregular forms.

Memory Verse: Review Genesis 1:10. Continue as directed in previous lessons by learning sections of the verse.

Math: Review number recognition of 6. Give each student at least 6 counters. Call out numbers 1-6 and have them make groups of the number. Have individual students point to the items in their group and count it for the entire class. Make a large die from a square cardboard box. Number each side of the cube. Roll the die and have the students make groups of counters that equal the number.

Teach oral counting 1-10. Use the Counting Train, Counting Pennies, or Counting Shapes visuals.

Do the Lesson 29 Math worksheet. Count each group of items and circle the correct number for the group.

Learn verse six of "This Old Man, He Played One."

This Old Man, He Played One

Verse 1
This old man, he played one, He played nick-nack on my thumb;
with a nick-nack paddy whack, give a dog a bone. This old man came rolling home.

Verse 2
This old man, he played two, He played nick-nack on my shoe;
with a nick-nack paddy whack, give a dog a bone. This old man came rolling home.

Verse 3
This old man, he played three, He played nick-nack on my on my knee;
with a nick-nack paddy whack, give a dog a bone. This old man came rolling home.

Verse 4
This old man, he played four, He played nick-nack on my door;
with a nick-nack paddy whack, give a dog a bone. This old man came rolling home.

Verse 5
This old man, he played five, He played nick-nack on my hive;
with a nick-nack paddy whack, give a dog a bone. This old man came rolling home.

Verse 6
This old man, he played six, He played nick-nack on my sticks;
with a nick-nack paddy whack, give a dog a bone. This old man came rolling home.

Color: Review the colors red, green, blue, black, white, yellow, brown, and pink.

Story Time: Read a story or stories of your choice.

Music: Review "Let's Make a Garden" and "God Made You, God Made Me." Repeat the song "Here We All Go Around The Rock."

Multimedia Resources: This week, listen and sing along to selections from the "Nathaniel the Grublet" CD.

Arts & Crafts: Do the Lesson 29 Arts & Crafts worksheet. Cut out the animal mix-up pieces, glue them on another sheet of paper and color the completed animals.

Physical Education: Continue the ball activities.

Homework: Send Lesson 29 Homework worksheet, Find Three Squares, home with students. Ask them to return the page tomorrow.

NOTES:

Activities in this Lesson: Bible Lesson, Social Studies, Science, Language Arts, Phonics, Reading, Writing, Memory Verse, Math, Shapes, Color, Story Time, Music, Field Trip/Outdoor Activity, Physical Education, Homework

Bible Reference: Genesis 1:9-10.

Bible Concept to Present: God made some special rocks when He made our earth. They are very special to us, because He did not make very many of them.

Multimedia Resources: Listen to the songs "Diamond In The Rough" and "Gifts In My Heart" from the "Bullfrogs and Butterflies: God Loves Fun" CD.

Bible Lesson: When God made our earth and the rocks in it, He made some very special rocks. He did not make very many of them, and they are very special to us. We call these rocks gem stones. God says in His Word that He will use some of these special kinds of rocks when He makes our new home in Heaven. I am glad God made some rocks to be very special. You may describe some of the gems and show your student any gems that you possess.

Social Studies: *Purchase some packages of little glass "gems" for the crowns.* Do Lesson 30 Social Studies worksheet. Say, We use special rocks in many ways. Usually we use them in jewelry. They are of value to us and cost very much money. Sometimes special gems will mean something special. A diamond means a promise. Queens and Kings use diamonds and other gems in their crowns. Gems used to be used in place of money to buy things. There are crowns that belong to the Queen of England that are worth millions of dollars. Let's make our own crowns today. Hand out the worksheet of the crown. First have the students color them. Then the students may cut out the pieces and staple, glue, or tape them into a crown. If you are having the students glue on fake gems, let the glue dry overnight before cutting out the pieces.

Science: Identify the various kinds of gems. Perhaps a trip to a museum will be of help in this. Take crayons, paper, and pencil to draw the various rocks and color them. Label the rocks.

Language Arts: Form a circle with masking tape on the floor. Have students stand beside the circle, in the circle or on the circle. Your goal is to have students verbalize where they are in relationship to the circle with position words. Do the same with a square shape.

Phonics: Review the letters Aa-Ii.

Teach the small letter *i*. Write some words beginning with the letter *i* on the board. Include words from stories or activities that tie this lesson to other things that have already been done. Underline the small *i* that begins the words. Read through the words and point out the shape of letter *i*. Have the students trace the *i* in the air as you trace the letter *i* beginning each word.
　　　Common words: if, in, is, it
　　　Vocabulary words: immediately, in a circle, in a line, in a little while, in a row, in front of, in the middle, inside

Do the Lesson 30 Phonics worksheet. Have the students put a pink triangle around the Gg letters, a blue circle around the Hh letters, and a white X on the Ii letters. Give them one direction at a time so they can focus on finding the correct letter shape. Begin with capital *G*, then lower case *g*, etc. Show them examples with flashcards or letters written on the board.

Reading: Dictate a simple letter, invitation, or thank you note.

Writing: For these two weeks focus on having the students trace the first two letters of their first name. During this time, write the students' names on all worksheets and papers making the first two letters dotted or something that can be traced.

Writing Skill Builders: Keep these objectives in mind as you direct the class. Dictate a caption for a photo or drawing. Incorporate writing strokes spiral, moon, and cross. Trace and then independently draw the outlines of geometric shapes and irregular forms.

Memory Verse: Review Genesis 1:10. Continue as directed in previous lessons by learning sections of the verse.

Math: Review number recognition of 6. Continue to teach the number 6 by counting items. Incorporate Physical Education into this exercise with the following ideas. Have students stand and hold their right hand up into the air beside their head. Trace with your hand the outline of the "Six." Now try to make your whole body into a "Six." Jump in the air six times. Stamp your right foot six times. Stamp your left foot six times. Get on the floor, roll your body into a ball, and roll over six times. Clap your hands six times.

Teach oral counting 1-10. Use the Counting Train, Counting Pennies, or Counting Shapes visuals.

Do the Lesson 30 Math worksheet. Instruct the students to trace the numbers, count each group, and then draw a line to the number for the group.

Shapes: Squares are found in many places. Look for squares around you. There are squares for windows in a house. Some books are square, too. Give your student several paper squares of various colors. Have him or her glue them to paper to make a house, windows in a house, etc. You may need to show the student how to place these items together. Review the "Sammy Square" finger play poem.

Do the Lesson 30 Shapes worksheet. Count and color the squares. Color at least one of the squares purple.

Color: Teach the color purple. Show them the purple color flashcard. Teach the color purple as in purple flowers. Bring some purple flowers to school or find some pictures of purple flowers to help teach this concept. Like the gems discussed in this lesson the color purple has often been associated with queens, kings, and royalty. Review the colors red, green, blue, black, white, yellow, brown, and pink.

Multimedia Resources: Listen to the song "Be Like Children" from "The Amazing Children" CD.

Story Time: Read a story or stories of your student's choice or ones they have brought from home.

Music: Review "Let's Make a Garden" "and "God Made You, God Made Me." Repeat the song from Lesson 28: "Here We All Go Around The Rock." You may also include "Heaven Is A Happy Place" from the "Horizons Preschool Music" CD.

Multimedia Resources: This week, listen and sing along to selections from the "Nathaniel the Grublet" CD.

Field Trip/Outdoor Activity: Call a few jewelry stores to see if they can give a tour to your students. Explain the scope of the Bible lessons to the jeweler. You might plan a picnic at a park after the visit.

Physical Education: Continue to use the balls for muscle coordination.

Homework: We've talked a lot today about squares. Did you find a lot of squares at your house last night? Share your homework page with the class.

NOTES:

Lesson 31

Week 7: Day 1

Activities in this Lesson: Bible Lesson, Social Studies, Science, Language Arts, Phonics, Reading, Writing, Memory Verse, Math, Shapes, Color, Story Time, Music, Arts & Crafts, Field Trip, Physical Education

Bible Reference: Genesis 1:9-10.

Bible Concept to Present: On the third day God made the soil. Soil is part of the dry land.

Bible Lesson: On the third day of Creation, God made dry land. Last week we learned about the rocks God made. God made something else very special when He made dry land. God made soil. Soil covers all our Earth. It is important that we have soil. Without soil plants could not live. If a plant were to try to live on a rock alone, it could not. The sun would be too hot and there would be no food, because rocks do not have the right food for plants. Soil is important for many things. God knew the soil He made would be needed by us. Thank You, God, for the soil you have made.

Social Studies: Soil is all around us. Take a walk. Look for the soil around you. Point out that there is soil under the grass, under the trees, under the houses and buildings. Everywhere on the Earth is soil. As you are outside discussing this aspect of soil, drift naturally into the Science lesson.

Science: Soil is made of many things. Soil has little pieces of rock in it. Wind, rain, and water washing off a rock over time will break off little pieces of rock. These collect with sand and clay to help make soil. When plants die, they rot and become a material we call humus. This humus is really just rotted plants. It becomes a part of soil, too. Animals help the soil too. Sometimes our soil contains small pieces of metal. If you have a magnet, run it over your soil to see if it contains filings of metal. Take a sample of soil and place it on wax paper. Now look closely at the soil sample. Ask students to identify the sand, rocks, and clay in the soil.

Language Arts: Finger Activity "There Was A Little Turtle." Say each line and have the students repeat it after you.

There Was A Little Turtle

There was a little turtle (Make a small circle with hands.)
    Who lived in a box (Make a box with both hands.)
He swam in the puddles (Wriggle hands.)
    And He climbed on the rocks (Climb fingers of one hand up over the other.)

He snapped at a mosquito (Clap hands.)
    He snapped at a flea (Clap hands.)
He snapped at a minnow (Clap hands.)
    And He snapped at me (Point at self.)

He caught the mosquito (Hold hand up, palm forward; quickly bend fingers shut.)
    He caught the flea (Repeat)
He caught the minnow (Repeat)
    But He didn't catch me (Bend fingers only half-way shut.)
      Vachel Lindsey (1879-1931) Public Domain

Phonics: Teach the letter Jj.

Show the students the letter Jj flashcard. Point out any student's name beginning with the letter *J*. Write some words beginning with the letter *J* on the board. Include any student names from the class that begin with letter *J*. Underline the capital *J* that begins the words. Read through the words and point out the shape of letter *J*. Have the students trace the *J* in the air as you trace the letter *J* beginning each name.

> Boys: Jack, Jackson, Jacob, Jaime, Jake, James, Jared, Jason, Javier, Jeffery, Jeffrey, Jeremiah, Jeremy, Jerry, Jesse, Jesus, Jimmy, Joe, Joel, John, Johnathan, Johnny, Jonathan, Jonathon, Jordan, Jorge, Jose, Joseph, Joshua, Josue, Juan, Jude, Julian, Julio, Justin
>
> Girls: Jaclyn, Jacqueline, Jade, Jamie, Jasmin, Jasmine, Jazmin, Jazmine, Jenna, Jennifer, Jessica, Jillian, Joanna, Jocelyn, Jordan, Julia, Julie, Justine
>
> Vocabulary words: January, Jr., July, June

Do the Lesson 31 Phonics worksheet. Complete the letter Jj worksheet. Have the students trace the letters Jj with their fingers. They should trace the letters with their fingers and say the names of the letters. Demonstrate the proper strokes for them on the board. Say the words for each of the pictures and look at the Jj letters that begin them.

Reading: Dictate a simple letter, invitation, or thank you note.

Multimedia Resources: View the Aa-Jj segments of "Rev-Up for Reading" from the "Rev-Up for Learning" DVD to drill letter recognition and sound. The students should say each letter sound along with the presentation.

Writing: For these two weeks focus on having the students trace the first three letters of their first name. During this time, write the students' names on all worksheets and papers making the first three letters dotted or something that can be traced.

Writing Skill Builders: Keep these objectives in mind as you direct the class. Incorporate writing strokes circle, moon, and cross. Trace and then independently draw the outlines of geometric shapes and irregular forms.

Multimedia Resources: View the Aa-Jj segments of "Rev-Up for Writing" from the "Rev-Up for Learning" DVD to review the writing of upper- and lowercase letters. The students should write each letter in the air along with the presentation. Since the first half of the presentation covers lowercase letters and the second half uppercase letters some navigation will be needed to skip to the letters that are covered in this lesson.

Memory Verse: Review Genesis 1:10. Be sure students can effectively state all the Memory Verses up to this point. Regular review of the memory verses will help students always remember the scriptures.

Math: Teach number recognition of 7. Show the students the number 7 flashcard. Begin to teach your student the concept of 7 by counting items. Take your math manipulative (blocks or whatever you have been using to count) and show your child seven. Practice counting 7 of varying items around your school. Look at the days of the week chart and count the number of days in a week and say the days in a week. Ask the students to name what day it is today. If you have hung cards for the week of the school year point out the Week 7 card.

Teach oral counting 1-10. Use the Counting Train, Counting Pennies, or Counting Shapes visuals.

Do the Lesson 31 Math worksheet. Notice that all of the numbers are displayed on the page and that the number 7 is highlighted with a background. As the students get better at number recognition you can call out a number and ask the students to point it out with their finger. Have the students trace the large number 7 with the proper strokes by following the arrows. Instruct the students to count each group of items and then trace the number.

Multimedia Resources: View "Rev-Up for Arithmetic" from the "Rev-Up for Learning" DVD to practice number recognition and counting 1-9.

Shapes: Let's find the squares in our room. Each student walks to a square and touches it. How many squares can we find? List them on the board.

Color: Continue to teach the color purple. Review the colors red, green, blue, black, white, yellow, brown, and pink.

Story Time: Read a story or stories of your choice.

Music: Review "Here We All Go Around the Rock," "Let's Make a Garden," and "Heaven Is A Happy Place."

Multimedia Resources: This week, listen and sing along to selections from "The Amazing Miracles" CD.

Arts & Crafts: Make a sand painting. You may either color your own sand by mixing it with dry tempera paint, or purchase small vials of colored sand. Choose a design of your own making, preferably simple. Have your students glue the sand onto the pictures in the directed colors.

Field Trip: Visit a nursery and have the staff explain to the students how they prepare the soil for plants. Find out what is mixed together for potting soil, for tree soil, for lawns, etc. As an alternative have someone come into the classroom to demonstrate how he/she prepares the soil for different plants.

Physical Education: Pretend to be a plant, planted in rich soil. Pretend to be the seed planted in the soil that is asleep. As the sun becomes warm, start to stretch up toward the sun; spread out arms to grow tall and bloom. Repeat this more than once.

NOTES:

Activities in this Lesson: Bible Lesson, Science, Language Arts, Phonics, Reading, Writing, Memory Verse, Math, Shapes, Color, Story Time, Music, Arts & Crafts, Outdoor Activity, Health & Safety, Physical Education, Optional Math/Language Arts/Bible/Arts & Crafts Activity

Bible Reference: Genesis 1:9-10.

Bible Concept to Present: Soil is different in different parts of the world.

Bible Lesson: Review yesterday's Bible lesson. God made many different kinds of soil. People describe soil types in all kinds of ways such as heavy, light, sandy, clay, loam, poor, or good. Soil scientists describe soil types by how much sand, silt, and clay are present. Particle size has a lot to do with a soil's drainage and nutrient holding capacity. All over the world, these same particles are in the soil. Some soil drains really well and is good for planting vegetables and flowers. Some soil drains very slowly and is very thick and hard.

Try this great website to find some interesting information about plants. http://www.urbanext.uiuc.edu/gpe/index.html

Science: *Prepare ahead – Bring soil and clay into class. Put the soil in one planter or jar and the clay in another.* Say, God made soil to absorb water, so that plants could drink. Add water to the clay and see if any is absorbed. Explain that "absorbed" means to soak into. Add water to the soil. See how the soil absorbs the water? Now, mix some of the soil into the clay. Try adding water again. Mixing loose soil into the clay makes the clay more absorbent.

Language Arts: Continue learning "There Was a Little Turtle" from yesterday. Say each line and have the students repeat it after you.

Phonics: Review the letter Jj.

Reading: Dictate a simple letter, invitation, or thank you note.

Writing: For these two weeks focus on having the students trace the first three letters of their first name. During this time, write the students' names on all worksheets and papers making the first three letters dotted or something that can be traced.

Writing Skill Builders: Keep these objectives in mind as you direct the class. Incorporate writing strokes circle, moon, and cross. Trace and then independently draw the outlines of geometric shapes and irregular forms.

Memory Verse: Review Genesis 1:10. Students should be practicing the whole memory verse, all three parts together. Let the students march around the building or house, shaking their rice film canisters, chanting the memory verse. Take special care with each word this time, making sure they have it memorized.

Math: Review number recognition of 7.

Teach oral counting 1-10. Use the Counting Train, Counting Pennies, or Counting Shapes visuals.

Do the Lesson 32 Math worksheet. Cut out the numbers from the strip. Count each group of objects and paste the correct number in the box.

Shapes: Do the Lesson 32 Shapes worksheet. Trace the squares, color the large square purple and color the small square pink. Complete the square on the bottom of the page and decorate it to make it look like a birthday present.

Color: Review the colors red, green, blue, black, white, yellow, brown, pink, and purple.

Story Time: Read a story or stories of your choice.

Music: Review "ABC Song," "Here We All Go Around the Rock," "Let's Make a Garden," and "Heaven Is A Happy Place."

Multimedia Resources: This week, listen and sing along to selections from "The Amazing Miracles" CD.

Arts & Crafts: Give the students playdough to create whatever they like.

Outdoor Activity: Take a walk. Make this a brisk walk, heading for any areas outside that might have different types of soil, or rocky ground versus dirt. A place where a fresh trench has been dug would be excellent for seeing layers in the soil. Let the students pick up handfuls of soil and feel it, crumbling it, smelling it. How does the earth smell? Do rocks smell?

Health & Safety: Ask, Did you know that lots of tiny, tiny animals live in soil? Bacteria and germs can also live in soil. Animal waste goes into the soil. Even though we love the dirt and planting things and smelling it, the thing is, dirt is dirty! We must always remember to wash our hands very well after digging in the dirt. This is especially true if we visit a farm where there are farm animals. If bacteria or germs are in the soil, they get on our hands. They then get on our food and into our mouths! Let's take turns washing our hands with lots of soapy water.

Physical Education: Jumping Beans. Give each student a ribbon stick. Instructions for making them are in Lesson 24. Use the ribbon sticks to demonstrate seeds that are placed into the ground and then pop up and grow into a plant. Have the students hold their ribbon sticks down on the floor, then they should pop up in the air like growing plants and wave their ribbons in the air like the leaves of a plant. The students could pantomime the following instruction. You could say, "First we dig up the soil, then we plant the seed (place ribbon stick on the floor), we add some water, and then the plant grows out of the soil (pick up ribbon stick and grow into the air). Review the sequence of digging, planting, watering, and growing several times.

Optional Math/Language Arts/Bible/Arts & Crafts Activity:

7 Dips in the Jordan: II Kings 5:1-14, read the Bible verses and tell the story.

Naaman had a bad disease called leprosy. God's prophet told him to dip in the Jordan River seven times and he would be healed. Sure enough, as he came up out of the water the seventh time he was well.

Do the Lesson 32 Bible Numbers worksheet. Give each student a sheet of white construction paper and the worksheet. Cut out the items on the worksheet and glue them to construction paper as illustrated in the drawing. Draw in the arms and face for the "7" dipping man. Draw in the rest of the picture.

NOTES:

Lesson 33

Week 7: Day 3

Activities in this Lesson: Bible Lesson, Social Studies/Science, Language Arts, Phonics, Reading, Writing, Math, Shapes, Color, Story Time, Music, Arts & Crafts, Outdoor Activity, Physical Education

Bible Reference: Genesis 1:9-10.

Bible Concept to Present: When God made the soil, He knew plants would need it to grow. He made the soil to help us.

Bible Lesson: Our God is such a wonderful God. He knew just what we would need before He even made us. When God made the dry land on the third day of Creation, He made the soil very special. He put special food in the soil that plants would need to grow and live. He also made the soil so that it could keep enough water in it to help the plants live. We need the plants to grow, because we eat plants, and animals eat plants too. God planned the soil, so that it would contain all the necessary food that plants would need. God loves us so much; He takes care of everything we need.

Social Studies/Science: Plants need special foods to grow, just like you do. If you did not have food, you would not grow. Plants are the same. Use some of the soil from yesterday and let each student transfer a plant into a small pot. Explain to your students as you do this that the soil has special food in it already for the plant to use to grow. Only after the plant has used all the food in the soil, does it need to be fed more. We call these special foods, minerals. Let your student plant the plant in the container. Water it well making sure there is a lid or container underneath. Explain proper drainage of plants. Let the students be responsible for watering the plant with your supervision. Set the plants along a window sill or in an area that gets some sun. It will take some time for the seeds to grow.

Multimedia Resources: Watch "Patience" from the *Character Builders Video Series*.

Language Arts: Finger Activity "Watch It Grow."

Watch It Grow

God sends the Sun to warm the seeds (Make hands to form small seed)
He sends the rain to make them swell (Motion for rain)
They burst their little brown coats (Push hands outward)
Up comes one little green shoot (Hold up one finger)
The others follow one by one (Hold up other fingers on same hand)
And that is how our gardens grow.

Phonics: Review the letters Aa-Jj.

Teach the small letter *j*. Write some words beginning with the letter *j* on the board. Include words from stories or activities that tie this lesson to other things that have already been done. Underline the small *j* that begins the words. Read through the words and point out the shape of letter *j*. Have the students trace the *j* in the air as you trace the letter *j* beginning each word.
    Common words: just
    Vocabulary words: jump, jungle

Reading: Dictate a simple letter, invitation, or thank you note.

Writing: For these two weeks focus on having the students trace the first three letters of their first name. During this time, write the students' names on all worksheets and papers making the first three letters dotted or something that can be traced.

Writing Skill Builders: Keep these objectives in mind as you direct the class. Incorporate writing strokes circle, moon, and cross. Trace and then independently draw the outlines of geometric shapes and irregular forms.

Memory Verse: Review Genesis 1:10. Say the entire verse.

Math: Review number recognition of 7. Continue to teach the concept of 7 by counting items. Equate items and things with the number 7. You may use the footprint idea if you desire to aid in teaching this.

Teach oral counting 1-10. Use the Counting Train, Counting Pennies, or Counting Shapes visuals.

Do the Lesson 33 Math worksheet. Count each group of items and circle the correct number under the items.

Shapes: Review "Sammy Square." Have your students build a square house with the blocks. Count the number of blocks for each wall, such as 7 blocks in each wall. Lay the blocks so they seem to be even. How many square blocks can you pile on top of one another to make a square tower?

Do the Lesson 33 Shapes worksheet. Color the large squares yellow, the small squares green, and the rest any other colors.

Color: Review the colors red, green, blue, black, white, yellow, brown, pink, and purple.

Story Time: Read a story or stories of your choice.

Music: Review the songs "Here We All Go Around the Rock" and "Heaven Is A Happy Place."

Multimedia Resources: This week, listen and sing along to selections from "The Amazing Miracles" CD.

Arts & Crafts: This will be so much fun! *Bring some clean earthworms to class,* enough for each student to have one. If they are in dirt, let the students help wash them off. *Mix a little non-toxic paint with at least half that amount of water or more.* Give each student a piece of white freezer paper. Place a drop of paint in the middle of each paper. Now place a worm in the middle of the drop of paint. Students will watch the worm move. Give the worms lots of time to "paint." When done, collect the worms and wash them off. Put them outside in the plant soil. They are wonderful soil workers.

Note: An alternate to this activity could be done with gummy worms, chocolate pudding, and a paper plate. Have the students "paint" on the plate with the worms and pudding. The worms and pudding can be eaten at the end of the activity.

Outdoor Activity: *Prepare ahead – Fill a large rectangular pan with soil or dirt. Or use foil containers so that each student has their own.* Take the students for a walk, collecting things to stand up in the dirt, such as twigs to represent trees, rocks for mountains, grass etc. Let the students create their own world. Encourage them to verbalize as they do this. Listen carefully to what they say so you will know what they are retaining.

Physical Education: Many forms of life exist in soil. Discuss a few of them. Now do some of the actions that would imitate those forms of life. Example: Crawl like a worm. Walk like a beetle. Roll like a Roly-Poly Bug. Jump like a grasshopper. Which does your student like the best? Why? Ask him and then note their answer. It will also be of interest to the student to dig up soil and look for some of those types of insects. Observe them.

NOTES:

Activities in this Lesson: Bible Lesson, Language Arts, Phonics, Reading, Writing, Memory Verse, Math, Color, Story Time, Music, Arts & Crafts, Physical Education

Bible Reference: Genesis 1:9-10

Bible Lesson: Review the Bible lesson from Lesson 33. God knew what we would need in order to live. There are seven basic requirements that plants need in order to grow. This is true for all living things. When God made the soil, He was providing for the plants that He would make. Plants need warmth, light, water, air, nutrients, time, and room. God made the light on Day 1, the air and clouds on Day 2, and the soil filled with nutrients on Day 3.

Illustration: Start a large Creation Mural today. Use banner paper, preferably a wide roll. Cut off a piece as long as your longest wall space. Divide the mural into eight even sections. Write Day 1, 2, 3, 4, and 5 on the first 5 sections. Then make Day 6 double wide. Day 7 is the last space. Let the students take turns drawing light, air and clouds, and soil in the first three days, in the correct day. Be sure to leave room for plants and trees in Day 3. Students will add to the mural in the next weeks and months.

Language Arts: Repeat "Watch It Grow" from Lesson 33.

Phonics: Review the letters Aa-Jj.

Do the Lesson 34 Phonics worksheet. Complete the letter Jj worksheet. Notice that all of the letters of the alphabet are displayed on the page and that the letters Jj are highlighted with a background. As the students get better at letter recognition you can call out a letter and ask the students to point it out with their finger. Trace the large letter and the small letter. The students can trace the letters between the guide lines. Review the pictures and the colored first letter of the words. The students can color the letters as desired.

Reading: Dictate a simple letter, invitation, or thank you note.

Writing: For these two weeks focus on having the students trace the first three letters of their first name. During this time, write the students' names on all worksheets and papers making the first three letters dotted or something that can be traced.

Writing Skill Builders: Keep these objectives in mind as you direct the class. Incorporate writing strokes circle, moon, and cross. Trace and then independently draw the outlines of geometric shapes and irregular forms.

Memory Verse: Review Genesis 1:10. If students are able, let them recite the memory verse alone. Don't pressure them to do it.

Math: Review number recognition of 7. Have the students lie on the floor and make 7's with their bodies. Review the Days of the Week chart, counting the 7 days in every week. Use the monthly calendar to count the 7 days in each week.

Practice counting with the "One Potato, Two Potatoes" chant. The students can hold up fingers while chanting.

One Potato, Two Potatoes

One potato, two potatoes, three potatoes four
Five potatoes, six potatoes, seven potatoes more
One potato, two potatoes, three potatoes four
Five potatoes, six potatoes, seven potatoes more

Teach oral counting 1-10. Use the Counting Train, Counting Pennies, or Counting Shapes visuals.

Do the Lesson 34 Math worksheet. Count each group of items and draw a line to the correct number.

Learn verse 7 of "This Old Man, He Played One."

This Old Man, He Played One

Verse 1
This old man, he played one, He played nick-nack on my thumb;
with a nick-nack paddy whack, give a dog a bone. This old man came rolling home.

Verse 2
This old man, he played two, He played nick-nack on my shoe;
with a nick-nack paddy whack, give a dog a bone. This old man came rolling home.

Verse 3
This old man, he played three, He played nick-nack on my on my knee;
with a nick-nack paddy whack, give a dog a bone. This old man came rolling home.

Verse 4
This old man, he played four, He played nick-nack on my door;
with a nick-nack paddy whack, give a dog a bone. This old man came rolling home.

Verse 5
This old man, he played five, He played nick-nack on my hive;
with a nick-nack paddy whack, give a dog a bone. This old man came rolling home.

Verse 6
This old man, he played six, He played nick-nack on my sticks;
with a nick-nack paddy whack, give a dog a bone. This old man came rolling home.

Verse 7
This old man, he played seven, He played nick-nack up in Heaven;
with a nick-nack paddy whack, give a dog a bone. This old man came rolling home.

Color: Review the colors red, green, blue, black, white, yellow, brown, pink, and purple.

Story Time: Read a story or stories of your choice.

Music: Review "Here We All Go Around the Rock" and some of the songs you've learned from the "Horizons Preschool Music" CD. Let the students make musical instruments.

Multimedia Resources: This week, listen and sing along to selections from "The Amazing Miracles" CD.

Arts & Crafts: *Prepare ahead – Tear pieces of brown construction paper in half horizontally, trying to make the tear a bit uneven.* Give each student a piece of pale blue construction paper, and a half sheet of the torn brown. Let them glue the brown on the edge of the blue, to look like soil. Now give them markers and let them add a Sun and clouds, reminding them that God made clouds and air on the second day. Let them add rocks and sand to the soil, as God made soil and everything in it on the third day. Collect the artwork to use for a later time, Lesson 47.

Do the Lesson 34 Arts & Crafts worksheet. Cut out the animal puzzle worksheet. Practice putting the puzzle together.

Physical Education: Soil is made of many things. There are rocks, sticks, old grass, dead leaves, roots, etc. in the soil. If you were a worm living in the soil you would have to move over, under, around, or through objects to travel in the soil. Set up an obstacle course of things that the students must go over, under, around, or through to get from the start to the finish. You can make a tunnel by draping a blanket over several chairs. Outline the sides of the course with jump ropes or string. Have the students travel the obstacle course and then discuss which items they had to go over, under, around, or through.

NOTES:

Lesson 35

Week 7: Day 5

Activities in this Lesson: Bible Lesson, Social Studies/Science, Language Arts, Phonics, Reading, Writing, Memory Verse, Math, Shapes, Color, Story Time, Music, Physical Education

Bible Reference: Genesis 1:9-10.

Bible Concept to Present: God's gift of soil is a very special gift. We are to take care of God's gift of soil.

Bible Lesson: God made such a wonderful gift when He gave us soil. He knew we would need soil to help us live. Soil is important to plants and animals and people. I am thankful God gave us soil. We need to take care of this special gift God has given to us. Long ago when only Indians lived in America, our soil was very thick. If you dug down, you would find nice top soil for many inches. Then people began to chop down the trees that helped keep the soil in its place. When people did this, the soil began to wash away with the rain, and it blew away with the wind. Soon the soil was not as thick as it used to be. Soil is so very important to us and we need to take care of it. It is important that plants cover the soil to keep it from blowing or washing away. As caretakers of God's world, we need to plant plants and trees to keep the soil where it belongs.

Illustration: Continue the large Creation Mural today. Use banner paper, preferably a wide roll. Cut off a piece as long as your longest wall space. Divide the mural into eight even sections. Write Day 1, 2, 3, 4, and 5 on the first 5 sections. Then make Day 6 double wide. Day 7 is the last space. Let the students take turns drawing light, air and clouds, and soil in the first three days, in the correct day. Be sure to leave room for plants and trees in Day 3. Students will add to the mural in the next weeks and months.

Social Studies/Science: We will combine these two subjects today in one activity. Find a place outside where some ground cover is needed. Work up the soil, fertilize it if necessary, and plant some ground cover. This can take many forms. Consult your nursery for ideas as to what would work best in your part of the country. As you do this work (include students), discuss how important it is to take care of our soil. It takes a very long time to make new soil. If we do not care for the soil God gave us, we will not have any. We cannot neglect this important job God has given us. If you live in the colder section of the United States, plant a small tree indoors, or plant the seeds for the ground cover for later. In the coming weeks we will be doing more planting. The area that you work up now does not need to be extremely large.

Language Arts: Review caring for the soil with the poem "God Made The Soil." Say each line and have the students repeat it after you.

God Made The Soil

God made the soil
He left it in our care
He made it for us
And for all to share

We must take care
Of God's wonderful gift
He's given to us.
Without it we would miss

The joys He wants us
To share and enjoy
And the wonderful things He has made
For all little girls and boys.

Phonics: Teach the letter Kk.

Show the students the letter Kk worksheet. Point out any student's name beginning with the letter *K*. Write some words beginning with the letter *K* on the board. Include any student names from the class that begin with letter *K*. Underline the capital *K* that begins the words. Read through the words and point out the shape of letter *K*. Have the students trace the *K* in the air as you trace the letter *K* beginning each name.

> Boys: Kaleb, Keith, Kenneth, Kevin, Kristopher, Kyle
> Girls: Kaitlin, Kaitlyn, Kara, Karen, Karina, Karla, Kasey, Kassandra, Katelyn, Katherine, Kathleen, Kathryn, Katie, Katrina, Kayla, Kaylee, Kelli, Kelly, Kelsey, Kendall, Kendra, Kiara, Kimberly, Kirsten, Krista, Kristen, Kristin, Kristina, Krystal, Kylie

Do the Lesson 35 Phonics worksheet. Complete the letter Kk worksheet. Have the students trace the letters Kk with their fingers. They should trace the letters with their fingers and say the names of the letters. Demonstrate the proper strokes for them on the board. Say the words for each of the pictures and look at the Kk letters that begin them.

Reading: Dictate a simple letter, invitation, or thank you note.

Writing: For these two weeks focus on having the students trace the first three letters of their first name. During this time, write the students' names on all worksheets and papers making the first three letters dotted or something that can be traced.

Writing Skill Builders: Keep these objectives in mind as you direct the class. Incorporate writing strokes circle, moon, and cross. Trace and then independently draw the outlines of geometric shapes and irregular forms.

Memory Verse: Review Genesis 1:10, Genesis 1:1, Genesis 1:3, and Genesis 1:6. Take some time today to review the verses you have learned so far. Praise students for their hard work.

Math: Review number recognition of 7. Continue to teach the number 7 by counting items. Have your students write the number. You will want to be certain that students count by rote, recognize the number of, and equate the number with the concept, of every number up through 7. The writing of these numbers is optional, depending upon the readiness of the child. Writing can take place in a pan of rice and cornmeal, or on a large sheet of paper.

Practice counting with the "One Potato, Two Potatoes" chant. Students stand in circles in groups of three to six. They put their clenched fists stretched out into the center of the circles. One student taps each fist in turn while chanting the rhymes. The fist that is tapped on "more" is out and is placed behind the player's back. When a player has both fists counted out, he should leave the game. The winner is the last one left in the game.

One Potato, Two Potatoes

One potato, two potatoes, three potatoes four
Five potatoes, six potatoes, seven potatoes more
One potato, two potatoes, three potatoes four
Five potatoes, six potatoes, seven potatoes more

Teach oral counting 1-10. Use the Counting Train, Counting Pennies, or Counting Shapes visuals.

Do the Lesson 35 Math worksheet. Instruct the students to trace the numbers, count each group, and then draw a line to the number for the group.

Shapes: Review triangles, circles, and squares with your students by having them sort triangles, circles, and squares into three different piles. Construction paper shapes will work for this. Then review the number seven. Have the students count seven items for you to be sure they know that seven equals seven.

Do the Lesson 35 Shapes worksheet. Count the squares. Count the circles. To reinforce the concepts of put together and altogether, tell the students that we are going to put the squares and circles together. Count both squares and circles. How many squares and circles are there altogether? Color the squares green, color the circles red, then color the party hat black. For variety you can have the students choose the colors.

Color: Review the colors red, green, blue, black, white, yellow, brown, pink, and purple.

Story Time: Read a story or stories of your student's choice or ones they have brought from home.

Music: Review "Here We All Go Around the Rock" and "Heaven Is A Happy Place."

Multimedia Resources: This week, listen and sing along to selections from "The Amazing Miracles" CD.

Physical Education: Your students will be working quite hard helping you to dig up the soil and plant the ground cover. If extra activity is needed on this day, take a brisk walk.

NOTES:

Activities in this Lesson: Bible Lesson, Science, Social Studies, Language Arts, Phonics, Reading, Writing, Memory Verse, Math, Shapes, Color, Story Time, Music, Arts & Crafts, Physical Education

Bible Reference: Genesis 1:11-13.

Bible Concept to Present: On the third day of Creation, God also made plants. One of the many types of plants are the grasses.

Bible Lesson: After God made the dry land, He began to make something very special to go into the dry land. God made the plants. God has made every plant you see around you. We are going to be discussing several kinds of plants, and we will first look at one special kind of plant God made. These plants are grasses. Some grasses are very tall, taller than you. Some grasses are short. Some grasses spread themselves along the ground. Others creep over rocks. Every kind of a grass we can think of God has made. Remember, soil needs to have something to cover it so that it does not blow away with the wind. God made the grasses so that the soil will not blow away or wash away with rains. I am happy God has made the grasses to help cover the ground, and keep the soil in place.

Science: Take a walk with your students and note the various kinds of grasses in the world around you. Anything that is low to the ground, that is not a bush type plant or a tree, is classified as a grass. Collect samples of the various grasses around you. Note the difference in blades, flowers, etc.

Note: We will use the classifications of grasses, herbs, and trees because this is how the Bible classifies the plant life. Save the sample you collect for the next lesson.

Social Studies: God made many plants. He made grasses to be very special plants. Many things need grasses to live. For example, cows and sheep eat grass. Do you know of anything else that eats grass and depends on grass to live? Make drawings to represent animals that eat grass.

Language Arts: After having gathered several types of grasses, place one of each in a row. Have students examine them carefully, noting the differences in each. Then, with eyes closed, have students describe one or two of the grass types you picked on your walk in Science. Save the grasses until tomorrow. Spread them on a piece of construction paper or poster board overnight.

Phonics: Review the letter Kk.

Teach the small letter *k*. Write some words beginning with the letter *k* on the board. Include words from stories or activities that tie this lesson to other things that have already been done. Underline the small *k* that begins the words. Read through the words and point out the shape of letter *k*. Have the students trace the *k* in the air as you trace the letter *k* beginning each word.
> Common words: keep, kind, know
> Vocabulary words: kick, knee

Reading: Dictate a simple letter, invitation, or thank you note.

Multimedia Resources: View the Aa-Kk segments of "Rev-Up for Reading" from the "Rev-Up for Learning" DVD to drill letter recognition and sound. The students should say each letter sound along with the presentation.

Writing: For these two weeks focus on having the students trace the first three letters of their first name. During this time, write the students' names on all worksheets and papers making the first three letters dotted or something that can be traced.

Writing Skill Builders: Keep these objectives in mind as you direct the class. Recognition of the initial letter of student's name. Incorporate the writing strokes of moon and cross. Trace and then independently draw the outlines of geometric shapes and irregular forms.

Multimedia Resources: View the Aa-Kk segments of "Rev-Up for Writing" from the "Rev-Up for Learning" DVD to review the writing of upper- and lowercase letters. The students should write each letter in the air along with the presentation. Since the first half of the presentation covers lowercase letters and the second half uppercase letters some navigation will be needed to skip to the letters that are covered in this lesson.

Memory Verse: I Peter 1:24-25.
"The grass withers, and the flower fall, but the word of the Lord stands forever." I Peter 1:24-25 NIV

The grass withereth, and the flower thereof falleth away: But the word of the Lord endureth for ever. I Peter 1:24-25 KJV

What a beautiful verse! Take some time to explain the verse to your students. Be sure to explain "withers" and "forever." Share with the children that when we memorize God's word, it will live forever in our hearts. This would be a good time to share a memory you have of memorizing scripture. Hand out Memory Verse Card 5 for students to take home.

Math: Teach number recognition of 8. Show the students the number 8 flashcard. Begin to teach your students the number 8 by counting items. Introduce them to counting to 8 and the symbol for 8. Count 8 of several different items. If you have more than one child, have them place their bodies on the floor so as to form a number 8. You may want to replace one child, so each student can see what the "Human Eight" looks like. If you have hung cards for the week of the school year, point out the Week 8 card.

Teach oral counting 1-10. Use the "Count Our Numbers" song.

Count Our Numbers
Original Author Unknown
Sung to: "Oh, My Darling Clementine"

Count our numbers, Count our numbers,
Count our numbers every day.
It is fun to count our numbers,
As a class every day.
One-two-three-four,
Five-six-seven-eight,
Nine and ten we'll count today.
It is fun to count together,
One to ten and then again.

Do the Lesson 36a Math worksheet. Notice that all of the numbers are displayed on the page and that the number 8 is highlighted with a background. As the students get better at number recognition you can call out a number and ask the students to point it out with their finger. Have the students trace the large number 8 with the proper strokes by following the arrows. Instruct the students to count each group of items and then trace the number.

Do the Lesson 36b Math worksheet. Instruct the students to draw a line between the groups that have the same number.

Multimedia Resources: View "Rev-Up for Arithmetic" from the "Rev-Up for Learning" DVD to practice number recognition and counting 1-9.

Shapes: Do the Lesson 36 Shapes worksheet. Count the squares, count the circles, and then count how many squares and circles there are altogether. Color the squares purple, the circles green, and the teapot yellow.

Color: Review the colors red, green, blue, black, white, yellow, brown, pink, and purple.

Story Time: Read a story or stories of your choice.

Music: Review "Let's Make A Garden" from Lesson 26 and "Heaven Is A Happy Place."

Multimedia Resources: This week, listen and sing along to selections from the "Bullfrogs and Butterflies: I've Been Born Again" CD.

Arts & Crafts: *Bring a small plastic plate for each student, preferably in different colors. Bring a small bag of grass seed and some little craft sponges, one for each student.* The sponges can be purchased at craft stores and are usually used for stamping. They come in all different shapes. Or you can get rectangular sponges. Give each student a plastic plate, a sponge, and a small amount of grass seed. Instruct them to put the sponge on the plate, and then spread the grass seed over the top of the sponge. Walk around the class with a pitcher of water, pouring water onto each sponge, just enough to wet them. Have the students set their plates on a shelf or counter. Each day, let them pour a little water on the sponge. Make one grass sponge for the teacher. DON'T add any water to it. As the days go by, check to see what the seeds with no water are doing. You will follow-up on this activity for several days.

Physical Education: Enjoy the grass throughout this exercise. Pretend the grass is a pool of water. Can you swim through it? Pretend the grass is a jungle. How will you get through? Pretend the grass is very fragile. How would you walk through it so as not to ruin it? Now pantomime a grass blade growing for your students. Begin in a little ball and slowly uncurl yourself as you begin to stretch up to the sun. Have your students imitate your actions. Verbalize what you are doing as you do it.

NOTES:

Lesson 37

Week 8: Day 2

Activities in this Lesson: Bible Lesson, Science, Language Arts, Phonics, Reading, Writing, Memory Verse, Math, Shapes, Color, Story Time, Music, Arts & Crafts, Physical Education, Optional Math/Language Arts/Bible/Arts & Crafts Activity

Bible Reference: Genesis 1:11-13.

Bible Concept to Present: When God created the plants, He created grass.

Bible Lesson: Review the story from yesterday. Grass is very important to everyone.

Illustration: Animals eat grass. Cows eat rich grass so that they can give good milk, and milk is good for everyone. Isn't it amazing that cows eat green, green grass to give us pure white milk? Many animals eat dried grass or hay. Dried grass can be saved for months if it is kept dry. Oats are a grass. Oats can also be dried and fed to animals. Horses love oats. Show students any pictures you have of cows or horses in a field of grass.

Science: *Bring some stalks of wheat to show the students.* They can be purchased in a craft store in bunches. Also bring out the grasses from yesterday. Say, Let's look at the grasses that we collected yesterday. Do they look different? Why do you think they look so droopy and shriveled up? They aren't connected to their plant any more. They aren't getting any water or nutrients through their roots. Living things need to get their basic needs met. Remember the seven basic needs? Plants need warmth, light, water, air, nutrients, time, and room. These plants weren't getting water or nutrients. So they had no strength to get light or air. When we pick flowers, they are beautiful for a few days, but then they will die. Some flowers and grasses are pretty when they are dried. Let each student have a stalk of wheat to examine. Pass the magnifying glass around. The students may pull the wheat apart to see how it is made.

Language Arts: Play a rhyming game. Rhyme the following words with HAY:

    My favorite thing to do is _____ . PLAY
    I wake up with the light of _____ . DAY
    When my team wins, I clap and say _____ . YEAH
    The month before June is _____ . MAY
    The way I talk to God is to _____ . PRAY
    Light from the Sun comes down in a _____ . RAY
    When I buy a treat, I first must _____ . PAY

Phonics: Review the letters Aa-Kk.

Do the Lesson 37 Phonics worksheet. Complete the letter Kk worksheet. Notice that all of the letters of the alphabet are displayed on the page and that the letters Kk are highlighted with a background. As the students get better at letter recognition you can call out a letter and ask the students to point it out with their finger. Trace the large letter and the small letter. The students can trace the letters between the guide lines. Review the pictures and the colored first letter of the words. The students can color the letters as desired.

Reading: Dictate a simple letter, invitation, or thank you note.

Writing: For these two weeks focus on having the students trace the first three letters of their first name. During this time, write the students' names on all worksheets and papers making the first three letters dotted or something that can be traced.

Writing Skill Builders: Keep these objectives in mind as you direct the class. Recognition of the initial letter of student's name. Incorporate the writing strokes of moon, and cross. Trace and then independently draw the outlines of geometric shapes and irregular forms.

Memory Verse: Review I Peter 1:24-25. Practice the memory verse, dividing it into three parts. Learn one part each day.

ONE	The grass withers
TWO	And the flowers fall
THREE	But the word of the Lord stands forever. I Peter 1:24-25

Math: Review number recognition of 8.

Teach oral counting 1-10. Use the Counting Train, Counting Pennies, Counting Shapes visuals, or a counting song.

Do the Lesson 37 Math worksheet. Count each group of objects and draw a line to the correct number.

Shapes: Review triangle, circle, and square shapes. Write a letter Kk on the board. Select a student to see how many triangles can be made by drawing lines to connect the points of the letter Kk. Ask the students to name a letter with a circle shape.

Color: Review the colors red, green, blue, black, white, yellow, brown, pink, and purple.

Story Time: Read a story or stories of your choice.

Music: Review "Count Our Numbers" (Math).

Multimedia Resources: This week, listen and sing along to selections from the "Bullfrogs and Butterflies: I've Been Born Again" CD.

Arts & Crafts: Let the students color with crayons on white paper. Instruct them to draw a field of wheat. What color would they like wheat to be? How much wheat can they put on their paper? What did the inside of the wheat look like?

Physical Education: Make motions like grass with ribbon sticks. Give each student a ribbon stick and have everyone spread out through the area. Use carpet squares for them to stand on to help them understand that they must not get into someone's self space. Practice a variety of motions similar to the motion of tall grass. Have the children move their hands and arms from left to right and back and forth in a high arching motion like a windshield wiper on a car. Move hands and arms in large circles, in front, to the sides and overhead. Make back and forth motions in front, to the sides and overhead. Make casting motions like you would with a fishing pole.

Optional Math/Language Arts/Bible/Arts & Crafts Activity:

8-Year-Old King: II Kings 22:1, 2, read the Bible verses and tell the story.
Josiah was eight years old when he became king. He was a good king. He always did what God wanted him to do.

Do the Lesson 37 Bible Numbers worksheet. Give each student a sheet of white construction paper and the worksheet. Cut out the items on the worksheet and glue them to construction paper as illustrated in the drawing. Draw in the arms, legs, and face for the "8" king. Draw in the rest of the picture.

NOTES:

Activities in this Lesson: Bible Lesson/Field Trip, Social Studies, Science, Language Arts, Phonics, Reading, Writing, Memory Verse, Math, Shapes, Color, Story Time, Music, Arts & Crafts, Physical Education

Bible Reference: Genesis 1:11-13.

Bible Concept to Present: There are many kinds of grasses that God made.

Bible Lesson/Field Trip: We have talked about how on the third day of Creation, God made the dry land. He made the rocks, sand, clay, and soil. We also talked about how God made plants, and especially grasses. Did you know that God made many kinds of grasses? Remember our walk we took during which we collected samples of kinds of grasses? Wasn't it neat to see how many grasses God made?

Today, we are going to see more grasses which God has made. We are going to go to a nursery to see many of the kinds of grasses God made. A nursery is where plants are grown and kept healthy. Let's go now to see this. While we are there I want you to notice the different kinds of grasses. And let's count how many different ones we see. Call ahead if you have more than five students. Visit a local nursery, preferably with an employee that can give your group a tour. Visit in the morning, and then have lunch at a park with grass.

Social Studies: Discuss with your students how people who work in nurseries work with plants all day. These people help us very much. They must know a lot about plants to do the work they do. Some of them have been to school for a long time to learn how to take care of the plants. As you are on the field trip, ask the nursery personnel questions about the plants, and how they care for them. Encourage your students to ask questions too.

Science: Note the various kinds of plants and how they resemble and are different from each other. You may wish to comment on which grasses are larger than others.

Be sure to water the grass sponges today. Add just enough water to each sponge so that it is wet. Let the students observe what is happening to the seeds.

Language Arts: Upon your return from the nursery, have the students describe what they have seen. What did they like the best? Try to get them to use descriptive terms. Ask leading questions regarding their interpretation of the smell and feel of the nursery.

After the field trip have the students dictate a thank you letter to send to the nursery. Encourage the students to share what they liked the most about what they saw. Include something from each student if possible in the letter. Write or type the letter out and go over the format of the letter with the class. Show them how to fold the letter and how to put it into the envelope. Show them the format of the information on the envelope. Remind the class that it is good to let people know that you are thankful for things that they do for them.

Phonics: Teach the letter Ll.

Show the students the letter Ll flashcard. Point out any student's name beginning with the letter *L*.

Write some words beginning with the letter *L* on the board. Include any student names from the class that begin with letter *L*. Underline the capital *L* that begins the words. Read through the words and point out the shape of letter *L*. Have the students trace the *L* in the air as you trace the letter *L* beginning each name.

Boys: Lance, Larry, Lawrence, Levi, Logan, Louis, Lucas, Luis, Luke
Girls: Lacey, Laura, Lauren, Leah, Leslie, Linda, Lindsay, Lindsey, Lisa, Lydia
Vocabulary words: Ladies (restroom)

Do the Lesson 38 Phonics worksheet. Complete the letter Ll worksheet. Have the students trace the letters Ll with their fingers. They should trace the letters with their fingers and say the names of the letters. Demonstrate the proper strokes for them on the board. Say the words for each of the pictures and look at the Ll letters that begin them.

Reading: Dictate a simple letter, invitation, or thank you note.

Writing: For these two weeks focus on having the students trace the first three letters of their first name. During this time, write the students' names on all worksheets and papers making the first three letters dotted or something that can be traced.

Writing Skill Builders: Keep these objectives in mind as you direct the class. Recognition of the initial letter of student's name. Incorporate the writing strokes of moon and cross. Trace and then independently draw the outlines of geometric shapes and irregular forms.

Memory Verse: Review I Peter 1:24-25. Work on the memory verse. Let the students march around the room, or outside, reciting the verse together.

Math: Review number recognition of 8. Continue to teach the number 8 by counting items. Have your student practice putting the number 8 in order with numbers 1-7.

Teach oral counting 1-10. Use the "One, Two Buckle My Shoe" rhyme.

One, Two, Buckle My Shoe

One, two, buckle my shoe
Three, four, knock at the door
Five, six, pick up sticks
Seven, eight, lay them straight
Nine, ten, a good fat hen

Do the Lesson 38 Math worksheet. Count each group of items and circle the correct number for the group.

Shapes: Do the Lesson 38 Shapes worksheet. Draw lines to connect pictures that look the same. They can color the pictures as they like.

Color: Teach the color orange. Show the students the orange color flashcard. Look for items around the room that are orange. Bring oranges for a snack.

Review the colors red, green, blue, black, white, yellow, brown, pink, and purple.

Story Time: Read a story or stories of your choice.

Music: Review "Count Our Numbers" (Math). Teach the following song to the tune of "I'm a Little Teapot."

I'm a Little Seed
Tune of I'm a Little Teapot

I'm a little seed all brown and dry
The dirt is my bed and that's where I lie
Till you give me water and plant food, too
Then I'll grow and grow for you
    ... Carol McSpadden Sheldon

Multimedia Resources: This week, listen and sing along to selections from the "Bullfrogs and Butterflies: I've Been Born Again" CD.

Arts & Crafts: Give students playdough. Ask them to design their own kinds of plant. What would their plants look like?

Physical Education: Continue to make motions like grass with ribbon sticks. Give each student a ribbon stick and have them spread themselves throughout the area. Use carpet squares for them to stand on to help them understand that they must not get into someone's self space. Practice a variety of motions similar to the motion of tall grass. Have the children move their hands and arms from left to right and back and forth in a high arching motion like a windshield wiper on a car. Move hands and arms in large circles, in front, to the sides and overhead. Make back and forth motions in front, to the sides and overhead. Make casting motions like you would with a fishing pole. Hold the ribbon in front and make sweeping motions. Do fast and slow movements.

NOTES:

Lesson 39

Activities in this Lesson: Bible Lesson, Language Arts, Science, Phonics, Reading, Writing, Math, Color, Story Time, Music, Arts & Crafts, Outdoor Activity, Health & Safety, Physical Education, Homework, Catch Up

Bible Reference: Genesis 1:9-13.

Bible Concept to Present: God has blessed us with a beautiful country.

Bible Lesson: Continue to review verses 9-13. Read all the verses to the students, reminding them of all that God made on the third day. Sing "America the Beautiful" to the class. Find a picture of "waves of grain." Many clip art collections have pictures of grain. Explain that the grasses grew very high, and when the wind blew, it looked like waves moving across the prairie. Years ago, wagon trains traveled across our country and left trails in the grasses. The wheels of the wagons pressed down the grass. For miles, you would be able to see lines in the grass from the passing wagons.

America the Beautiful

Oh, Beautiful for spacious skies
For amber WAVES OF GRAIN
For purple mountains majesties
Above the fruited plain
America, America
God shed His grace on thee
And crown thy good with brotherhood
From sea to shining sea.

Illustration: Did you know we can eat seed sprouts? Make some bean sprouts as a class. This project will take several days. Bring some ranch dressing at one lunch time and let the students sample the sprouts.

Go to: http://www.sproutpeople.com/index.html. This website is the home of a sprout company. There are instructions on this site for growing sprouts. Here are some of their basic instructions:

Put 2/3 cup of seed into a bowl or into a seed sprouter.
Add 2-3 times as much cool (60-70 degree) water.
Mix seeds up to assure even water contact for all.
Allow seeds to soak for 6-12 hours.

Note: Though, when sprouted individually, some of the seeds in this mix require less soak time. They will do fine in the context of this mix when soaked 6-12 hours.

Empty the seeds into a sprouter.
Drain off the soak water.
Rinse thoroughly with cool (60-70°) water.
Drain thoroughly.

This also works with beans. Small mung beans work well. Thank God for the miracle of sprouting.

Language Arts: Following a sequence of instructions like a recipe is an important skill for your students to learn. Have the students act out and repeat the steps of the sprout recipe.

Science: Let's take a look at our grass seed. Let each student carry their grass sponge back to their desk or table. Now, have each student gently pull out a small amount of grass seed (you might need helpers for this experiment) and lay them on a plate. Is anything happening to any of the grass seeds? Some should be splitting open or sprouting. Pass a good magnifying glass around and let the students study their seed samples. What is it that signaled the seeds to open? Water. Seeds can stay dry and whole for years and years, but when they meet water, they use the water to start the special process of sprouting and growing into a plant. Set the grass sponges back on the counter to grow some more. Check each sponge to be sure it is wet.

Phonics: Review the letter Ll.

Do the Lesson 39 Phonics worksheet. Complete the letter Ll worksheet. Notice that all of the letters of the alphabet are displayed on the page and that the letters Ll are highlighted with a background. As the students get better at letter recognition you can call out a letter and ask the students to point it out with their finger. Trace the large letter and the small letter. The students can trace the letters between the guide lines. Review the pictures and the colored first letter of the words. The students can color the letters as desired.

Reading: Dictate a simple letter, invitation, or thank you note.

Writing: For these two weeks focus on having the students trace the first three letters of their first name. During this time, write the students' names on all worksheets and papers making the first three letters dotted or something that can be traced.

Writing Skill Builders: Keep these objectives in mind as you direct the class. Recognition of the initial letter of student's name. Incorporate the writing strokes of moon and cross. Trace and then independently draw the outlines of geometric shapes and irregular forms.

Memory Verse: Review I Peter 1:24-25. Practice the memory verse, dividing it into three parts.

Math: Review number recognition of 8.

Teach oral counting 1-10. Use any of the different counting visuals, songs, or rhymes.

Teach verse 8 to the song "This Old Man, He Played One."

This Old Man, He Played One

Verse 1
This old man, he played one, He played nick-nack on my thumb;
with a nick-nack paddy whack, give a dog a bone. This old man came rolling home.

Verse 2
This old man, he played two, He played nick-nack on my shoe;
with a nick-nack paddy whack, give a dog a bone. This old man came rolling home.

Verse 3
This old man, he played three, He played nick-nack on my on my knee;
with a nick-nack paddy whack, give a dog a bone. This old man came rolling home.

Verse 4
This old man, he played four, He played nick-nack on my door;
with a nick-nack paddy whack, give a dog a bone. This old man came rolling home.

Verse 5
This old man, he played five, He played nick-nack on my hive;
with a nick-nack paddy whack, give a dog a bone. This old man came rolling home.

Verse 6
This old man, he played six, He played nick-nack on my sticks;
with a nick-nack paddy whack, give a dog a bone. This old man came rolling home.

Verse 7
This old man, he played seven, He played nick-nack up in Heaven;
with a nick-nack paddy whack, give a dog a bone. This old man came rolling home.

Verse 8
This old man, he played eight, He played nick-nack on my gate;
with a nick-nack paddy whack, give a dog a bone. This old man came rolling home.

Do the Lesson 39 Math worksheet. Trace the numbers and then draw lines to match the group of the same number.

Color: Continue to teach the color orange. Review the colors red, green, blue, black, white, yellow, brown, pink, and purple.

Story Time: Read a story or stories of your choice.

Music: Review "Count Our Numbers" (Math). Repeat "I'm a Little Seed." Help the students to memorize it.

Multimedia Resources: This week, listen and sing along to selections from the "Bullfrogs and Butterflies: I've Been Born Again" CD.

Arts & Crafts: Do the Lesson 39 Arts & Crafts worksheet. Cut out the animal puzzle. Practice putting the puzzle together.

Outdoor Activity: This would be a wonderful day for a walk through a field of grass. If you have one nearby, take a walk to make trails in the grass. If possible, find a high point, even a rock, and look at the trails that students have made in the grass.

Health & Safety: *Bring whole wheat, high fiber bread, small paper plates, plastic knives and soft margarine.* Eating the right food is our responsibility to our bodies. God gave us grasses to help us get the vitamins we need for strong bodies. If we don't eat the wonderful grasses He made for us, our bodies won't work well. God gave us wheat, oats, barley, maize and rye as our main grass foods. Give each student a piece of whole wheat bread on a plate and one plastic knife. Let the students cut their piece of bread in half. With one half, tear the bread into small pieces, looking at the seeds and fiber in the bread. Explain that there are 90% more vitamins in this bread than in white bread. Let the students eat the other half of the slice.

Physical Education: Continue to make motions like grass with ribbon sticks. Give each student a ribbon stick and have everyone spread out through the area. Use carpet squares for them to stand on to help them understand that they must not get into someone's self space. Practice a variety of motions similar to the motion of tall grass. Have the children move their hands and arms from left to right and back and forth in a high arching motion like a windshield wiper on a car. Move hands and arms in large circles, in front, to the sides and overhead. Make back and forth motions in front, to the sides and overhead. Make casting motions like you would with a fishing pole. Hold the ribbon in front and make sweeping motions. Do fast and slow movements. Give the students some free time at the end to run and wave as they wish with the ribbon sticks. Remind them to look for others and to not get into another child's space.

Homework: Give students Lesson 39 Homework "America the Beautiful" worksheet to take home. It doesn't need to be returned.

Catch Up: Do any assignment that you didn't have time for earlier in the month.

NOTES:

Lesson 40
Week 8: Day 5

Activities in this Lesson: Bible Lesson, Social Studies, Science, Language Arts, Phonics, Reading, Writing, Memory Verse, Math, Shapes, Color, Story Time, Music, Outdoor Activity, Health & Safety, Physical Education

Bible Reference: Genesis 1:11-13.

Bible Concept to Present: Grass makes seeds so there will be more grass.

Bible Lesson: Inside of every type of grass God made, He gave the capability to do a very special thing. God made each grass so it would make seeds. Seeds are very important so that grasses can continue to live. Grass does not live very long, so when it is ready to die and dry up, it puts out seeds. The seeds then fall to the ground and sprout, and make more grass. One blade of grass will give off many seeds. I am thankful God made it so that we will always have grasses. I am thankful God gave us seeds.

Social Studies: People who work with plants will often grow grass just for the seeds that it produces. Then they collect the seeds and package them and sell them to us. Without these people doing their jobs, it would be hard for us to have seeds to plant when we needed grass. They do very important work.

Science: Do you remember how there were so many kinds of grass? Did you know that each grass produces its own kind of seeds? It does. Each plant produces its very own kind of seed. This means that when we want a certain type of grass, we can get that kind of seed, and it will make that kind of a grass. Seeds are very special. Inside of the little grass seed is the ability to grow more grass just like the kind of plant from where the seed came. Note various kinds of grass seeds. Some nurseries have them in bulk and you can note the differences in the seeds. Gather as many as possible. Glue them on a piece of paper to show the differences in seeds of grasses. Many of the plants in a garden are considered grass-type plants, because they are close to the ground.

Purchase some garden seeds. Take a few of them and place them in a clear glass. Layer damp paper towels around them, but be sure that the seeds can be seen from the outside of the glass. Place under the sink or in a dark place. Note the changes in the seeds over a period of days.

Language Arts: Glue seeds of a garden plant on one side of a 3x5 card and a picture of that plant on the other. Select seeds that are very different in shape and size. Have students identify the plant by its mature picture and by its seed. Explain that each plant has its own seed.

Phonics: Review the letters Aa-Ll.

Teach the small letter *l*. Write some words beginning with the letter *l* on the board. Include words from stories or activities that tie this lesson to other things that have already been done. Underline the small *l* that begins the words. Read through the words and point out the shape of letter *l*. Have the students trace the *l* in the air as you trace the letter *l* beginning each word.

> Common words: land, large, last, late, learn, left, let, life, light, like, line, little, live, long, look, low
> Vocabulary words: lake, larger, largest, later, leaf, leg, less than, lip, living, long ago, longer, longest, loud, lungs

Do the Lesson 40 Phonics worksheet. Do the Letter Find worksheet. Have the students put an orange square around the Jj letters, a purple circle around the Kk letters, and a yellow triangle on the Ll letters. Give them one direction at a time so they can focus on finding the correct letter shape. Begin with capital J, then lower case j, etc. Show them examples with flashcards or letters written on the board.

Reading: Dictate a simple letter, invitation, or thank you note.

Writing: For these two weeks focus on having the students trace the first three letters of their first name. During this time, write the students' names on all worksheets and papers making the first three letters dotted or something that can be traced.

Writing Skill Builders: Keep these objectives in mind as you direct the class. Recognition of the initial letter of student's name. Incorporate the writing strokes of moon and cross. Trace and then independently draw the outlines of geometric shapes and irregular forms.

Memory Verse: Review I Peter 1:24-25. Finish this week's memory work. Let the students recite to the class if they want to.

Math: Review number recognition of 8. Continue to teach the number 8 by counting items. Count to 8, sequence to 8, and write the number 8 in the cornmeal box.

Teach oral counting 1-10. Use any of the different counting visuals, songs, or rhymes.

Do the Lesson 40 Math worksheet. Instruct the students to count each group and then draw a line to match groups with the same number.

Shapes: Do Lesson 40 Shapes worksheet. Point out the circle, square, and dotted lines on the worksheet. Tell the students to cut from the circle to the square following the dotted lines as closely as is possible.

Color: Review the colors red, green, blue, black, white, yellow, brown, pink, purple, and orange.

Story Time: Read a story or stories of your student's choice or ones they have brought from home.

Music: Review "I'm a Little Seed," "Count Our Numbers (Math)," and "America the Beautiful."

Multimedia Resources: This week, listen and sing along to selections from the "Bullfrogs and Butterflies: I've Been Born Again" CD.

Outdoor Activity: Take another walk to the grassy field. Stand on the high point and see if you can see the trails from yesterday. Can you? Probably not. The grass lifts its head up during the night, erasing the trails made by the student walkers.

Health & Safety: Bring an apple, some strawberries, and some seeds. Bring sunflower seeds, in shell and out of shell, pumpkin seeds, and sesame seeds. Explain that some seeds we eat, some we don't. Some seeds grow in the inside of food; some grow on the outside. Show the students the seeds of an apple. Let them see the "star" inside when you cut the apple across the center. Show them the strawberries, with the seeds on the outside. Have a seed snack today. Give each student some seeds on a napkin. Give them enough to get a good taste of the different seeds. We will study more about seeds later.

Physical Education: Do a brisk aerobic workout today. Start with a few warm-up stretches. Stretch to the right, left, front, and back doing each four times. Then hop to the right three times, then to the left three times. Nest hop forward three times and backwards three times. Jump in place for two counts. Now jog around the room while you sing "Jesus Loves Me." Begin now to slow down. Walk slower around the room as you quote one of your memory verses. At the end of the verse, your heart should have begun to slow its rapid beating somewhat. Now lay down on the floor (or grass) and stretch your arms to the sides of you. Reach out and then pull them in. Lift each leg and bring it toward your chest. Do this twice. Now lay very, very still.

NOTES:

AOP's Commitment to Quality—Tell us how we are doing

As a publisher dedicated to providing high quality educational materials we invite you to tell us how we are doing. Please visit our website at www.aop.com to give us your comments, concerns, and/or compliments concerning Horizons Preschool. Contact information can be found in the support area for Horizons at the AOP website.

Activities in this Lesson: Bible Lesson, Social Studies, Science, Language Arts, Phonics, Reading, Writing, Memory Verse, Math, Shapes, Color, Story Time, Music, Arts & Crafts, Field Trip, Physical Education

Bible Reference: Genesis 1:11-13.

Bible Concept to Present: When God made the plants, He made the grasses. He also made herbs. Herbs are bushes, including those bushes that give fruit.

Bible Lesson: Our God is so wonderful. Do you remember when I told you about the grasses God made? Well, God made other kinds of plants as well. The kinds of plants we will study about this week are very special plants. They are called herbs in the Bible, but we often call them bushes today. Bushes are very important to our earth. They help to keep the soil from washing or blowing away. They also give food for us and for animals and birds. They provide homes for animals and birds. I am thankful God gave us bushes and herbs.

Multimedia Resources: Listen to the song "Everything I See" from the "Bullfrogs and Butterflies: God Loves Fun" CD.

Social Studies: Herbs are important for the life of animals and birds, as well as for people. We use herbs to eat, to cook, and we use their fruits for dessert. Birds eat herbs, too. They make homes for themselves in the branches of bushes. Other animals live under a bush and depend on the bush for shelter. Discuss the kinds of birds and animals that depend upon bushes for food and shelter.

Science: *Prepare ahead – Find a small bush and pull it up by the roots. If the ground is dry, you may want to first soak the dirt with a dribble from a hose overnight. Gently pull it out, roots and all. Wash the bush and roots well, removing all dirt and bugs. Set it aside on a piece of cloth or poster board.* Show students the bush. Let them examine the root system. Provide the magnifying glass for students that want to use it. Say, Herbs or bushes all have some things in common. They all have a root system. Roots are at the bottom of a bush. They go deep into the ground to get water and food for the bush. The branches of a bush carry the water and food to the leaves of the bush. A bush has roots, branches, and leaves. Show students a picture of a bush and ask them where the root system would be. Where would a bird live in the bush? Where would a mouse live?

Let's look at some of our own living roots. Get the grass sponges. Instruct the students to carefully pull up a small bunch of grass. Lay the pieces of grass out and separate them. What do the grass roots look like today? Are they bigger? Water the sponges before putting them back on the shelf.

Check on the garden seeds that were prepared for sprouting in Lesson 40.

Language Arts: Review the seed cards prepared for Lesson 40.

Phonics: Teach the letter Mm.

Show the students the letter Mn flashcard. Point out any student's name beginning with the letter *M*. Write some words beginning with the letter *M* on the board. Include any student names from the class that begin with letter *M*. Underline the capital *M* that begins the words. Read through the words and point out the shape of letter *M*. Have the students trace the *M* in the air as you trace the letter *M* beginning each name.

> Boys: Malik, Manuel, Marc, Marco, Marcos, Marcus, Mario, Mark, Martin, Mason, Mathew, Matthew, Max, Maxwell, Micah, Michael, Micheal, Miguel, Mitchell
>
> Girls: Mackenzie, Madeline, Madison, Makayla, Mallory, Margaret, Maria, Mariah, Marisa, Marissa, Mary, Maya, Mayra, Mckenzie, Meagan, Megan, Meghan, Melanie, Melissa, Mercedes, Meredith, Mia, Michaela, Michelle, Mikayla, Miranda, Molly, Monica, Monique, Morgan
>
> Vocabulary words: March, May, Men's (restroom), Miss, Monday, Mr., Mrs., Ms.

Do the Lesson 41 Phonics worksheet. Complete the letter Mm worksheet. Have the students trace the letters Mm with their fingers. They should trace the letters with their fingers and say the names of the letters. Demonstrate the proper strokes for them on the board. Say the words for each of the pictures and look at the Mm letters that begin them.

Reading: Dictate a description to accompany one's drawings of people, objects, events, or activities, derived from experience or imagination. Follow a simple recipe.

Multimedia Resources: View the Aa-Mm segments of "Rev-Up for Reading" from the "Rev-Up for Learning" DVD to drill letter recognition and sound. The students should say each letter sound along with the presentation.

Writing: For these two weeks focus on having the students trace all the letters of their first name. During this time, write the students' names on all worksheets and papers making all the letters dotted or something that can be traced.

Writing Skill Builders: Keep these objectives in mind as you direct the class. Drawing horizontal and vertical lines between two points. Incorporate writing strokes cane and hook.

Multimedia Resources: View the Aa-Mm segments of "Rev-Up for Writing" from the "Rev-Up for Learning" DVD to review the writing of upper- and lowercase letters. The students should write each letter in the air along with the presentation. Since the first half of the presentation covers lowercase letters and the second half uppercase letters some navigation will be needed to skip to the letters that are covered in this lesson.

Memory Verse: Genesis 8:22.

> "As long as the earth endures, seedtime and harvest...will never cease."
> Genesis 8:22 NIV
>
> While the earth remaineth, seedtime and harvest,...shall not cease.
> Genesis 8:22 KJV

Make cards with the words of the verse on them. Explain the memory verse to your class. Make sure they understand "endures," "harvest," and "cease." Give students the word cards. Have them arrange the words in order, helping them read the words. Though they can't read every word, it is good for them to see the written words. Make sure they memorize the reference, too. Let the students take home their Memory Verse Card 6.

Math: Teach number recognition of 9. Show the students the number 9 flashcard. Begin to teach the number 9 by counting items. Count in sequence to 9. Represent the concept on 9 with the symbol of 9. If you have hung cards for the week of the school year point out the Week 9 card.

Teach oral counting 1-10. Use any of the different counting visuals, songs, or rhymes.

Do the Lesson 41 Math worksheet. Have the students trace the large number 9 with the proper strokes by following the arrows. Instruct the students to count each group of items and then trace the number. Instruct the students to draw a line between the groups that have the same number.

Multimedia Resources: View "Rev-Up for Arithmetic" from the "Rev-Up for Learning" DVD to practice number recognition and counting 1-9.

Shapes: Review the square shape.

Do the Lesson 41 Shapes worksheet. Color the shapes at the bottom of the sheet, cut them out, and paste them under the correct group.

Color: Review the colors red, green, blue, black, white, yellow, brown, pink, purple, and orange.

Story Time: Read a story or stories of your choice.

Music: Review "I'm a Little Seed," "Count Our Numbers (Math)," and "America the Beautiful." Teach the following song to the tune of "Are You Sleeping, Brother John?" (Frère Jacques)

We Are Planting
Tune of Frère Jacques

We are planting
We are planting
Seeds to grow
Seeds to grow
Soon we will have green plants
Soon we will have green plants
Just to show
Just to show
  ... Carol McSpadden Sheldon

Multimedia Resources: This week, listen and sing along to selections from the "Music Machine: The Fruit Of The Spirit" CD.

Arts & Crafts: Do one or both of the following activities.

This one is pretend: Have the students make a bush from construction paper. Make the bark from brown construction paper, the leaves from green. Glue onto another paper. In the bush, place a bird's nest and a bird. Under the tree place a rodent in a nest of thin fringed paper.

This one is with real stuff: Gather leaves of bushes, bark, stems, etc. Permit students to glue them onto paper in any form they desire.

Field Trip: Take a field trip to a local grocery store to look at things from plants in the produce section. Compare textures, colors, shapes, and sizes of the different fruits and vegetables. Have the produce manager explain how to select good fruits and vegetables and how to store them at home. Perhaps the bakery can provide a free cookie as a treat. As an alternative, have a grocery store produce manager bring in some fruits and vegetables and do a similar activity in the classroom.

Physical Education: If we were to dramatize a bush, we would squat. Show your students how to squat. Next do a duck waddle in the squatted position. Pretend to squat in the sunshine, in the shade, beside a house, under a larger tree.

NOTES:

Activities in this Lesson: Bible Lesson, Science, Language Arts, Phonics, Reading, Writing, Memory Verse, Math, Color, Story Time, Music, Arts & Crafts, Outdoor Activity, Physical Education, Optional Math/Language Arts/Bible/Arts & Crafts Activity

Bible Reference: Genesis 1:11-13.

Bible Concept to Present: God made many things on the third day.

Bible Lesson: Review the lesson from Lesson 41. Give each student paper and poster pens. Instruct them to draw some of the things they have learned about the third day of Creation. Remind them of bushes and what grows on and lives in bushes. Remind them about berries and parsley and cilantro and rosemary. Remind them that plants and trees are homes for animals.

Science: *Bring some herbs and spices for the children to smell.* Go through your own collection at home for samples: oregano, rosemary, bay leaves, thyme, parsley, etc. Get some fresh cilantro, it smells wonderful! Spices are dry seeds, pods, or vegetables. Bring what you have: cinnamon, nutmeg, pepper, cocoa, etc. Let the children smell and compare everything.

Check on the garden seeds that were prepared for sprouting in Lesson 40.

Language Arts: *If you can purchase some herbs in bulk or at a craft store inexpensively, let the students create a painting with glue and herbs.* Have them write the word HERBS on their piece of paper, then sprinkle the glue with different kinds of herbs. This makes a form of potpourri paper that will smell good wherever it is hung.

Phonics: Review the letter Mm.

Teach the small letter *m*. Write some words beginning with the letter *m* on the board. Include words from stories or activities that tie this lesson to other things that have already been done. Underline the small *m* that begins the words. Read through the words and point out the shape of letter *m*. Have the students trace the *m* in the air as you trace the letter *m* beginning each word.

> Common words: made, make, man, many, may, me, mean, men, might, more, most, mother, move, much, must, my
> Vocabulary words: map, medium, middle, month, more than, morning, mouth

Do the Lesson 42 Phonics worksheet. Complete the letter Mm worksheet. Notice that all of the letters of the alphabet are displayed on the page and that the letters Mm are highlighted with a background. As the students get better at letter recognition you can call out a letter and ask the students to point it out with their finger. Trace the large letter and the small letter. The students can trace the letters between the guide lines. Review the pictures and the colored first letter of the words. The students can color the letters as desired.

Reading: Dictate a description to accompany one's drawings of people, objects, events, or activities, derived from experience or imagination. Follow a simple recipe.

Writing: For these two weeks focus on having the students trace all the letters of their first name. During this time, write the students' names on all worksheets and papers making all the letters dotted or something that can be traced.

Writing Skill Builders: Keep these objectives in mind as you direct the class. Drawing horizontal and vertical lines between two points. Incorporate writing strokes cane and hook.

Memory Verse: Review Genesis 8:22. Review with the word cards. Give students the word cards. Have them arrange the words in order, helping them read the words. Though they can't read every word, it is good for them to see the written words. Make sure they memorize the reference, too.

Math: Review number recognition of 9.

Teach oral counting 1-10. Use any of the different counting visuals, songs, or rhymes.

Do the Lesson 42 Math worksheet. They can color the fish after connecting the dots.

Color: Review the colors red, green, blue, black, white, yellow, brown, pink, purple, and orange.

Story Time: Read a story or stories of your choice.

Music: Review "I'm a Little Seed," "Count Our Numbers (Math)," "America the Beautiful," and "We Are Planting."

Multimedia Resources: This week, listen and sing along to selections from the "Music Machine: The Fruit Of The Spirit" CD.

Arts & Crafts: Give the students playdough. Let them create whatever they want.

Outdoor Activity: If there are any berries growing, go on a walk to pick some. If this is not possible, bring a pint of strawberries or other berries to class. Remind the students that berries grow on bushes. Enjoy eating the berries together.

Physical Education: Hot Circles. Lay out different colored hula hoops, one for each student. This activity will practice jumping using both feet and landing on two feet from the inside to the outside of the hoops. Have the students stand in a hoop to start the game. Call out a circle color as being "hot" and the students in those hoops must jump out and get into different color hoop. Set a limit of four students in one hoop at a time. Choose a circle as hot by saying, "red circles are hot!" Keep calling circles as hot until there is no more space, then call the color of the full circle. Watch for jumping skill and movement in a safe manner.

Optional Math/Language Arts/Bible/Arts & Crafts Activity:

9 Unthankful Men: Luke 17:12-19, read the Bible verses and tell the story.

One day Jesus was going into a village. Ten men who had leprosy asked Jesus to make them well. Jesus healed the ten men, but nine of them forgot to thank Jesus. Only one remembered to say "thank you."

Do the Lesson 42 Bible Numbers worksheet. Give each student a sheet of white construction paper and the worksheet. Cut out the items on the worksheet and glue them to construction paper as illustrated in the drawing. Draw in the arms, legs, and face for the "9" happy man. Draw in the rest of the picture.

Note: Look ahead to Lesson 44. You need to prepare the bread for the bird feeders.

NOTES:

Lesson 43

Activities in this Lesson: Bible Lesson, Social Studies, Science, Language Arts, Phonics, Reading, Writing, Memory Verse, Math, Shapes, Color, Story Time, Music, Arts & Crafts, Physical Education

Bible Reference: Genesis 1:11-13.

Bible Concept to Present: God made many kinds of herbs when He created the plant world.

Bible Lesson: Not all bushes are alike. Some of the bushes God made are bigger than others. Some have big strong branches. Some just seem to have stems and leaves. Some bushes have flowers. Some do not. Some bushes hide their seeds in fruit. Some bushes have big seeds and some have little seeds. Do you like blackberries? Blackberries are very good in pie, aren't they? Did you know that blackberries come from a bush? But not all bushes give us blackberries, do they? Some bushes give us raspberries and some bushes do not grow anything that we can eat. I am thankful God made many different bushes for us to enjoy.

Social Studies: A farmer is a person who plants seeds in the ground to produce more plants, and then sells the seeds from those plants to earn money. A farmer works with the soil, and it is very important that a farmer knows how to plant seeds and care for plants. Farmers are important to us because they grow our food. Discuss farm life. Discuss how farmers get up early, feed the animals, milk the cows, then go to the fields to plant the seeds or work up the field. Often they do not go to bed until very late. A farmer must enjoy their work, or the time spent would not be worth the amount of money they make. Pretend to be a farmer. What would you do first in the day? How would you plant the field? Dramatize this.

Science: Bushes give seeds. This is how they have little baby bushes. Some of the seeds from bushes are inside a soft shell. Some are on the outside of a soft shell. We call these soft shells fruit. A blackberry has seeds all over the outside of it. A tomato has its seeds on the inside of the fruit. When either a blackberry seed or a tomato seed are buried in soil, it will produce a plant. If you have access to both types of fruit, plant them (not too deep). Keep them watered, and see what happens. Let the students have the responsibility of watering, with reminders from you. Note how both seeds sprout and produce a plant.

Check on the garden seeds that were prepared for sprouting in Lesson 40.

Language Arts: Rhyme words with the following: tomato, berry, seed, and plant.

       Before dinner would you please peel this large _____ ? POTATO
       The storm had a cloud that looked like the funnel of a _____ . TORNADO
       Plants have energy which our bodies _____ . NEED
       The farmer gave his horse some oats for _____ . FEED
       Coming out of the hill of dirt in the yard was an _____ . ANT
       When the circus comes to town we can see the big _____ . ELEPHANT

Phonics: Teach the letter Nn.

Show the student the letter Nn flashcard. Point out any student's name beginning with the letter *N*. Write some words beginning with the letter *N* on the board. Include any student names from the class that begin with letter *N*. Underline the capital *N* that begins the words. Read through the words and point out the shape of letter *N*. Have the students trace the *N* in the air as you trace the letter *N* beginning each name.

> Boys: Nathan, Nathaniel, Nicholas, Nicolas, Noah
> Girls: Nancy, Naomi, Natalie, Natasha, Nichole, Nicole
> Vocabulary words: November

Do the Lesson 43 Phonics worksheet. Complete the letter Nn worksheet. Have the students trace the letters Nn with their fingers. They should trace the letters with their fingers and say the names of the letters. Demonstrate the proper strokes for them on the board. Say the words for each of the pictures and look at the Nn letters that begin them.

Reading: Dictate a description to accompany one's drawings of people, objects, events, or activities, derived from experience or imagination. Follow a simple recipe.

Writing: For these two weeks focus on having the students trace all the letters of their first name. During this time, write the students' names on all worksheets and papers making all the letters dotted or something that can be traced.

Writing Skill Builders: Keep these objectives in mind as you direct the class. Drawing horizontal and vertical lines between two points. Incorporate writing strokes cane and hook.

Memory Verse: Review Genesis 8:22. Let the students use their film canisters filled with rice to march around the room or the yard, singing their verse.

Math: Review number recognition of 9. Continue to teach the number 9 by counting items.

Teach oral counting 1-10. Use any of the different counting visuals, songs, or rhymes.

Do the Lesson 43 Math worksheet. Demonstrate how the students should draw the candles on the cupcakes. Have them circle the cupcake that has the same number as their age.

Shapes: Introduce the shape of a rectangle today. Show the student the rectangle shape flashcard. Again, make a stick puppet similar to those we used for the triangle, circle, and square. Make this puppet a rectangle. Use the "I'm a Rectangle" poem that follows.

I'm a Rectangle

I'm a rectangle
Ron is my name
I have four sides
They are not the same

Count one long side (tap side)
Then count two (tap side
Count a short side (tap side)
One more will do. (tap remaining side)

Four sides in all
On me you'll find
Now do you know me?
Please use your mind.

My name is Ron
That's who I am
Now what's my shape?
Tell me if you can.

Do the Lesson 43a Shapes worksheet. Have the students trace the rectangle.

Do the Lesson 43b Shapes worksheet. Count and color the rectangles. Color some of them gray.

Color: Teach the color gray. This is the final color to be learned this year. Show the student the gray color flashcard. Find items in the room that are gray. Look for items of clothing that are gray.

Review the colors red, green, blue, black, white, yellow, brown, pink, purple, and orange.

Story Time: Read a story or stories of your choice.

Music: Review "I'm a Little Seed," "Count Our Numbers (Math)," "America the Beautiful," and "We Are Planting." Teach the following song to the tune of "London Bridge is Falling Down."

I'm Just a Little Tiny Seed
Tune of London Bridge is Falling Down

I'm just a little tiny seed (Crouch down as a tiny seed, and then stretch up to "grow.")
Tiny seed
Tiny seed
I'm just a little tiny seed
Learning, growing, knowing

Soon I will be big and strong (Stretch arms into the air and wave them back and forth.)
Big and strong
Big and strong
Soon I will be big and strong
Giving fruit all day long
    ... Carol McSpadden Sheldon

Multimedia Resources: This week, listen and sing along to selections from the "Music Machine: The Fruit Of The Spirit" CD.

Arts & Crafts: Cut out several types of seed pictures from a seed catalog. Permit students to paste them at random on a sheet of paper, making a seed collage. The Usborne *First Book of Nature* has a great article on fruits and seeds.

Physical Education: Run a foot race. If you have more than one student, include them all in the race. This does not need to be long or strenuous. Rather, work to make it a fun time to pace yourself and enjoy the activity together. Use a rectangle shaped route for the race.

NOTES:

Lesson 44

Week 9: Day 4

Activities in this Lesson: Bible Lesson, Language Arts/Music, Phonics, Reading, Writing, Memory Verse, Math, Color, Story Time, Music, Arts & Crafts, Language Arts/Arts & Crafts, Outdoor Activity, Physical Education

Bible Reference: Genesis 1:11-13.

Bible Concept to Present: God provided for us. He made sure we would always have plants by giving every plant seeds.

Bible Lesson: Review the story from Lesson 43. Explain that every kind of bush and grass has seeds. Some of the seeds are hard and some are soft. God made every variety.

Science: *Bring in some unusual fruits and seeds: guava, avocado, papaya, tomato, coconut.* Talk about how unusual some things are that God made. What would it be like if He only made one kind of fruit? Cut the fruits and give everyone a taste. The guava is very hard to cut. The tomato seeds are enclosed in gel. Papaya seeds look like fish eggs.

The coconut is the biggest seed. It was originally encased in a hard shell. Coconuts are wonderful examples of God's care and provision for plants to make more plants. This fruit of the coco palm begins life on a tree that towers from 60 to 100 feet high. It's an incredibly nutritious and useful food—providing milk, meat, sugar, and oil and acting as its own food dish and cup. Its husk can also be burned as a fuel to cook the fruit and its milk. Break the coconut open in front of the students. Start with scissors. Using one blade of the scissors, probe the three "eyes" on the end of the coconut until you locate the soft one. Drain the coconut water. Now put the coconut into a plastic bag, the bags that grocery stores use. Then put it in another plastic bag, so it is doubled. Take the class outside to a concrete step or wall. Holding the double bag by the handle, smack the coconut against the concrete. Do this several times, to break the shell into pieces. Any coconut meat that clings to the shell may be loosened by inserting a knife in between meat and husk. Let all of your students enjoy some coconut meat. Thank God for coconuts.

Check on the garden seeds that were prepared for sprouting in Lesson 40.

Language/Music: Sing "America, the Beautiful." See if students have it memorized. Talk about what the song means, that America has every kind of landscape. Thank God that we were born in a country like America. (Or apply to your country.)

Phonics: Review the letter Nn.

Do the Lesson 44 Phonics worksheet. Complete the letter Nn worksheet. Notice that all of the letters of the alphabet are displayed on the page and that the letters Nn are highlighted with a background. As the students get better at letter recognition you can call out a letter and ask the students to point it out with their finger. Trace the large letter and the small letter. The students can trace the letters between the guide lines. Review the pictures and the colored first letter of the words. The students can color the letters as desired.

Reading: Dictate a description to accompany one's drawings of people, objects, events, or activities, derived from experience or imagination. Follow a simple recipe.

Writing: For these two weeks focus on having the students trace all the letters of their first name. During this time, write the students' names on all worksheets and papers making all the letters dotted or something that can be traced.

Writing Skill Builders: Keep these objectives in mind as you direct the class. Drawing horizontal and vertical lines between two points. Incorporate writing strokes cane and hook.

Memory Verse: Review Genesis 8:22. Repeat the verse several times during the school day.

Math: Review number recognition of 9.

Teach oral counting 1-10. Use any of the different counting visuals, songs, or rhymes.

Do the Lesson 44 Math worksheet. Can the students correctly identify the shapes under the steps? (Rectangles)

Teach verse 9 to the song "This Old Man."

This Old Man, He Played One

Verse 1
This old man, he played one, He played nick-nack on my thumb;
with a nick-nack paddy whack, give a dog a bone. This old man came rolling home.

Verse 2
This old man, he played two, He played nick-nack on my shoe;
with a nick-nack paddy whack, give a dog a bone. This old man came rolling home.

Verse 3
This old man, he played three, He played nick-nack on my on my knee;
with a nick-nack paddy whack, give a dog a bone. This old man came rolling home.

Verse 4
This old man, he played four, He played nick-nack on my door;
with a nick-nack paddy whack, give a dog a bone. This old man came rolling home.

Verse 5
This old man, he played five, He played nick-nack on my hive;
with a nick-nack paddy whack, give a dog a bone. This old man came rolling home.

Verse 6
This old man, he played six, He played nick-nack on my sticks;
with a nick-nack paddy whack, give a dog a bone. This old man came rolling home.

Verse 7
This old man, he played seven, He played nick-nack up in Heaven;
with a nick-nack paddy whack, give a dog a bone. This old man came rolling home.

Verse 8
This old man, he played eight, He played nick-nack on my gate;
with a nick-nack paddy whack, give a dog a bone. This old man came rolling home.

Verse 9
This old man, he played nine, He played nick-nack on my spine;
with a nick-nack paddy whack, give a dog a bone. This old man came rolling home.

Shapes: Review the shape of a rectangle. Look for rectangles in everyday objects. Review "I'm a Rectangle" poem.

Color: Continue to teach the color gray. Review the colors red, green, blue, black, white, yellow, brown, pink, purple, and orange.

Story Time: Read a story or stories of your choice.

Music: Continue learning the song "I'm Just a Little Tiny Seed." Review "We Are Planting" and "I'm a Little Seed."

Multimedia Resources: This week, listen and sing along to selections from the "Music Machine: The Fruit Of The Spirit" CD.

Prepare ahead, see Lesson 42. – *Using heavy white bread, cut slices with a simple cookie cutter shape, like hearts or stars. Poke a hole in the top of each slice with a straw. Cut enough for each student to have one. Bring some ribbon cut into 12" pieces, plastic knives and a large jar of peanut butter.*
Let the slices dry overnight. This must be done ahead of time! Give each student a piece of dry bread and a piece of ribbon. Help them tie the ribbon on the bread, inserting it through the hole. Give each student a plastic knife. Put a spoon full of peanut butter on their bread and instruct them to spread it evenly. They must be very careful not to tear or break the bread. Give them each some leftover grass seed from last week. Tell them to spread it all over the peanut butter with their knife.

Take time to water the grass sponges.

Arts & Crafts: Do the Lesson 44 Arts & Crafts worksheet. Count the number of pieces in the puzzle. Cut out the pieces. Practice putting the puzzle together.

Language Arts/Arts & Crafts: Go to the library and get *Planting a Rainbow* by Lois Elhert. Say, When we plant seeds, we often get flowers. What is your favorite color of flower? We're going to read a book about flowers. Read the book. Ask, Who was working in the garden with mother? Give the students colored construction paper, scissors, and glue sticks. Let them design their favorite flowers.

Outdoor Activity: Take the class on a walk to hang the Bread Bird Feeders. Find a place away from the feeders to sit and wait for the birds or students may put them in zippered sandwich bags and take them home.

Physical Education: Play Hot Circles again. This time have the students jump both in and out of the circles. Lay out different colored hula hoops, one for each student. This activity will practice jumping using both feet and landing on two feet from one side to the other side of the hoops. Have the students stand in a hoop to start the game. Call out a circle color as being "hot" and the students in those hoops must jump out and jump into a different color hoop. Set a limit of four students in one hoop at a time. Choose a circle as hot by saying, "red circles are hot!" Keep calling circles as hot until there is no more space, then call the color of the full circle. Watch for jumping skill and movement in a safe manner.

NOTES:

Lesson 45

Week 9: Day 5

Activities in this Lesson: Bible Lesson, Social Studies, Science, Language Arts, Phonics, Reading, Writing, Memory Verse, Math, Shapes, Color, Story Time, Music, Arts & Crafts, Physical Education

Bible Reference: Genesis 1:11-13.

Bible Concept to Present: God made the bushes to have seeds so there would be more bushes.

Bible Lesson: God made the bushes, or herbs, in our world to be very special. He knew that there would need to be a way for the bushes to create more bushes. So He gave bushes the ability to make seeds. Inside of each seed is everything that is needed to make another bush. God made the soil as a place for the seed to rest and grow. Each kind of bush has its own seeds. Some seeds are found on the outside of the fruit. Others are found on the inside of the fruit. Wherever the seeds are found, the seeds will grow that kind of plant. In this way, God was sure that what He created would continue to grow. I am happy that God thought of such a wonderful idea.

Social Studies: We use the seeds from bushes in many ways. Sometimes we eat them. An example of this would be a tomato plant. In eating the fruit of the bush, we eat the seeds. We eat the seeds of a sunflower plant, too. Consider the use of cotton seeds, tomato seeds, sunflower seeds, and vanilla bean seeds. After you have told how each is used, have your students choose one to illustrate in a sketch as to what the plant looks like, where the seeds are kept and how we use them.

Science: *Obtain a gardening book* that will list and show pictures of various types of herb and bush plants. Note the differences in the leaves and fruit of each. If you live in a locality where you are able to go outdoors, do so, and gather several types of leaves from bushes. Place them under paper, and by rubbing the side of a crayon over the leaf, make a leaf rubbing of the various types of leaves of bushes. The larger the leaf, the better the detail. You may point out to your student how the veins vary in location on each one, but how each leaf contains veins to transport the nutrients.

Make a final check on the garden seeds that were prepared for sprouting in Lesson 40.

Language Arts: Play the game of "Upset the Fruit Basket." Have two of several kinds of fruit cut from construction paper, or use plastic or real fruit. Place the fruit on a tray. Have students match fruit with its own kind. As the student matches them, have him place them into a basket. Upon the completion of all the fruit being matched, students may upset the basket, and it becomes a free-for-all to gather as many as one child can.

Phonics: Review the letters Aa-Nn.

Teach the small letter *n*. Write some words beginning with the letter *n* on the board. Include words from stories or activities that tie this lesson to other things that have already been done. Underline the small *n* that begins the words. Read through the words and point out the shape of letter *n*. Have the students trace the *n* in the air as you trace the letter *n* beginning each word.
> Common words: name, near, need, never, new, night, no, north, now, number
> Vocabulary words: nail, narrow, neck, next, next to, nickel, night, nine, nineteen, ninth, none, nose, not living

Reading: Dictate a description to accompany one's drawings of people, objects, events, or activities, derived from experience or imagination. Follow a simple recipe.

Writing: For these two weeks focus on having the students trace all the letters of their first name. During this time, write the students' names on all worksheets and papers making all the letters dotted or something that can be traced.

Writing Skill Builders: Keep these objectives in mind as you direct the class. Drawing horizontal and vertical lines between two points. Incorporate writing strokes cane and hook.

Memory Verse: Review Genesis 8:22. Repeat the activity with the word cards.

Math: Review number recognition of 9. Continue to teach the number 9 by counting items.

Teach oral counting 1-10. Use any of the different counting visuals, songs, or rhymes.

Do the Lesson 45 Math worksheet. Instruct the students to trace the numbers, count each group, and then draw a line to the number for the group.

Shapes: Do a rectangle search around the room. Let the students call out the name of every rectangular object. Write them on the board.

Do the Lesson 45 Shapes worksheet. Count the shapes on the sheet that are the same. Draw lines to connect the rectangles that are the same inside. They can color the worksheet as they wish.

Color: Continue to teach the color gray. Review the colors red, green, blue, black, white, yellow, brown, pink, purple, and orange.

Story Time: Read a story or stories of your student's choice or ones they have brought from home.

Music: Review "We Are Planting" and "I'm a Little Seed." Continue learning the song "I'm Just a Little Tiny Seed."

Multimedia Resources: This week, listen and sing along to selections from the "Music Machine: The Fruit Of The Spirit" CD.

Arts & Crafts: *You'll need whole cloves, small oranges and ribbon.* Explain to students that cloves come from a bush type plant. Using the ribbon, tie it around the oranges twice, as if you were dividing each orange into quarters. In the four spaces, push the stick-like part of the clove into the orange. Fill the entire area with cloves. It is important for the preservation of the orange that you not leave empty spaces. Complete all the sections of the orange. It will take some time to complete. You may make this a two day project. Tie the ribbon in a bow on the top with a loop so as to hang it in a closet. You now have a pomander for the closet or a nice gift for Grandma.

Physical Education: Begin to develop the ability to walk briskly for a period of time. Walk a block or so to begin with and continue this practice while gradually adding a block over the period of the week. If a child has health problems, consult a doctor previous to doing this. Do not expect students to do what you will not do. Enjoy the walk. Discuss plants as you go. Continue this activity throughout the next week.

NOTES:

Activities in this Lesson: Bible Lesson, Social Studies, Science, Language Arts, Phonics, Reading, Writing, Memory Verse, Math, Shapes, Color, Story Time, Music, Arts & Crafts, Field Trip, Physical Education

Bible Reference: Genesis 1:11-13.

Bible Concept to Present: On the third day of Creation, God made the trees.

Bible Lesson: Can you tell me what God made on the first day of Creation? Hold up the #1 Days of Creation Number to remind them. That's right. God made light. What did God make on the second day of Creation? Hold up the #2 Days of Creation Number to remind them. Yes. God made the air. On the third day of Creation, what did God make? Hold up the #3 Days of Creation Number to remind them. You are right. God made the dry land and plants. We have talked about two kinds of plants. We talked about plants that do not grow very tall, like the grasses. We talked about plants that grow a bit bigger than the grasses, as a bush does. God made great big plants, too. He made them to grow very tall. Some are so very tall, we have to look way up to see them. He called these kinds of plants trees. God made some trees to be a little bit tall, some are medium tall, and some are very, very tall. Did you know that some trees are so tall; you must look very carefully to even see the top of them? These trees grow in Northern California and are called Giant Sequoia trees. They have been growing for many, many years. Some of them were growing when Jesus lived here on earth. God made the trees for many reasons. He planned some trees to give us fruit to eat. He planned some trees for wood for our homes. God gave us a very wonderful gift when He made trees for us.

Multimedia Resources: Listen to the songs "Je T'aime King Of Kings" and "Just One God Is He" from "Sir Oliver's Song" CD.

Social Studies: We use trees in many ways. One of the most common uses for trees is in building houses. Visit a lumber yard. Show students all the ways trees are cut to make different parts of our homes.

Science: God made the trees very special. See the Lesson 46 Resource page. Point out the various parts of the tree. Emphasize that God made each part of a tree especially for a certain use. Discuss the need for bark, for the roots, the branches, the trunk of the tree, the leaves, and the fruit of the tree. There is a chapter on trees in Usborne's *First Book of Nature*.

Language Arts: Read Joyce Kilmer's "Trees," a poem. Although students will be too young to really understand this poem, the appreciation for good literature must be developed at a young age. So read it, and share with your students how much you like the poem.

Trees

I think that I shall never see
A poem as lovely as a tree.
A tree whose hungry mouth is pressed
Against the earth's sweet flowing breast.
A tree that looks to God all day
And lifts her leafy arms to pray.
A tree that may in summer wear
A nest of robins in her hair.

Upon whose bosom snow has lain;
Who intimately lives with rain.
Poems are made by fools like me
But only God can make a tree!
        Joyce Kilmer

You may use the following poem as well. Review the position words that begin each phrase.

In the Tree

In the tree is a nest for Mr. Bluebird
From the tree hangs a hive for Mr. Bee
Under the tree is the hole for Mr. Bunny
From the tree comes a house for me.
        ... Author Unknown

Phonics: Teach the letter Oo.

Show the students the letter Oo flashcard. Point out any student's name beginning with the letter *O*. Write some words beginning with the letter *O* on the board. Include any student names from the class that begin with letter *O*. Underline the capital *O* that begins the words. Read through the words and point out the shape of letter *O*. Have the students trace the *O* in the air as you trace the letter *O* beginning each name.
        Boys: Omar, Oscar
        Girls: Olivia
        Vocabulary words: October, Office

Do the Lesson 46 Phonics worksheet. Complete the letter Oo worksheet. Have the students trace the letters Oo with their fingers. They should trace the letters with their fingers and say the names of the letters. Demonstrate the proper strokes for them on the board. Say the words for each of the pictures and look at the Oo letters that begin them.

Reading: Dictate a description to accompany one's drawings of people, objects, events, or activities, derived from experience or imagination. Follow a simple recipe.

Multimedia Resources: View the Aa-Oo segments of "Rev-Up for Reading" from the "Rev-Up for Learning" DVD to drill letter recognition and sound. The students should say each letter sound along with the presentation.

Writing: For these two weeks focus on having the students trace all the letters of their first name. During this time, write the students' names on all worksheets and papers making all the letters dotted or something that can be traced.

Writing Skill Builders: Keep these objectives in mind as you direct the class. Incorporate writing strokes cane and hook.

Multimedia Resources: View the Aa-Oo segments of "Rev-Up for Writing" from the "Rev-Up for Learning" DVD to review the writing of upper- and lowercase letters. The students should write each letter in the air along with the presentation. Since the first half of the presentation covers lowercase letters and the second half uppercase letters some navigation will be needed to skip to the letters that are covered in this lesson.

Memory Verse: Continue learning Genesis 8:22. Use the word cards.

Math: Teach number recognition of 0.

Review oral counting 1-10. Use any of the different counting visuals, songs, or rhymes.

Ask counting questions that have 0 as an answer. For example ask how many elephants or how many swimming pools are in the room. Have the students ask similar questions for which 0 is the correct answer. Give each student several counters or blocks. Ask them to move 0 counters to the other side of the table. Ask them to move other numbers of counters and then ask for 0 again. Ask them how many counters are under the table or on top of the door to the room. Any question that has 0 for an answer is OK to use. Show the students the letter 0 flashcard.

Do the Lesson 46 Math worksheet. Count each group. Instruct the students to draw a line between the groups that have the same number.

Multimedia Resources: View "Rev-Up for Arithmetic" from the "Rev-Up for Learning" DVD to practice number recognition and counting 1-9 and 0.

Shapes: Continue giving your students exposure to rectangles. Cut several rectangles out of paper, as well as several circles. Have students make rectangle cars with circle wheels. Vary the sizes so that they become familiar with differing sizes of the same shape. You may also obtain a shoe box, place circles on it for wheels, and make a three dimensional car. Let your students experience some playtime with this.

Color: Review the colors red, green, blue, black, white, yellow, brown, pink, purple, orange, and gray.

Story Time: Read a story or stories of your choice.

Music: Review "We Are Planting," "I Am a Little Seed," and "I Am Just a Tiny Seed."

Multimedia Resources: This week, listen and sing along to selections from "Sir Oliver's Song" CD.

Arts & Crafts: Have your students draw a tree and label or tell you the parts, simply, as they are able.

Field Trip: Visit a nursery to see the different types of trees that they have available. Talk about the bark, the branches, the leaves and other obvious differences. You could also take a walk in a park that is nearby.

Physical Education: Continue working on your brisk walking as suggested in Lesson 45.

NOTES:

Lesson 47
Week 10: Day 2

Activities in this Lesson: Bible Lesson, Science/Outdoor Activity, Language Arts, Phonics, Reading, Writing, Memory Verse, Math, Health & Safety/Shapes, Color, Story Time, Music, Arts & Crafts, Physical Education, Optional Math/Language Arts/Bible/Arts & Crafts Activity

Bible Reference: Genesis 1:11-13.

Bible Concept to Present: Trees are awesome creations of God. Some trees have been on the earth since the time of Christ.

Bible Lesson: Review yesterday's story. *Bring a picture of a giant redwood tree.* Talk again about how big and how old these trees are. There are only a few stands left in California. They are now protected so that they can't be cut down. See http://www.pcimagenetwork.com/tree/pc.html, for a picture of a cut redwood, showing the rings. Explain to the students that trees usually grow a new ring every year. So if we count the rings, we know how old the tree is. The site for Muir Woods, California, also has some good information. http://www.nps.gov/muwo/ Think about the giant redwoods, high on the California hills, watching the first ships entering San Francisco Bay. They were there when the Russians came to Fort Ross. They were there when the earth shook with the 1906 earthquake. When you walk through Muir woods, you feel a sense of the history, and awe toward a powerful Creator. Try in some way to get the students to experience the majesty of these mighty trees.

Science/Outdoor Activity: Take a walk. Find some branches. Try to find some that are big enough to see the rings when you cut them. Cut them with a serrated knife or small saw. Show students the rings. Look at the bark on each branch, comparing different barks and colors. Try to find an old stump; it will have some wonderful ring history. A thick ring means that there was a lot of rain that year. Experts can tell what year goes with each ring. A black ring could be the result of a fire.

Language Arts: Write some words on the board associated with "trees." Let the students volunteer the words. List anything and everything to do with trees. Examples: bees, bee hives, branches, roots, leaves, maple syrup, bark, birds, bird nests, owls, bugs, cicadas, oranges, apples, lemons, walnuts, plums, shadows, blowing leaves, changing leaves, yellow leaves, etc. After writing the words on the board, let the students draw their favorite "tree" things. Encourage those that can write to write the names under their drawings. Review the poems "Trees" by Joyce Kilmer and "In a Tree."

Phonics: Review the letter Oo.

Reading: Dictate a description to accompany one's drawings of people, objects, events, or activities, derived from experience or imagination. Follow a simple recipe.

Writing: For these two weeks focus on having the students trace all the letters of their first name. During this time, write the students' names on all worksheets and papers making all the letters dotted or something that can be traced.

Writing Skill Builders: Keep these objectives in mind as you direct the class. Incorporate writing strokes cane and hook.

Memory Verse: Review Genesis 8:22. Let the children act out the verse.

Math: Review number recognition of 0.

Review oral counting 1-10. Use any of the different counting visuals, songs, or rhymes.

Do the Lesson 47a Math worksheet. Connect the dots from 0 to 9 to form the tree.

Do the Lesson 47b Math worksheet. Notice that the numbers 0-12 are displayed on the page and that the number 0 is highlighted with a background. As the students get better at number recognition you can call out a number and ask the students to point it out with their finger. Have the students trace the large number 0 with the proper stroke by following the arrow. Instruct the students to count each box of 0 items and then trace the number.

Health & Safety/Shapes/Arts & Crafts: Review traffic lights and the meanings of the colors.
Do Lesson 47a and 47b Arts & Crafts worksheets. The Traffic Light craft. Paint with sponges, fingers, brushes or cotton swabs, or color the rectangle black and the circles red, yellow and green. Cut out the circles and the rectangle. Paste the circles on the rectangle to make the traffic lights.

Color: Review the colors red, green, blue, black, white, yellow, brown, pink, purple, orange, and gray.

Story Time: Read a story or stories of your choice.

Music: Review "We Are Planting" and "I Am Just a Tiny Seed."

Multimedia Resources: This week, listen and sing along to selections from "Sir Oliver's Song" CD.

Arts & Crafts: Give the students playdough. Let them make their own trees.

Bring out the soil pictures made for Lesson 34. Let the students add trees to their picture. Another choice is to let them bring in tiny branches from their walk and glue them onto their pictures.

Physical Education: Play the game Red light Green light. Continue to walk briskly.

Optional Math/Language Arts/Bible/Arts & Crafts Activity:

> **0 Manna Found:** Exodus 16:26-27, read the Bible verses and tell the story.
>
> For six days God provided the people in the wilderness with manna. On the sixth day they were to gather enough for two days. The seventh day, the Sabbath, was holy and set apart for God. Those who did not gather extra on the sixth day were surprised when they went to gather manna on the Sabbath. The Bible says that they found none. Zero manna was on the ground the seventh day.

Do the Lesson 47 Bible Numbers worksheet. Give each student a sheet of white construction paper and the worksheet. Cut out the items on the worksheet and glue them to construction paper as illustrated in the drawing. Draw in the arms, legs, and face for the "0" manna man. Draw in the rest of the picture.

Multimedia Resources: Listen to the song "Here Comes a Miracle" from "The Amazing Miracles" CD.

NOTES:

Activities in this Lesson: Bible Lesson, Health & Safety, Social Studies, Science, Language Arts, Phonics, Reading, Writing, Memory Verse, Math, Shapes, Color, Story Time, Music, Arts & Crafts, Physical Education

Bible Reference: Genesis 1: 11-13.

Bible Concept to Present: When God made the trees He made many kinds of trees.

Bible Lesson: God made many kinds of trees for us to enjoy. Some trees He made to give us special foods. We eat oranges, apples, and bananas. All of these come from different trees. God made some trees to be very tall. He made some trees to be very small. Some trees are very big around. Some trees are skinny. The leaves on some trees are big. On other trees, the leaves are small. Let's go for a walk now and discover the differences in trees. Let's gather some of the different leaves as we go.

Health & Safety: Say, As we walked today, we gathered a lot of leaves to look at and study. We need to be careful and immediately wash our hands after gathering leaves. Some leaves can give us a skin rash. We wash off any powder or moisture from the leaves. Everyone, wash your hands with lots of soapy water.

Social Studies: Trees are used to make many things. We talked about how trees are used to make houses and we went to the lumber yard to look at all the different ways wood is used. Trees are also used to make paper. People take little chips of wood and grind them up. Then they are pressed together and run through big rollers. This makes the paper thin. We use paper for many things. We use it for writing and drawing. We use it for tissue, to wipe our hands, wash our windows, and clean up spills. We use it to wrap gifts. Let's see how many ways we use paper. (Go for a walk through the school or house looking for paper products.)

Science: As you are taking your walk for Bible, gather some of the leaves. When you return to class, discuss how they all are different. Have the students trace the veins of the leaves with their fingers. Lay all the leaves out on white paper, grouping similar leaves together. Save the leaves for crafts. Have the students wash their hands.

Language Arts: Look in your library for poetry dealing with trees. Did you find anything you particularly liked? The following poems deal with trees.

OAK TREE

Here is an oak tree, straight and tall
And here are its branches wide,
Here is a nest of twigs and moss
With three little birds inside
The breezes blow, and the little leaves play
But the branches keep the little nest safe
As they sway and sway
And rock the little birds to sleep.

THE TREE

I am a tall tree
I reach toward the sky.
Where bright stars twinkle
And clouds float by.
As the wild winds blow,
They bend forward,
Laden with snow.
When they sway gently
I like it best.
Then I rock birdies to sleep
In their nest.

Phonics: Review the letters Aa-Oo.

Teach the small letter *o*. Write some words beginning with the letter *o* on the board. Include words from stories or activities that tie this lesson to other things that have already been done. Underline the small *o* that begins the words. Read through the words and point out the shape of letter *o*. Have the students trace the *o* in the air as you trace the letter *o* beginning each word.

> Common words: of, off, old, on, only, or, other, our, out, over, own
> Vocabulary words: ocean, once upon a time, one, orange, outside, oval

Do the Lesson 48 Phonics worksheet. Have the students put a gray rectangle around the Mm letters, a purple circle around the Nn letters, and a green X on the Oo letters. Give them one direction at a time so they can focus on finding the correct letter shape. Begin with capital *M*, then lower case *m*, etc. Show them examples with flashcards or letters written on the board.

Reading: Dictate a description to accompany one's drawings of people, objects, events, or activities, derived from experience or imagination. Follow a simple recipe.

Writing: For these two weeks focus on having the students trace all the letters of their first name. During this time, write the students' names on all worksheets and papers making all the letters dotted or something that can be traced.

Writing Skill Builders: Keep these objectives in mind as you direct the class. Incorporate writing strokes cane and hook.

Memory Verse: Continue learning Genesis 8:22. Say the verse together several times during the school day.

Math: Teach oral counting backward, 10-0. Review number recognition of 0.

Use the "Ten Green Bottles" song to help teach counting backwards.

Ten Green Bottles
Written By: Unknown (Copyright Unknown)

Ten green bottles
Hanging on the wall
Ten green bottles
Hanging on the wall
And if one green bottle
Should accidentally fall
There'll be nine green bottles
Hanging on the wall

Nine green bottles
Hanging on the wall
Nine green bottles
Hanging on the wall
And if one green bottle
Should accidentally fall
There'll be eight green bottles
Hanging on the wall

Eight green bottles
Hanging on the wall
Eight green bottles
Hanging on the wall
And if one green bottle
Should accidentally fall
There'll be seven green bottles
Hanging on the wall

Seven green bottles
Hanging on the wall
Seven green bottles
Hanging on the wall
And if one green bottle
Should accidentally fall
There'll be six green bottles
Hanging on the wall

Six green bottles
Hanging on the wall
Six green bottles
Hanging on the wall
And if one green bottle
Should accidentally fall
There'll be five green bottles
Hanging on the wall

Five green bottles
Hanging on the wall
Five green bottles
Hanging on the wall
And if one green bottle
Should accidentally fall
There'll be four green bottles
Hanging on the wall

Four green bottles
Hanging on the wall
Four green bottles
Hanging on the wall
And if one green bottle
Should accidentally fall
There'll be three green bottles
Hanging on the wall

Three green bottles
Hanging on the wall
Three green bottles
Hanging on the wall
And if one green bottle
Should accidentally fall
There'll be two green bottles
Hanging on the wall

Two green bottles
Hanging on the wall
Two green bottles
Hanging on the wall
And if one green bottle
Should accidentally fall
There'll be one green bottle
Hanging on the wall

One green bottle
Hanging on the wall
One green bottle
Hanging on the wall
If that one green bottle
Should accidentally fall
There'll be no green bottles
Hanging on the wall

Review oral counting 1-10. Use any of the different counting visuals, songs, or rhymes.

Do the Lesson 48 Math worksheet. Count each group of items and circle the correct number for the group.

Shapes: Review rectangles today with students. They should be able to state what a rectangle is upon sight. Take two sheets of paper and make doors in one by cutting two sides into the paper and folding the third side. Under each door, let your student draw a person in their family. Stress that the doors are rectangles.

Do the Lesson 48 Shapes worksheet. Trace the rectangles, count the rectangles in each drawing, and match pictures that are the same.

Color: Review the colors red, green, blue, black, white, yellow, brown, pink, purple, orange, and gray.

Story Time: Read a story or stories of your choice.

Music: Review "I Am Just a Tiny Seed." Learn the song "My God Is So Big" from the "Horizons Preschool Music" CD.

Multimedia Resources: This week, listen and sing along to selections from "Sir Oliver's Song" CD.

Arts & Crafts: Place small pieces of crayon shavings around the leaves that were collected on the walk on waxed paper. Now place another sheet of wax paper over this. Press with a warm iron until the crayons have melted and the wax has formed around the leaf. After this is cool, place strips of paper stapled around the outside of the picture for a frame. Hang in a window. The light will come through to create a lighted stained-glass effect.

Do the Lesson 48 Arts & Crafts worksheet. Color the tree house.

Give the students colored pencils. Permit them to create as they desire. One idea to give them is to design a tree house of their own.

Physical Education: Continue to walk briskly for a period of time each day.

NOTES:

Activities in this Lesson: Bible Lesson, Language Arts, Phonics, Reading, Writing, Memory Verse, Math, Shapes, Color, Story Time, Music, Arts & Crafts, Science/Health & Safety, Physical Education, Homework

Bible Reference: Genesis 1:11-13.

Bible Concept to Present: God planned for man to use trees to build homes.

Bible Lesson: Review the story from Lesson 47. God knew we would use trees. He knew we would use them for houses and for paper. He knew that many people would be architects, people who design houses and buildings. God made trees strong and thick. There were trees covering much of the land years ago. Pioneers, the first Americans, cut these trees down to make houses and fences. Some families made their houses totally out of trees. These houses were called "log cabins."

Illustration: *Bring a set of LINCOLN LOGS® or similar toys to class.* Let the students try to build a log cabin.

Language Arts: *If possible, bring in an evergreen bush or branch.* Say, What happens to trees during the year? Do the trees change? Talk about the seasons and the changes that occur. Talk about some trees that don't change much, evergreens like pines, fir, cypress, juniper, and spruce. Pass some of the evergreen around for students to smell. What does it smell like? Christmas! Review the poems "Oak Tree" and "The Tree."

Phonics: Review the letters Aa-Oo.

Do the Lesson 49 Phonics worksheet. Complete the letter Oo worksheet. Notice that all of the letters of the alphabet are displayed on the page and that the letters Oo are highlighted with a background. As the students get better at letter recognition you can call out a letter and ask the students to point it out with their finger. Trace the large letter and the small letter. The students can trace the letters between the guide lines. Review the pictures and the colored first letter of the words. The students can color the letters as desired.

Reading: Dictate a description to accompany one's drawings of people, objects, events, or activities, derived from experience or imagination. Follow a simple recipe.

Writing: For these two weeks focus on having the students trace all the letters of their first name. During this time, write the students' names on all worksheets and papers making all the letters dotted or something that can be traced.

Writing Skill Builders: Keep these objectives in mind as you direct the class. Incorporate writing strokes cane and hook.

Memory Verse: Finish learning Genesis 8:22. Let the students recite if they want to.

Math: Teach oral counting backward, 10-0. Sing the "Ten Green Bottles" song.

Review number recognition of 0.

Review oral counting 1-10. Use any of the different counting visuals, songs, or rhymes.

Do the Lesson 49 Math worksheet. Connect the dots to make the sailboat and color the picture. Count how many triangles are in the drawing.

Shapes: Review rectangles today with students.

Color: Review the colors red, green, blue, black, white, yellow, brown, pink, purple, orange, and gray.

Story Time: Read a story or stories of your choice.

Music: Review "My God is So Big" and "I Am Just a Tiny Seed."

Multimedia Resources: This week, listen and sing along to selections from "Sir Oliver's Song" CD.

Arts & Crafts: *Bring in a variety of noodles.* Talk about the flour in noodles. We dry the noodles so that they will keep a long time. Then cooking them in boiling water makes the noodles soft so we can eat them. Let the students glue noodles on construction paper with tacky glue. They may paint the noodles with poster pens.

Let the students take their grass sponge home. Encourage them to tell their families what they learned about grasses and roots. This can be told and given to a relative or shut-in as a gift.

Science/Health & Safety: *Bring in some dry corn or wheat kernels, a small round rock and a flat rock.* Let the students grind the grain. Place the grain on the flat rock and roll the round rock over the grain to crush it. Talk about bread, a staple food in every culture. There are so many kinds of bread. What is your favorite? Pita bread, crackers, white bread, wheat bread, corn bread, muffins, nut breads, and buns for burgers or hot dogs. Explain that noodles are also made from ground up grain. Bread is very good for us. It fills us up and gives our body energy for activities.

Physical Education: Continue to walk briskly for a period of time each day.

Homework: Pass out the Lesson 49 Homework worksheet, the Plant Eating Chart. Talk about what the students will be doing with the chart. We eat plants every day in many of the foods we eat. The students will bring back their chart in one week.

NOTES:

Activities in this Lesson: Bible Lesson, Social Studies, Science, Language Arts, Phonics, Reading, Memory Verse, Math, Shapes, Color, Story Time, Music, Arts & Crafts, Field Trip, Physical Education

Bible Reference: Genesis 1:11-13.

Bible Concept to Present: God made the trees to have seeds so that each type of tree would have little trees.

Bible Lesson: When God made the plants He made each of them with seeds so that each plant would make new plants like itself. God made grasses to be like this. He made bushes to be like this. He made trees to be like this. Yes, God made the trees to have seeds, too. If you were to cut open an orange, you would see an orange seed inside. The same is true for apples and cherries. All of these fruits come from trees. All of them have seeds inside their fruit. Sometimes trees have seeds that are not on the inside of the fruit. Walnuts are from trees, and they have a hard outer shell. Sometimes the seeds of a tree are hard to see. In a pine cone, for example, the seeds are harder to see. There are many seeds within one pine cone. An avocado is a fruit which has only one seed in it. Inside of each seed from the avocado is the ability to make a tree just like the tree the seed came from. An apple seed will only make an apple tree. An apple seed would never make a cherry tree; neither would a cherry seed make an apple tree. God made each seed so it would make the exact kind of tree from which it came. I am happy God planned for each seed to be special.

Social Studies: Several of the seeds from trees are edible. Seeds are very good for us for they contain protein. List several of the seeds or nuts from trees that people eat. Using a bag of *mixed bird seed* let the students make a drawing on construction paper with seeds and glue. Be sure your students understand that unless you tell them that the seeds may be eaten, seeds from any plant should not be eaten.

Science: Purchase some beans. Place a dampened paper towel in a glass bottle. Now place two bean seeds between the dampened paper towel and the glass. Leave in a darkened place (under the sink is great) for two days. Take out the glass and observe the changes in the seed. The seeds should have begun to sprout. Tell your students that the part of the plant that is beginning to grow now will be the root of the plant. Let the seed continue to sprout, noticing stem and leaves. Discuss how every seed grows its own type of plant.

Note: You will want to mention to your students that the bean seed is not a tree seed. The length of time it requires a tree seed to germinate is prohibitive as a useful illustration for small children.

Language Arts: Play a game called "Find the Fruit." Take the fruit patterns you made in Lesson 45. Hide them all over in one large room. Have students find all the fruit. Give your students a basket to place the fruit in, encouraging them to take turns. This is similar to "Hide the Thimble."

Phonics: Teach the letter Pp.

Show the students the letter Pp flashcard. Point out any student's name beginning with the letter *P*.

Write some words beginning with the letter *P* on the board. Include any student names from the class that begin with letter *P*. Underline the capital *P* that begins the words. Read through the words and point out the shape of letter *P*. Have the students trace the *P* in the air as you trace the letter *P* beginning each name.

> Boys: Parker, Patrick, Paul, Pedro, Peter, Philip, Phillip, Preston
> Girls: Paige, Patricia, Priscilla

Do the Lesson 50 Phonics worksheet. Complete the letter Pp worksheet. Have the students trace the letters Pp with their fingers. They should trace the letters with their fingers and say the names of the letters. Demonstrate the proper strokes for them on the board. Say the words for each of the pictures and look at the Pp letters that begin them.

Reading: Dictate a description to accompany one's drawings of people, objects, events, or activities, derived from experience or imagination. Follow a simple recipe.

Writing: For these two weeks focus on having the students trace all the letters of their first name. During this time, write the students' names on all worksheets and papers making all the letters dotted or something that can be traced.

Writing Skill Builders: Keep these objectives in mind as you direct the class. Incorporate writing strokes cane and hook.

Memory Verse: Finish learning Genesis 8:22. Let the students recite if they want to.

Math: Teach oral counting backward, 10-0. Use a variation of the "Ten Green Bottles" song called "Ten Brown Beavers." You can probably make up other variations yourself using colors and objects that have been studied like "There were ten pink piglets, playing in the mud."

Ten Brown Beavers
Tune of Ten Green Bottles

There were ten brown Beavers building up a dam
Ten brown Beavers building a dam
And if one brown Beaver left and swam,
There'd be nine brown Beavers building up a dam.
(Continue going 8,7,6,5,4,3,2,1, then....)
There'd be no brown Beavers left to build up a dam.

Review number recognition of 0.

Review oral counting 1-10. Use the "Ants Go Marching" song.

The Ants Go Marching

The ants go marching one by one, hurrah, hurrah,
The ants go marching one by one, hurrah, hurrah,
The ants go marching one by one,
The little one stopped to suck his thumb.
And they all go marching down, to the ground, to get out, of the rain.
Boom, boom, boom, boom, boom, boom, boom.

Two by two	- ... to tie his shoe.
Three by three	- ... to climb a tree.
Four by four	- ... to sleep some more.
Five by five	- ... to joke and jive.
Six by six	- ... to do some tricks.
Seven by seven	- ... to point to Heaven.
Eight by eight	- ... to shut the gate.
Nine by nine	- ... to read a sign.
Ten by ten	- ... to start over again. - ... to say THE END.

Do the Lesson 50 Math worksheet. Instruct the students to trace the numbers, count each group, and then draw a line to the number for the group.

Shapes: Review rectangles today with students.

Do the Lesson 50 Shapes worksheet. Discuss the one-to-one correspondence between a shape on the left of the page and a similar shape on the right side of the page. Count the number of shapes on each side of the page. Select students to name the shapes from top to bottom on each side of the paper. Draw lines to connect the shapes that are the same.

Color: Review the colors red, green, blue, black, white, yellow, brown, pink, purple, orange, and gray.

Story Time: Read a story or stories of your student's choice or ones they have brought from home.

Music: Review "My God is So Big." Teach the following song to the tune of "Three Blind Mice."

I Am a Tree
Tune of Three Blind Mice

I am a tree (Crouch on ground)
I am a tree
My arms stretch and grow (Stretch out arms)
My arms stretch and grow
Watch me, watch me and up I go (Spring up)
I am a tree
I am a tree

Multimedia Resources: This week, listen and sing along to selections from "Sir Oliver's Song" CD.

Arts & Crafts: *Bring enough pine cones for each student to have one. If you gather pine cones from outside with the students, bake the pine cones for one hour at low heat to kill any insects inside.* Pass out Lesson 50 Arts & Crafts worksheet. Have the students color the parts of the turkey before cutting them out. Attach to the pine cones with tacky glue.

Field Trip: Visit a lumber yard to see the different types of products that are made from wood. You can cover the same topic by looking around the room for things made from wood but nothing substitutes for the smell of a real lumber yard. A person who does hobby work with wood might bring in some of their items to show to the students.

Physical Education: Continue to walk briskly. Have you progressed in the ability of how far you and your students can walk without tiring?

NOTES:

Activities in this Lesson: Bible Lesson, Social Studies, Science, Language Arts, Phonics, Reading, Writing, Memory Verse, Math, Shapes, Color, Story Time, Music, Arts & Crafts, Physical Education

Bible Reference: Genesis 1:11-13.

Bible Concept to Present: When God made the plants, He made them for food for us to enjoy.

Bible Lesson: God made the plants on the third day of Creation. I am so happy that He did. He gave us grasses, bushes and trees. From these types of plants we get food which our body needs. When God first made man, the only kind of food he ate was plants. We call some plants we use as food, vegetables. Vegetables are plants that are usually closer to the ground. Vegetables give us important nutrients for our body. Some vegetables are corn, peas, beans, lettuce, cabbage, turnips, and carrots. God made all of these for us. They, too, have seeds to help them make more of their kind. Fruit is another kind of food from plants. Oranges, apples, cherries, lemons, and grapefruit are all kinds of fruit that we eat. We need both fruits and vegetables to grow strong. Let's thank God now for the fruits and vegetables He has made for us.

Social Studies: Our bodies need fruits and vegetables to stay healthy. How do you serve fruits and vegetables? How many of them do you eat raw? How many of them do you cook? Which is better for you? Discuss all of these with your students, and if you wish you may discuss one or two vitamins which are contained in fruits and vegetables. For example, vitamin C is found in oranges and parsley. Carrots are a good source of vitamin A which is known to be very good for our eyes.

Science: Some of the vegetables that we eat are the leaves of plants (lettuce), some are the roots (turnips, beets, radishes), some are the stems (celery), some are the fruit (tomato), and some are the seeds. Cut out pictures of several plants from a gardening magazine. Classify them according to the leaf, stem, fruit, root, or seed of a plant. Which foods do we classify as a grain? How do we use grains?

Language Arts: Do this finger activity:

Picking Apples

Here's a little apple tree (Left arm up, fingers spread)
I look up and I can see (Look at fingers)
Big red apples, ripe and sweet (Cup hands to hold apple)
Big red apples, good to eat! (Raise hands to mouth)
Shake the little apple tree (Shake the tree with right hand)
See the apples fall on me (Raise cupped hands and let fall gently on head several times)

Here's a basket, big and round (Make circle with arms)
Pick the apples from the ground (Pick up and put in basket)
Here's an apple I can see (Look up to the tree.)
I'll reach up. It's ripe and sweet (Reach up to left thumb with right hand)
That's the apple I will eat! (Hands to mouth)

Phonics: Review the letter Pp.

Teach the small letter *p*. Write some words beginning with the letter *p* on the board. Include words from stories or activities that tie this lesson to other things that have already been done. Underline the small *p* that begins the words. Read through the words and point out the shape of letter *p*. Have the students trace the *p* in the air as you trace the letter *p* beginning each word.

> Common words: page, part, people, picture, place, plant, play, point, port, press, put
> Vocabulary words: penny, pink, please, present, purple

Reading: Dictate a description to accompany one's drawings of people, objects, events, or activities, derived from experience or imagination. Follow a simple recipe.

Multimedia Resources: View the Aa-Pp segments of "Rev-Up for Reading" from the "Rev-Up for Learning" DVD to drill letter recognition and sound. The students should say each letter sound along with the presentation.

Writing: For these two weeks focus on having the students write the first letter of their first name freehand. During this time, write the students' names on all worksheets and papers leaving space for the first letter and make the rest dotted or something that can be traced. They should have their Name Plates to look at as they do this.

Writing Skill Builders: Keep these objectives in mind as you direct the class. Incorporate writing strokes cane and hook.

Multimedia Resources: View the Aa-Pp segments of "Rev-Up for Writing" from the "Rev-Up for Learning" DVD to review the writing of upper- and lowercase letters. The students should write each letter in the air along with the presentation. Since the first half of the presentation covers lowercase letters and the second half uppercase letters some navigation will be needed to skip to the letters that are covered in this lesson.

Memory Verse: This week review all of the verses learned so far. Genesis 1:1, Genesis 1:3, Genesis 1:6, Genesis 1:10, I Peter 1:24-25, and Genesis 8:22. The students might like to learn a Bible thought this week: *He gives us all things to enjoy.*

Math: Teach number recognition of 10. Show the students the number 10 flashcard. Begin to teach the number 10 by counting items. Find 10 of a number of items and have your student count them. Concentrate on teaching the counting only of 10 today. Say the "Ten Little Fingers" finger play.

Ten Little Fingers

I have ten little fingers and they all belong to me! (hold up 10 fingers)
I can make them do things, would you like to see? (point to eyes)
I can shut them up tight, or open them wide. (hold up and close, open hand)
I can hold them in front, or make them all hide. (open in front, close)
I can hold them up high, I can put them down low. (open high, open low)
I can hide them in back, then hold them just so. (open behind back, open by side at attention)

Teach oral counting backward, 10-0. Review oral counting 1-10. Use any of the different counting visuals, songs, or rhymes.

Do the Lesson 51a Math worksheet. Notice that all of the numbers are displayed on the page and that the number 10 is highlighted with a background. As the students get better at number recognition you can call out a number and ask the students to point it out with their finger. Have the students trace the large number 10 with the proper strokes by following the arrows. Instruct the students to count each group of items and then trace the number.

Do the Lesson 51b Math worksheet. Instruct the students to draw a line between the groups that have the same number.

Multimedia Resources: View "Rev-Up for Arithmetic" from the "Rev-Up for Learning" DVD to practice number recognition and counting 1-10.

Shapes: Review rectangles today with students.

Do the Lesson 51 Shapes worksheet. Select students to name the shapes top to bottom on both sides of the sheet. Select students to describe the items inside the shapes. Have them use complete sentences. Instruct the students to draw a line between shapes that are the same.

Color: Review the colors red, green, blue, black, white, yellow, brown, pink, purple, orange, and gray.

Story Time: Read a story or stories of your choice.

Music: Review "I Am a Tree," "Ten Brown Beavers" (Math), "The Ants Go Marching" (Math), and "My God is So Big." Work on the song from the "Horizons Preschool Music" CD, "He Plants Me Like A Seed."

Multimedia Resources: This week, listen and sing along to selections from the "Music Machine: All About Love" CD.

Arts & Crafts: *Bring in some women's magazines.* Cut out several pictures of foods to eat. Let the students find the pictures in old magazines. After they have cut them out, let the students paste them onto a paper plate.

Bring in green peppers, several large mushrooms, potatoes, and broccoli. Wash the veggies and dry them well. Pour a thin layer of paint into several white foam deli trays. Provide an assortment of colors. Cut each vegetable in half, in a direction to make the most interesting cut surface. Let the students stamp with the vegetable stamps on white construction paper. Guide the students to press the stamps gently but firmly to make the best impressions.

Physical Education: Begin to teach a few stretching exercises to your students. Lie flat on the floor. Reach your arms as high above the head as you can. Now stretch up as if reaching for something way above you. Now lift each leg, one at a time upwards toward the sky. Now sit up. With your legs straddled in front of you, stretch your body to the right, now to the left. See if you can touch your toes. Grab your toes and stretch to the count of five. Then release and grab the other toe and stretch to the count of five. Now fold your legs in front of you so that you are sitting cross-legged. Stretch the trunk of your body to the right, to the left and to the center. Continue to stretch to the ceiling for five counts and to the floor for five counts. Shake out your limbs and rest.

NOTES:

Activities in this Lesson: Bible Lesson, Language Arts, Phonics, Reading, Writing, Memory Verse, Math, Shapes, Color, Story Time, Music, Arts & Crafts, Outdoor Activity, Health & Safety, Physical Education, Optional Math/Language Arts/Bible/Arts & Crafts Activity

Bible Reference: Genesis 1:11-13.

Bible Concept to Present: God loved variety. God gave us many tastes and textures in the fruit and vegetables He made for us.

Bible Lesson: Review yesterday's story. *Bring one kind of each growing style of fruit or vegetable: root, stalk, leaf, flower, and fruit. Cut them into bite size pieces.* God made vegetables and fruit in all sizes. Some grow way up high in trees, some grow in bushes, some grow on the ground, and some even grow underground! Tell me some fruits that grow high in trees. Tell me some fruits or vegetables that grow on bushes. Now tell me some vegetables that grow close to the ground. And finally, what vegetables do we eat that are really roots and grow underground? Let the students guess then provide them with more answers. Now let the students taste the different kinds of produce.

Language Arts: Say the alphabet together. Talk about vegetables and fruits. What letter of the alphabet do they start with? Let's start with A and see if we can name one vegetable or fruit for each letter. Allow students some time to guess, and then provide an answer. Be prepared the answer the "What's that?" question about some of the fruits on the list.

A = apple, apricot, artichokes, asparagus, avocado;
B = banana, blackberry, broccoli;
C = cantaloupe, cherry, coconut, cranberry, cauliflower, celery, carrot;
D = date, durian, dill;
E = endive, egg plant, elderberry, eggfruit;
F = fig, fennel, filbert;
G = grape, gooseberry, grapefruit, guava, green beans;
H = haw (hawthorn), huckleberry, honeydew, horseradish; **I** = Ita palm, Indian corn;
J = June berry, jicama, jackfruit;
K = kiwi, kumquat, key lime;
L = lemon, lime, lettuce;
M = mango, mulberry, mandarins, mushrooms;
N = nuts, navy beans, nectarine;
O = orange, onion, olive;
P = ineapple, pear, plum, pomegranate, pumpkin, peach, persimmon, prickly pear, papaya, peas, potato, pepper;
Q = quince, quinoa;
R = rhubarb, raspberry, radish;
S = trawberry, sunflower seeds, saguaro, spinach, soybeans, spinach; **T** = turnip, tomato, tangerine;
U = ugli fruit;
V = voacanga, velvet apple;
W = wasabi, white radish, watercress, walnut, watermelon;
X = ximenia fruit, xigua;
Y = yam, yucca;
Z = zucchini

Repeat the "Picking Apples" action verse from yesterday's Language Arts.

Phonics: Review the letters Aa-Pp.

Do the Lesson 52 Phonics worksheet. Complete the letter Pp worksheet. Notice that all of the letters of the alphabet are displayed on the page and that the letters Aa are highlighted with a background. As the students get better at letter recognition you can call out a letter and ask the students to point it out with their finger. Trace the large letter and the small letter. The students can trace the letters between the guide lines. Review the pictures and the colored first letter of the words. The students can color the letters as desired.

Reading: Dictate a description to accompany one's drawings of people, objects, events, or activities, derived from experience or imagination. Follow a simple recipe.

Writing: For these two weeks focus on having the students write the first letter of their first name freehand. During this time, write the students' names on all worksheets and papers leaving space for the first letter and make the rest dotted or something that can be traced. They should have their Name Plates to look at as they do this.

Writing Skill Builders: Keep these objectives in mind as you direct the class. Incorporate writing strokes cane and hook.

Memory Verse: This week review all of the verses learned so far. Genesis 1:1, Genesis 1:3, Genesis 1:6, Genesis 1:10, I Peter 1:24-25, and Genesis 8:22. The students might like to learn a Bible thought this week: *He gives us all things to enjoy.*

Math: Review number recognition of 10.

Review oral counting 1-10 and 10-0. Use any of the different counting visuals, songs, or rhymes.

Do the Lesson 52 Math worksheet. Cut out the numbers from the strip. Count each group of objects and paste the correct number in the box.

Shapes: Review rectangles today with students.

Color: Review the colors red, green, blue, black, white, yellow, brown, pink, purple, orange, and gray.

Story Time: Read a story or stories of your choice.

Music: Review "He Plants Me Like a Seed," "I Am a Tree," "Ten Brown Beavers (Math)," "The Ants Go Marching (Math)," and "My God is So Big."

Multimedia Resources: This week, listen and sing along to selections from the "Music Machine: All About Love" CD.

Arts & Crafts: Go to the Creation Mural. Let the students take turns adding some fruits and vegetables to Day 3 of Creation. They may be creative, drawing just the fruit or the fruit on the tree.

Give the students playdough. Let them create their favorite vegetable.

Field Trip: Take a trip to the grocery store or a vegetable stand nearby. Walk the vegetable and fruit aisles, especially noticing unusual items. Talk about how the store sells the produce, usually by the pound. Put something on the scale and let the students see it being weighed. Buy some carrots or celery to eat later.

Health & Safety: Even when vegetables and fruit seem clean, they need to be washed. They travel a long way to get to our stores. They grow in dirt. They are often sprayed to keep bugs off. Wash the carrots and celery carefully in water. Show students how to hand wash each piece of produce. Slice the items and share with all the students. Some ranch dip would be nice, too!

Physical Education: Continue to teach a few stretching exercises to your students. Lie flat on the floor. Reach your arms as high above the head as you can. Now stretch up as if reaching for something way above you. Now lift each leg, one at a time upwards toward the sky. Now sit up. With your legs straddled in front of you, stretch your body to the right, now to the left. See if you can touch your toes. Grab your toes and stretch to the count of five. Then release and grab the other toe and stretch to the count of five. Now fold your legs in front of you so that you are sitting cross-legged. Stretch the trunk of your body to the right, to the left and to the center. Continue to stretch to the ceiling for five counts and to the floor for five counts. Shake out your limbs and rest.

Optional Math/Language Arts/Bible/Arts & Crafts Activity:

10 Girls: Matthew 25:1-13, read the Bible verses and tell the story.

Ten girls were invited to a wedding. While they were waiting for the bridegroom, five of the girls' lamps went out. They didn't have enough oil. While they were gone to get oil, the bridegroom came and the five girls whose lamps were still burning went to the wedding.

Do the Lesson 52 Bible Numbers worksheet. Give each student a sheet of white construction paper and the worksheet. Cut out the items on the worksheet and glue them to construction paper as illustrated in the drawing. Draw in the arms, legs, and faces for the "10" girls. Draw in the rest of the picture.

NOTES:

Activities in this Lesson: Bible Lesson, Social Studies, Language Arts, Phonics, Reading, Writing, Math, Language Arts/Math, Shapes, Colors, Story Time, Music, Arts & Crafts, Physical Education

Bible Reference: Genesis 1:11-13.

Bible Concept to Present: When God made the plants He made them for our use. We use the plants or products from the plants for the purpose of clothing and shelter.

Bible Lesson: When God made plants He made them for a very specific purpose. They not only are needed for our food, but they also are used by us for houses and clothing. Cotton is one of the plants that we use to make clothes. The cotton plant gives us a seed fiber that can be spun into thread. From this thread, our clothes are made. Plants are used in the making of our homes, too. We discussed before how trees were used for the wood in our homes. In some places of the world, the grasses themselves are bundled together and made into roofs for the houses. Sometimes sticks are used for the walls. God knew we would need the things which plants provide when He made the plants. Let's thank God for the things plants provide for us by reading this poem:

Thank You Lord

Thank You Lord for the plants you give
For us to use and enjoy.
Thank You for the fruits we eat
The food for every girl and boy.

Thank You for the plants that make
Clothes for us to wear.
To keep us warm in the winter-time
Until the days turn fair.

Thank You for the trees that make
The house in which we live.
Thank You Lord, for everything
That to us you give.

Social Studies: We use plants in more ways than just for clothes and shelter. We use plants for medicine also. We have learned much about what is good for our health. In the days when your great-grandparents lived, plants were used often for medicine. It was all they had. For example, cherry bark was often boiled and the juices used for treating colds. Seeds from a mustard plant were ground together to make a paste and put with onions in a bag under a child when he was sick with a cold and cough. We don't use these particular plants now for medicine, but we still use plants. For example, aspirin is a part of a plant. Penicillin is made from mold, which is a type of plant.

Language Arts: Notice the types of plants that we use for shelter, clothes, and medicine. Try to help your students identify some of them by looking at pictures with them. Ask them to identify plants used only for shelter, etc.

Phonics: Teach the letter Qq. They should trace the letters with their fingers and say the names of the letters.

Show students the Qq flashcard. Point out any student's name beginning with the letter *Q*. Write some words beginning with the letter *Q* on the board. Include any student names from the class that begin with letter *Q*. Underline the capital *Q* that begins the words. Read through the words and point out the shape of letter *Q*. Have the students trace the *Q* in the air as you trace the letter *Q* beginning each name.

> Boys: Qabil, Qadir, Qaiser, Qiao, Qshawn, Quacey, Quanah, Quennel, Quentin, Quico, Quillan, Quincy, Quinlan, Quinn, Quinton, Qusay
>
> Girls: Qiao, Qona, Qrystal, Qrysti, Qrystin, Qsari, Queena, Queenie, Querida, Questa, Queta, Quilla, Quin

Do the Lesson 53 Phonics worksheet. Complete the letter Qq worksheet. Have the students trace the letters Qq with their fingers. They should trace the letters with their fingers and say the names of the letters. Demonstrate the proper strokes for them on the board. Say the words for each of the pictures and look at the Qq letters that begin them.

Reading: Dictate a description to accompany one's drawings of people, objects, events, or activities, derived from experience or imagination. Follow a simple recipe.

Writing: For these two weeks focus on having the students write the first letter of their first name freehand. During this time, write the students' names on all worksheets and papers leaving space for the first letter and make the rest dotted or something that can be traced. They should have their Name Plates to look at as they do this.

Writing Skill Builders: Keep these objectives in mind as you direct the class. Incorporate writing strokes cane and hook.

Memory Verse: This week review all of the verses learned so far. Genesis 1:1, Genesis 1:3, Genesis 1:6, Genesis 1:10, I Peter 1:24-25, and Genesis 8:22. The students might like to learn a Bible thought this week: *He gives us all things to enjoy*.

Math: Review number recognition of 10.

Review oral counting 1-10 and 10-0. Use any of the different counting visuals, songs, or rhymes.

Do the Lesson 53 Math worksheet. Count the objects in each group and then circle the correct number.

Language Arts/Math: Make a fishing pole from a dowel rod. On the end of the dowel rod, place a string. On the end of the string, add a magnet. Use the patterns on the Lesson 53 Resource page to cut out several fish from cardstock. On the back of the fishes, place a magnet that will attract the magnet on the fishing pole. Place numbers 0-10 on the fishes. If your students are capable, circle a part of the fish on each fish pattern. (Examples: fins, head, eyes, scales) Let the children go "fishing." The child will tell you the number on the fish they catch. Some students will tell you the part of the fish that is circled.

Shapes: Review triangles, circles, squares, and rectangles with students.

Do the Lesson 53 Shapes worksheet. Trace each of the shapes, cut them out and paste them on a sheet of paper in order of big, bigger and biggest.

Color: Review the colors red, green, blue, black, white, yellow, brown, pink, purple, orange, and gray.

Story Time: Read a story or stories of your choice.

Music: Review "He Plants Me Like a Seed," "I Am a Tree," "Ten Brown Beavers (Math)," "The Ants Go Marching (Math)," and "My God is So Big."

Multimedia Resources: This week, listen and sing along to selections from the "Music Machine: All About Love" CD.

Arts & Crafts: Have the students build a sample of a house made of sticks and gathered grasses, similar to the ones the Indians used. You may need to place the sticks in a clay foundation so that they will hold. Encyclopedias will have an illustration of this type of home. Look under California Indians or Africa.

Give your students craft sticks and playdough and permit them to create.

Physical Education: Teach the students to play hopscotch. Lay out the hopscotch court as shown. Each player has a marker such as a stone, beanbag, shell, button, etc. The first player stands behind the starting line to toss her or his marker in square 1. Hop over square 1 to square 2 and then continue hopping to square 8, turn around, and hop back again. Pause in square 2 to pick up the marker, hop in square 1, and out. Then continue by tossing the stone in square 2. All hopping is done on one foot unless the hopscotch design is such that two squares are side-by-side. Then two feet can be placed down with one in each square. A player must always hop over any square where a maker has been placed. A player is out if the marker fails to land in the proper square, the hopper steps on a line, the hopper looses balance when bending over to pick up the marker and puts a second hand or foot down, the hopper goes into a square where a marker is, or if a player puts two feet down in a single box. The player puts the marker in the square where he or she will resume playing on the next turn, and the next player begins. Sometimes a dome-shaped "rest area" is added on one end of the hopscotch pattern where the player can rest for a second or two before hopping back through. The goal is to get to the top square with the least amount of rolls of the rock. You can allow the students to hop on both feet if balance is a problem for them. This activity can also provide review in the numbers being learned.

NOTES:

Activities in this Lesson: Bible Lesson, Language Arts, Phonics, Reading, Writing, Memory Verse, Math, Shapes, Color, Story Time, Music, Arts & Crafts, Outdoor Activity, Physical Education, Homework

Bible Reference: Genesis 1:11-13.

Bible Concept to Present: It is amazing how much we can do with just one creation, cotton!

Bible Lesson: Review the lesson from yesterday and the "Thank You, Lord" poem. When God made cotton, He knew we would use it for lots and lots of things. All of us have worn something made with cotton in our lives. Probably every day!

Illustration: *Bring in a garment made of cotton that says "Cotton" on the label. Also bring some cotton balls, enough for every student to have one, and a small piece of cotton broadcloth.* Show the students the garment made of cotton. Cotton can be used alone, or mixed with other materials. Hand out the cotton balls. Let the students try to pull strings out of the cotton balls. But God didn't give us the cotton material on a roll. People have to work very hard to make the cotton into cloth. God expects us to work for what we have. Turn the garment inside out. Show students the seams and talk about sewing cotton material together. Even the thread is made of cotton. Take the square of broadcloth and start pulling out some of the threads. Let the students pull out threads. Show them that the material is actually made of rows and rows of crossed cotton threads. They are put together in what is called "weaving."

Language Arts: Tell the "Cotton" story. Let the students act it out the second time you read it.

Cotton

People have been weaving cotton cloth for thousands of years. First, farmers plant the cotton. They go up and down the rows of soil, spreading seeds. With rain and sun, the cotton plants grow. When the cotton bushes are grown, they are covered with puffs of cotton. Workers go up and down the rows, pulling the cotton off of the bushes. It can hurt, because the cotton bushes have thorns. The farmer takes the cotton to the market in a big truck. A factory buys the cotton. In the factory, workers spin the cotton into cloth on big machines. Many different weights and colors of cotton are made. These cotton fabrics are sent to the clothing factory. There, the material is cut into pieces and sewn into garments like shirts, pants, and dresses. They are put in plastic bags and shipped away to the stores, where children go shopping with their family to buy new clothes.

Get the book *Eating the Alphabet,* by Lois Ehlert, from the library. Read to the class. Use the index of fruits and vegetables to find out where they originated. Find the country on a globe.

Phonics: Review the letter Qq.

Do the Lesson 54 Phonics worksheet. Complete the letter Qq worksheet. Notice that all of the letters of the alphabet are displayed on the page and that the letters Qq are highlighted with a background. As the students get better at letter recognition you can call out a letter and ask the students to point it out with their finger. Trace the large letter and the small letter. The students can trace the letters between the guide lines. Review the pictures and the colored first letter of the words. The students can color the letters as desired.

Reading: Dictate a description to accompany one's drawings of people, objects, events, or activities, derived from experience or imagination. Follow a simple recipe.

Writing: For these two weeks focus on having the students write the first letter of their first name freehand. During this time, write the students' names on all worksheets and papers leaving space for the first letter and make the rest dotted or something that can be traced. They should have their Name Plates to look at as they do this.

Writing Skill Builders: Keep these objectives in mind as you direct the class. Incorporate writing strokes cane and hook.

Memory Verse: This week review all of the verses learned so far. Genesis 1:1, Genesis 1:3, Genesis 1:6, Genesis 1:10, I Peter 1:24-25, and Genesis 8:22. The students might like to learn a Bible thought this week: *He gives us all things to enjoy.*

Math: Review number recognition of 10.

Review oral counting 1-10 and 10-0. Use any of the different counting visuals, songs, or rhymes.

Do the Lesson 54 Math worksheet. Count each group of items and draw a line to the correct number.

Teach verse 10 of the song "This Old Man."

This Old Man, He Played One

Verse 1
This old man, he played one, He played nick-nack on my thumb;
with a nick-nack paddy whack, give a dog a bone. This old man came rolling home.

Verse 2
This old man, he played two, He played nick-nack on my shoe;
with a nick-nack paddy whack, give a dog a bone. This old man came rolling home.

Verse 3
This old man, he played three, He played nick-nack on my on my knee;
with a nick-nack paddy whack, give a dog a bone. This old man came rolling home.

Verse 4
This old man, he played four, He played nick-nack on my door;
with a nick-nack paddy whack, give a dog a bone. This old man came rolling home.

Verse 5
This old man, he played five, He played nick-nack on my hive;
with a nick-nack paddy whack, give a dog a bone. This old man came rolling home.

Verse 6
This old man, he played six, He played nick-nack on my sticks;
with a nick-nack paddy whack, give a dog a bone. This old man came rolling home.

Verse 7
This old man, he played seven, He played nick-nack up in Heaven;
with a nick-nack paddy whack, give a dog a bone. This old man came rolling home.

Verse 8
This old man, he played eight, He played nick-nack on my gate;
with a nick-nack paddy whack, give a dog a bone. This old man came rolling home.

Verse 9
This old man, he played nine, He played nick-nack on my spine;
with a nick-nack paddy whack, give a dog a bone. This old man came rolling home.

Verse 10
This old man, he played ten, He played nick-nack once again;
with a nick-nack paddy whack, give a dog a bone. This old man came rolling home.

Shapes: Review triangles, circles, squares, and rectangles with students.

Do the Lesson 54 Shapes worksheet. Point out the circle, square, and dotted lines on the worksheet. Tell the students to cut from the circle to the square following the dotted lines as closely as is possible.

Color: Review the colors red, green, blue, black, white, yellow, brown, pink, purple, orange, and gray.

Story Time: Read a story or stories of your choice.

Music: Review "He Plants Me Like a Seed," "I Am a Tree," "Ten Brown Beavers (Math)," "The Ants Go Marching (Math)," and "My God is So Big."

Multimedia Resources: This week, listen and sing along to selections from the "Music Machine: All About Love" CD.

Arts & Crafts: *Prepare ahead – Buy some large embroidery needles, needles with a blunt tip. Also buy some different colors of yarn. Buy a yard or more of loosely woven linen.* Cut it into pieces, giving each student a large piece. Cut the yarn into long pieces. Let the students have fun. They can edge the linen with yarn stitches. They can make shapes. You will need helpers if you have a big class. Talk about cotton as they work.

Physical Education: Continue to learn to play Hopscotch. Try using different things as game pieces. Pieces of chain, coins, paper clips. See what works best.

Homework: Send Lesson 54 Homework Cotton Items worksheet home with the students. Instruct them to bring it back tomorrow. The students should have brought their eating charts back. Remind them to bring them tomorrow.

NOTES:

Lesson 55

Week 11: Day 5

Activities in this Lesson: Bible Lesson, Social Studies, Language Arts, Phonics, Reading, Writing, Memory Verse, Math, Shapes, Color, Story Time, Music, Science/Arts & Crafts, Physical Education, Homework

Bible Reference: Genesis 1:11-13.

Bible Concept to Present: God gave the plants He made for us to care for. If we do not care for them, they will become extinct.

Bible Lesson: God made our wonderful world with every kind of a plant you could ever dream about. We have beautiful flowering plants such as the orchid. We have tall grasses, short grasses, tall bushes, short bushes, tall trees, and short trees. Every kind of a plant that God made He made for us to enjoy. Plants must be cared for. We must take care of the plants God gave us. If we ruin the air that plants need, or put unnatural things in our soil the plants cannot live in it. Our plants will die and we will not have them any more. When an entire type of plant dies, it is called *extinction*. We must care for our world so that our plants do not become extinct. We want other people to enjoy what God has made, too.

Multimedia Resources: Watch the video, "Music Machine: Benny's Biggest Battle," which is a lesson in self-control.

Social Studies: God gave us the plants to enjoy, but we must take care of them. Plan a trip to a location that you know needs some yard work. This might be the school grounds or the home of an elderly friend or neighbor. Plan to spend some time pulling weeds and watering. Explain that some plants need our care. Make sure students know what area has weeds and what area doesn't have weeds. Remind them of their health lesson and instruct them to wash their hands well when they are all finished.

Language Arts: Play a concentration game with your students. Start by naming a type of fruit. Then have your student name a fruit. When it is your turn again, repeat your first choice, then the student's, then your second choice. Keep this up as long as your students can repeat all the types of fruit mentioned. Your goal is for the students to remember the list in order, going as long as possible. Start over and play again.

Give students a digital recording device and record ideas on how to care for the world which God has made, especially for the plants.

Read *Eating the Alphabet* again. Have students share which fruits and vegetables are their favorites as you read.

Phonics: Review the letters Aa-Qq.

Teach the small letter *q*. Write some words beginning with the letter *q* on the board. Include words from stories or activities that tie this lesson to other things that have already been done. Underline the small *q* that begins the words. Read through the words and point out the shape of letter *q*. Have the students trace the *q* in the air as you trace the letter *q* beginning each word.
    Common words: qualify, quality, quantity, queen, quick, quit, quite, quiver
    Vocabulary words: quarter, quiet

Do the Lesson 55 Phonics worksheet. Have the students put an orange square around the Pp letters and a blue circle around the Qq letters. Give them one direction at a time so they can focus on finding the correct letter shape. Begin with capital *P*, then lower case *p*, etc. Show them examples with flashcards or letters written on the board.

Reading: Dictate a description to accompany one's drawings of people, objects, events, or activities, derived from experience or imagination. Follow a simple recipe.

Writing: For these two weeks focus on having the students write the first letter of their first name freehand. During this time, write the students' names on all worksheets and papers leaving space for the first letter and make the rest dotted or something that can be traced. They should have their Name Plates to look at as they do this.

Writing Skill Builders: Keep these objectives in mind as you direct the class. Incorporate writing strokes cane and hook.

Memory Verse: This week review all of the verses learned so far. Genesis 1:1, Genesis 1:3, Genesis 1:6, Genesis 1:10, I Peter 1:24-25, and Genesis 8:22. Students might like to learn a Bible thought this week: *He gives us all things to enjoy.*

Math: Review number recognition of 10. Use the pattern Lesson 55 Resource page to cut out 10 shells. Have your students count the shells, and then, if capable, number them 1 - 10.

Review oral counting 1-10 and 10-0. Use any of the different counting visuals, songs, or rhymes.

Do the Lesson 55 Math worksheet. Instruct the students to trace the numbers, count each group, and then draw a line to the number for the group.

Shapes: Review triangles, circles, squares, and rectangles with students.

Color: Review the colors red, green, blue, black, white, yellow, brown, pink, purple, orange, and gray.

Story Time: Read a story or stories of your student's choice or ones they have brought from home.

Music: Review "He Plants Me Like a Seed," "I Am a Tree," "Ten Brown Beavers (Math)," "The Ants Go Marching (Math)," and "My God is So Big."

Multimedia Resources: This week, listen and sing along to selections from the "Music Machine: All About Love" CD.

Science/Arts & Crafts: Divide a sheet of paper into four parts. In each section have the students draw ways they can help to care for plants. The following can serve as ideas:

1. Keep the plant in good light.
2. Water the plant.
3. Feed the plant food that is good for the plant.
4. Put the plant in a bigger container if needed.

Physical Education: Continue to play hopscotch.

Homework: Did you have fun writing down the foods you ate? Did you find out that lots and lots of foods contain plant parts? Tell us some of the foods you ate. Let's thank God for plants and our good food that He provides.

NOTES:

Activities in this Lesson: Bible Lesson, Social Studies, Science/Language Arts, Phonics, Reading, Writing, Memory Verse, Math, Shapes, Color, Story Time, Music, Arts & Crafts, Health & Safety, Physical Education

Bible Reference: Genesis 1:14-19.

Bible Concept to Present: God made the sun.

Bible Lesson: Let's review the days of Creation that we have learned. Use the Days of Creation Numbers. Before God the Father, God the Son, and God the Holy Spirit began to create our world, all was dark. Then, on Day One of Creation, God made light. On the second day of Creation, God made the air to separate the waters that were above and below the earth. He also made clouds on the second day. On the third day, God made the dry land, the rocks, the plants and seeds for the plants to continue to make new plants. All of this happened on the third day of Creation. On the fourth day of Creation, God made something very wonderful. He made something very big. He made something very, very bright. He made something we cannot live without. Do you know what He made on Day Four of Creation? He made the Sun. Hold up the #4 Days of Creation Numbers. The Sun is a very big star in our sky. Although there are stars in the Milky Way that are brighter than our Sun, the Sun is the closest star to us. The Moon is not brighter than the Sun. The Sun is the closest, brightest star in our sky. But the Sun is also a long way away from us. If you got on a spaceship now and traveled to the Sun, you would be older than I am before you got there. The Sun is so very far away. We would not want to be any closer to the Sun than we are. If we were closer, we would burn up. And if we were further away, we would freeze. God knew He would need to put the Sun just exactly where it is now. He made the Sun to be very hot, and to be just the right distance away from us. I am so happy to have God for my Heavenly Father, for He is such a wise God.

Multimedia Resources: Listen to the songs "God's Wonderful Love" and "I Know Somebody Who Knows" from the "Bullfrogs and Butterflies: God is Great" CD. Listen to the song "Je T'aime King Of Kings" from "Sir Oliver's Song" CD.

Social Studies: The Sun does many good things for us. It is the Sun that keeps our Earth warm. We use the Sun to dry clothes and dry foods. We use the Sun to keep us warm. Man has even found a way to heat our homes with the sun. This kind of heat is called solar heat. The sun gives us our light by day. It is very important for us to have the sun, for without it we would not live. Discuss the ways we use the sun.

Science/Language Arts: People who take trips into space are called astronauts. Because people have gone up into space, we know much more about our world than your great-grandparents knew. Astronauts are a very special kind of people. They are a kind of a scientist. A scientist is someone who studies science. Astronauts study about the sun and its planets. Astronauts go up in space capsules to find out about the Sun and its planets. Let's pretend to be an astronaut now.

Note: You may make an astronaut suit from duct tape, aluminum foil, oatmeal boxes, paper bags, and construction paper. Tell students how the astronauts float about the capsule, how they have work to do inside the capsule, when it is in flight, and the type of food they would eat. The Usborne book *Rockets and Space Flight* has lots of information about astronauts. Point out the pictures of a spacesuit. Go through a countdown process, having students count down from 10 – 0, and then BLAST OFF!

Let them continue to fantasize about the trip. Encourage stories with little or no correction of false-hood at the time of the story. If you wish to correct a misunderstanding, do it after some time has passed and in such a way so that the child personally is not put in a derogatory position.

Phonics: Teach the letter Rr.

Show the students the letter Rr flashcard. Point out any student's name beginning with the letter *R*. Write some words beginning with the letter *R* on the board. Include any student names from the class that begin with letter *R*. Underline the capital *R* that begins the words. Read through the words and point out the shape of letter *R*. Have the students trace the *R* in the air as you trace the letter *R* beginning each name.

> Boys: Rafael, Randy, Raul, Raymond, Ricardo, Richard, Ricky, Riley, Robert, Roberto, Rodney, Ronald, Ruben, Russell, Ryan
>
> Girls: Rachael, Rachel, Raven, Rebecca, Rebekah, Renee, Rosa

Do the Lesson 56 Phonics worksheet. Complete the letter Rr worksheet. Have the students trace the letters Rr with their fingers. They should trace the letters with their fingers and say the names of the letters. Demonstrate the proper strokes for them on the board. Say the words for each of the pictures and look at the Rr letters that begin them.

Reading: Dictate a description to accompany one's drawings of people, objects, events, or activities, derived from experience or imagination. Follow a simple recipe.

Multimedia Resources: View the Aa-Rr segments of "Rev-Up for Reading" from the "Rev-Up for Learning" DVD to drill letter recognition and sound. The students should say each letter sound along with the presentation.

Writing: For these two weeks focus on having the students write the first letter of their first name freehand. During this time, write the students' names on all worksheets and papers leaving space for the first letter and make the rest dotted or something that can be traced. They should have their Name Plates to look at as they do this.

Writing Skill Builders: Keep these objectives in mind as you direct the class. Incorporate writing strokes cane and hook.

Multimedia Resources: View the Aa-Rr segments of "Rev-Up for Writing" from the "Rev-Up for Learning" DVD to review the writing of upper- and lowercase letters. The students should write each letter in the air along with the presentation. Since the first half of the presentation covers lowercase letters and the second half uppercase letters some navigation will be needed to skip to the letters that are covered in this lesson.

Memory Verse: Genesis 1:16a.

God made two great lights-the greater light to govern the day... Genesis 1:16a NIV

And God made two great lights; the greater light to rule the day... Genesis 1:16a KJV

One of the most interesting facts about Creation is that God made light on the first day but didn't make the Sun until the fourth day. Cut a circle out of yellow construction paper. Print the words of the verse on individual strips of white paper. Let the students help glue the circle onto a big piece of blue construction paper. Then glue the strips around the circle, in order, like rays of the Sun. Read the verse strips together, pointing to each word. Pass out Memory Verse Card 7 for the students to take home. Explain that you will be learning more of this verse in weeks to come. Save the Sun for a later time.

Math: Review number recognition of 10. Review the counting of numbers 1-10 for this entire week. If your students are capable, you may play a game of hide and seek with the numbers. Place 10 numbers down on the table in order. Have a student look at the numbers. Tell the students to cover theri eyes before you remove a number. Have the student guess which number you removed.

Review oral counting 1-10 and 10-0. Use any of the different counting visuals, songs, or rhymes.

Do the Lesson 56 Math worksheet. Instruct the students to begin at the left and color the correct number of squares in each strip. Review colors by telling them a color to use for each strip. Demonstrate how to do this on the board if the students need the help.

Multimedia Resources: View "Rev-Up for Arithmetic" from the "Rev-Up for Learning" DVD to practice number recognition and counting 1-10.

Shapes: Review triangles, circles, squares, and rectangles with the students.

Do the Lesson 56 Shapes worksheet. Count the triangles and the rectangles. Count the triangles and rectangles altogether. Trace the triangles and rectangles on the dotted lines. Color the shapes. Cut out the shapes and paste them on another sheet of paper to make the sailboat.

Color: Review the colors red, green, blue, black, white, yellow, brown, pink, purple, orange, and gray.

Story Time: Read a story or stories of your choice.

Music: Review "He Plants Me Like a Seed," "I Am a Tree," "Ten Brown Beavers" (Math) and "The Ants Go Marching" (Math). Learn the "Countdown" song on the "Horizons Preschool Music" CD.

Multimedia Resources: This week, listen and sing along to selections from the "Bullfrogs and Butterflies: God Loves Fun" CD.

Arts & Crafts: Give your students clay (may be purchased clay, but should be yellow and be able to dry in the sun) and have them fashion a Sun similar to one you have made as a sample. After making the suns, place them in the sun to dry. This will give you a chance to discuss the drying power of the sun.

Health & Safety: We use many foods that are dried by the sun. Some of them are included on trips that astronauts take. Breakfast bars contain dried grains and are high in protein. They have been taken into space for food. Purchase breakfast bars or a bar that is similar. Also purchase a bag of dried fruit. Provide one bar and one piece of fruit per student. Discuss the texture of the bar. How does dried food taste? How is the fruit different from fresh fruit?

Physical Education: Astronauts need to be in good shape physically to be able to go into space. We need to be in good shape, too. Astronauts have to do exercises to help them stay in good physical shape. Choose an exercise of your choice and spend a period of time today working on being in good physical shape.

NOTES:

Activities in this Lesson: Bible Lesson, Language Arts, Phonics, Reading, Writing, Memory Verse, Math, Shapes, Color, Story Time, Music, Arts & Crafts, Science/Outdoor Activity, Health & Safety/Science, Physical Education, Homework

Bible Reference: Genesis 1:14-19.

Bible Concept to Present: The Sun is part of our life every day.

Bible Lesson: Review the introduction of day four of Creation. The Sun that God made not only provides light, it provides heat. Explain to the students that our air around the Earth helps protect us from the Sun's heat. Without the layers of air, it would be much to hot on Earth. Even though we can't see the air, there are layers and layers of air that go way, way up into the sky. The Sun's rays have to shine down through the air layers.

Multimedia Resources: Listen to the song "God Is So Big" from the "Music Machine: The Majesty of God" CD.

Illustration: Put a large flashlight in the center of the room, facing the ceiling. Turn out the lights. Explain that we are pretending that the flashlight is the Sun and the students are the Earth. Let the students spin as they walk around the flashlight in a big circle. Talk about the Earth spinning around the Sun. Try to help them understand the light of the Sun moving over the earth.

Language Arts: Let's play a rhyming game again today. Help me finish these sentences with a word that rhymes with "sun."

> I usually eat my hot dog on a _____ . BUN
> The kid that wins the race can yell, "I _____ ." WON
> It's nice to finish all my work and say, "I'm _____ ." DONE
> I love the things we do in school because they're _____ . FUN
> When the sun is shining, I like to make my legs move fast and _____ . RUN

Phonics: Review the letter Rr.

Reading: Dictate a description to accompany one's drawings of people, objects, events, or activities, derived from experience or imagination. Follow a simple recipe.

Writing: For these two weeks focus on having the students write the first letter of their first name freehand. During this time, write the students' names on all worksheets and papers leaving space for the first letter and make the rest dotted or something that can be traced. They should have their Name Plates to look at as they do this.

Writing Skill Builders: Keep these objectives in mind as you direct the class. Incorporate writing strokes cane and hook.

Memory Verse: Review Genesis 1:16a. Use the crafr (Sun with verse) you made yesterday in Lesson 56 to review the memory verse. Explain that this is really half of the verse, and that students will be learning the rest of the verse later in the month. Make sure that the children understand that the Sun is "...the greater light...."

Math: Review number recognition of 10.

Review oral counting 1-10 and 10-0. Use any of the different counting visuals, songs, or rhymes.

Do the Lesson 57 Math worksheet. Count the dots on each of the tiles and match it to the correct number.

Shapes: Review triangles, circles, squares, and rectangles with students.

Color: Review the colors red, green, blue, black, white, yellow, brown, pink, purple, orange, and gray.

Story Time: Read a story or stories of your choice.

Music: Review "Countdown." Learn "What's the Weather." This is something that you can sing everyday with your class. Select a different student to be the "weatherman" each day. After singing their name in the song they should go outside to "check" the weather for the class. When the song is done have the "weatherman" report on the weather. Verse 1 or the entire song could be repeated until the "weatherman" gets back.

What's The Weather?
Tune of Clementine

Verse 1
What's the weather?
What's the weather?
What's the weather like today?
Tell us (child's name),
What's the weather?
What's the weather like today?

Verse 2
Is it sunny? (hold arms above head in a circle)
Is it cloudy? (cover eyes with hands)
Is it rainy out today? (flutter fingers downward)
Is it snowy? (wrap arms around body and shiver)
Is it windy? ("blow children over" with a swoop of your arms)
What's the weather like today?

Multimedia Resources: This week, listen and sing along to selections from the "Bullfrogs and Butterflies: God Loves Fun" CD.

Arts & Crafts: *Bring gold glitter and popsicle sticks to class.* Instruct the students to draw a circle on a piece of pale blue construction paper. Have them spread some glue on their circle using popsicle sticks. Give them a bit of gold glitter in the middle of their circle. Instruct them to spread the glitter all around the circle making their own glittering Sun. Carefully set the Sun art on the floor. Bring out the little individual flashlights for each student. Let them shine the lights on their Sun picture.

Science/Outdoor Activity: The Sun makes our weather. Weather happens all the time. Our weather can be so different every day: cold or hot, windy or calm, rainy or dry. Sometimes, we don't even pay attention to our weather, yet it is affecting our lives. Sometimes, the weather can get really bad and we have a storm. The Sun and its heat play a big part in making our weather. Let's go outside and see what the weather is like today.

Health & Safety/Science: *Prepare ahead – Needed: one inexpensive wood frame, as used for art canvas; one yard cheesecloth, cut in half; aluminum foil; twine; two pieces of 4 x 4 lumber; bananas.* Put this project together in the classroom, with students watching. Tell them you are going to dry some fruit in the sun. This is a way to preserve fruit for a long time, for hiking trips or vacations, or just for snacks. Cover the frame with half of the piece of cheesecloth. Staple the cheesecloth to the edges of the frame. Wrap some twine around the frame, corner to corner as shown. This will give some strength to the cheesecloth. Peel and slice the bananas into 1/4 inch slices. Carefully lay the bananas on the cheesecloth. Gently lay the other piece of cheesecloth over the bananas. Find a place in the bright sun where you can prop the frame up on the 4 x 4's. Air needs to circulate around the frame. Cover the ground or concrete with foil. At the end of class, bring the frame inside. Turn each banana slice over. Put the solar dryer outside every day for several days, until the bananas are brittle. Plan to serve them as a snack on the fourth day with honey. (It might be wise to spray the ground first with bug spray the day before this activity.)

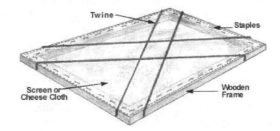

Physical Education: Choose another exercise or several exercises of your choice and spend a period of time today working on being in good physical shape.

Homework: Instruct students to take home Lesson 57 Homework worksheet. They will watch the weather for a month, filling in the squares with a sun, clouds, or some rain.

NOTES:

Lesson 58

Week 12: Day 3

Activities in this Lesson: Bible Lesson, Social Studies, Science, Language Arts, Phonics, Reading, Writing, Memory Verse, Math, Shapes, Color, Story Time, Music, Arts & Crafts, Physical Education

Bible Reference: Genesis 1:14-19.

Bible Concept to Present: The Sun, which God made on the Fourth Day, gives us our daytime.

Bible Lesson: When God made the Sun, He made it to be very bright. He also made it for a very specific reason. The Bible says that God made the Sun to be the closest, brightest light to make our day. Is it daytime now? Yes, it is. And it is daytime because the Sun is in the sky. When we no longer see the Sun, it is not daytime, but nighttime. In times long ago, man thought that the Sun ran across the sky each day. We know now that is not true. The Sun does not move across the Earth each day, we do. That's right. Our Earth spins. Let's get the globe, and I will show you how this happens, and how we get daytime. Using a flashlight to pretend it is the Sun, let's see where the light is. My finger is now on the place where we live, and the light or the Sun is shining on us. Now let's slowly turn the globe and see what happens with our light. Oh! Look! The light is no longer on where we live. It is now away from us. Where we live would now be dark or night time. Isn't it wonderful how God made our world to turn so that it gives everyone a chance to have daytime? It always takes the same amount of time for our Earth to spin, so our time is always the same. Our days always have 24 bits of time in them. We call those bits of time, hours. I am happy God made the hours of our day and the Sun to give us daytime.

Multimedia Resources: Listen to the song "Tick Tock" from "The Amazing Miracles" CD.

Social Studies: The Sun makes it possible to have daytime. We need the daytime for several reasons. Would you like to have nighttime all the time? I wouldn't. On sheets of paper draw some of the things you do in daytime. Label the drawings as students tell you about each one.

Science: We measure our time by how long it takes our Earth to spin around once. While we are spinning around, the Sun shines on different parts of the Earth. We call the time the Sun is above us, shedding its light on us daytime. We call the time the Sun is away from us nighttime. We divide time up into segments. We call the biggest segment of time in a day, an hour. An hour is divided up into minutes, and a minute is divided up into seconds. All of this time depends on the Sun and how long it takes our Earth to spin.

Language Arts: Do this action rhyme:

Stars

Over there the Sun gets up (extend arm horizontally, to the east if possible)
And marches all the day (raise arm slowly)
And noon, it stands right overhead (point straight up)
At night, it goes away. (lower arm slowly and drop down to west if possible)

Phonics: Review the letters Aa-Rr.

Teach the small letter *r*. Write some words beginning with the letter *r* on the board. Include words from stories or activities that tie this lesson to other things that have already been done. Underline the small *r* that begins the words. Read through the words and point out the shape of letter *r*. Have the students trace the *r* in the air as you trace the letter *r* beginning each word.
    Common words: read, real, right, round, run
    Vocabulary words: rectangle, red, river, roots

Reading: Dictate a description to accompany one's drawings of people, objects, events, or activities, derived from experience or imagination. Follow a simple recipe.

Writing: For these two weeks focus on having the students write the first letter of their first name freehand. During this time, write the students' names on all worksheets and papers leaving space for the first letter and make the rest dotted or something that can be traced. They should have their Name Plates to look at as they do this.

Writing Skill Builders: Keep these objectives in mind as you direct the class. Incorporate writing strokes cane and hook.

Memory Verse: Review Genesis 1:16a. Use the craft (Sun with verse) you made in Lesson 56 to review the memory verse. Explain that this is really half of the verse, and that students will be learning the rest of the verse later in the month. Make sure that the children understand that the sun is "...the greater light...."

Math: Teach oral counting 1-20. Review number recognition of 10. Continue to review numbers 1-10. Play the hide and seek game again today.

Teach oral counting 11-20. As a visual you may want to add cars to the Counting Train or you can simply use beads on a string or wire, or an abacus. The focus is not on number recognition but on oral counting.

Review oral counting 1-10 and 10-0. Use any of the different counting visuals, songs, or rhymes.

Do the Lesson 58 Math worksheet. Follow the Snake Path by coloring the correct number of steps. Do the worksheet together as a class by saying the color and how many steps need to be colored. How many students made it to the finish line?

Teach the students to recognize and be aware when it is daytime and when it is nighttime. Classify things that occur during the daytime and during the nighttime. Perhaps you will wish to cut from magazines or draw things that you do in daytime and nighttime. You may wish to have your students separate these and place those things that occur in daytime on a yellow sheet of paper that represents the Sun. Place the night time activities on a black piece of paper to represent the night.

Shapes: Teach the star shape. Look at the stars in the American flag. Many other countries also have stars on their flags. Search for flags of the world on the internet or in other resource materials for examples to show the students. Color either the flag of Chile or the flag Panama and review the shapes and colors in the flags.

Do the Lesson 58 Shapes worksheet. Have the students trace the star. Color the flag of Chili like the sample.

Color: Review the colors red, green, blue, black, white, yellow, brown, pink, purple, orange, and gray.

Story Time: Read a story or stories of your choice.

Music: Continue with "Countdown." Continue "What's the Weather."

Multimedia Resources: This week, listen and sing along to selections from the "Bullfrogs and Butterflies: God Loves Fun" CD.

Arts & Crafts: *Using construction paper cut out some basic shapes of things you do at certain times.* A suggestion would be: breakfast at 7, playtime at 9, lunch at 12, dinner at 5, bedtime at 8. Use shapes of a bowl and spoon for breakfast, balls and blocks for playtime, a plate or sandwich for lunch, a plate for dinner, and a bed for bedtime. Place them in a time line as to when you do these things. Then scramble them. Let the students place them back into order. An older child may place the time notation beside the activity suggested. Use these shapes again for tomorrow's lesson.

Physical Education: Take a walk today and time yourself. Walk a block at a regular pace and record the time it takes you to walk that distance. Then try to beat your time on following walks.

Homework: Remind the students to keep working on their Lesson 57 Homework worksheet where they record the weather each morning by drawing a sun, clouds, or rain.

NOTES:

Activities in this Lesson: Bible Lesson, Outdoor Activity, Social Studies, Science, Language Arts, Phonics, Reading, Writing, Memory Verse, Math, Shapes, Color, Story Time, Music, Arts & Crafts, Physical Education

Bible Reference: Genesis 1:14-19.

Bible Concept to Present: God keeps all of His Creation running smoothly and precisely.

Bible Lesson: Review yesterday's lesson. Isn't it amazing that God keeps the Earth spinning around the Sun at the same speed, year after year after year? Years and years ago, before electricity or batteries, people used the Sun to help them tell the time and the seasons. Remember when we studied shadows? And we learned that the shadow of the Sun can tell us the time? What if we look outside and see very short shadows? We know it is around noon. What if we see very long shadows? We know it is early morning or late afternoon.

Multimedia Resources: Listen to the songs "I Will Praise You Lord" from the "Bullfrogs and Butterflies: God is Great" CD and "Today Is My Favorite Day" from the "Bullfrogs and Butterflies: God Loves Fun" CD.

Outdoor Activity: Let's go outside and see how long our shadow is. Will my shadow be longer than yours?

Social Studies: Help students understand how long an hour is. Bring in a small timer. Set the timer for one hour. Let the timer go off. Talk about how long the hour was. Then set it again. Reset the alarm throughout the day, always talking about how long the hour was and what students did in the hour of time.

You may have to do most of this project, as it is too hard for the children to do completely on their own. Make each student a clock. Use the Lesson 59 Time worksheet. Cut on the dotted line. Cut out the clock hands. If desired, glue the pattern to card stock to make a sturdier clock. Poke a little hole in the clock and the two hands with a pencil. Using a brad, attach the clock little/short hand to the clock. Save the big/longer hands for later. Give one to each student. Let them move the hands. Show them how the clock works for the hour times.

Multimedia Resources: Listen to the song "Tick Tock" from the "The Amazing Miracles" CD.

Science: *Prepare ahead – Bring a shallow metal pan, a shallow glass pan, and have water available.* Say, The sun's rays contain lots of energy. Energy is important. Energy is light, heat, sound, motion, growth, and electricity. Do you think we can use the sun's energy? Yes, we can. The sun's energy, called Solar Energy, is used to heat homes, heat water, and cook. We are going to see if we can trap some of the sun's energy. Take the two pans outside and fill them with an inch of cool water. Set them on a level surface out in the sun. Let the students feel the temperature of the water. Back in the classroom, check the time. Plan to go back outside in several hours. Let the students feel the water temperature and note it is hot, containing the sun's heat energy. Did the kind of pan make a difference? Go to a tree or rock in the area. Feel the side of the tree facing the sun. Then feel the side of the tree away from the sun.

"Energy is the ability to do work. It can come in the forms of heat and light. There are two types of energy: working energy and stored energy. Stored energy becomes working energy when we use it."
http://www.eere.energy.gov/erec/factsheets/savenrgy.html

Language Arts: Instruct students to look around the room. How many things can you see that use energy? Do an energy search around the school or home. Write the items on the board. Repeat the words and follow with your finger so that students can see the words.

Do this action rhyme.

Mister Sun

Oh Mister Sun, Sun, Mister golden Sun (arms circle overhead)
    Please shine down on me (flutter fingers down)
Oh Mister Sun, Sun, Mister golden Sun (arms circle overhead)
    Hiding behind a tree (cover eyes)
These little children are asking you (tap fingers on chest)
    To please come out so we can play with you (wave hand "come")
Oh Mister Sun, Sun, Mister golden Sun (arms circle overhead)
    Please shine down on me. (flutter fingers downward)
                    Author Unknown

Review the "Stars" action rhyme from Lesson 58.

Phonics: Review the letters Aa-Rr.

Do the Lesson 59 Phonics worksheet. Complete the letter Rr worksheet. Notice that all of the letters of the alphabet are displayed on the page and that the letters Rr are highlighted with a background. As the students get better at letter recognition you can call out a letter and ask the students to point it out with their finger. Trace the large letter and the small letter. The students can trace the letters between the guide lines. Review the pictures and the colored first letter of the words. The students can color the letters as desired.

Reading: Dictate a description to accompany one's drawings of people, objects, events, or activities, derived from experience or imagination. Follow a simple recipe.

Writing: For these two weeks focus on having the students write the first letter of their first name freehand. During this time, write the students' names on all worksheets and papers leaving space for the first letter and make the rest dotted or something that can be traced. They should have their Name Plates to look at as they do this.

Writing Skill Builders: Keep these objectives in mind as you direct the class. Incorporate writing strokes cane and hook.

Memory Verse: Continue to work on Genesis 1:16a. *Write the words of the verse on rectangles of paper.* Let the students arrange the words in the correct order, helping them to read.

Math: Review number recognition of 10. Play a game called "Guess that Number" with your students. On a chalkboard, begin to write a number, but stop part way through. See if a student can guess what number you are writing. Complete numbers 1-10 in a mixed up order. Your objective is that the students be able to recognize the formation of the number and the number name.

Review oral counting 1-20 and 10-0. Use any of the different counting visuals, songs, or rhymes.

Do the Lesson 59 Math worksheet. Count the dots on each of the tiles and match it to the correct number.

Shapes: Review the star shape. Give each student a round cracker, a square saltine, a triangle corn chip, a rectangle wafer cookie, and a star shaped marshmallow. Talk about these shapes that we see everyday. Ask the following questions and have the students hold up the correct shape to answer the question. After answering the questions the students may eat their shapes.

> What shape is round? (circle)
> What shape has 0 corners? (circle)
> What shape has three corners? (triangle)
> What shape has four sides that look different? (rectangle)
> What shape has curved edges? (circle)
> What shape has four sides that are all the same? (square)
> What shape has five corners? (star)
> What shape has 3 sides? (triangle)
> What shapes have 4 corners? (square, rectangle)

Do the Lesson 59 Shapes worksheet. Have the students trace the circle. All of the letters in the word *circle* have been covered. Point out the letter *r* in the word *circle*. Have the students trace the letters in the word *circle*.

Color: Review the colors red, green, blue, black, white, yellow, brown, pink, purple, orange, and gray.

Story Time: Read a story or stories of your choice.

Music: Continue with "Countdown." Continue "What's the Weather."

Multimedia Resources: This week, listen and sing along to selections from the "Bullfrogs and Butterflies: God Loves Fun" CD.

Arts & Crafts: Bring out the shapes of things that are done at specific times during the day from yesterday. Let the students practice putting the shapes in the correct order. When they can do it well, time them. Help them to understand how long a minute is and that there are sixty minutes in an hour.

Physical Education: Repeat the block walk taken yesterday and time yourself. Try to beat your time.

NOTES:

Lesson 60

Activities in this Lesson: Bible Lesson, Social Studies, Science/Language Arts/Physical Education, Phonics, Reading, Writing, Memory Verse, Math, Shapes, Color, Story Time

Bible Reference: Genesis 1: 14-19.

Bible Concept to Present: The Sun which God made helps us to have seasons.

Bible Lesson: When God made our Sun and Earth, He made them so that the Earth spins around. We talked about this when we were learning about how we get our daytime. Will you show me now how the Earth gets its daytime? You may use the globe for the Earth and the flashlight for the Sun.

Note: You want your child to be able to recall that the Earth spins around and around and that the Sun stays in one position. It is the spinning of the Earth that brings our days.

Now I want to tell you another wonderful fact about our Earth and Sun. Our Earth not only spins around and around, it also moves around the Sun like this. (Take the globe and move it in a circle around the flashlight. The diagram on Lesson 60 Resource page will also help you to explain this to your students.) The Earth's relationship to the Sun determines our seasons. It is so wonderful that God gives us a change in season. I would not like it if it were always winter. We would get so tired of the cold. And if it were always summer, it would be so hot and we would be tired of the hot weather. I am glad God gave us a change in seasons. Aren't you?

Social Studies: Our seasons are very important to us. They are important for our plants. Many plants need the cold to help them produce seeds. The seasons are important to animals too, because many animals sleep all winter long. If there were not a winter time they would get very tired! (Name an animal that hibernates.) Each season is important to us. Briefly discuss with students the four seasons. We will be studying each season in depth during the coming weeks. We suggest you use this time now to begin preparing students for the study to come. Discuss what season it is now and that there is more than one season.

Science/Language Arts/Physical Education: You may take this time to go into detail as to how the seasons come to be. For instance, following a study of the illustration on Lesson 60 Resource page, you could set up an area for Season Play. Mark a large circle on the floor (A driveway will work nicely for this.) Place an X on the four stopping points of the Earth for each season. You may pretend to be the Sun, and let a student be the Earth. Let them walk around the circle. When they come to an X on the circle, they may then pretend to be the season. For example, where summer would be, wave hand as if to fan and pretend to be summer. On winter, a shiver would do. In fall, pretend to play with leaves. In spring, sounds like a bird. Repeat this several times. You may also make this a game if you have enough children. Let the children walk around the circle with music playing until the music stops. Then whatever X they are on, they must tell you by pantomime the season that they are on.

Do the Lesson 60 Language Arts worksheet. Identify the items on the worksheet. Talk about what season they belong to. Have the students trace the lines to match the items for the same season.

Phonics: Teach the letter Ss.

Show the students the letter Ss flashcard. Point out any student's name beginning with the letter *S*. Write some words beginning with the letter *S* on the board. Include any student names from the class that begin with letter *S*. Underline the capital *S* that begins the words. Read through the words and point out the shape of letter *S*. Have the students trace the *S* in the air as you trace the letter *S* beginning each name.

Boys: Samuel, Scott, Sean, Sebastian, Sergio, Seth, Shane, Shawn, Skyler, Spencer, Stephen, Steven
Girls: Sabrina, Samantha, Sandra, Sara, Sarah, Savannah, Selena, Shannon, Shelby, Sierra, Sophia, Stephanie, Summer, Susan, Sydney
Vocabulary words: Saturday, September, STOP, Sunday

Do the Lesson 60 Phonics worksheet. Complete the letter Ss worksheet. Have the students trace the letters Ss with their fingers. They should trace the letters with their fingers and say the names of the letters. Demonstrate the proper strokes for them on the board. Say the words for each of the pictures and look at the Ss letters that begin them.

Reading: Dictate a description to accompany one's drawings of people, objects, events, or activities, derived from experience or imagination. Follow a simple recipe.

Writing: For these two weeks focus on having the students write the first letter of their first name freehand. During this time, write the students' names on all worksheets and papers leaving space for the first letter and make the rest dotted or something that can be traced. They should have their Name Plates to look at as they do this.

Writing Skill Builders: Keep these objectives in mind as you direct the class. Incorporate writing strokes cane and hook.

Memory Verse: Finish memory work on Genesis 1:16a today. Let those students recite that want to do so.

Math: Review number recognition of 10. Play a game called *Guess that Number* with your students. On a chalkboard, begin to write a number, but stop part way through. See if a student can guess what number you are writing. Complete numbers 1-10 in a mixed up order. Your objective is that the students be able to recognize the formation of the number and the number name.

Review oral counting 1-20 and 10-0. Use any of the different counting visuals, songs, or rhymes.

Do the Lesson 60 Math worksheet. Count the dots on each of the tiles and trace the number.

Continue to classify things according to time. You may also begin to teach the months of the year.

A little song will do this nicely. Using the tune to "Old MacDonald Had A Farm," sing the following words:

Months of the Year
Tune of "Old McDonald Had A Farm"

There are twelve months in our year
E I E I O
January is the first
E I E I O
Then February, March,
April, May,
June, July,
August, September,
October, November,
E I E I O
And then comes the last
Our favorite of all is
De-cem-ber
Yes, December
E I E I O

Shapes: Review the star shape. Look for star shaped objects in the classroom.

Color: Review the colors red, green, blue, black, white, yellow, brown, pink, purple, orange, and gray.

Story Time: Read a story or stories of your student's choice or ones they have brought from home.

Music: Review "What's the Weather" and "Countdown." Begin to teach your students the hymn "Great Is Thy Faithfulness" on the "Horizons Preschool Music" CD.

Multimedia Resources: This week, listen and sing-along to selections from "Bullfrogs and Butterflies: God Loves Fun" CD.

Homework: Remind the students to keep working on their Lesson 57 Homework worksheet where they record the weather each morning by drawing a sun, clouds, or rain.

NOTES:

Activities in this Lesson: Bible Lesson, Social Studies, Science, Language Arts, Phonics, Reading, Writing, Memory Verse, Math, Shapes, Color, Story Time, Music, Arts & Crafts, Health & Safety, Physical Education

Bible Reference: Genesis 1:14-19.

Bible Concept to Present: When God made the Sun, He also gave us the season of summer.

Bible Lesson: God is so good to us to give us the Sun and the seasons. Yesterday we talked about how God made it so the Sun can help us have seasons. Today we want to talk about the season of summer. There are twelve months in the year. The months of June, July and August are the season of summer. This is actually a time of year when we are furthest from the Sun. We are closest in January and furthest in July. But the Earth has a tilt to it, so the part of the Earth that tilts toward the Sun has summer. It is the time of the year when our Earth is the hottest. The summertime is a wonderful time for plants, animals and people. The summer helps plants to grow big and tall, and many plants give their fruit during the summer. We enjoy the summer in many ways. The summer is a time to swim and play in the sprinklers. It is a time to plant gardens and work outdoors in the yard. Summer is a wonderful gift from God.

Social Studies: Summer is such a wonderful time. In the summer we do many things outdoors. We do not need coats in the summer. It is much too hot. Make a calendar display of the 12 months of the year. On separate sheets of paper, print the month of the year, and let the students add the symbol. You may need to draw the symbol in or make it on construction paper. In this lesson you will make symbols for the summer months. In future lessons you will make symbols for the other months. The students may make a symbol to represent each month of summer.

This is a list of the symbols suggested for summer:

    June - June 14 is Flag Day. Make a drawing of a flag.
    July - July 4th is Independence Day. Make a drawing of firecrackers.
          Glitter may be added for the fire.
August - The "growing " plant that you make as suggested in the following Observation Project
          can be the symbol for August, since in August many plants are growing very fast.

Science: Summer is when our part of the Earth, the United States, is tilted toward the Sun. Use the Lesson 60 Resource sheet to illustrate this. The heat from the Sun affects our Earth in many ways. For example, the heat from the Sun makes the plants dry up faster and you must water them more often. It also makes the plants grow faster than any other time of the year. By following the description in the craft, make the plant "grow."

Language Arts: Play a game called Pass The Sun. Use a yellow tennis ball or a circle of yellow paper to represent the Sun. Pass the "Sun" very quickly from one person to another. This will indicate the reaction time of your student. If they are extremely slow at this, continue to play it for a few days until you see an improvement in motor control.

Do this action rhyme.

Beach Poem

Ocean breeze blowing, (wave hands from one side to the other)
Feet kick and splash, (kick feet)
Ocean waves breaking (smack fist into open hand)
On rocks with a crash. (smack fist into open hand)
Boys finding sea shells, (bend over, pretend to pick up shells)
Girls sifting sand, (pretend to dig in sand with hands)
Friends building castles (make shapes with hands)
As high as they can. (reach high with one hand on tip-toe)
I stretch my arms out (stretch arms to sides)
Far as they'll reach. (stretch arms to sides)
Oh, my what fun (jump with glee)
On this day at the beach. (jump with glee)

Do the Lesson 61 Language Arts worksheet. Identify the clothes for the children on the worksheet. Talk about clothes that are worn in the summer and why they are worn during that time of the year. Have the students draw a circle around the clothes that are worn in the summer. This activity can be supplemented with paper doll patterns that can be printed from the internet or obtained from other sources. Have the students cut out the paper dolls and dress them with clothes appropriate for the summer season.

Phonics: Review the letter Ss.

Teach the small letter *s*. Write some words beginning with the letter *s* on the board. Include words from stories or activities that tie this lesson to other things that have already been done. Underline the small *s* that begins the words. Read through the words and point out the shape of letter *s*. Have the students trace the *s* in the air as you trace the letter *s* beginning each word.

Common words: said, same, saw, say, school, sea, see, self, sentence, set, she, should, show, side, small, so, some, sound, spell, stand, start, state, still, story, study, such, sun
Vocabulary words: salty, same, schedule, second, seed, seven, seventeen, seventh, short, shorter, shortest, shoulder, six, sixteen, sixth, slow, smaller, smallest, smell, soft, some, sometimes, sorry, sour, square, star, stem, stomach, stop, subtraction, sweet

Reading: Associate spoken and written language by matching written word labels with spoken words. Segment a spoken sentence into separate, distinct words. Point to words as distinct units on a page of print.

Multimedia Resources: View the Aa-Ss segments of "Rev-Up for Reading" from the "Rev-Up for Learning" DVD to drill letter recognition and sound. The students should say each letter sound along with the presentation.

Writing: For these two weeks focus on having the students write the first two letters of their first name freehand. During this time, write the students' names on all worksheets and papers leaving space for the first two letters and make the rest dotted or something that can be traced. They should have their Name Plates to look at as they do this.

Writing Skill Builders: Keep these objectives in mind as you direct the class. Incorporate writing strokes bowl, bridge, and diagonal lines.

Multimedia Resources: View the Aa-Ss segments of "Rev-Up for Writing" from the "Rev-Up for Learning" DVD to review the writing of upper- and lowercase letters. The students should write each letter in the air along with the presentation. Since the first half of the presentation covers lowercase letters and the second half uppercase letters some navigation will be needed to skip to the letters that are covered in this lesson.

Memory Verse: Psalm 90:12

Teach us to number our days aright, that we may gain a heart of wisdom.
Psalm 90:12 NIV

So teach us to number our days, that we may apply our hearts unto wisdom.
Psalm 90:12 KJV

Introduce this week's memory verse. Explain any words that the students don't know well. Talk about God's wisdom. Our goal should be to gain a heart of wisdom, no matter how old we are. Pass out Memory Verse Card 8 for the students to take home.

Math: Review number recognition of 10. Review oral counting 1-20 and 10-0.

Do the Lesson 61 Math worksheet. Count the items one group at a time together with the students. After counting the items have them draw the line to the number.

Continue to learn the names of the months.

Multimedia Resources: View "Rev-Up for Arithmetic" from the "Rev-Up for Learning" DVD to practice number recognition and counting 1-20.

Shapes: Review the star shape. Give examples of places where stars are seen on toys or clothing.

Do the Lesson 61 Shapes worksheet. This is a color by number worksheet. Give the students a number and the corresponding color. Allow enough time for them to complete each color.

Color: Review the colors red, green, blue, black, white, yellow, brown, pink, purple, orange, and gray.

Story Time: Read a story or stories of your choice.

Music: Review "Months of the Year (Math)," "Great Is Thy Faithfulness," "What's the Weather," and "Countdown."

Multimedia Resources: This week, listen and sing along to selections from "The Birthday Party" CD. This week, watch *The Kingdom Under the Sea* adventure "The Gift," which is a Christmas story.

Arts & Crafts: Make a plant grow in summer. Take a piece of 5 1/2 x 8 1/2 green construction paper. Roll it semi-tightly into a tube, rolling so that you are at an angle. Tape the sides of the tube at the bottom, being careful not to wrap the tape around the thicknesses of the tube. Make a fringe at the top of the tube by cutting the layers of paper. Now pull from the inside the layers of paper. They should pull upward and form a spiral with the fringes on the top of each piece. It should look similar to a palm tree.

Make a summer scene. Glue actual sand to the bottom of a piece of paper with blue construction paper at the top. You may wish to add Saran™ wrap over the blue paper for a look of water. Glue securely all edges. On the sand, add an umbrella on a toothpick for a sun shade, a piece of terry cloth or old towel for a towel, and if desired a chenille wire man for the beach-goer.

SECOND CHOICE: Use the Lesson 61 Resource page. Make four copies on light colored paper. Attach the four copies to one sheet of poster board. Label the four trees: Spring, Summer, Fall, and Winter. Give the students paper in greens, yellows, oranges, and tans. Instruct them to cut out small leaves, letting them be creative. Let the students help you add leaves in appropriate colors to the seasonal trees.

Health & Safety: Summer is a fun time but we must be careful to remain healthy in the summer months. The sun is very powerful and can burn our skin. We need to protect our skin with lotion before going out into the sun for long periods of time. We also must never look directly at the Sun. It would hurt our eyes very badly. Sunglasses help to protect our eyes from the sun.

Physical Education: What is a favorite summer activity? Let the students decide what it is and then imitate it for your physical movement today. For example, for swimming, pretend to swim across the pool and back.

NOTES:

Activities in this Lesson: Bible Lesson, Language Arts, Phonics, Reading, Writing, Memory Verse, Math, Shapes, Color, Story Time, Music, Arts & Crafts, Physical Education, Homework, Catch Up

Bible Reference: Genesis 1:14-19.

Bible Concept to Present: We need to be continually thankful for all that God made.

Bible Lesson: Continue to emphasize the facts of Creation. God made the Sun on the fourth day. The Sun is always in our sky, comes up on schedule, and sets on schedule. We can take it for granted sometimes. Explain what "taking for granted" means. Our memory verse reminds us to be careful how we spend our days. The wisdom and faith we have is our gift to God. It is exciting to learn about His Creation.

Multimedia Resources: Watch "Thankfulness" from the *Character Builders Video Series*.

Language Arts: Repeat the "Beach Poem" about the beach from yesterday. Give the students paper and poster pens. Read the poem again very slowly. Let the students draw things they hear in the poem. Ask, who has been to the beach? Trips to the beach are wonderful summer fun. You may also give students big pieces of construction paper, or old towels. Take an imaginary trip to the beach. "Lie in the sun" and "put on lotion," talking about protecting from sunburn. "Drink a drink of cold lemonade" and "run into the water." Let the students pretend.

Play the game "Pass The Sun" again from Lesson 61.

Do the Lesson 62 Language Arts worksheet. Identify the items on the worksheet. Talk about activities that take place in the summer. Have the students draw a circle around the activities that happen in the summer.

Phonics: Review the letters Aa-Ss.

Do the Lesson 62 Phonics worksheet. Complete the letter Ss worksheet. Notice that all of the letters of the alphabet are displayed on the page and that the letters Ss are highlighted with a background. As the students get better at letter recognition you can call out a letter and ask the students to point it out with their finger. Trace the large letter and the small letter. The students can trace the letters between the guide lines. Review the pictures and the colored first letter of the words. The students can color the letters as desired.

Reading: Associate spoken and written language by matching written word labels with spoken words. Segment a spoken sentence into separate, distinct words. Point to words as distinct units on a page of print.

Writing: For these two weeks focus on having the students write the first two letters of their first name freehand. During this time, write the students' names on all worksheets and papers leaving space for the first two letters and make the rest dotted or something that can be traced. They should have their Name Plates to look at as they do this.

Writing Skill Builders: Keep these objectives in mind as you direct the class. Incorporate writing strokes bowl, bridge, and diagonal lines.

Memory Verse: Review Psalm 90:12. Explain any words that the students don't know well. Talk about God's wisdom. Our goal should be to gain a heart of wisdom, no matter how old we are. Give students their Lesson 62 Memory Verse worksheet. Let them trace the word "wisdom" inside the heart, then color as they wish.

Math: Review number recognition of 10. Review oral counting 1-20 and 10-0.

Shapes: Review the star shape.

Color: Review the colors red, green, blue, black, white, yellow, brown, pink, purple, orange, and gray.

Story Time: Read a story or stories of your choice.

Music: Review "Months of the Year (Math)," "Great Is Thy Faithfulness," "What's the Weather," and "Countdown." Sing the following words to "You are My Sunshine."

You are My Sunshine
You are my sunshine,
Bright, yellow sunshine.
You bring me sunlight,
All through the days.
You help the seasons go,
You make the plants grow.
Please be my sunshine always.

Multimedia Resources: This week, listen and sing along to selections from "The Birthday Party" CD. This week, watch *The Kingdom Under the Sea* adventure "The Gift," which is a Christmas story.

Arts & Crafts: Take the big Sun memory verse that you made for Lesson 56. With the students, go to the big Creation Mural and glue the Sun onto Day 4. Glue it mid-mural, leaving room for the Moon and stars, to be added later.

Give the students playdough. Let them create something they would use at the beach.

Physical Education: Repeat the block walk taken a few days ago and time yourself. Try to beat your time.

Explore walking in different directions. Spread out carpet squares, hula hoops or something to use for bases, one for each student. Have the students start on a base. You will beat a drum and the students will walk in and around the bases until the drum beat stops. When it stops the students should get on a base and freeze. Allow them to share bases but do not allow pushing or shoving. When they are walking they can walk anyplace in the area except on the bases and they should walk in time to the drum beat. Repeat using different walking directions such as walking backward, sideways, or diagonally. Increase and decrease the tempo of the drumbeat.

Catch Up: Do any assignment that you didn't have time for earlier in the month.

NOTES:

Lesson 63

Activities in this Lesson: Bible Lesson, Social Studies, Science, Language Arts, Phonics, Reading, Writing, Memory Verse, Math, Shapes, Color, Story Time, Music, Arts & Crafts, Physical Education, Additional Study

Bible Reference: Genesis 1:14-19.

Bible Concept to Present: Fall is one of the seasons which God gave to us when He made the Sun.

Bible Lesson: Fall is the time of the year when the Earth begins to get cooler. In Fall, the leaves begin to turn colors and the grasses begin to die. September, October, and November are months of Fall. In the Fall time of the year, we need to wear our coats and jackets and long sleeves on our blouses and shirts. We sometimes need to wear something on our heads, too. Fall is the time of the year when some animals begin to look for a place to sleep for the winter. Birds fly from the colder parts of the United States to states where it is warmer. People begin to get their homes ready for winter by filling cracks around doors and windows and being sure their furnaces work. Fall is a lovely time of the year. We celebrate Thanksgiving in the Fall to celebrate the bringing in of all the garden and field crops. I am thankful God gave Fall to us.

Social Studies: Discuss things you do in Fall. Discuss the holidays that occur in Fall. Have the students make the necessary symbols for the calendar display that was started in Lesson 61.
September – Books and a ruler to represent the start of school. October – Pumpkins to represent Fall. November – a Turkey to represent Thanksgiving. You may wish to mention at this point that fall is also referred to as autumn.

Science: Though the Earth is actually closer to the Sun in the fall, the tilt of the Earth tilts the United States away from the Sun's heat. Our country is somewhat cooler in Fall, but not as cool as winter. Plants begin to die and turn brown. Many plants will finish ripening their fruits and we have a harvest in fall. If you do not live in the cooler sections of the United States where leaves change colors drastically, obtain pictures from National Geographic, library books, or online for showing your students what the colored trees look like. This is one of the most gorgeous times of the year for the eastern and northern U.S.

Language Arts: Do the following action rhymes.

AUTUMN

Leaves are floating softly down. (Wiggle fingers from high in the air to down low by the floor)
They make a carpet on the ground. (Wave hands over the floor)
Then swish, the wind comes whistling by, (Brush hands in a sweeping motion over the floor)
And send them dancing to the sky. (Wiggle fingers and raise arms high in the air)

GENTLY FALLING LEAVES

Little leaves fall gently down, (Wiggle fingers from high in the air to waist)
Red and yellow, orange and brown,
Whirling, whirling round and round, (Move arms in a churning motion at waist level)
Quietly without a sound,
Falling softly to the ground, (Wiggle fingers from waist down to ground)
Down - and down - and down - and down.

Do the Lesson 63 Language Arts worksheet. Identify the clothes for the children on the worksheet. Talk about clothes that are worn in the fall and why they are worn during that time of the year. Have the students draw a circle around the clothes that are worn in the fall. This activity can be supplemented with paper doll patterns that can be printed from the internet or obtained from other sources. Have the students cut out the paper dolls and dress them with clothes appropriate for the fall season.

Phonics: Teach the letter Tt.

Show the students the letter Tt flashcard. Point out any student's name beginning with the letter *T*. Write some words beginning with the letter *T* on the board. Include any student names from the class that begin with letter *T*. Underline the capital *T* that begins the words. Read through the words and point out the shape of letter *T*. Have the students trace the *T* in the air as you trace the letter *T* beginning each name.

> Boys: Tanner, Taylor, Terry, Thomas, Timothy, Todd, Tony, Travis, Trenton, Trevor, Trey, Tristan, Troy, Tyler
> Girls: Tabitha, Tamara, Tara, Tatiana, Taylor, Teresa, Tessa, Tiara, Tiffany, Tori
> Vocabulary words: Thursday, Tuesday

Do the Lesson 63 Phonics worksheet. Complete the letter Tt worksheet. Have the students trace the letters Tt with their fingers. They should trace the letters with their fingers and say the names of the letters. Demonstrate the proper strokes for them on the board. Say the words for each of the pictures and look at the Tt letters that begin them.

Reading: Associate spoken and written language by matching written word labels with spoken words. Segment a spoken sentence into separate, distinct words. Point to the words as distinct units on a page of print.

Writing: For these two weeks focus on having the students write the first two letters of their first name freehand. During this time, write the students' names on all worksheets and papers leaving space for the first two letters and make the rest dotted or something that can be traced. They should have their Name Plates to look at as they do this.

Writing Skill Builders: Keep these objectives in mind as you direct the class. Incorporate writing strokes bowl, bridge, and diagonal lines.

Memory Verse: Review Psalm 90:12. Review the memory verse. Write the words on big pieces of construction paper. Let the students move around, holding the words, until they are in the correct order. Help those that can't read well yet. Let the students arrange the words across the floor.

Math: Review number recognition of 10. Review oral counting 1-20 and 10-0.

Continue teaching the months of the year and recognition of day and nighttime activities.

Do the Lesson 63 Math worksheet. Instruct the students to begin at the left and color the correct number of squares in each strip. Review colors by telling them a color to use for each strip.

Shapes: Review the star shape.

Do the Lesson 63 Shapes worksheet. Count the number of points on the starfish. Color the starfish.

Color: Review the colors red, green, blue, black, white, yellow, brown, pink, purple, orange, and gray.

Story Time: Read a story or stories of your choice.

Music: Review "You are My Sunshine," "Months of the Year (Math)," "Great Is Thy Faithfulness," and "What's the Weather."

Multimedia Resources: This week, listen and sing along to selections from "The Birthday Party" CD. This week, watch *The Kingdom Under the Sea* adventure "The Gift," which is a Christmas story.

Arts & Crafts: You may also make a Fall picture to place beside the seashore summer picture. For Fall, cut several colored leaves out of construction paper and glue in a heap on the paper. Next, take a twig from outdoors or toothpicks and make them into the shape of a rake. Glue the toothpick rake onto the paper by the pile of leaves.

Physical Education: What are favorite Fall activities? Imitate them.

Additional Study: Should you desire, you may study a specific plant or animal and what it does in the various seasons. We do not provide further study material for you, but if you desire you may research a plant such as a maple tree and an animal such as a bear. You could also cut out a picture of a bear and place it in various seasons along with a picture of a tree in various stages. At each season you could mention what the bear was doing and in what stages the tree was. This type of education is important for the child's awareness. We encourage you to try some of your own creative ideas along this line.

Homework: Remind the students to keep working on their Lesson 57 Homework worksheet where they record the weather each morning by drawing a sun, clouds, or rain.

NOTES:

Activities in this Lesson: Bible Lesson, Social Studies, Language Arts, Phonics, Reading, Writing, Memory Verse, Math, Shapes, Color, Story Time, Music, Health & Safety, Physical Education

Bible Reference: Genesis 1:14-19.

Bible Concept to Present: We need to be aware of the seasons around us. The seasons and seasonal changes affect our lives.

Bible Lesson: Continue reviewing God's part in creating the seasons. Did God make the seasons for everyone? Fall is a time when farmers are busy. The vegetables and fruit are ripe and ready for picking. Fall is a beautiful time. We enjoy fall, because winter is coming fast. Winter can be very different depending on where you live. Many farmers can rest in the winter time. But some farmers plant a second crop in winter. Winter can be very beautiful, white with snow.

Social Studies: Work on telling time with the students. Put the little/short hands on the clocks. Let the students move the clock hands as you show them how both hands work for hourly time.

Write the words Summer, Fall, Winter, and Spring on the board. Have the students tell you what we wear during each season. If you did the optional paper doll activity suggested in Lesson 61 ask, "What did you learn about what the clothes that we wear during different times of the year?" If you did not do the paper doll activity, then brainstorm clothing choices for the different seasons. Write the clothing words on the board, whether every student can read them or not. Continue until there are several items of clothing listed for each season.

Language Arts: Snow is really big fluffy snowflakes, all piled together. First read this poem about snow. Then repeat the poem, letting the students act like snowflakes.

SNOWFLAKES

Merry little snowflakes
Falling through the air.
Resting on the steeple
And the tall trees everywhere.
Covering roofs and fences
Capping every post,
Covering the hillside,
Where we like to coast.
Merry little snowflakes
Do their very best
To make a soft, white blanket
So bud and flowers will rest.
But when the bright spring sunshine
Says it's come to stay
Those merry little snowflakes
Quickly run away!

Review "Autumn" and "Gently Falling Leaves" poems.

Do the Lesson 64 Language Arts worksheet. Identify the items on the worksheet. Talk about activities that take place in the fall. Have the students draw a circle around the activities that happen in the fall.

Phonics: Review the letter Tt.

Do the Lesson 64 Phonics worksheet. Complete the letter Tt worksheet. Notice that all of the letters of the alphabet are displayed on the page and that the letters Tt are highlighted with a background. As the students get better at letter recognition you can call out a letter and ask the students to point it out with their finger. Trace the large letter and the small letter. The students can trace the letters between the guide lines. Review the pictures and the colored first letter of the words. The students can color the letters as desired.

Reading: Associate spoken and written language by matching written word labels with spoken words. Segment a spoken sentence into separate, distinct words. Point to words as distinct units on a page of print.

Writing: For these two weeks focus on having the students write the first two letters of their first name freehand. During this time, write the students' names on all worksheets and papers leaving space for the first two letters and make the rest dotted or something that can be traced. They should have their Name Plates to look at as they do this.

Writing Skill Builders: Keep these objectives in mind as you direct the class. Incorporate writing strokes bowl, bridge, and diagonal lines.

Memory Verse: Review Psalm 90:12 with the students. Let them use their film canister shakers and chant the verse, walking in a circle.

Math: Review number recognition of 10. Review oral counting 1-20 and 10-0.

Do the Lesson 64 Math worksheet. The students are to draw the correct number of objects for each number.

Shapes: Review the star shape.

Do the Lesson 64 Shapes worksheet. Complete the Dot-to-dot A-J star.

Color: Review the colors red, green, blue, black, white, yellow, brown, pink, purple, orange, and gray.

Story Time: Read a story or stories of your choice.

Music: Review "You are My Sunshine," "Months of the Year (Math)," and "Great Is Thy Faithfulness."

Multimedia Resources: This week, listen and sing along to selections from "The Birthday Party" CD. This week, watch *The Kingdom Under the Sea* adventure "The Gift," which is a Christmas story.

Health & Safety: *Bring some hand cream to share.* Say, We hear a lot about protecting our skin in the summer. But we must help our skin in the winter, too. Winter cold can be very rough on our skin. Our hands get chapped and red. Our noses are sometimes red from using lots of tissues. Daily body cream applied to our hands and face can make our skin feel smooth and comfortable. Give each student a little bit of cream to rub into their hands.

Physical Education: What are your favorite winter activities? Imitate them. Think of sledding and building snowmen, or walking in the rain. Do this activity outside if weather permits.

NOTES:

Lesson 65

Week 13: Day 5

Activities in this Lesson: Bible Lesson, Social Studies, Science, Language Arts, Phonics, Reading, Writing, Memory Verse, Math, Shapes, Color, Music, Story Time, Creative Cooking, Physical Education

Bible Reference: Genesis 1:14-19.

Bible Concept to Present: God gave us the winter season when He made the Sun.

Bible Lesson: The seasons which God made are so wonderful. We have talked about summer. Review with Seasons flashcards. Can you tell me how we know when summer arrives? Very good. How about Fall? How do we know when Fall is here? And what months are the months of summer? What are the months of Fall? Very Good. You are listening so carefully, I am very proud of you. Winter is another season which God gave to us. The months of December, January and February are winter months. In some parts of the world, the ground becomes frozen in winter. The lakes and rivers freeze over with ice. The roads become covered with ice. You could not go outside without a coat on because it is very, very cold. If you live in the Southern part of the United States, the wintertime is the time when it rains. It is colder there too, but it does not snow, and people do not have to wear quite as warm coats. There is no ice on the roads there, for it is too warm. In the southern part of the United States certain flowers begin to bloom. But where ever you live, winter is the coldest time of the year.

Social Studies: People need to be able to be indoors during the winter. Winter is very cold. We need to wear hats, and mittens and warm coats. Add to the month display started in Lesson 61. December - place a Christmas tree. January - a snowman. February - pictures of Lincoln and Washington or a valentine.

Also make a picture to represent Winter. A hill covered with cotton ball snow with a sled at the top of the hill, or an ice pond (blue paper with plastic wrap over it) with chenille wire or pipe cleaner figures skating on the pond. (Be sure to dress your figures with construction paper clothes.)

Science: During the winter, the Sun's rays hit the Earth in a less direct manner. Do you remember this picture I showed you earlier when I told you about how we get our seasons? (See Lesson 60 Resource page.) Find where the Earth is during the winter in relationship to the Sun. Very Good! You have been listening carefully and learning very much. Use Lesson 65 Science worksheet to illustrate a winter scene. Cotton may go around the tree at the bottom to represent snow. Discuss the tree and why it has no leaves. Show them how the cotton can pull apart and thin out.

Language Arts: The following action rhymes may be done with your students. Add appropriate actions.

LET'S BUILD A SNOWMAN

First the body
And then the head.
A stovepipe hat
And a scarf of red.
Pebbles for eyes,
And a carrot nose,
And a mouth made of raisins
In two smiling rows.

JACK FROST

Who comes creeping in the night,
    When the moon is clear and bright?
Who paints tree leaves red and gold,
    When the autumn days turn cold?
Up the hill and down he goes
    In and out the brown corn rows,
Making music crackling sweet,
    With his little frosty feet.
        Jack Frost!

Review "Snowflakes" poem.

Do the Lesson 65 Language Arts worksheet. Identify the clothes for the children on the worksheet. Talk about clothes that are worn in the winter and why they are worn during that time of the year. Have the students draw a circle around the clothes that are worn in the winter. This activity can be supplemented with paper doll patterns that can be printed from the internet or obtained from other sources. Have the students cut out the paper dolls and dress them with clothes appropriate for the winter season.

Phonics: Review the letters Aa-Tt.

Teach the small letter *t*. Write some words beginning with the letter *t* on the board. Include words from stories or activities that tie this lesson to other things that have already been done. Underline the small *t* that begins the words. Read through the words and point out the shape of letter *t*. Have the students trace the *t* in the air as you trace the letter *t* beginning each word.
    Common words: take, tell, than, that, the, their, them, then, there, these, they, thing, think, this, thought, through, time, to, too, tree, try, turn
    Vocabulary words: taller, tallest, taste, teeth, ten, tenth, thank you, thick, thin, three, third, thirteen, throw, to the side, today, toe, tomorrow, tongue, tooth, top, touch, towards, triangle, twelve, twenty, two

Do the Lesson 65 Phonics worksheet. Have the students put a blue star around the Rr letters, a brown rectangle around the Ss letters, and a yellow X on the Tt letters. Give them one direction at a time so they can focus on finding the correct letter shape. Begin with capital *R*, then lower case *r*, etc. Show them examples with flashcards or letters written on the board.

Reading: Associate spoken and written language by matching written word labels with spoken words. Segment a spoken sentence into separate, distinct words. Point to words as distinct units on a page of print.

Writing: For these two weeks focus on having the students write the first two letters of their first name freehand. During this time, write the students' names on all worksheets and papers leaving space for the first two letters and make the rest dotted or something that can be traced. They should have their Name Plates to look at as they do this.

Writing Skill Builders: Keep these objectives in mind as you direct the class. Incorporate writing strokes bowl, bridge, and diagonal lines.

Memory Verse: Finish memory work on Psalm 90:12 today. Let those students recite that want to do so.

Math: Review number recognition of 10. Review oral counting 1-20 and 10-0.

Do the Lesson 65 Math worksheet. Connect the dots to form the helicopter. Color the drawing as you wish.

Review, for the final time, the months of the year and the activities of day and night. Praise your students highly for the progress they have made.

Shapes: Review the star shape.

Color: Review the colors red, green, blue, black, white, yellow, brown, pink, purple, orange, and gray.

Story Time: Read a story or stories of your student's choice or ones they have brought from home.

Music: Review "You are My Sunshine," "Months of the Year (Math)," and "Great Is Thy Faithfulness."

Multimedia Resources: This week, listen and sing along to selections from "The Birthday Party" CD. This week, watch *The Kingdom Under the Sea* adventure "The Gift," which is a Christmas story.

Creative Cooking: Make popcorn. Using a recipe similar to the marshmallow covering you use for rice crispies, cover the popcorn with the marshmallow topping. Form immediately into a popcorn snowman. Your students will enjoy this if you display the snowman in a Winter setting, such as a cotton snow bank. Candy corns can serve as eyes (push the pointed end in the popcorn) and nose (place the pointed end out). Can stars be made out of the candy corns? A hat and scarf may be made of construction paper. Involve the students in all you can. This is an activity we did every winter as we were growing up. It is part of our warm memories; a time spent doing something special.

Physical Education: Continue the walking in different directions activity. Spread out carpet squares, hula hoops or something to use for bases, one for each student. Have the students start on a base. You will beat a drum and the students will walk in and around the bases until the drum beat stops. When it stops the students should get on a base and freeze. Allow them to share bases but do not allow pushing or shoving. When they are walking they can walk anyplace in the area except on the bases and they should walk in time to the drum beat. Repeat using different walking directions such as walking backward, sideways or diagonally. Increase and decrease the tempo of the drumbeat.

Homework: Remind the students to keep working on their Lesson 57 Homework worksheet where they record the weather each morning by drawing a sun, clouds, or rain.

NOTES:

Activities in this Lesson: Bible Lesson, Social Studies, Science, Language Arts, Phonics, Reading, Writing, Memory Verse, Math, Shapes, Color, Story Time, Music, Physical Education

Bible Reference: Genesis 1:14-19.

Bible Concept to Present: God gave us a wonderful gift of spring when He gave us the Sun.

Bible Lesson: God has given us such wonderful gifts when He gave us the seasons. We have talked about the seasons of Summer, Fall, and Winter. God also gave us the season of Spring. Spring comes in the months of March, April, and May. In Spring, the Sun's rays hit our section of the Earth more directly (refer to the picture on the Lesson 60 Resource page). In spring we can put on lighter jackets. The Earth begins to seem to come alive again. The birds return from their winter homes, the bears come awake from their winter sleep. Plants begin to shoot up out of the ground, and some plants begin to bloom. Trees begin to show their new leaves and blossoms. It is a very special time of the year. Many animals have babies in the spring. God is so good to give us spring to see all the beautiful things He has made.

Social Studies: Spring is a wonderful time for people. We can smell the flowers, see the baby animals and feel the warming of the sun on our faces. Conclude your calendar display started in Lesson 61 by placing the symbols for spring. March - a kite in the wind. April - an umbrella with rain coming down. May - a beautiful flower. For the spring season, make a row of flowers (patterns may be used from Lesson 66 Resource page) and place a fuzzy bee above the flower. The bee may be made by winding a black and yellow chenille wire around a pencil and gluing a wiggly eye on it.

Science: Spring occurs when the Sun's rays hit our part of the Earth more directly compared to winter, but not as directly as compared to summer. Have your students show you on Lesson 60 Resource page the position of the Earth for spring. Praise them highly if they can do this.

Language Arts: The following action rhymes may be done with your students. Add appropriate actions.

THE STORM

Clouds are swiftly floating by,
Dark and darker grows the sky.
Pitter-patter sounds the rain
Splashing on the windowpane.
Wind is blowing, "oo-oo-ooo!"
Rattling doors and windows, too.
Tom's umbrella is so small
It does not keep him dry at all.
Pouring, pouring, hours and hours,
Water for the thirsty flowers.
Waiting children say "We fear
That the sky will never clear."
"Look! Sunshine! A pleasant day!
Now we can go out and play."

PITTER PATTER

Pitter, patter falls the rain,
On the roof and window pain.
Softly, softly it comes down,
Makes a stream that runs around.
Flowers lift their heads and say:
"A nice cool drink for us today."

FALLING RAINDROPS

Raindrops, raindrops
Falling all around.
Pitter-patter on the rooftops,
Pitter-patter on the ground.
Here is my umbrella.
It will keep me dry.
When I go walking in the rain,
I hold it up so high.

Review the action the rhymes "Let's Build a Snowman" and "Jack Frost."

Do the Lesson 66 Language Arts worksheet. Identify the clothes for the children on the worksheet. Talk about clothes that are worn in the spring and why they are worn during that time of the year. Have the students draw a circle around the clothes that are worn in the spring. This activity can be supplemented with paper doll patterns that can be printed from the internet or obtained from other sources. Have the students cut out the paper dolls and dress them with clothes appropriate for the spring season.

Phonics: Teach the letter Uu.

Point out any student's name beginning with the letter *U*. Write some words beginning with the letter *U* on the board. Include any student names from the class that begin with letter *U*. Underline the capital *U* that begins the words. Read through the words and point out the shape of letter *U*. Have the students trace the *U* in the air as you trace the letter *U* beginning each name.
   Boys: Uaine, Uang, Uba, Ubadah, Uberto, Uday, Udo, Ugo, Ulf, Ulick, Ulric, Umberto
   Girls: Udele, Ujana, Ula, Ulan, Ulani, Ulema, Ulla, Ultima, Uma, Umay
   Vocabulary words: United States

Do the Lesson 66 Phonics worksheet. Complete the letter Uu worksheet. Have the students trace the letters Uu with their fingers. They should trace the letters with their fingers and say the names of the letters. Demonstrate the proper strokes for them on the board. Say the words for each of the pictures and look at the Uu letters that begin them.

Reading: Associate spoken and written language by matching written word labels with spoken words. Segment a spoken sentence into separate, distinct words. Point to words as distinct units on a page of print.

Multimedia Resources: View the Aa-Uu segments of "Rev-Up for Reading" from the "Rev-Up for Learning" DVD to drill letter recognition and sound. The students should say each letter sound along with the presentation.

Writing: For these two weeks focus on having the students write the first two letters of their first name freehand. During this time, write the students' names on all worksheets and papers leaving space for the first two letters and make the rest dotted or something that can be traced. They should have their Name Plates to look at as they do this.

Writing Skill Builders: Keep these objectives in mind as you direct the class. Incorporate writing strokes bowl, bridge, and diagonal lines.

Multimedia Resources: View the Aa-Uu segments of "Rev-Up for Writing" from the "Rev-Up for Learning" DVD to review the writing of upper- and lowercase letters. The students should write each letter in the air along with the presentation. Since the first half of the presentation covers lowercase letters and the second half uppercase letters some navigation will be needed to skip to the letters that are covered in this lesson.

Memory Verse: Psalm 89:1.

> I will sing of the LORD's great love forever; Psalm 89:1 NIV

> I will sing of the mercies of the LORD for ever: Psalm 89:1 KJV

Introduce this week's memory verse. Talk about what "forever" means. This line of God's word is in many songs. God often mentions us singing to Him, singing Him praises. "When you do music, make sure you sing as to the Lord in Praise to Him. Make a rainbow umbrella. Hand out Lesson 66 Memory Verse worksheet. Let the students color the sections as they learn the verse.

	NIV	KJV
PURPLE	I will sing	I will sing
BLUE	of the Lord's	of the mercies
GREEN	great	of the
YELLOW	love	LORD
ORANGE	forever!	for ever:
RED	Psalm 89:1	Psalm 89:1

Hand out Memory Verse Card 9, for the students to take home.

Math: Teach number recognition of 11. Show the students the number 11 flashcard. If your students have mastered the ability to identify numbers 1 - 10, and can write them, teach the number 11. Have them count out 11 of an item and show them the number 11.

Review oral counting 1-20 and 10-0.

Teach patterns. Use shape patterns to extend simple patterns. Keep this simple by alternating 2 different shapes. The concept can also be taught using letters of the alphabet. (Example: ACACAC ?)

Do Lesson 66a Math worksheet. Do the first row of patterns together with the students. Say the pattern aloud and ask the students for what comes next.

Do the Lesson 66b Math worksheet. Notice that all of the numbers are displayed on the page and that the number 11 is highlighted with a background. Have the students trace the large number 11 with the proper strokes by following the arrows. Instruct the students to count each group of items and then trace the number.

Do the Lesson 66c Math worksheet. Instruct the students to draw a line between the groups that have the same number.

Multimedia Resources: View "Rev-Up for Arithmetic" from the "Rev-Up for Learning" DVD to practice number recognition and counting 1-20.

Shapes: Review the star shape.

Color: Review the colors red, green, blue, black, white, yellow, brown, pink, purple, orange, and gray.

Story Time: Read a story or stories of your choice.

Music: Review "You are My Sunshine," "Months of the Year" (Math), and "Great Is Thy Faithfulness."

Multimedia Resources: This week, listen and sing along to selections from "Once Upon A Christmas" CD. This week, watch *The Kingdom Under the Sea* adventure "The Gift," which is a Christmas story.

Physical Education: What do your students enjoy doing in Spring? Ask them to share their ideas. Let them imitate these actions.

NOTES:

Activities in this Lesson: Bible Lesson, Outdoor Activity, Language Arts, Phonics, Reading, Writing, Memory Verse, Math, Shapes, Color, Story Time, Music, Arts & Crafts, Physical Education, Optional Math/Language Arts/Bible/Arts & Crafts Activity

Bible Reference: Genesis 1:14-19.

Bible Concept to Present: There is happiness and joy just in having the sun shine.

Bible Lesson: Review the days of Creation. Emphasize how important the sun is to us. Talk about the sunshine being rays of good cheer. It is true that people that don't see the sun much can be very unhappy. There is joy and happiness in the sunshine. That's why spring is so joyous. Spring is often the first time people have seen the sun for a while. They have had months of clouds and rain and snow. How wonderful those first rays of the sun feel on our face, after a long, cold winter. If the sun is shining, go to a window and feel the rays of the sun on your faces. Take some deep breaths. Doesn't that just feel happy?

Outdoor Activity: Take a walk. Start in the classroom with grumpy faces. Have students make their grumpiest face. Then, as you walk out into the sunshine (presuming there is some!), everyone changes their grumpy face into a happy face. Sing some songs to the Lord and say the memory verse.

Multimedia Resources: Watch "Joy" from the *Character Builders Video Series*.

Language Arts: Learn this little poem about the seasons. Be sure that students know the names of the seasons, and the order in which they occur. After going over the poem several times, let the students experiment with making up rhymes.

Seasons

Fall, winter, spring, and summer
Seasons we enjoy together.
Winter, spring, summer, and fall
Thank you God, who made them all!
Spring and summer, fall and winter
Filled with fun that we remember.
Summer, fall and winter, spring
God can do just anything!

Review the action rhymes "The Storm," "Pitter Patter," and "Falling Raindrops."

Do the Lesson 67 Language Arts worksheet. Identify the items on the worksheet. Talk about activities that take place in the winter. Have the students draw a circle around the activities that happen in the winter.

Phonics: Review the letter Uu.

Do the Lesson 67 Phonics worksheet. Complete the letter Uu worksheet. Notice that all of the letters of the alphabet are displayed on the page and that the letters Uu are highlighted with a background. As the students get better at letter recognition you can call out a letter and ask the students to point it out with their finger. Trace the large letter and the small letter. The students can trace the letters between the guide lines. Review the pictures and the colored first letter of the words. The students can color the letters as desired.

Reading: Associate spoken and written language by matching written word labels with spoken words. Segment a spoken sentence into separate, distinct words. Point to words as distinct units on a page of print.

Writing: For these two weeks focus on having the students write the first two letters of their first name freehand. During this time, write the students' names on all worksheets and papers leaving space for the first two letters and make the rest dotted or something that can be traced. They should have their Name Plates to look at as they do this.

Writing Skill Builders: Keep these objectives in mind as you direct the class. Incorporate writing strokes bowl, bridge, and diagonal lines.

Memory Verse: Practice the memory verse Psalm 89:1. Color the umbrella on the Lesson 66 Memory Verse worksheet as words are learned. When students memorize the verse, allow them to dot some glitter glue on their picture as rain.

Math: Review number recognition of 11. Review oral counting 1-20 and 10-0.

Do the Lesson 67 Math worksheet. Trace the numbers. Count the items and draw lines to match the items with the number.

Shapes: Review the star shape.

Color: Review the colors red, green, blue, black, white, yellow, brown, pink, purple, orange, and gray.

Story Time: Read a story or stories of your choice.

Music: Review "You are My Sunshine" and "Great Is Thy Faithfulness."

Multimedia Resources: This week, listen and sing along to selections from the "Once Upon a Christmas" CD. This week, watch *The Kingdom Under the Sea* adventure "The Gift," which is a Christmas story.

Arts & Crafts: Give the students large sheets of black construction paper and chalk. Instruct them to draw their favorite season, including trees and the sky with weather conditions. Talk about the four seasons as they draw.

Physical Education: Follow the Lines. Find an area where there are lots of lines, a gym floor, joints in a sidewalk, or joint lines on a tile floor. The students start by finding any line in the area. You will play music and they will walk on the lines until the music stops. When the music stops they must freeze in place. Give some instructions so they know what to do if two students end up on a collision course. Another option would be to use lines that go back and forth across the area so that collisions are not possible. Have the students use walking, skipping, hopping, etc. as they travel the lines.

Multimedia Resources: A good song for a skipping activity is "Hip and a Hey" from the "Nathaniel the Grublet" CD.

Optional Math/Language Arts/Bible/Arts & Crafts Activity:

11 Stars: Genesis 37:5-11, read the Bible verses and tell the story.

Eleven stars bowed down to Joseph in his dream. Joseph had two dreams. In the first dream he and his family were harvesting grain. As they tied the grain into bundles for drying Joseph saw the bundles (sheaves) of everyone's grain bowing down to his. In the second dream Joseph saw the sun, moon and eleven stars bow down to him. No one understood this dream until many years later when Joseph's family came to Egypt and bowed down to him because he was giving them food during a time when food was not growing.

Do the Lesson 67 Bible Numbers worksheet. Give each student a sheet of white construction paper and the worksheet. Cut out the items on the worksheet and glue them to construction paper as illustrated in the drawing. Draw in the arms, legs, and faces for the "11" stars that Joseph saw bowing down. Draw in the rest of the picture.

Multimedia Resources: Listen to the song "Joseph" from "The Amazing Children" CD.

NOTES:

Lesson 68

Week 14: Day 3

Activities in this Lesson: Bible Lesson, Social Studies, Science, Language Arts, Phonics, Reading, Writing, Memory Verse, Math, Shapes, Color, Story Time, Music, Arts & Crafts, Creative Cooking, Physical Education

Bible Reference: Genesis 1:14-19.

Bible Concept to Present: The Sun is Earth's source of warmth. It is necessary for the life of plants.

Bible Lesson: When God made our Sun, He gave us our seasons. He gave us the wonderful, warm summer, the cool fall, the cold winter, and the refreshing spring. We have all of these seasons because God gave us the Sun. Did you know that the Sun also helps plants to grow? The Sun is very important to plants. Without the Sun, the plants would not grow. If plants did not grow, we would not have lettuce to eat, or carrots, or potatoes. There would be no pizza either. The tomatoes could not grow for the pizza sauce, nor the wheat grow for the flour for making the crust. If there were no plants, animals would not have anything to eat. And without animals or plants, we would not have anything to eat. Plants are very important to us. And all plants need the Sun. God loved us so much when He gave the Sun. He knew we would need the Sun very much. He knew the plants would need the Sun, too. And He knew we would need the plants. Just knowing that God cares so much for me, makes me feel very, very happy. Do you feel happy too?

Social Studies: Plants are very important to people. Take an inventory of your kitchen and notice all the things which are provided by plants. Mention them all to your students as you show them to them. You may want to have your students classify foods according to grains, dried vegetables or fruits, canned vegetables or fruits, etc. Encourage them to verbally express what they are doing and why they are classifying the food in that manner. If necessary keep this simple by classifying cereals versus macaroni.

Science: Plants need the Sun. To reinforce this concept, tell the students that without the Sun, plants cannot live. They would not have light, or warmth, and both are needed for the plant to grow. Take a plant (one you are willing to risk) and place it in a dark freezer. You will need to tell your student that when the door is shut on the freezer, it is dark and very cold in there, just as it would be on Earth if there were no Sun. Check the plant after a few hours and set it back into the room. Notice the results.

Language Arts: Read the following story to your students. You will want to inform them that you will only be telling part of the story, and that they will need to listen carefully so that they can complete the story for you.

Billy Bean Seed

Billy Bean was a seed. He lived in a box with other members of his family. Billy liked living in his box house, but sometimes, when he listened to the other beans talk, he was sure he was missing something. Some of the older beans told Billy about being put in a dark bed and that when this happened, he would change. Billy wasn't sure he wanted to change, but then he decided not to worry too much since he still lived in the box.

One day, Billy was awakened by a bright light shining in his box. The next thing he knew, he felt the warm sunshine on his body, and then he was being placed in a bed. Soon the dark soil covered him. Billy missed the nice warm sunlight. He missed his box house. After a few days, Billy noticed that his skin was getting tight. Soon there was a tear in his skin, and he found a nice green stem growing out of his body. Billy liked the new change in his body. He felt the warm sunlight through the soil. He stretched his new stem up and up and up until he reached the very top of his dark bed. Then one more push and POP! He was through the soil and into the bright sunlight. Billy kept stretching and stretching up and up and up. Billy was happy to reach towards the Sun. The Sun was his friend.

Billy and Sun played together all day long, day after day. Billy grew bigger and bigger. Then one day, Billy didn't feel the warm sun. It was cold, and his friend the Sun was nowhere in sight. He looked up to the sky and saw a big cloud. The cloud started to cry on him. The rain felt so cold. Billy wished the Sun would come and make him warm again. The next morning, Billy looked up into the sky and guess what he saw! Billy saw, (Let the students finish the story. Whatever the students say happens is correct. Discuss what they answer. If, after they have completed the story, they want you to complete the story, you may tell them that Billy noticed that he now has pretty flowers growing from him. Continue with the sequence of a growing plant.)

Review "Seasons" poem from Lesson 67.

Do the Lesson 68 Language Arts worksheet. Identify the items on the worksheet. Talk about activities that take place in the spring. Have the students draw a circle around the activities that happen in the spring.

Phonics: Review the letters Aa-Uu.

Teach the small letter *u*. Write some words beginning with the letter *u* on the board. Include words from stories or activities that tie this lesson to other things that have already been done. Underline the small *u* that begins the words. Read through the words and point out the shape of letter *u*. Have the students trace the *u* in the air as you trace the letter *u* beginning each word.
    Common words: under, up, us, use

Reading: Associate spoken and written language by matching written word labels with spoken words. Segment a spoken sentence into separate, distinct words. Point to words as distinct units on a page of print.

Writing: For these two weeks focus on having the students write the first two letters of their first name freehand. During this time, write the students' names on all worksheets and papers leaving space for the first two letters and make the rest dotted or something that can be traced. They should have their Name Plates to look at as they do this.

Writing Skill Builders: Keep these objectives in mind as you direct the class. Incorporate writing strokes bowl, bridge, and diagonal lines.

Lesson 68
(Cont.)

Memory Verse: Practice the memory verse Psalm 89:1. Color the umbrella on the Lesson 66 Memory Verse worksheet as words are learned. When students memorize the verse, allow them to dot some glitter glue on their picture as rain.

Math: Review number recognition of 11. Continue to teach the number 11 by counting items.

Do the Lesson 68 Math worksheet. Connect the dots and color the picture.

Review oral counting 1-20 and 10-0.

Shapes: Review triangle, circle, square, rectangle, and star shapes.

Do the Lesson 68 Shapes worksheet. Trace the shapes, name them and color the drawings.

Color: Review the colors red, green, blue, black, white, yellow, brown, pink, purple, orange, and gray.

Story Time: Read a story or stories of your choice.

Music: Review "You are My Sunshine," "Great Is Thy Faithfulness," and "He Plants Me Like a Seed."

Multimedia Resources: This week, listen and sing along to selections from the "Once Upon a Christmas" CD. This week, watch *The Kingdom Under the Sea* adventure "The Gift," which is a Christmas story.

Arts & Crafts: This would be a great day to make a pizza from colors of clay. The plants discussed in the Bible story provide wonderful ingredients for pizza.

Creative Cooking: Pizza day! Make homemade or cook frozen pizzas for lunch today. Make at least one pizza from scratch. The students will have a wonderful time talking about and placing the vegetables you use for the toppings on the pizza.

Physical Education: Repeat the Follow the Lines activity. Find an area where there are lots of lines, a gym floor, joints in a sidewalk or joint lines on a tile floor. The students start by finding any line in the area. You will play music and they will walk on the lines until the music stops. When the music stops they must freeze in place. Give some instructions so they know what to do if two students end up on a collision course. Another option would be to use lines that go back and forth across the area so that collisions are not possible. Have the students use walking, skipping, hopping, etc. as they travel the lines.

Homework: Remind the students to keep working on their Lesson 57 Homework worksheet where they record the weather each morning by drawing a sun, clouds, or rain.

NOTES:

Activities in this Lesson: Bible Lesson, Language Arts, Phonics, Reading, Writing, Memory Verse, Math, Shapes, Color, Story Time, Music, Arts & Crafts, Health & Safety, Physical Education, Homework

Bible Reference: Genesis 1:14-19.

Bible Concept to Present: God controls the mighty Sun and the huge Earth as they rotate through space. He makes the Earth tilt at exactly the right angle.

Bible Lesson: Have the students stand around you, with you as the Sun and them as the Earth. Say, God made the Sun and the Earth to move in perfect harmony. As they circle around you, remind them that the Earth travels around the Sun in exactly the same orbit every year, with the same timing. The Earth tilts at exactly the same angle. These huge bodies in the sky are completely in God's control. What a mighty and powerful God we have!

Science: Ask, When does summer come, what month? June. But does it ever come in January? No. Does it come in October? No. Summer always comes at the same time, so we know it is coming. Farmers know when to plant the seeds. Sometimes the weather can be different, even though the seasons are the same. What has our weather been like? Have you been keeping your daily weather diary? Let the students share.

Language Arts: Encourage the students to share about the weather. Help them to use *weather* words as they share. Let them respond and fill in the blanks at the end of each sentence. They may also act them out.

Drip, drip, drop, drop. Water falling from the sky. It is _____ . RAINING
Brrrr, cold. Things are blowing, trees are bending. It is _____ . WINDY
Beautiful, soft pieces floating down. Each one is different. But they pile up and pile up very high. It is _____ . SNOWING
Lift my face and feel the warmth. Bright and clear. It is _____ . SUNNY
Thunder crashes! Wind smashes! Rain pounds the window. It is _____ . STORMY

Do the Lesson 69 Language Arts worksheet. Identify the items on the worksheet. Talk about activities that take place during the different seasons of the year. Have the students trace the lines to match items from the same season.

Phonics: Review the letters Aa-Uu.

Reading: Associate spoken and written language by matching written word labels with spoken words. Segment a spoken sentence into separate, distinct words. Point to words as distinct units on a page of print.

Writing: For these two weeks focus on having the students write the first two letters of their first name freehand. During this time, write the students' names on all worksheets and papers leaving space for the first two letters and make the rest dotted or something that can be traced. They should have their Name Plates to look at as they do this.

Writing Skill Builders: Keep these objectives in mind as you direct the class. Incorporate writing strokes bowl, bridge, and diagonal lines.

Lesson 69
(Cont.)

Memory Verse: Continue learning the memory verse Psalm 89:1. Color the umbrella on the Lesson 66 Memory Verse worksheet as words are learned.

Math: Review number recognition of 11. Review oral counting 1-20 and 10-0.

Review patterns. Use shape patterns to extend simple patterns. Keep this simple by alternating 2 different shapes. The concept can also be taught using letters of the alphabet. (AACAACAAC __?__)

Do Lesson 69a Math worksheet. Do the first row of patterns together with the students. Say the pattern aloud and ask the students for what comes next.

Do the Lesson 69b Math worksheet. Trace the numbers and then draw lines to match the group of the same number.

Learn verse eleven to "This Old Man."

This Old Man, He Played One

Verse 1
This old man, he played one, He played nick-nack on my thumb;
with a nick-nack paddy whack, give a dog a bone. This old man came rolling home.

Verse 2
This old man, he played two, He played nick-nack on my shoe;
with a nick-nack paddy whack, give a dog a bone. This old man came rolling home.

Verse 3
This old man, he played three, He played nick-nack on my on my knee;
with a nick-nack paddy whack, give a dog a bone. This old man came rolling home.

Verse 4
This old man, he played four, He played nick-nack on my door;
with a nick-nack paddy whack, give a dog a bone. This old man came rolling home.

Verse 5
This old man, he played five, He played nick-nack on my hive;
with a nick-nack paddy whack, give a dog a bone. This old man came rolling home.

Verse 6
This old man, he played six, He played nick-nack on my sticks;
with a nick-nack paddy whack, give a dog a bone. This old man came rolling home.

Verse 7
This old man, he played seven, He played nick-nack up in Heaven;
with a nick-nack paddy whack, give a dog a bone. This old man came rolling home.

Verse 8
This old man, he played eight, He played nick-nack on my gate;
with a nick-nack paddy whack, give a dog a bone. This old man came rolling home.

Verse 9
This old man, he played nine, He played nick-nack on my spine;
with a nick-nack paddy whack, give a dog a bone. This old man came rolling home.

Verse 10
This old man, he played ten, He played nick-nack once again;
with a nick-nack paddy whack, give a dog a bone. This old man came rolling home.

Verse 11
This old man, he played eleven, He played knick knack up in Heaven,
with a Knick, knack, paddy whack, Give the dog a bone; This old man came rolling home.

Shapes: Review triangle, circle, square, rectangle, and star shapes.

Color: Review the colors red, green, blue, black, white, yellow, brown, pink, purple, orange, and gray.

Story Time: Read a story or stories of your choice.

Music: Review favorite songs learned this year.

Multimedia Resources: This week, listen and sing along to selections from the "Once Upon a Christmas" CD. This week, watch *The Kingdom Under the Sea* adventure "The Gift," which is a Christmas story.

Arts & Crafts: *Cut pieces of yellow and/or gold yarn into 3-4 inch pieces, enough for each student to have at least ten pieces. Cut out 3 inch circles of yellow construction paper, one for each student.* Give students a large piece of pale blue construction paper. Talk about the Sun's light coming to us in the form of rays. Rays of light come out from all over the Sun's surface. Instruct students to glue the circle in the middle of their paper. Then let them have fun gluing the strips of yarn all around their Sun, just like rays of light. It will be messy, but that's OK.

Provide the students with crayons and white paper. Review the story about Billy. Have the students draw Billy as a seed in a box, as a seed in the soil, cracking open, sprouting, then pushing through to the surface as a plant. Let the students be creative but remind them to put a Sun in the sky.

Health & Safety: We will be learning about the Sun and its warmth tomorrow. The Sun helps keep us warm. A fire can also keep us warm, but we must learn that only adults can strike a match or start a fire. When children play with fire, tragedy can result. Once a fire gets started, it is very hard to put out. Our community pays a lot of money so that there are always fire fighters available to fight fires. Never, ever try to start a fire. If there is an accident, and your clothes catch fire, you must remember to STOP, DROP, ROLL. Show the students the Lesson 69 Resource page. Let's say that together: STOP, DROP, ROLL. Now let's all practice. Let the students practice over and over again, until they have the movement memorized. Explain that if they see someone else with clothes on fire, they must yell STOP, DROP, ROLL to that person.

Physical Education: Airplane Tilt. Do a follow the leader activity with the students pretending to be airplanes. They should walk, skip, hop or jump with their arms held out to their sides. When they are going straight their arms should be straight out. When they make a turn their arms should tilt in the direction of the turn. Do this as a follow the leader activity with all of the students copying the movements of the leader.

Homework: Give the students Lesson 69 Homework worksheet. Make sure they know they don't have to bring it back tomorrow.

NOTES:

Activities in this Lesson: Bible Lesson, Social Studies, Science, Language Arts, Phonics, Reading, Writing, Memory Verse, Math, Shapes, Color, Story Time, Music, Arts & Crafts, Health & Safety, Physical Education

Bible Reference: Genesis 1: 14-19.

Bible Concept to Present: We need the Sun to live.

Bible Lesson: We have talked about how important the Sun is to the life of plants and animals. It is also very, very important to us. It is the Sun that warms up our Earth. If we did not have the Sun, our Earth would be frozen. It would be like a big, big icicle. We would not have any flowers growing, or animals, or trees. Our world would be dark, because the Sun gives us our daytime. What would keep us warm if we had no Sun? What would we eat? God knew we would need the Sun to help us live. He knew it would keep us warm, and make food for us to eat. God showed us how very much He loved us when He made the Sun for us. Let's thank God now for the Sun.

Social Studies: The Sun is important for our life. Life cannot exist on a totally frozen planet or a dark planet. Refer to the experiment you did in Lesson 68 of this week. Relate to students that just as the plant needed the warmth and light to live, so do we. State that God is good to us. He will never let us be without the Sun to warm us and provide food and light for us.

Science: Reinforce in conversation how we need the light from the Sun for the food we eat, and how we need the warmth from the Sun to keep us warm. Have your students draw their conception of the Sun with a picture to represent how the Sun helps us. Discuss the ways we get heat here on Earth. This is not to be an in depth discussion; a simple drawing of heat sources will be sufficient. Some examples are: fire, electricity, natural gas, coal, etc.

Language Arts: Show your students the pictures of sources of heat which you taught in Science. Ask them leading questions such as: For what do we use fire? How does fire help us? How can fire harm us? How does the sun feel to you? During what time of the year does the sun feel hotter? What do you like to do when the sun feels hot? Describe how a plant would feel in the hot sun. Your goal is for the student to verbalize. There are no right or wrong answers. Should you find a student has misconceptions, make a note of it and correct them at a later time.

Phonics: Teach the letter Vv.

Show the students the letter Vv flashcard. Point out any student's name beginning with the letter *V*. Write some words beginning with the letter *V* on the board. Include any student names from the class that begin with letter *V*. Underline the capital *V* that begins the words. Read through the words and point out the shape of letter *V*. Have the students trace the *V* in the air as you trace the letter V beginning each name.

> Boys: Victor, Vincent
> Girls: Valerie, Vanessa, Veronica, Victoria

Do the Lesson 70 Phonics worksheet. Complete the letter Vv worksheet. Have the students trace the letters Vv with their fingers. They should trace the letters with their fingers and say the names of the letters. Demonstrate the proper strokes for them on the board. Say the words for each of the pictures and look at the Vv letters that begin them.

Reading: Associate spoken and written language by matching written word labels with spoken words. Segment a spoken sentence into separate, distinct words. Point to words as distinct units on a page of print.

Writing: For these two weeks focus on having the students write the first two letters of their first name freehand. During this time, write the students' names on all worksheets and papers leaving space for the first two letters and make the rest dotted or something that can be traced. They should have their Name Plates to look at as they do this.

Writing Skill Builders: Keep these objectives in mind as you direct the class. Incorporate writing strokes bowl, bridge, and diagonal lines.

Memory Verse: Let each student recite the memory verse Psalm 89:1, if they will. Let them finish their umbrella picture.

Math: Review number recognition of 11. Review the number 11 today. You may plan an "Eleven Hunt" in which students gather 11 of an item, such as 11 beans, 11 rocks, or 11 flowers. Can they write the number 11 and sequence numbers 1 -11?

Review oral counting 1-20 and 10-0.

Do the Lesson 70 Math worksheet. Instruct the students to trace the numbers, count each group, and then draw a line to the number for the group.

Shapes: Review triangle, circle, square, rectangle, and star shapes.

Color: Review the colors red, green, blue, black, white, yellow, brown, pink, purple, orange, and gray.

Story Time: Read a story or stories of your student's choice or ones they have brought from home.

Music: Continue with the review of songs you have already learned through this program.

Multimedia Resources: This week, listen and sing along to selections from the "Once Upon a Christmas" CD. This week, watch *The Kingdom Under the Sea* adventure "The Gift," which is a Christmas story.

Arts & Crafts: Give the students colored markers. Let them draw their interpretation of light and warmth.

Health & Safety: Review if there is an accident, and your clothes catch fire, you must remember to STOP, DROP, ROLL. Show the students the Lesson 69 Resource page. Let's say that together: STOP, DROP, ROLL. Now let's all practice. Let the students practice over and over again, until they have the movement memorized. Explain that if they see someone else with clothes on fire, they must yell STOP, DROP, ROLL to that person. Role play with two students where one accidentally catches on fire and the other shouts the STOP, DROP, ROLL instruction to them. Learn the "Stop, Drop, and Roll" song.

Stop, Drop, and Roll
Original Author Unknown
Tune of Hot Cross Buns

Stop, drop, and roll,
Stop, drop, and roll,
If your clothes ever catch on fire,
Stop, drop, and roll.

Physical Education: Repeat the Airplane Tilt activity. Do a follow the leader activity with the students pretending to be airplanes. They should walk, skip, hop or jump with their arms held out to their sides. When they are going straight their arms should be straight out. When they make a turn their arms should tilt in the direction of the turn. Do this as a follow the leader activity with all of the students copying the movements of the leader.

Homework: Remind the students to keep working on their Lesson 57 Homework worksheet where they record the weather each morning by drawing a sun, clouds, or rain.

NOTES:

AOP's Commitment to Quality—Tell us how we are doing

As a publisher dedicated to providing high quality educational materials we invite you to tell us how we are doing. Please visit our website at www.aop.com to give us your comments, concerns, and/or compliments concerning Horizons Preschool. Contact information can be found in the support area for Horizons at the AOP website.

Lesson 71

Week 15: Day 1

Activities in this Lesson: Bible Lesson, Social Studies, Science, Language Arts, Phonics, Reading, Writing, Memory Verse, Math, Shapes, Color, Story Time, Music, Arts & Crafts, Health & Safety, Physical Education

Bible Reference: Genesis 1:14-19.

Bible Concept to Present: God made the Moon for nighttime.

Bible Lesson: We know that God made the Sun on the 4th day of Creation. Did you know that God did not just make the Sun? He also made another light. This light is not as big as the Sun, but it is important for us too. This light shines at night. Can you guess the name of this light? That is a very good guess. This light is the Moon. When God made the Sun for daytime, He made the Moon for nighttime. The Moon is not as bright as the Sun, but it is just as important. If we had no Moon, our nights would be very, very dark. The Moon helps us in other ways, too. I am thankful God made the Moon to give me light at night.

Social Studies: The Moon helps us in many ways. One very important thing it does for us is to give us light at night. If we did not have the Moon, we would have a very dark night. The Moon helps the plants to grow at night too. Make a cut out of the Moon. Yellow construction paper should be used, and placed on a black background. Incorporate the teaching in Science below. Make the Moon in its various phases.

Science: Our Moon gets its light from the Sun. The Moon is always moving and so is the Earth. The relationship of the Earth and the Moon makes a difference as to how much of the lighted side of the Moon we see. We have included an illustration on Lesson 71 Resource page to explain this. Show your students a whole moon, a half moon and a quarter moon. Using a globe, shine the light of a flashlight over the globe to where the light hits a ball held on the other side at different angles as illustrated on the Lesson 71 Resource page. Then, using yellow construction paper, cut out that shape from the paper. Glue all moon phases on black construction paper.

Find a calendar that includes the phases of the Moon. Discuss the current phase of the Moon.

Language Arts: Ask your students: "What do you think the Moon is made of?" Let the children guess. What shape does it look like? There is a legend that said the Moon was made of green cheese. Ask, Do you think this is true. Why or why not?

Read the following action poem:

Moon Ride

Do you want to go up with me to the Moon? (point to friend, self, then to sky)
Let's get in our rocket ship and blast off soon! (pretend to climb in ship, swish hands quickly)
Faster and faster we reach to the sky (jump and reach)
Isn't it fun to be able to fly? (stretch arms out)
We're on the Moon, now all take a look (look down)

Phonics: Review the letter Vv.

Teach the small letter *v*. Write some words beginning with the letter *v* on the board. Include words from stories or activities that tie this lesson to other things that have already been done. Underline the small *v* that begins the words. Read through the words and point out the shape of letter *v*. Have the students trace the *v* in the air as you trace the letter *v* beginning each word.

Common words: very

Reading: Associate spoken and written language by matching written word labels with spoken words. Segment a spoken sentence into separate, distinct words. Point to words as distinct units on a page of print.

Multimedia Resources: View the Aa-Vv segments of "Rev-Up for Reading" from the "Rev-Up for Learning" DVD to drill letter recognition and sound. The students should say each letter sound along with the presentation.

Writing: For these two weeks focus on having the students write the first three letters of their first name freehand. During this time, write the students' names on all worksheets and papers leaving space for the first three letters and make the rest dotted or something that can be traced. They should have their Name Plates to look at as they do this.

Writing Skill Builders: Keep these objectives in mind as you direct the class. Incorporate writing strokes bowl, bridge, and diagonal lines.

Multimedia Resources: View the Aa-Vv segments of "Rev-Up for Writing" from the "Rev-Up for Learning" DVD to review the writing of upper- and lowercase letters. The students should write each letter in the air along with the presentation. Since the first half of the presentation covers lowercase letters and the second half uppercase letters some navigation will be needed to skip to the letters that are covered in this lesson.

Memory Verse: Genesis 1:16a.
God made two great lights—the greater light to govern the day and the lesser light to govern the night. Genesis 1:16a NIV

And God made two great lights; the greater light to rule the day, and the lesser light to rule the night: Genesis 1:16a KJV

This week we are adding to a verse we already learned. Explain any words that students might not understand, especially "lesser" and "govern." Later we will learn more of the verse. Let the students take Memory Verse Card 10 home.

Math: Teach number recognition of 12. Show students the number 12 flashcard. Begin to teach counting to the number 12. Count 12 of an item, such as toothpicks, spaghetti, etc. Listen carefully as each student counts to be certain that they are counting consecutively to twelve and not missing any numbers.

Review oral counting 1-20 and 10-0.

Do the Lesson 71a Math worksheet. Notice that all of the numbers are displayed on the page and that the number 12 is highlighted with a background. Have the students trace the large number 12 with the proper strokes by following the arrows. Instruct the students to count each group of items and then trace the number.

Do the Lesson 71b Math worksheet. Instruct the students to draw a line between the groups that have the same number.

Multimedia Resources: View "Rev-Up for Arithmetic" from the "Rev-Up for Learning" DVD to practice number recognition and counting 1-20.

Shapes: Review triangle, circle, square, rectangle, and star shapes.

Color: Review the colors red, green, blue, black, white, yellow, brown, pink, purple, orange, and gray.

Story Time: Read a story or stories of your choice.

Music: Continue with the review of songs you have already learned through this program.

Multimedia Resources: This week, listen and sing along to selections from "The Birthday Party" CD. This week, watch *The Kingdom Under the Sea* adventure "The Gift," which is a Christmas story.

Arts & Crafts: *Bring enough thick sliced cheese for each student to have several slices.* There is an old tale that the Moon was made of green cheese. While we know this is not true, cheese makes a wonderful medium with which to create. Give your students several pieces of processed cheese that has been sliced. Let them create as desired.

Health & Safety: Review STOP, DROP, ROLL. Review the "Stop, Drop, and Roll" song.

Teach the students that if they are in a building that is on fire and the room is full of smoke that they must "Get Low and Go" to reach safety. Discuss escape routes and how to get to exits of buildings. Practice this concept by hanging a sheet down low so that the students can crawl under it to safety.

Physical Education: Play an active game of your choice with your students today. Your goal is at least 25 minutes of exercise.

NOTES:

Activities in this Lesson: Bible Lesson, Science, Language Arts, Phonics, Reading, Writing, Memory Verse, Math, Shapes, Color, Story Time, Music, Arts & Crafts, Physical Education

Bible Reference: Genesis 1:14-19.

Bible Concept to Present: The evening sky can bring us peace as we consider the Heavens and the God who created them.

Bible Lesson: Say, God made so many beautiful things. He didn't have to make them beautiful, but He did. It is so peaceful to sit outside at night and look at the Moon rising in the east. The Moon rises in the east, just like the Sun. But the Moon has a different orbit. It is in the sky at different places and different times.

Illustration: Hand out the student flashlights. It is very interesting that the Moon really has no light of its own. It is simply reflecting the light from the Sun. Remember when we talked about reflected light when we studied light? Shine your flashlights around the room. What in the room reflects light back to you? That is what the Moon does. The rays of light from the Sun hit the Moon, then the rays come down to us. So moonlight is really sunlight.

Multimedia Resources: Watch "Peace" from the *Character Builders Video Series*.

Science: *Cut out a very small white circle, a small green circle and a very big yellow circle.* You want these to represent the Moon, the Earth and the Sun. Talk to the students about the size of the Moon and the Sun. Explain that even though the Sun might look smaller than the Moon, it is much, much, much bigger! It is simply very far away. Lay the Sun on the floor in the middle of the room. Go to the edge and place the Earth. Talk about orbits and the Earth revolving around the Sun. Then add the little Moon. Explain that the Moon is revolving around the Earth as the Earth is revolving around the Sun. Let the students move the pieces around. Save the circles for another day.

Language Arts: This is an old rhyme that children have been saying for years and years. Learn the rhyme together.

I See the Moon

I see the Moon and the Moon sees me.
God bless the Moon and God bless me.

Review "Moon Ride" action poem from Lesson 71.

Phonics: Review the letters Aa-Vv.

Do the Lesson 72 Phonics worksheet. Complete the letter Vv worksheet. Notice that all of the letters of the alphabet are displayed on the page and that the letters Vv are highlighted with a background. As the students get better at letter recognition you can call out a letter and ask the students to point it out with their finger. Trace the large letter and the small letter. The students can trace the letters between the guide lines. Review the pictures and the colored first letter of the words. The students can color the letters as desired.

Reading: Associate spoken and written language by matching written word labels with spoken words. Segment a spoken sentence into separate, distinct words. Point to words as distinct units on a page of print.

Writing: For these two weeks focus on having the students write the first three letters of their first name freehand. During this time, write the students' names on all worksheets and papers leaving space for the first three letters and make the rest dotted or something that can be traced. They should have their Name Plates to look at as they do this.

Writing Skill Builders: Keep these objectives in mind as you direct the class. Incorporate writing strokes bowl, bridge, and diagonal lines.

Memory Verse: Study the memory verse Genesis 1:16a. Let one student be the Sun and another the Moon.

EVERYONE SAYS:	God made two great lights—
THE SUNS SAY:	the greater light to govern the day
THE MOONS SAY:	and the lesser light to govern the night.

If you only have one student, then you can be the Sun and let him/her be the Moon.

Math: Review number recognition of 12. Review oral counting 1-20 and 10-0.

Do the Lesson 72 Math worksheet. Cut out the numbers from the strip. Count each group of objects and paste the correct number in the box.

Shapes: Review triangle, circle, square, rectangle, and star shapes.

Color: Review the colors red, green, blue, black, white, yellow, brown, pink, purple, orange, and gray.

Story Time: Read a story or stories of your choice.

Music: Review "My God is So Big" on the "Horizons Preschool Music" CD.

Multimedia Resources: This week, listen and sing along to selections from "The Birthday Party" CD. This week, watch *The Kingdom Under the Sea* adventure "The Gift," which is a Christmas story.

Arts & Crafts: Instruct the students on some scissors practice. Hand out children's scissors to everyone. Give each student a piece of white construction paper and one paper cup. Show the students how to use the cup as a pattern for a circle. Let them draw several circles on their paper. Show the children the moon phases you made yesterday. Let them cut out some moon phases.

Go to the Creation Mural or get it out again. Add the Moon to Day 4. Use the different phases of the Moon the students have cut out, gluing them onto the mural in order, in an arch, as if the Moon was going across the sky in stages. Be sure to save room for the stars, to be added next week.

Give the students playdough. Let them create the phases of the Moon.

Physical Education: Play another active game of your choice with your students. Your goal is at least 25 minutes of exercise.

Optional Math/Language Arts/Bible/Arts & Crafts Activity:

12 Baskets: Matthew 14:13-21, Mark 6:30-44, read the Bible verses and tell the story.

Twelve baskets of food were leftover after Jesus' miracle. One day Jesus fed more than five thousand people with five loaves and two fishes. There were twelve baskets full of food left over. Jesus could do this because He was God's Son.

Do the Lesson 72 Bible Numbers worksheet. Give each student a sheet of white construction paper and the worksheet. Cut out the items on the worksheet and glue them to construction paper as illustrated in the drawing. Draw in the arms, legs, and faces for the "12" baskets gathered by the disciples. Draw in the rest of the picture.

This concludes the optional Bible Numbers activities. If you chose not to do them they would fit in well as a review of numbers over the next couple of weeks.

Health & Safety: Review STOP, DROP, ROLL. Review the "Stop, Drop, and Roll" song.

Review "Get Low and Go." Review escape routes and how to get to exits of buildings. Practice this concept by hanging a sheet down low so that the students can crawl under it to safety.

NOTES:

Lesson 73

Week 15: Day 3

Activities in this Lesson: Bible Lesson, Social Studies, Science, Language Arts, Phonics, Reading, Writing, Memory Verse, Math, Shapes, Color, Story Time, Music, Health & Safety, Physical Education

Bible Reference: Genesis 1:14 -19.

Bible Concept to Present: The Moon which God made is very important to us.

Bible Lesson: God made the Moon to be very special for us. The Moon not only gives us light at the nighttime, but it also helps the plants to grow. Did you know that there are some people who look at the Moon and wait for it to look just right before they will plant seeds and then they wait for just the right sort of Moon before they will pick their crops? They believe the Moon helps the plants to grow faster and bigger. The Moon also makes a difference in how big the waves of the ocean are and how far they come up onto the land. Have you ever been to the beach and seen the waves come up very high onto the land? The Moon helps them to do this. The Moon also helps them to stay further away from the land. We call this high and low tide. The Moon is very important to us. God knew we would need it for light, for helping the ocean waves, and for helping plants to grow. I am thankful God made the Moon to help us.

Social Studies: A very long time ago when our country was new, there was a man who was a printer and a scientist (explain these terms). His name was Benjamin Franklin, and he printed a magazine called *Poor Richard's Almanac*. It was a book that told people when to plant their seeds and when to harvest their crops according to the fullness of the Moon. Years later, Benjamin Franklin became one of the men who helped to made America a strong country. God helped Benjamin Franklin to learn about the world around him. This quote from Benjamin Franklin is great. It talks about what we studied last week! "Do not anticipate trouble, or worry about what may never happen. Keep in the sunlight." And here is another one: "Early to bed and early to rise makes a man healthy, wealthy, and wise."

Science: The Moon shines all the time, we just do not see it because the daytime light is brighter than the nighttime light. To illustrate this, take a flashlight into a dark room. You can see the light of the flashlight. Now take it into the sunlight. You cannot see it as easily because the light from the Sun is bigger than the light from the flashlight. Equate to the Sun being the larger light and the Moon being the lesser light. God planned it this way. It is as the Bible says.

Language Arts: American astronauts have been on the Moon. Pretend now to be an astronaut and land on the Moon. What do you see? What does it smell like? Do they have a McDonald's on the Moon? Why not? Encourage your students to express and imagine. The Usborne book *Rockets and Space Flight* has lots of information about space flight. Review the story of the first Moon missions.

Review "I See the Moon" rhyme.

Phonics: Teach the letter Ww.

Show students the letter Ww flashcard. Point out any student's name beginning with the letter *W*.

Write some words beginning with the letter *W* on the board. Include any student names from the class that begin with letter *W*. Underline the capital *W* that begins the words. Read through the words and point out the shape of letter *W*. Have the students trace the *W* in the air as you trace the letter *W* beginning each name.

Boys: Wade, Waggoner, Wallace, Walter, Wendell, Wesley, Whitley, William, Willis, Woody, Wyatt
Girls: Wanda, Waneta, Wendy, Whitney, Wilma, Winifred, Winona
Vocabulary words: WALK, WAIT, Wednesday

Do the Lesson 73 Phonics worksheet. Complete the letter Ww worksheet. Have the students trace the letters Ww with their fingers. They should trace the letters with their fingers and say the names of the letters. Demonstrate the proper strokes for them on the board. Say the words for each of the pictures and look at the Ww letters that begin them.

Reading: Associate spoken and written language by matching written word labels with spoken words. Segment a spoken sentence into separate, distinct words. Point to words as distinct units on a page of print.

Writing: For these two weeks focus on having the students write the first three letters of their first name freehand. During this time, write the students' names on all worksheets and papers leaving space for the first three letters and make the rest dotted or something that can be traced. They should have their Name Plates to look at as they do this.

Writing Skill Builders: Keep these objectives in mind as you direct the class. Incorporate writing strokes bowl, bridge, and diagonal lines.

Memory Verse: Study the memory verse Genesis 1:16a. Reverse the roles of letting students be the Sun and the Moon.

EVERYONE SAYS: God made two great lights—
THE SUNS SAY: the greater light to govern the day
THE MOONS SAY: and the lesser light to govern the night.

If you only have one student, then you can be the Moon and let him/her be the Sun.

Math: Review number recognition of 12. 12 of an item is a dozen. We call a group of 12 eggs a dozen. We call 12 cookies a dozen. Show students 12 buttons: 4 red, 4 white and 4 black. (Or whatever colors you have in 4's) Practice counting to 12, then dividing them into color groups.

Review oral counting 1-20 and 10-0.

Do the Lesson 73 Math worksheet. Count each group of items and circle the correct number for the group.

Shapes: Teach the heart shape.

Do the Lesson 73 Shapes worksheet. Have the students trace the heart. All of the letters in the word *heart* have been covered. Point out the letters in the word *heart*. Have the students trace the letters in the word *heart*.

Multimedia Resources: Listen to the song "Your Heart" from the "Bullfrogs and Butterflies: I've Been Born Again" CD.

Color: Review the colors red, green, blue, black, white, yellow, brown, pink, purple, orange, and gray.

Story Time: Read a story or stories of your choice.

Music: Review "My God is So Big."

Multimedia Resources: This week, listen and sing along to selections from "The Birthday Party" CD. This week, watch *The Kingdom Under the Sea* adventure "The Gift," which is a Christmas story.

Health & Safety: Review STOP, DROP, ROLL. Review the "Stop, Drop, and Roll" song. Review "Get Low and Go."

Physical Education: Practice skipping. This requires motor coordination that is important for the child to develop. You may vary the time spent according to the needs of the child.

Homework: Remind the students to keep working on their Lesson 57 Homework worksheet where they record the weather each morning by drawing a sun, clouds, or rain.

NOTES:

Activities in this Lesson: Bible Lesson, Science, Language Arts, Phonics, Reading, Writing, Memory Verse/Outdoor Activity, Math, Shapes, Color, Story Time, Music, Arts & Crafts, Health & Safety, Physical Education

Bible Reference: Genesis 1:14-19.

Bible Concept to Present: The Moon is a big part of our life.

Bible Lesson: Say, You will hear people talk about "The Man on the Moon." Several valleys and mountains on the Moon make it look like there is a face up there. Have you ever seen the face on the Moon? There really isn't a face up there. The mountains God made just make some interesting shadows. God knows every mountain He made on the Moon.

Social Studies: Mankind has looked at the Moon, written about the Moon and sung about the Moon for all of history. Years ago, the idea of traveling to the Moon was laughable. Then many countries tried to be the first to put a man on the Moon. First, a man had to travel around the Earth in a special space vehicle. Then several men flew to the Moon using rockets and a space capsule. Many astronauts believe in God and are awed by the Moon that God created.

One of the things the Moon astronauts did was read the Bible from space. On Apollo 8, one of the Moon missions, the first scripture was read from space. "On the fourth day [of the mission], Christmas Eve, communications were interrupted as Apollo 8 passed behind the moon, and the astronauts became the first men to see the moon's far side. Later that day, during the evening hours in the United States, the crew read the first 10 verses of Genesis on television to earth and wished viewers 'goodnight, good luck, a Merry Christmas and God bless all of you - all of you on the good earth.' Subsequently, *TV Guide* for May 10-16, 1969, claimed that one out of every four persons on earth - nearly 1 billion people in 64 countries - heard the astronauts' reading and greeting, either on radio or on TV; and delayed broadcasts that same day reached 30 additional countries." * Read the first ten verses of Genesis chapter one to the students.

There are maps of the Moon landscape, just as there are maps of the Earth. If possible, get a map of the Moon, even a small one. Show it to the class. Show the class Lesson 74b Resource page.

Science: Be prepared to write on the board. Say, When people travel in space to go to the Moon, they have to bring everything with them that they will need. That is a lot of things. What things do you think astronauts need in space? Write their suggestions on the board. Be sure that air, water, food and heat are mentioned. Many of our food products come from research in making space foods. Tang® orange drink was first made for the astronauts. Granola bars and energy drinks were made for them, too. Now there is a space station up in space, orbiting our Earth. Astronauts in the space station have to be sure they bring everything they need. If they run out of something, they have to wait for another shuttle flight to bring it up to them.

Language Arts: There are hundreds of poems and songs written about the Moon. Let's make some rhymes. Tell me the word that rhymes with moon to finish the sentence.

When I sit down to dinner, I use a knife, fork and _____ . SPOON
I love lunch time, when it's time to eat. That time is called _____ . NOON

When I am really happy, I whistle a little _____ . TUNE

At my last birthday party, a friend of mine popped my _____ . BALLOON

When we were at the zoo, we saw a very big, ugly monkey called a _____ . BABOON

Many, many brides chose to get married in the summer, in the month of _____ . JUNE

Phonics: Review the letter Ww.

Do the Lesson 74 Phonics worksheet. Complete the letter Ww worksheet. Notice that all of the letters of the alphabet are displayed on the page and that the letters Ww are highlighted with a background. Trace the large letter and the small letter. The students can trace the letters between the guide lines. Review the pictures and the colored first letter of the words. The students can color the letters as desired.

Reading: Associate spoken and written language by matching written word labels with spoken words. Segment a spoken sentence into separate, distinct words. Point to words as distinct units on a page of print.

Writing: For these two weeks focus on having the students write the first three letters of their first name freehand. During this time, write the students' names on all worksheets and papers leaving space for the first three letters and make the rest dotted or something that can be traced. They should have their Name Plates to look at as they do this.

Writing Skill Builders: Keep these objectives in mind as you direct the class. Incorporate writing strokes bowl, bridge, and diagonal lines.

Memory Verse/Outdoor Activity: Review the memory verse Genesis 1:16a. Take a walk. Sing or chant the verse as you walk. Have students point to the Sun as you get to that line of the verse. Look and see if the Moon is visible.

Math: Review number recognition of 12. Conclude the teaching of the numbering 1 -12.

Do the Lesson 74 Math worksheet. Cut out the butterfly, mix up the pieces and put the puzzle together in number order.

Learn verse twelve of "This Old Man, He Played One"

This Old Man, He Played One

Verse 1
This old man, he played one, He played nick-nack on my thumb;
with a nick-nack paddy whack, give a dog a bone. This old man came rolling home.

Verse 2
This old man, he played two, He played nick-nack on my shoe;
with a nick-nack paddy whack, give a dog a bone. This old man came rolling home.

Verse 3
This old man, he played three, He played nick-nack on my on my knee;
with a nick-nack paddy whack, give a dog a bone. This old man came rolling home.

Verse 4
This old man, he played four, He played nick-nack on my door;
with a nick-nack paddy whack, give a dog a bone. This old man came rolling home.

Verse 5
This old man, he played five, He played nick-nack on my hive;
with a nick-nack paddy whack, give a dog a bone. This old man came rolling home.

Verse 6
This old man, he played six, He played nick-nack on my sticks;
with a nick-nack paddy whack, give a dog a bone. This old man came rolling home.

Verse 7
This old man, he played seven, He played nick-nack up in Heaven;
with a nick-nack paddy whack, give a dog a bone. This old man came rolling home.

Verse 8
This old man, he played eight, He played nick-nack on my gate;
with a nick-nack paddy whack, give a dog a bone. This old man came rolling home.

Verse 9
This old man, he played nine, He played nick-nack on my spine;
with a nick-nack paddy whack, give a dog a bone. This old man came rolling home.

Verse 10
This old man, he played ten, He played nick-nack once again;
with a nick-nack paddy whack, give a dog a bone. This old man came rolling home.

Verse 11
This old man, he played eleven, He played knick knack up in Heaven,
with a Knick, knack, paddy whack, Give the dog a bone; This old man came rolling home.

Verse 12
This old man, he played twelve, He played knick knack, dig and delve,
with a Knick, knack, paddy whack, Give the dog a bone; This old man came rolling home

Shapes: Review the heart shape. Use the hearts in the Lesson 74 Resource page to play a concentration game of matching hearts that are the same.

Color: Review the colors red, green, blue, black, white, yellow, brown, pink, purple, orange, and gray.

Story Time: Read a story or stories of your choice.

Music: Review "My God is So Big."

Multimedia Resources: This week, listen and sing along to selections from "The Birthday Party" CD. This week, watch *The Kingdom Under the Sea* adventure "The Gift," which is a Christmas story.

Arts & Crafts: Give each student a large piece of white construction paper. Say, Pretend that this paper is your suitcase. You are packing the suitcase to go to the Moon. What things would you take? Draw all of the things you would pack in your suitcase.

Health & Safety: The most important thing the astronauts need in space is good air. We have to have air to breathe. We have to breathe many times a minute. Can you feel your breath going in and out? Spaceships have equipment that cleans the air for the astronauts. We must always try to breathe clean air. If the air outside is smoky or dirty, we should stay inside. Some big cities have dirty air. This air makes people sick. Sometimes they have to wear breathing masks to clean the air before it goes into their body. Some people smoke cigarettes. This means they are pulling smoky air into the wonderful lungs that God made for them. The best thing to do is never smoke a cigarette. We want to keep our lungs clean.

Physical Education: Moon Walk. Take an imaginary moon walk. Find an area with some obstacles for pretend mountains and go exploring on a moon walk. Walk up and down the mountains.

NOTES:

*http://www.astronautix.com/details/apoo8829.htm

Activities in this Lesson: Bible Lesson, Social Studies, Science, Language Arts, Phonics, Reading, Writing, Memory Verse, Math, Shapes, Color, Story Time, Music, Arts & Crafts, Physical Education

Bible Reference: Genesis 1:14-19.

Bible Concept to Present: When God created our Moon, He knew it would be visited some day by man.

Bible Lesson: God made our Moon very special. He made it just like he wanted to. And when He made it, He knew that one day people would visit it. The first man to walk on the Moon was named Neil Armstrong. Mr. Armstrong believed in God and believed that God made the Moon. When he walked on the Moon, Mr. Armstrong said "In the beginning God created the heaven and earth." He was quoting from the Bible about how God had made the Moon. God helped Mr. Armstrong to learn about the Moon. God wants us to know about the world He has made too.

Social Studies: People who travel to the Moon are called Astronauts. Astronauts are scientists (explain term) who travel into space. Astronauts must know much about the Moon. They must know much about math too. To be an astronaut you must have studied very hard. Astronauts wear special suits when they travel in space and eat special food. They travel in a special ship called a spaceship. It looks like a rocket. God helps Astronauts to learn about the world He has made.

Science: When Neil Armstrong set foot on the Moon, he did not walk like we do. Instead he bounced. The Moon is different from the Earth, so the way people walk on the Moon is different too. It is like having very little weight. The Moon is also dusty. It has no water on it so no trees or flowers can grow there. No animals can live there. We could not live on the Moon.

Language Arts: Take a pretend trip to the Moon again today. Concentrate on the student expressing what they "see" on this pretend trip. Dramatize the trip. Incorporate with Social Studies.

Phonics: Review the letters Aa-Ww.

Teach the small letter *w*. Write some words beginning with the letter *w* on the board. Include words from stories or activities that tie this lesson to other things that have already been done. Underline the small *w* that begins the words. Read through the words and point out the shape of letter *w*. Have the students trace the *w* in the air as you trace the letter *w* beginning each word.

    Common words: want, was, water, way, we, well, went, were, what, when, where, which, while, who, why, will, with, word, work, world, would, write

    Vocabulary words: waist, walk, watch, week, weekend, white, wide, wind, woods, wrist

Do the Lesson 75 Phonics worksheet. Do the Letter Find worksheet. Have the students put a red heart around the Uu letters, a purple X on the Vv letters, and a black circle around the Ww letters. Give them one direction at a time so they can focus on finding the correct letter shape. Begin with capital *U*, then lowercase *u*, etc. Show them examples with flashcards or letters written on the board.

Reading: Associate spoken and written language by matching written word labels with spoken words. Segment a spoken sentence into separate, distinct words. Point to words as distinct units on a page of print.

Writing: For these two weeks focus on having the students write the first three letters of their first name freehand. During this time, write the students' names on all worksheets and papers leaving space for the first three letters and make the rest dotted or something that can be traced. They should have their Name Plates to look at as they do this.

Writing Skill Builders: Keep these objectives in mind as you direct the class. Incorporate writing strokes bowl, bridge, and diagonal lines.

Memory Verse: Finish memory work on Genesis 1:16a today. Let those students recite that want to do so.

Math: Review number recognition of 12. Review oral counting 1-20 and 10-0.

Review patterns. Use shape patterns to extend simple patterns. Try using 3 different shapes. The concept can also be taught using letters of the alphabet. (AMCAMCAM _?_)

Do Lesson 75a Math worksheet. Do the first row of patterns together with the students.

Do the Lesson 75b Math worksheet. Instruct the students to trace the numbers, count each group, and then draw a line to the number for the group.

Shapes: Review the heart shape. Use the hearts in the Lesson 74 Resource page to play a concentration game of matching hearts that are the same.

Color: Review the colors red, green, blue, black, white, yellow, brown, pink, purple, orange, and gray.

Story Time: Read a story or stories of your student's choice or ones they have brought from home.

Music: Review "Countdown" and "My God Is So Big."

Multimedia Resources: This week, listen and sing along to selections from "The Birthday Party" CD. This week, watch *The Kingdom Under the Sea* adventure "The Gift," which is a Christmas story.

Arts & Crafts: Give the students laundry baskets, cardboard, chairs, or anything else available and let them create a spaceship. Encourage them to pretend that they are astronauts. Help them verbalize what is happening. What will they eat? What will they wear? What are they now seeing?

If possible, provide each student with a cardboard box. You might cut windows into the boxes ahead of time. Let the students use poster pens and make the box into a space vehicle. Use the circles you saved from an earlier project to represent the Earth, the Moon and the Sun. Set the Earth and the Moon on opposite sides of the room and let the students "fly" back and forth. Save the circles for another day.

Physical Education: Super Ball Bounce. Obtain a number of super balls. Since the gravity on the Moon is less than on Earth it is different walking on the Moon. Bounce some regular balls and then give the students some super balls to bounce and chase pretending that they are on the Moon. Do this in an enclosed area so the balls don't get lost. To lessen the chance of an accident, this may need to be done in a relay format so that not so many balls are bouncing around at one time.

Homework: Remind the students to keep working on their Lesson 57 Homework worksheet where they record the weather each morning by drawing a sun, clouds, or rain.

NOTES:

Lesson 76

Week 16: Day 1

Activities in this Lesson: Bible Lesson, Social Studies, Science, Language Arts, Phonics, Reading, Writing, Memory Verse, Math, Shapes, Color, Story Time, Music, Arts & Crafts, Physical Education, Homework, Additional Stories

Bible Reference: Genesis 1:14-19.

Bible Concept to Present: On the fourth day of Creation, God made the Sun and Moon. He also made the stars.

Bible Lesson: Can you tell me what God created on the first day of Creation? Review with the Days of Creation Numbers. On the second day? On the third day? Very good. You also know that on the fourth day of Creation, God made the Sun and Moon. Did you know that God made the stars on the fourth day, too? He did. When we look up into the sky at night, we can see many, many stars. God made them all. Although there are many stars, God made each one of them. Stars send their light to us here on Earth from very far away. Isn't it wonderful to see the stars at night? God is so good to us. Let's thank Him for the stars.

Multimedia Resources: Listen to the song "Some Invisible Things Are Real" from the "Music Machine: The Majesty of God" CD.

Social Studies: People who study the stars are called astronomers. These people study how far the stars are from one another, and how far they are from us. They study to find out what a star is made of and how stars change. An astronomer is a scientist. They use the laws of science to study the stars which God has made.

Science: What gives the stars their light? There is a special energy in stars. When little bits of the star join together they release lots of energy and it makes a bright light. Did you know that stars are always in the sky? They continually shine. But we don't always see them because the sunshine of the day is brighter than the light from the stars. Did you know that our Sun is a star? Stars send their light to us from very, very far away. If we got into a rocket ship to travel to the stars we would have to travel for many years. The stars are even further away from us than our Sun. This evening, go out into the night and look at the stars. Express how wonderful God was to make so many stars and how big He is to make them so far away.

Language Arts: Sing the familiar song: "Twinkle, Twinkle Little Star" to your students. There is a Christian version of this poem in *The Christian Mother Goose Book of Nursery Rhymes* by Marjorie Ainsborough Decker. You may also quote other "Star" poetry you know, such as "Star Light, Star Bright." You will want students to memorize one or two "Star" poems throughout the next two weeks.

Phonics: Teach the letter Xx.

Show students the letter Xx flashcard. Point out any student's name beginning with the letter *X*. Write some words beginning with the letter *X* on the board. Include any student names from the class that begin with letter *X*. Underline the capital *X* that begins the words. Read through the words and point out the shape of letter *X*. Have the students trace the *X* in the air as you trace the letter *X* beginning each name.

Boys: Xander, Xanti, Xarles, Xavier, Xenon
Girls: Xantara, Xanthe, Xaria, Xaviera, Xena, Xhosa, Xia, Xiang, Xiu, Xylia
Vocabulary word: Xerox, X-ray

Do the Lesson 76 Phonics worksheet. Complete the letter Xx worksheet. Have the students trace the letters Xx with their fingers. They should trace the letters with their fingers and say the names of the letters. Demonstrate the proper strokes for them on the board. Say the words for each of the pictures and look at the Xx letters that begin them. There are two sounds for Xx in the words.

Reading: Associate spoken and written language by matching written word labels with spoken words. Segment a spoken sentence into separate, distinct words. Point to words as distinct units on a page of print.

Multimedia Resources: View the Aa-Xx segments of "Rev-Up for Reading" from the "Rev-Up for Learning" DVD to drill letter recognition and sound. The students should say each letter sound along with the presentation.

Writing: For these two weeks focus on having the students write the first three letters of their first name freehand. During this time, write the students' names on all worksheets and papers leaving space for the first three letters and make the rest dotted or something that can be traced. They should have their Name Plates to look at as they do this.

Writing Skill Builders: Keep these objectives in mind as you direct the class. Incorporate writing strokes bowl, bridge, and diagonal lines.

Multimedia Resources: View the Aa-Xx segments of "Rev-Up for Writing" from the "Rev-Up for Learning" DVD to review the writing of upper- and lowercase letters. The students should write each letter in the air along with the presentation. Since the first half of the presentation covers lowercase letters and the second half uppercase letters some navigation will be needed to skip to the letters that are covered in this lesson.

Memory Verse: Genesis 1:16
God made two great lights... the greater light to govern the day and the lesser light to govern the night. He also made the stars. Genesis 1:16 NIV

And God made two great lights; the greater light to rule the day, and the lesser light to rule the night: He made the stars also. Genesis 1:16 KJV

This week, we are adding to a verse we already learned. Students will be learning a very long verse, isn't that great? Think about all God created on the fourth day. He made the Sun and put it in the sky. He made the Moon. Then He made every star, and gave every one of them a name. (Psalm 147:4) Have students take Memory Verse Card 11 home.

Math: Teach telling time to the hour. Review number recognition 1-12. The clock is what we use to tell time. The front of the clock is called the face, and the pieces that move around it are called the hands. The big hand is the minute hand and the little hand is the hour hand. When the big hand is on the 12, the little hand tells us what hour it is. An hour is 60 minutes. Set the clock to several different hours and ask the students what time it is. Have students come up to the clock and set several different times to the hour.

Do the Lesson 76 Math worksheet. Circle the correct number of objects for each number.

Multimedia Resources: View "Rev-Up for Arithmetic" from the "Rev-Up for Learning" DVD to practice number recognition and counting 1-20.

Shapes: Review the heart shape.

Color: Review the colors red, green, blue, black, white, yellow, brown, pink, purple, orange, and gray.

Story Time: Read a story or stories of your choice.

Music: Review "My God Is So Big."

Multimedia Resources: This week, listen and sing along to selections from the "Once Upon a Christmas" CD. This week, watch *The Kingdom Under the Sea* adventure "The Gift," which is a Christmas story.

Arts & Crafts: Give the students yellow clay. Let them create as desired.

Physical Education: Make a balance beam by placing cement or wood blocks under a 2 x 4 that is six feet long. It might be necessary to put some padding around the cement blocks or just lay the 2 x 4 on the floor or sidewalk. During this week let the students practice the following:

1. Walk forward on the beam, placing one foot in front of the other to do so.
2. Walk backward on the beam.
3. Walk forward to the half way point of the beam, and then turn around and walk back to the point of origination.
4. Walk forward with the left foot always in front of the right foot.
5. Walk forward with hands held on hips.
6. Walk backward with hands held on hips.
7. Walk forward, pick up a rock in the middle of the beam.
8. Walk forward, kneel on one knee, rise and continue to walk to the end of the beam.
9. Walk forward with a light book balanced on the head.
10. Walk backward with a light book balanced on the head.

Homework: Say, Remember that everyone is working on a weather chart? Bring your chart in to school tomorrow. We will see what kind of weather we have had for a month.

Additional Star Stories: The story of Jesus' birth and the appearance of the special star. (Matthew chapter 2) Abraham who was promised his descendants would be as the stars in the sky. (Genesis 15:5) Joseph's dream about the stars. (Genesis 37:9)

NOTES:

Activities in this Lesson: Bible Lesson, Science/Language Arts, Homework/Science Review, Language Arts, Phonics, Reading, Writing, Memory Verse, Math, Shapes, Color, Story Time, Music, Arts & Crafts, Physical Education

Bible Reference: Genesis 1:14-19.

Bible Concept to Present: God named every star with beautiful names.

Bible Lesson: Review the Bible lesson from Lesson 76. God named every star. He gave some of them beautiful names.

Science/Language Arts: The stars look alike, don't they? But they are really all very different. They are different sizes and different levels of brightness. Some are huge and are very, very bright. Some of them even change, sometimes growing brighter, then becoming dimmer. Some of the stars have very interesting and famous names. Let's see if you can say their names.

The closest star to us: Alpha Centauri
Some of the brightest stars: Sirius, Canis Major, Canopus, Rigel Orion, Beta Centauri
The star that expands and shrinks: Betelgeuse Orion
What star is our biggest help in navigation and direction? The North star, Polaris.

Homework/Science Review: Did everyone remember to bring the weather chart? Let's talk about them. Did you have fun keeping track of the weather every day? Does everyone's chart agree? Or did some of you have different weather? Did you know that there are people that study the weather? And report it on television? They have to study for many years, studying the clouds and the air currents. There are some weather events that are very bad. Hurricanes and tornadoes are very strong storms. We are so fortunate that weather experts can now tell us when a bad storm is coming so we can be prepared.

Language Arts: Here is a star poem to share and discuss. It is the traditional "Twinkle, Twinkle Little Star" with a second verse.

The Star
by Jane Taylor

Twinkle, twinkle little star, How I wonder what you are!
Up above the world so high, Like a diamond in the sky.
As your bright and tiny spark, Lights the traveler in the dark—
Though I know not what you are, Twinkle, twinkle little star.

Here's a famous song about a star. Can it really happen?

Catch a Falling Star
by Paul Vance/Lee Pockriss, 1957
Catch a falling star and put it in your pocket
Never let it fade away.
Catch a falling star and put it in your pocket
Save it for a rainy day.

Continue to work on the star poems that you introduced in Lesson 76.

Phonics: Review the letter Xx.

Teach the small letter *x*. Write some words beginning with the letter *x* on the board. Include words from stories or activities that tie this lesson to other things that have already been done. Underline the small *x* that begins the words. Read through the words and point out the shape of letter *x*. Have the students trace the *x* in the air as you trace the letter *x* beginning each word.

Common word: xylophone

Do the Lesson 77 Phonics worksheet. Complete the letter Xx worksheet. Notice that all of the letters of the alphabet are displayed on the page and that the letters Xx are highlighted with a background. Trace the large letter and the small letter. The students can trace the letters between the guide lines. Review the pictures and the colored first or last letter of the words. The students can color the letters as desired. There are two sounds for Xx in the words.

Reading: Associate spoken and written language by matching written word labels with spoken words. Segment a spoken sentence into separate, distinct words. Point to words as distinct units on a page of print.

Writing: For these two weeks focus on having the students write the first three letters of their first name freehand. During this time, write the students' names on all worksheets and papers leaving space for the first three letters and make the rest dotted or something that can be traced. They should have their Name Plates to look at as they do this.

Writing Skill Builders: Keep these objectives in mind as you direct the class. Incorporate writing strokes bowl, bridge, and diagonal lines.

Memory Verse: Review Genesis 1:16. What a powerful memory verse we are learning. What does the memory verse tell us about God? He made the Sun, the Moon, and the stars. He is powerful and strong. He cares about us. Everyone say the verse together.

Math: Review telling time to the hour. Review number recognition 1-12. Throughout the day set the clock to different times and ask the students to tell you what time you have set the clock to. If you have an actual clock on the wall, occasionally ask the students to tell you the time when it moves to the hour. Have the students count aloud the number of girls in the class, boys in the class, students with brown hair, blond hair, shirt or blouse color, etc.

Do the Lesson 77 Math worksheet. Draw lines to match the numbers on the sheet.

Shapes: Review the heart shape.

Color: Review the colors red, green, blue, black, white, yellow, brown, pink, purple, orange, and gray.

Story Time: Read a story or stories of your choice.

Music: Review "My God Is So Big."

Multimedia Resources: This week, listen and sing along to selections from the "Once Upon a Christmas" CD. This week, watch *The Kingdom Under the Sea* adventure "The Gift," which is a Christmas story.

Arts & Crafts: *Prepare ahead: Make copies of Lesson 77 Resource page so that you have one star per student.* Cut the paper on the lines. Have scissors and glue sticks for each student. Also have one container of glitter. Say, Today we will be practicing our cutting. We will cut out stars and add them to the Creation Mural. First, cut out your stars. Then spread glue all over it. Raise your hand when you are ready, and I will come and pour some glitter on the glue. Carefully go to the trash and pour off the extra glitter. Bring the star up to the mural and we will glue them on. (Remember to have students wash their hands after the project.)

Physical Education: Continue the balance beam exercises.

NOTES:

Lesson 78

Week 16: Day 3

Activities in this Lesson: Bible Lesson, Music, Social Studies, Science, Language Arts, Phonics, Reading, Writing, Memory Verse, Math, Shapes, Color, Story Time, Music, Creative Cooking, Arts & Crafts, Physical Education

Bible Reference: Genesis 1:16 and Psalms 147:4.

Bible Concept to Present: Only God knows how many stars there are in the sky.

Bible Lesson: Our God is such a big God. He is big enough to make the Sun, the Moon, and the stars. And He is big enough to place them far, far away from us and from each other. God made many, many stars. Did you know that there has never been a man anywhere who has been able to count the stars? No person knows how many stars there are. But God does. God knows exactly how many stars there are. He knows how many stars there are because he made them. In the Bible, it says that "God counts the number of the stars." Only God knows how many stars there are. Aren't you happy that God can count the stars? God is a very BIG God.

Social Studies: People who study stars look through strong telescopes to see the stars. A telescope makes the stars look closer to the person looking through it. Show students a picture of a telescope. If you have a pair of binoculars, let the children look through those and explain that the telescope makes the stars look even closer than the binoculars do.

Science: Scientists have told us that there are many, many stars that we do not even see. There are many stars, too far away for even the strongest telescope to see. Because the stars are so far away and there are so many, there is no way to count them. How far can your students count? Even if they could count to a billion, they could not count all the stars in the sky. Draw a parallel between how many stars there are and how big our God is.

Language Arts: Continue to work on the star poems from Lessons 76 and 77.

Phonics: Teach the letter Yy.

Show students the letter Yy flashcard. Point out any student's name beginning with the letter *Y*. Write some words beginning with the letter *Y* on the board. Include any student names from the class that begin with letter *Y*. Underline the capital *Y* that begins the words. Read through the words and point out the shape of letter *Y*. Have the students trace the *Y* in the air as you trace the letter *Y* beginning each name.

> Boys: Yaakov, Yael, Yadid, Yanni, Yaro, Yaser, Yazid, Yitro, York, Yosef, Yoshi, Yul, Yuma, Yuri, Yves
> Girls: Yama, Yan, Yana, Yasmin, Yatima, Yesenia, Yelena, Yessica, Yetta, Yettie, Yori, Yoshiko, Yvette, Yvonne
> Vocabulary word: Yellow Pages

Do the Lesson 78 Phonics worksheet. Complete the letter Yy worksheet. Have the students trace the letters Yy with their fingers. They should trace the letters with their fingers and say the names of the letters. Demonstrate the proper strokes for them on the board. Say the words for each of the pictures and look at the Yy letters that begin them.

Reading: Associate spoken and written language by matching written word labels with spoken words. Segment a spoken sentence into separate, distinct words. Point to words as distinct units on a page of print.

Writing: For these two weeks focus on having the students write the first three letters of their first name freehand. During this time, write the students' names on all worksheets and papers leaving space for the first three letters and make the rest dotted or something that can be traced. They should have their Name Plates to look at as they do this.

Writing Skill Builders: Keep these objectives in mind as you direct the class. Incorporate writing strokes bowl, bridge, and diagonal lines.

Memory Verse: Review Genesis 1:16. What a powerful memory verse we are learning. What does the memory verse tell us about God? He made the Sun, the Moon, and the stars. He is powerful and strong. He cares about us. Everyone say the verse together.

Math: Review telling time to the hour. Review number recognition 1-12. Explain a digital clock to the students. Tell them that the first number is the hour and that the numbers following the dots are the minutes. You are only teaching time to the hour but the students should be able to read minutes to the numbers that you have covered so far. Set a digital clock to different times and ask the students to read the time.

Do the Lesson 78 Math worksheet. Instruct the students to begin at the left and color the correct number of squares in each strip. Review colors by telling them a color to use for each strip.

Shapes: Review the heart shape.

Do the Lesson 78 Shapes worksheet. Find the path through the ABC maze.

Color: Review the colors red, green, blue, black, white, yellow, brown, pink, purple, orange, and gray.

Story Time: Read a story or stories of your choice.

Music: Review "My God Is So Big" and "Great Is Thy Faithfulness."

Multimedia Resources: This week, listen and sing along to selections from the "Once Upon a Christmas" CD. This week, watch *The Kingdom Under the Sea* adventure "The Gift," which is a Christmas story.

Arts & Crafts: Do the Lesson 78 Arts & Crafts worksheet. If you have many students, you will need help with this project. *Prepare ahead – Cut yarn into various size lengths, enough for each student to have six pieces.* Instruct the students to first color the Sun, Moon and stars. Provide crayons or markers. The page can be glued to a sheet of construction paper for added strength. Then let the students carefully cut out the pieces. Use a small hole punch to punch holes where indicated. Tie the mobile together.

Creative Cooking: *Plan ahead – Bring Chicken and Stars soup, enough for all students to have some in a paper cup. Bring plastic spoons.* Serve the soup warm as a snack, perhaps with crackers. Ask, What are these stars made of? They were hot and now they are cooling down. If possible let the children help you heat the soup.

Tell the students that when God made the stars they were very hot to begin with, then they cooled down. Some stars are hotter than others are even now. The color of the stars will tell you how hot they are. Blue is the hottest star, yellow the next hottest, then orange, red, and finally black.

Physical Education: Continue to practice the Balance Beam exercises.

NOTES:

Activities in this Lesson: Bible Lesson, Language Arts, Phonics, Reading, Writing, Memory Verse, Math, Shapes, Color, Story Time, Music, Arts & Crafts, Creative Cooking, Physical Education, Homework

Bible Reference: Genesis 1:14-19.

Bible Concept to Present: God wants us to be shining stars for Him.

Bible Lesson: Review yesterday's lesson. God was happy that He made stars, millions and millions of stars. Read Genesis 1:16-18 again. God saw that it was good, and the Sun, Moon and stars praise God. "Praise Him, sun and moon, praise Him, all you shining stars, Praise Him, you highest heavens..." Psalm 148:3-4a. God want us to shine like the stars. "Do everything without complaining or arguing so that you may become blameless and pure, children of God without fault... [as] you shine like stars in the universe." Philippians 2:14-15.

Arts & Crafts: *Prepare ahead: Bring one foil pan for each student. Cut out a star from Lesson 77 Resource page to use as a pattern. With a black Sharpie pen, outline a star on each foil pan. Bring some string and nails for each student.* Give students scissors, a nail, a piece of string, and a square of cardboard bigger than the star. Say, We can be shining stars for God. Let's hang some shining stars in our room. First, cut out the star outlined on the foil. Cut very carefully. Now, lay your foil star on the piece of card-board. Poke one hole in the top of a point, big enough for string to go through. Then poke little holes everywhere, in any pattern you like. Put the string through the hole and tie it. Hang from the ceiling or board.

Language Arts: Stars are very, very far away from Earth. They are very hot, but they are out in the middle of a vast, cold space. How would you feel if you were a star? Let the students express some thoughts about stars.

Continue to work on the star poems from Lessons 76 and 77.

Phonics: Review the letter Yy.

Teach the small letter *y*. Write some words beginning with the letter *y* on the board. Include words from stories or activities that tie this lesson to other things that have already been done. Underline the small *y* that begins the words. Read through the words and point out the shape of letter *y*. Have the students trace the *y* in the air as you trace the letter *y* beginning each word.

> Common words: year, yes, yo-yo, you, your
> Vocabulary words: yellow, you're welcome

Do the Lesson 79 Phonics worksheet. Complete the letter Yy worksheet. Notice that all of the letters of the alphabet are displayed on the page and that the letters Yy are highlighted with a background. Trace the large letter and the small letter. The students can trace the letters between the guide lines. Review the pictures and the colored first letter of the words. The students can color the letters as desired.

Lesson 79
(Cont.)

Reading: Associate spoken and written language by matching written word labels with spoken words. Segment a spoken sentence into separate, distinct words. Point to words as distinct units on a page of print.

Writing: For these two weeks focus on having the students write the first three letters of their first name freehand. During this time, write the students' names on all worksheets and papers leaving space for the first three letters and make the rest dotted or something that can be traced. They should have their Name Plates to look at as they do this.

Writing Skill Builders: Keep these objectives in mind as you direct the class. Incorporate writing strokes bowl, bridge, and diagonal lines.

Memory Verse: Students should know this verse by today, Genesis 1:16. They have worked very hard to learn it. Play a game with them. Say a line of the verse, leaving out a word. Let them guess the word. Let the students recite the verse to the class if they are ready.

Math: Review telling time to the hour. Review number recognition 1-12. Draw a large clock on the board. Have the students come up and draw hands on the clock for a time to the hour that you have given to them.

Give each of the students a number of counters. Using their Name Plates, have them count the number of letters in their name. Then have them count out the same number of counters. Take away the extra counters. With one to one correspondence have the students place one counter on top of each letter in their name. How many counted correctly? Have the students compare their names with one another. Decide who has more, less, or the same number of letters in their names.

Do the Lesson 79 Math worksheet. Count the dots on each of the tiles and match it to the correct number.

Shapes: Review the heart shape.

Color: Review the colors red, green, blue, black, white, yellow, brown, pink, purple, orange, and gray.

Story Time: Read a story or stories of your choice.

Music: Learn the song "Jesus Loves Me."

Jesus Loves Me
by Anna Bartlett Warner and William Batchelder Bradbury (public domain)

1. Jesus Loves Me this I Know
   For the Bible tells me so.
   Little ones to him belong,
   They are weak but He is strong.
(chorus)
   Yes, Jesus loves me,
   Yes, Jesus loves me,
   Yes, Jesus loves me,
   The Bible tells me so.

2. Jesus loves me! He who died,
    Heaven's gate to open wide;
    He will wash away my sin,
    Let His little child come in.
    (repeat chorus)

3. Jesus loves me! Loves me still,
    When I'm very weak and ill;
    From His shining throne on high,
    Comes to watch me where I lie.
    (repeat chorus)

4. Jesus loves me! He will stay,
    Close beside me all the way;
    He's prepared a home for me,
    And some day His face I'll see.
    (repeat chorus)

Multimedia Resources: This week, listen and sing along to selections from the "Once Upon a Christmas" CD. This week, watch *The Kingdom Under the Sea* adventure "The Gift," which is a Christmas story.

Arts & Crafts: Have the students cut out white and yellow stars from construction paper. Get out the circles from last week, the Earth, Moon, and Sun. Put the Sun in the middle of the room. Then put the Earth and Moon half way out to the walls. Let the students lay their stars all around the edges of the room, representing the stars in the sky. Talk about how far away the stars are from us. Save the Earth, Sun, Moon, and stars for another day.

Creative Cooking: You might choose to make the cookie dough today, to be cut out tomorrow.

Physical Education: Continue the balance beam exercises.

Homework: Let the students take home Lesson 79 Homework worksheet. The Shining Stars worksheet. This is a way for the parents to encourage good behavior at home by rewarding their student with a star. They don't have to bring it back.

NOTES:

Lesson 80

Week 16: Day 5

Activities in this Lesson: Bible Lesson, Social Studies, Science, Language Arts, Phonics, Reading, Writing, Memory Verse, Math, Shapes, Color, Story Time, Music, Creative Cooking, Physical Education

Bible Reference: Genesis 1:16 and Job 38:31-33.

Bible Concept to Present: When God made the stars, He put them into families called constellations, and large groups of families called a galaxy.

Bible Lesson: When God made the many, many stars, He put some of them closer to one another in sky. Some of these stars make some very funny shapes. Man has looked at some of these stars and called them different names. One group of stars looks like a soup dipper. So it was named the Big Dipper. Another looks like a bear. So man named it The Bear. God knows the names of these families of stars, too. In the Bible, God calls them by name. I am happy to have a God who knows the names of the groups of stars.

A small family of stars is called a constellation. Can you say that word? Con-stel-la-tion. It's a big word that means a group or family of stars. When there are many, many families of stars together, we call it a galaxy. We have many stars that we can see in our constellation. All the stars we can see make up our galaxy which has a name, too. It is named the Milky Way. So we have a galaxy named the Milky Way and inside of that galaxy are many smaller constellations with different names.

Science: On Lesson 80 Science worksheet you will find an illustration of two constellations. Have your students place star stickers on the stars and then trace the lines to clarify the shape of the constellation. Let the students name the different constellations as they see them. Place emphasis on the fact that there are many of these constellations in the galaxy of the Milky Way.

Social Studies: The Indians had many stories about the stars. They believed that the stars were gods. They thought that the stars had powers and could hurt them if they did not do what the stars wanted. We know that this is not true. We know that God is the one who made the stars, and that God is the one who loves us. We know the stars cannot hurt us, and that they are not gods. I am happy to know that God made the stars.

Title: Grizzly Bear
Tribe: Shoshoni
Region: Wyoming, Southern Idaho
Object: Cygnus
A grizzly bear (Cygnus) climbed up a tall mountain to go hunting in the sky. As he climbed the snow and ice clung to the fur of his feet and legs. Crossing the sky the ice crystals trailed behind him forming the Milky Way.

Title: Coyote's Eyeball
Tribe: Lummi
Region: Wyoming, Pacific Northwest
Object: Arcturus
The Coyote liked to show off to the girls by juggling his eyeballs. One day he threw one so high it stuck in the sky (Arcturus).

Language Arts: Continue to work on the star poems from Lessons 76 and 77.

Phonics: Teach the letter Zz.

Show the students the letter Zz flashcard. Point out any student's name beginning with the letter Z. Write some words beginning with the letter Z on the board. Include any student names from the class that begin with letter Z. Underline the capital Z that begins the words. Read through the words and point out the shape of letter Z. Have the students trace the Z in the air as you trace the letter Z beginning each name.

> Boys: Zaccheus, Zachary, Zachariah, Zachery, Zander, Zared, Zareh, Zeno, Ziv, Zohar, Zubin, Zulu
> Girls: Zabrina, Zada, Zanta, Zara, Zarina, Zaza, Zea, Zinnia, Zipporah, Ziva, Zoe, Zora, Zuna, Zuri, Zurina, Zuzana, Zytka
> Vocabulary word: Zip Code

Teach the small letter z. Write some words beginning with the letter z on the board. Include words from stories or activities that tie this lesson to other things that have already been done. Underline the small z that begins the words. Read through the words and point out the shape of letter z. Have the students trace the z in the air as you trace the letter z beginning each word.

> Common words: zebra, zigzag, zip, zoo, zoom
> Vocabulary word: zero

Do the Lesson 80a Phonics worksheet. Complete the letter Zz worksheet. Have the students trace the letters Zz with their fingers. They should trace the letters with their fingers and say the names of the letters. Demonstrate the proper strokes for them on the board. Say the words for each of the pictures and look at the Zz letters that begin them.

Do the Lesson 80b Phonics worksheet. Complete the letter Zz worksheet. Notice that all of the letters of the alphabet are displayed on the page and that the letters Zz are highlighted with a background. Trace the large letter and the small letter. The students can trace the letters between the guide lines. Review the pictures and the colored first letter of the words. The students can color the letters as desired.

Reading: Associate spoken and written language by matching written word labels with spoken words. Segment a spoken sentence into separate, distinct words. Point to words as distinct units on a page of print.

Writing: For these two weeks focus on having the students write the first three letters of their first name freehand. During this time, write the students' names on all worksheets and papers leaving space for the first three letters and make the rest dotted or something that can be traced. They should have their Name Plates to look at as they do this.

Writing Skill Builders: Keep these objectives in mind as you direct the class. Incorporate writing strokes bowl, bridge, and diagonal lines.

Memory Verse: Finish up Genesis 1:16 today. Let the students recite the verse to the class if they are ready.

Math: Review telling time to the hour. Review number recognition 1-12. Set a digital clock to the hour. Ask a student to come up and set an analog clock to the same time. Do this several times.

Shapes: Review the heart shape.

Color: Review the colors red, green, blue, black, white, yellow, brown, pink, purple, orange, and gray.

Story Time: Read a story or stories of your student's choice or ones they have brought from home.

Music: Review "Jesus Loves Me."

Multimedia Resources: This week, listen and sing along to selections from the "Once Upon a Christmas" CD. This week, watch *The Kingdom Under the Sea* adventure "The Gift," which is a Christmas story.

Creative Cooking: Make a batch of your favorite cut-out cookies. Have the students cut stars from the dough. Bake them and then decorate each in a different way. Just as each cookie is decorated in a different way and no two are alike, so it is with the stars. There are no two stars alike. Some are big, some are little, no two are the same. God not only made many, many stars, He also made each of them different.

Physical Education: Continue the balance beam exercises.

NOTES:

Activities in this Lesson: Bible Lesson, Social Studies, Science, Language Arts, Phonics, Reading, Writing, Memory Verse, Math, Shapes, Color, Story Time, Music, Arts & Crafts, Field Trip, Physical Education

Bible Reference: Genesis 1:16.

Bible Concept to Present: When God made the stars, He made some of them to be brighter than others.

Bible Lesson: When God made the stars in the sky, He made some of them different from others. If you could look at the stars through a telescope, you would be able to see that some stars are brighter than other stars. Even when we look at the stars at night, it appears that some stars are brighter than others. Scientists call the degree of brightness of a star "magnitude." First magnitude stars are the brightest stars of the heavens. Second magnitude stars are very bright, but not quite as bright as first magnitude stars. Tomorrow we are going to learn about certain stars and which stars are brighter than others. I am happy to see how God made the stars different from each other, and how He made some stars to be brighter than others.

If it is possible, go outside tonight and view the stars, looking for the brightest stars you can see. Children enjoy posters of the stars, too, if they understand the correlation between the map and the heavens. There are often excellent maps of the stars sold in museums.

Social Studies: We previously discussed what an astronomer was and what he did. Review this information with your students and then pretend to go on a star search. Create a toy "telescope" from a cardboard tube, such as a tube from wrapping paper or paper towel. Let the students be the astronomers and "look at the stars." After this, inform them about how the stars are used to help guide ships out on the ocean. Let the students be the ones who tell you which direction to turn the ship. It is important to remember that at the Preschool level the play experiences are very important. It is in this way that the child internalizes what they learn.

Science: What makes some stars brighter than others? If the star is very hot (such as a blue star) the star will be brighter. Briefly discuss with your students hot and cold. You will want to point out that the hotter the fire is, the brighter it is.

Language Arts: Play the game "Hot and Cold." Name an article that you think of that is hot. Have students name one that is cold. Then you name one that is hot. They name one that is cold. Let this be a type of "popcorn" session where the ideas "pop." Reverse roles and let the students name hot items while you name cold.

Continue to work on the star poems from Lessons 76 and 77.

Phonics: Teach the initial short sound of Aa. Review letter recognition Aa-Zz.

The phonics focus up to this point has been on letter recognition. With this lesson the sound of the letter will become the focus. The shape of the letter indicates the letter name. The shape and position of the letter in a word also indicates the sound of the letter. Begin with the initial short sound of Aa.

Write several initial short Aa words on the board: at, am, an, as, ax, add, Adam, ant, apple, alligator, atom, etc. Underline the initial letter Aa and say the words. Ask the students for other words that start with the same sound.

Use the "A Was an Apple Pie" poem to review the letters of the alphabet and initial sounds. Discuss the symbol and meaning of ampersand. (&) You can have the students call out the next letter of the alphabet as you say each line of the poem. For example:

Students say:	A
Teacher says:	was an apple pie
Students say:	B
Teacher says:	bit it, etc.

A was an Apple Pie

A was an apple pie,
B bit it,
C cut it,
D dealt it,
E eat it, (say with a short e)
F fought for it,
G got it,
H had it,
I inspected it,
J jumped for it,
K kept it,
L longed for it,
M mourned for it,
N nodded at it,
O observed it, (say with a short o)
P peeped in it,
Q quartered it,
R ran for it,
S stole it,
T took it,
U upset it,
V viewed it,
W wanted it,
X, Y, Z, and ampersand
All wished for a piece in hand.

Reading: Blend two parts of a compound word or two syllables. Represent "in written form," following an actual experience: directions for completing a recipe or craft, scientific observations of experiments, or events.

Multimedia Resources: View the Aa-Zz segments of "Rev-Up for Reading" from the "Rev-Up for Learning" DVD to drill letter recognition and sound. The students should say each letter sound along with the presentation.

Writing: For the remainder of the year the students should write their first name freehand. They should have their Name Plates to look at as they do this.

Do the Lesson 81 Writing worksheet. Instruct the students to use a pencil and to follow the lines as closely as they can. Review pencil holding and writing techniques.

Writing Skill Builders: Keep these objectives in mind as you direct the class. Incorporate writing strokes wave, X, star, and zigzag line.

Multimedia Resources: View the Aa-Zz segments of "Rev-Up for Writing" from the "Rev-Up for Learning" DVD to review the writing of upper- and lowercase letters. The students should write each letter in the air along with the presentation.

Memory Verse: Revelation 22:16.

> I, Jesus, … am … the bright Morning Star. Revelation 22:16 NIV

> I Jesus … am … the bright and morning star. Revelation 22:16 KJV

Place emphasis on the fact that Jesus' coming is the very best event that has occurred to mankind. God called Him the "bright morning star," the brightest star that ever was. Does this mean that Jesus was really a star? No. Just that He was like a bright star – His life would show others light. For each day a student can say the verse, give them a star sticker to put on their star page, Lesson 81 Memory Verse worksheet. Let the students take this page home at the end of the week. Let the students take home Memory Verse Card 12 tonight.

Math: Review telling time to the hour. Review number recognition 1-12. Set an analog clock to the hour. Ask a student to come up and write the same time on a wipe off digital clock. Do this several times.

Do the Lesson 81 Math worksheet. Match the analog clock to the digital clock that shows the same time.

Multimedia Resources: View "Rev-Up for Arithmetic" from the "Rev-Up for Learning" DVD to practice number recognition and counting 1-20.

Shapes: Review the heart shape.

Color: Review the colors red, green, blue, black, white, yellow, brown, pink, purple, orange, and gray.

Story Time: Read a story or stories of your choice.

Music: Review "Jesus Loves Me."

Multimedia Resources: This week, listen and sing along to selections from the "Music Machine: Benny's Biggest Battle" CD.

Arts & Crafts: Read Lesson 81 Resource page. Decide whether you will make one class Star of David or let each student make a star. If you have several students, you will need help. Say, This star is called, "The Star of David." Stars have had special meanings through history. This star represents the Jewish Religion. Jesus was Jewish. Help your students make the star, permitting them to do as much of the work as they can. Refrain from doing anything that they can do for themselves.

Field Trip: If you have a planetarium near you, they often will have a time for the public to view the stars through their telescope. Call your local colleges, or Chamber of Commerce, for information. Although much of what is presented will be above your student's learning level, bits and pieces of information are absorbed, and the students will enjoy the outing.

Physical Education: Did you know that the stars sing together? They do. They are praising the Lord, just like we do. Gather band instruments that you have available, or if you do not have any, give your students some pan lids. Play some lively music on the CD player. Let the children be a 'Star' that sings praise to the Lord as they 'dance' across the sky. Let the children break the normal bounds of noise level. After a few minutes of this, put on some quiet music and concentrate on 'dancing' to praise the Lord as some of the more quiet stars might do.

NOTES:

Activities in this Lesson: Bible Lesson, Language Arts, Social Studies, Phonics, Reading, Writing, Memory Verse, Math, Shapes, Color, Story Time, Music, Arts & Crafts, Physical Education, Catch Up

Bible Reference: Genesis 1:14-16.

Bible Concept to Present: Stars are so important that they are used as symbols for importance.

Bible Lesson: Review yesterday's lesson. Stars were very important to God. Even though God made the stars a certain brightness, sometimes what man does makes a difference in how the stars look. If the air is dirty, or there are lots and lots of city lights around, we can't see many stars. In the country, we can see millions of stars. The air is clean and there aren't many lights. What is your town like? Can you see lots and lots of stars at night, or just a few?

Language Arts: *Look in magazines for pictures of any advertisements that use stars. Bring any jewelry or products you might have that are stars or use stars.* We use stars as symbols. A star on a product means it is important. Many religions use stars as symbols. The Dallas Cowboy football team has a big star on their helmet. The old Texaco gas company used a big red star. What about our national flag? Stars on our flag represent the fifty states. Many newspapers are called star, like *The Western Star Journal*. Actors and actresses are called "Movie Stars" because they shine or they are important in the movies. In the military, the number of stars on your shoulder shows how important you are. A "Four Star General" is very important. Police uniforms have stars. Hotels are rated by stars, "four star" being very good. Show the students Lesson 82 Resource page of military medals with stars.

Continue to work on the Star poems from Lessons 76 and 77.

Social Studies: *Find actual pictures taken by the Hubble Telescope. Print some for your students.* http://hubblesite.org/newscenter/ Astronomers are scientists that study space. They study the stars and send space cameras to take pictures. Because of the space program, space shuttles and satellites, we have wonderful pictures of space and star systems. The Hubble Telescope is set up out on a satellite orbiting Earth. Shuttle astronauts have gone up into space to repair the Hubble Telescope. We have also sent many unmanned space vehicles or probes out to visit the planets.

Phonics: Review the initial short sound of Aa. Review letter recognition Aa-Zz.

Do the Lesson 82 Phonics worksheet. The Short Sound of Aa. Review the letter sound with the picture and words on the worksheet. Ask the students for other words that begin with the same sound. Discuss the position of the letters on the guidelines. Give them specific instructions for how the letter should be traced. Trace the letters and say the short sound of Aa. Observe the students as they trace the letters and help them with the letter strokes.

Reading: Blend two parts of a compound word or two syllables. Represent "in written form," following an actual experience: directions for completing a recipe or craft, scientific observations of experiments, or events.

Writing: For the remainder of the year the students should write their first name freehand. They should have their Name Plates to look at as they do this.

Writing Skill Builders: Keep these objectives in mind as you direct the class. Incorporate writing strokes wave, X, star, and zigzag line.

Memory Verse: Review Revelation 22:16. *Write the words of the verse very clearly on strips of paper. Tape them around the room.* Let the students find the words, then lay them on the floor in order. Help them to read the harder words.

Math: Review telling time to the hour. Review number recognition 1-12. Ask one student to set the time on an analog clock and have another student write the same time on a wipe off digital clock. Do this several times.

Do the Lesson 82 Math worksheet. Match the analog clock to the digital clock that shows the same time.

Shapes: Review the heart shape.

Do the Lesson 82 Shapes worksheet. Find the path from the mother hen to her baby chicks.

Color: Review the colors red, green, blue, black, white, yellow, brown, pink, purple, orange, and gray.

Story Time: Read a story or stories of your choice.

Music: Review "Jesus Loves Me."

Multimedia Resources: This week, listen and sing along to selections from the "Music Machine: Benny's Biggest Battle" CD.

Arts & Crafts: Give the students playdough. Let them create some playdough stars.

Bring one toilet paper tube per student. Provide each one with black construction paper circles, big enough to cover the tube ends. Help the students tape or glue the black circles over the ends of the tubes, slashing edges to fit. Let the students punch holes in the black paper, representing stars. As they look at a light through the open end of the tube, it will look like they are looking at stars.

Physical Education: Catch a Falling Star. For this activity you will need a launch board and a star shaped bean bag. A small ball, bean bag or koosh type ball will also work. The students will place the bean bag on the low end of the launch board. They will then go around and stomp on the high end of the launch board, sending the bean bag into the air where they can attempt to catch it.

To make a launch board use good quality plywood, 1/4 inch or thicker, 30 inches long and 5 inches wide. Seven inches from one end, attach a 5-inch-long, 1 1/2 inch-diameter dowel stick or PVC pipe with glue and screws or bolts. Felt glued to the underside ends of the board make it quieter when it is stomped on.

Place a small ball or beanbag on the launch end of the board. If using a ball, drill a 2-inch hole in the end of the board to place the ball.

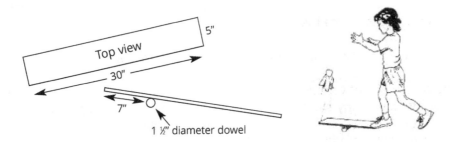

Top view
5"
30"
7"
1 ½" diameter dowel

Catch Up: Do any assignment that you didn't have time for earlier in the month.

NOTES:

Lesson 83

Week 17: Day 3

Activities in this Lesson: Bible Lesson, Science, Language Arts/Arts & Crafts, Phonics, Reading, Writing, Memory Verse, Math, Shapes, Color, Story Time, Music, Arts & Crafts, Outdoor Activity, Physical Education

Bible Reference: Genesis 1:16 and Psalms 147:4.

Bible Concept to Present: When God made the stars, He named them.

Bible Lesson: On the fourth day of Creation, God made all the stars in the skies. He made many, many stars. We don't even know how many stars God made, but God does. He made each star to be different from the others. Some stars are very bright, and some are not quite as bright. Do you remember what we call the brightest stars? We call them first magnitude stars.

Did you know that God not only made each star, but He also named each star? That's right. Just like you and I each have a name, so every star God made has a name. God knows each of the stars just like He knows you and me. There are names like Pollus, Castor, Betelgeuse (pronounced Bettlejuice), and Rigel. You could say these stars have last names, too. Betelgeuse is found in the constellation of Orion, as is Rigel. Castor and Pollus are found in the constellation of Zodiac. Just as God knows each star's name, He knows your name too. Our God is so wonderful. I love Him very much, don't you?

Science: We discussed before how some stars are brighter than others and that we call these first magnitude stars. In the constellation of Orion, Betelgeuse is a first magnitude star. That means it is the brightest star in Orion. Betelgeuse is a sort of a flag to help scientists find the other stars in Orion. Because of its brightness, it helps scientists see it first, and then they use it as a mark to find other stars.

Language Arts/Arts & Crafts: Give the students a piece of paper, some glue, and some glitter. Have them put 'stars' at random over the paper by placing the glue and then the glitter on the paper. Do not require a certain order for the stars. Your only requirement is that some of the stars be brighter than others. Then have the students name the brightest stars they have made. Write the names down beside the stars as the children say them. You desire is for the child to verbalize why they have named the star as they have.

Continue to work on the star poems from Lessons 76 and 77.

Phonics: Review the initial short sound of Aa. Review letter recognition Aa-Zz.

Do the Lesson 83 Phonics worksheet. The Short Sound of Aa. Review the letter sound with the picture and words on the worksheet. Ask the students for other words that begin with the same sound. Give them specific instructions for how the letter should be traced. Allow time for tracing the letters and observe their progress. If you have the students do one row at a time, the worksheet can be carried over to various parts of the day or another day.

Reading: Blend two parts of a compound word or two syllables. Represent "in written form," following an actual experience: directions for completing a recipe or craft, scientific observations of experiments, events.

Writing: For the remainder of the year the students should write their first name freehand. They should have their Name Plates to look at as they do this.

Writing Skill Builders: Keep these objectives in mind as you direct the class. Incorporate writing strokes wave, X, star, and zigzag line.

Memory Verse: Review Revelation 22:16. Give the students the Lesson 83 Memory Verse worksheet. Give them markers, crayons, star stickers and glitter glue. Let them decorate the verse, saying it together with you several times.

Math: Review telling time to the hour. Review number recognition 1-12. Ask one student to set the time on an analog clock and have another student write the same time on a wipe off digital clock. Do this several times.

Shapes: Review triangle, circle, square, rectangle, star, and heart shapes.

Do the Lesson 83 Shapes worksheet. Trace the shapes. Give the students the instruction for coloring the shapes. Do one shape at a time and give them time to find and color the shape. Color the circle red. Color the heart yellow. Color the triangle orange. Color the square blue. Color the rectangle green. Color the star your favorite color.

Color: Review the colors red, green, blue, black, white, yellow, brown, pink, purple, orange, and gray.

Story Time: Read a story or stories of your choice.

Music: Review "Jesus Loves Me."

Multimedia Resources: This week, listen and sing along to selections from the "Music Machine: Benny's Biggest Battle" CD.

Arts & Crafts: Have the students make a string of beads that can be used for counting and addition/subtraction practice in future lessons. They will need a piece of string or cord and 20 beads with holes through them. You can get wooden beads at a craft store. Tie a knot in one end of the string for them and have them string the 20 beads and tie another knot in the other end for them. Leave extra string between the knots for the students to slide the beads back and forth. This should be stored in their pencil box or cubby.

Outdoor Activity: Take a long walk. Talk about the stars in the sky. Share with students that the stars are there, up in the sky, right now. But the Sun is so bright, we can't see them. The stars are always there above us. Just like our Heavenly Father is always there, protecting and caring for us.

Physical Education: Teach your children a few ballet steps. Put music on the player that is calm. Follow the steps below for a few of the steps. You will want to repeat these steps several times.

NOTES:

Lesson 84

Week 17: Day 4

Activities in this Lesson: Bible Lesson, Language Arts, Social Studies, Science, Phonics, Reading, Writing, Memory Verse/Outdoor Activity, Math, Shapes, Color, Story Time, Music, Music/Physical Education, Arts & Crafts

Bible Reference: Genesis 1:3; 6:9-11; 16.

Bible Concept to Present: God made so many things that we have studied, and we are only on Day 4!

Bible Lesson: Take some time to review all of the days of Creation up to now. You can use the Days of Creation Numbers.

> Day 1 = light, earth
> Day 2 = air and clouds
> Day 3 = land, soil, rocks, plants, trees
> Day 4 = Sun, Moon, stars

Go to the Creation Mural and use it as a reminder. Say, God made a lot of wonderful things for us in four days. He cared for and loved His Creation. He even named the Sun, the Moon and every star. He knows our name, too.

Illustration: God loves us so much. He gives us our very own names. Give each student white construction paper and poster pens. Ask them to write their names. They may decorate the letters as they wish. Suggest that they decorate with a Sun, Moon, and stars.

Language Arts: Everything has a name. Walk around the room and say the name of every item. Let the students do this, too. Explain that everything, even our actions, have a name. We can act angry, it has a name. We can act happy, it has a name. Call out actions and let the students act them out. Some things we can't see have names. What are some things that have names that we can't see? Love. Peace. Time. Air.

Continue to work on the star poems from Lessons 76 and 77.

Have the students form the letters of their names with playdough.

Social Studies: An astronomer studies space and cosmic bodies in space. Basically, an astronomer studies the universe. They use telescopes, computers and complex measuring devices to locate the position of stars and planets. Astronomers also study comets, galaxies, and the birth and death of stars many light years away. Astronomers must study lots of math and science.

Years and years ago, astronomers named the constellations. They didn't "discover" them, as the constellations are only imaginary pictures made by connecting stars together with lines. These named groups of stars helps astronomers and others to locate individual stars. There are many constellations.

Science: Review. Go back to Lesson 15. Read the "Thank You God for Light" poem again. Remind students that the Sun, Moon, and stars are all forms of light. God created light on the first day. We are so thankful for all of the light God gave us.

Phonics: Review the initial short sound of Aa. Review letter recognition Aa-Zz.

Have the students brainstorm words that begin or include the letter Aa. Write these words on the board. Model the correct letter formation as you write the letters on the board. The students should practice forming the letter Aa on a blank sheet of paper. Students who are ready can practice copying complete words from the board.

Do the Lesson 84 Phonics worksheet. The Short Sound of Aa. Review the letter sound with the picture and words on the worksheet. Ask the students for other words that begin with the same sound. Trace the letters and say the short sound of Aa. Observe the students as they trace the letters and help them with the letter strokes. If you have the students do one row at a time, the worksheet can be carried over to various parts of the day or another day.

Reading: Blend two parts of a compound word or two syllables. Represent "in written form," following an actual experience: directions for completing a recipe or craft, scientific observations of experiments, events.

Writing: For the remainder of the year the students should write their first name freehand. They should have their Name Plates to look at as they do this.

Writing Skill Builders: Keep these objectives in mind as you direct the class. Incorporate writing strokes wave, X, star, and zigzag line.

Memory Verse/Outdoor Activity: Continue working on Revelation 22:16. Take a walk and recite the verse together.

Math: Review telling time to the hour. Review number recognition 1-12. Use the Counting Beads made in yesterday's craft to review counting 1-12. Have the students slide one bead at a time from one side of the string to the other as you count from 1-12.

Talk about the daily schedule. Show the students the times that you have put on the schedule for the different activities of the day. Read an activity, point to the time and have the students set a clock to the correct hour.

Do the Lesson 84 Math worksheet. Match the analog clock to the digital clock that shows the same time.

Shapes: Review triangle, circle, square, rectangle, star, and heart shapes.

Color: Review the colors red, green, blue, black, white, yellow, brown, pink, purple, orange, and gray.

Story Time: Read a story or stories of your choice.

Music: Review "Jesus Loves Me."

Multimedia Resources: This week, listen and sing along to selections from the "Music Machine: Benny's Biggest Battle" CD.

Music/Physical Education: Play some classical music. Let the students practice their dance moves with the music.

Arts & Crafts: Give the students black construction paper and at least ten silver or gold star stickers. Instruct them to be creative and make their own constellation. Let them draw a picture, then place the star stickers around the edges of the drawing. They can then name their "constellation."

NOTES:

Activities in this Lesson: Bible Lesson, Social Studies/Science, Language Arts, Phonics, Reading, Writing, Memory Verse, Math, Shapes, Color, Story Time, Music, Physical Education

Bible Reference: Genesis 1:16.

Bible Concept to Present: When God made the stars He made all the stars at one time. It only took Him one day to make the Sun, Moon, and stars. Our God is a very BIG God.

Bible Lesson: On the fourth day of Creation, God made the Sun. He made the Moon. He made the stars. God made the stars in a very special way. He didn't just make one star and then another star and so on until He had made all the millions of stars in our sky. No, God made things very special. Now you and I know that when we make cookies, we can only cut out one cookie at a time, can't we? We don't have the ability to just wave our hands and have all the cookies be done in an instant do we? When God made the stars, He made all of them in one instant. It did not take him days and days to make all the stars. No. God made them all with a word. That tells me that God is very BIG and very POWERFUL. God can do things that no one else can do. Our God is very, very BIG. He is very, very powerful. He is very, very wise. And He loves you and me very, very much. I am glad to have such a big, powerful and wise God for my friend.

Multimedia Resources: Listen to the song "Friends Forever" from the "Bullfrogs and Butterflies: God Loves Fun" CD.

Social Studies/Science: Stars help us in many ways. Did you know that the stars move across the sky at the same time every day? They do this year in and year out. Because of this, man has used the stars as a kind of heavenly calendar. Calendars tell us the time of the year it is, they tell us the day it is, and they tell us how long until the end of the year. We use calendars today. They are different from the first calendars made, but just as important. Our calendars look like this (Hold a calendar up for the children to see). The regularity of the stars helps us to be able to have a calendar.

Do the Lesson 85 Social Studies worksheet. If the students are capable, give them poster pens and let them color the little squares. Cut the squares out and paste them on the appropriate day of the calendar. Let the students take their pages home.

Language Arts: Review the star poems from the last two weeks. Talk about words that rhyme. Let the students make up some rhymes.

Phonics: Review the initial short sound of Aa. Review letter recognition Aa-Zz.

Do the Lesson 85a Phonics worksheet. Have the students put a green circle around the Xx letters, a blue triangle around the Yy letters, and a brown square around the Zz letters. Give them one direction at a time so they can focus on finding the correct letter shape. Begin with capital *X*, then lower case *x*, etc. Show them examples with flashcards or letters written on the board.

Do the Lesson 85b Phonics worksheet. The Short Sound of Aa. Review the letter sound with the picture and words on the worksheet. Ask the students for other words that begin with the same sound. Trace the letters and say the short sound of Aa. Observe the students as they trace the letters and help them with the letter strokes. If you have the students do one row at a time, the worksheet can be carried over to various parts of the day or another day.

Reading: Blend two parts of a compound word or two syllables. Represent "in written form," following an actual experience: directions for completing a recipe or craft, scientific observations of experiments, events.

Writing: For the remainder of the year the students should write their first name freehand. They should have their Name Plates to look at as they do this.

Writing Skill Builders: Keep these objectives in mind as you direct the class. Incorporate writing strokes wave, X, star, and zigzag line.

Memory Verse: Students should know their verse, Revelation 22:16. Let them recite if they are ready.

Math: Review telling time. Review number recognition 1-12. Use the Counting Beads to review counting 1-12. Have the students slide one bead at a time from one side of the string to the other as you count from 1-12.

Talk about the daily schedule. Show the students the times that you have put on the schedule for the different activities of the day. Read an activity, point to the time and have the students write the time on a wipe off digital clock to the correct hour. Set an alarm clock to go off on the hour. When it goes off ask the students what time it is.

Shapes: Review triangle, circle, square, rectangle, star, and heart shapes.

Do the Lesson 85 Shapes worksheet. Have the students trace the lines as closely as they can from the circle to the square. Give each instruction and allow enough time for the students to do their work.

Color: Review the colors red, green, blue, black, white, yellow, brown, pink, purple, orange, and gray.

Story Time: Read a story or stories of your student's choice or ones they have brought from home.

Music: Review "My God is So Big" and "Jesus Loves Me." Review other favorite music.

Multimedia Resources: This week, listen and sing along to selections from the "Music Machine: Benny's Biggest Battle" CD.

Physical Education: Continue ballet steps.

Arts & Crafts: Let the students take home their foil stars today from Lesson 79.

NOTES:

Activities in this Lesson: Bible Lesson, Social Studies, Phonics, Reading, Writing, Memory Verse, Math, Shapes, Color, Story Time, Music, Science/Arts & Crafts, Arts & Crafts, Physical Education

Bible Reference: Genesis 1:16-18.

Bible Concept to Present: When God made the Sun, Moon, and stars, He also made other bodies in the heavens.

Bible Lesson: When God made the Sun, Moon, and stars on the fourth day of Creation, God also made other bodies to be in the heavens. These bodies have funny names. God made comets, and He also made planets. A comet is like a star, only we rarely see it. Some comets come in sight of Earth only once in 75 years. Planets are like our Earth, only in other parts of the sky. They orbit (explain term) around the Sun just like the Earth does. Comets orbit around the Sun, too. God put many heavenly bodies in the sky when He made the heavens. God is a very big God. He is a God big enough to make many heavenly bodies in the sky all in one day. Let's thank God now for all the things He made in our sky.

Social Studies: Many things that God made to put in our sky orbit around the Sun. The planets, the comets and the Earth all orbit around the Sun. The Bible says that God made a great light. That great light is the Sun. Let's begin a project that will help you to understand how everything is placed in the heavens. For classes with several students, each student may make a planet or two. Divide up the eight planets and one Sun between your students.

Phonics: Teach the initial sound of Bb. Review the initial sound of Aa. Review letter recognition Aa-Zz.

Write several initial Bb words on the board: baa, bad, bag, ball, ban, bat, bed, Bible, bit, Bob, boy, box, bug, bus, etc. Underline the initial letter Bb and say the words. Ask the students for other words that start with the same sound.

Continue to use the "A Was an Apple Pie" poem to review the letters of the alphabet and initial sounds.

Reading: Blend two parts of a compound word or two syllables. Represent "in written form," following an actual experience: directions for completing a recipe or craft, scientific observations of experiments, events.

Multimedia Resources: Review "Rev-Up for Reading" from the "Rev-Up for Learning" DVD to drill letter recognition and sound. The students should say each letter sound along with the presentation.

Writing: For the remainder of the year the students should write their first name freehand. They should have their Name Plates to look at as they do this.

Do the Lesson 86 Writing worksheet. Instruct the students to use a pencil and to follow the lines from the circle to the square as closely as they can. Review pencil holding and writing techniques.

Writing Skill Builders: Keep these objectives in mind as you direct the class. Incorporate writing strokes wave, X, star, and zigzag line.

Multimedia Resources: Review "Rev-Up for Writing" from the "Rev-Up for Learning" DVD to review the writing of upper- and lowercase letters.

Memory Verse: Psalm 148:13.

> Let them praise the name of the Lord ... His splendor is above the earth and the heavens. Psalm 148:13 NIV

> Let them praise the name of the LORD: ... his glory is above the earth and heaven. Psalm 148:13 KJV

Talk about this week's verse. Explain any words that the students might not know, like "splendor." Send Memory Verse Card 13 home with students.

Math: Review telling time to the hour. Teach 1 + 1 = 2

Talk about and demonstrate the way that we write time for the hour. (4 o'clock) Once they said "7 Of-the-clock" to show that they were not using the Sun to tell the time of day. This was shortened to "7 O'clock." With the clock we have the same amount of time each hour of the day. Telling time by the Sun does not give the same amount of time for different parts of the day like the time between sunrise and sunset. A clock divides the day into equal parts called hours.

Do the Lesson 86a Math worksheet. Match the analog clock to the o'clock time.

Show the students a plus (+) sign. Tell them that it means addition. Addition is putting things together. If a recipe calls for 1 cup + 1 tablespoon of flour then we put together 1 cup plus 1 tablespoon of flour in the bowl. This could be demonstrated for the students. When you add you have more. Show the students an equal (=) sign. Tell them that it means equals. When things are put together, addition, it makes more. Have two students come to the front and hold a plus sign up between them. Say, "Jane is one student and Dick is one student. If we add them together what does that equal?" Have two more students come to the front. Hold the equal sign after Dick and Jane and have the two new students stand in a group after the equal sign. Have the students count the number in the new group. Say, "one plus one equals, two" and count the two students in the new group. Do this with several groups of students.

Do the Lesson 86b Math worksheet. Count the number of objects in the box with the number 1. Trace the number 1 following the proper top to bottom stroke. Count the objects in each box at the bottom of the page. Color the set that shows 1.

Multimedia Resources: View "Rev-Up for Arithmetic" from the "Rev-Up for Learning" DVD to practice number recognition, counting and addition 1-20.

Shapes: Review triangle, circle, square, rectangle, star, and heart shapes.

Color: Review the colors red, green, blue, black, white, yellow, brown, pink, purple, orange, and gray.

Story Time: Read a story or stories of your choice.

Music: Learn the song "He's Still Working On Me" from the "Horizons Preschool Music" CD.

Multimedia Resources: This week, listen and sing along to selections from "The Amazing Book" CD.

Science/Arts & Crafts: This project will continue through this entire week. Your objective is for students to see how the planets line up with the Sun. You will want to involve students in the painting and gluing of the objects used. For today, you will take the following materials, and begin to prepare them. There will not be too much discussion as to specifics concerning the planets today. You will want your students to know that the balls you are preparing will be representing the planets and the Sun. The next two days you will be teaching more in depth.

Materials Needed:

      1 - 10 inch diameter foam ball
      1 - 8 inch diameter foam ball
      1 - 6 inch diameter foam ball
      2 - 3 inch diameter foam balls
      3 - 1 1/2 inch diameter foam balls
      1 - 7/8 inch diameter foam ball
      Nine colors of paint
      String and thumbtacks

Have the students paint the foam balls. You will want the largest ball to be yellow. The remaining balls may be the colors your student desires. The use of tempera paint is best, and if you purchase the dry paint, you may mix your own colors as needed. It is true that Mars is usually red and the Earth is usually green and blue. Permit these to dry overnight. If you do not have foam balls available, paper mache covered balloons will work. For a paper mache recipe, consult the craft section of your library or the internet.

As you are doing this work, ask your students the following questions:

1. Show me which ball is the biggest.
2. Which heavenly body do you think is the biggest?
3. Which ball is next in size?
4. Show me the next smallest sized ball (Continue this until the student has sequenced all the balls)
5. How do you think the paint stays on the balls?
6. Why do you think the biggest ball is being painted yellow?

Instructional Note: Mr. Earnest Collings did some research on the integration of subjects in the early 1900s. He found that when subjects are taught in an interrelated way, through a project, the child retains approximately 40% more of the lesson. The above project is designed to teach Social Studies (as we will be teaching the child his relationship to the universe) Science (in the placement of and teaching on the planets) Language Arts (in the expression and description of what the child is doing and verbalization as far as relationships) and Math (in the descriptions of distance, biggest, smallest, counting of the planets, etc.)

Arts & Crafts: Have the students cut out the Lesson 86 Arts & Crafts worksheet. These will be used in future lessons to demonstrate addition and subtraction.

Physical Education: The planets are circles, as is the Earth. On concrete, place masking tape in the shape of a circle. Have students walk around the circle, stepping only on the tape. Now give them a ball. Standing on the outside of the circle, let the students bounce the ball to you with the ball bouncing inside the circle once. They may begin using two hands, then go to one hand. Can they make the ball bounce twice within the circle? Are they capable of catching the ball as it bounces back from you using two hands? Continue this type of exercise through this week. Count the consecutive times a student catches the ball and can properly throw the ball.

NOTES:

Activities in this Lesson: Bible Lesson, Social Studies, Science, Language Arts, Phonics, Reading, Writing, Memory Verse/Arts & Crafts, Math, Shapes, Color, Story Time, Music, Science/Arts & Crafts, Physical Education

Bible Reference: Genesis 1:16-18.

Bible Concept to Present: God made the stars, but they are not all the same. He made many kinds of stars.

Bible Lesson: Review the lesson from yesterday. Mention asteroids, minor planets that orbit the Sun between Mars and Jupiter. Mention meteors, small pieces of rock that are traveling through space. There are also many, many things in space that we don't understand. There are different kinds of stars. Some that have collapsed are called Black Holes. There are star clusters. There are objects smaller than stars but bigger than planets, called Brown Dwarfs. There are Neutron Stars, high energy cosmic rays and energy bursts. There is even a black hole in the center of our Milky Way. Scientists try and try to figure out everything about the universe, but they will never succeed without knowing the God that created it all.

Social Studies: All astronomers would love to discover something in space: another planet, a comet or something unusual. When a scientist discovers something, they usually can name it. But God knew the name from the days of Creation. Probably the most famous of all comets, Halley's Comet, is the exception to the rule that the person/people who discover the comet get to have it named after them. Edmund Halley did not exactly discover Halley's Comet, but instead he correctly predicted when it would return (1758). Since he correctly calculated its return it was named after him. If you're fairly young you should be able to see it. It will next pass by Earth in 2061. How old will you be in 2061?

Science: Pluto is a dwarf planet in the solar system, and was considered the ninth full planet from the Sun until it was reclassified on August 24, 2006 according to the International Astronomical Union's (IAU) redefinition of planet. Pluto could be reclassified again as the prototype of a yet-to-be-named family of objects that appear beyond Neptune. Pluto was considered for many years to be the ninth planet but as other bodies, much smaller than planets, were discovered it became obvious to scientists that the classification needed to be changed. This is the nature of science. A rule or law is often suggested and then scientist go to work either proving or disproving the rule. This can sometimes change the rule.

Language Arts: Ask, How many things have we learned so far about space and our universe? Write the names on the board, whether students can read them or not. Help them remember all that they have learned so far.

Phonics: Review the initial sound of Bb. Review the initial sound of Aa. Review letter recognition Aa-Zz.

Do the Lesson 87a Phonics worksheet. The Sound of Bb. Review the letter sound with the picture and words on the worksheet. Ask the students for other words that begin with the same sound. Discuss the position of the letters on the guidelines. Give them specific instructions for how the letter should be traced. Trace the letters and say the sound of Bb. Observe the students as they trace the letters and help them with the letter strokes. If you have the students do one row at a time, the worksheet can be carried over to various parts of the day or another day.

Do the Lesson 87b Phonics worksheet. Help the badger get to the ball. Follow the path of the maze to find the ball sound of *b*.

Reading: Blend two parts of a compound word or two syllables. Represent "in written form," following an actual experience: directions for completing a recipe or craft, scientific observations of experiments, events.

Writing: For the remainder of the year the students should write their first name freehand. They should have their Name Plates to look at as they do this.

Writing Skill Builders: Keep these objectives in mind as you direct the class. Incorporate writing strokes wave, X, star, and zigzag line.

Memory Verse/Arts & Crafts: Work on this week's memory verse, Psalm 148:13. Give students colored markers and large white construction paper. Let them draw the verse, showing God's splendor above the earth and the heavens.

Math: Review telling time to the hour. Review 1 + 1 = 2. Give the students the dog bones that they cut out yesterday and a bowl to put them in. Have them place 1 bone in the bowl while saying "one plus one" and have them place another bone in the bowl, "equals" and have them count "one, two, bones in the bowl." Do this several times.

Do the Lesson 87a Math worksheet. As they trace the ones have them say "one plus one equals" and have them look at and read, "two."

Do the Lesson 87b Math worksheet. Match the analog clock to the o'clock time.

Shapes: Review triangle, circle, square, rectangle, star, and heart shapes.

Color: Review the colors red, green, blue, black, white, yellow, brown, pink, purple, orange, and gray.

Story Time: Read the "Hickory, Dickory, Dock" story.

Hickory, Dickory, Dock
From *Mother Goose in Prose* by L. Frank Baum (Lyman Frank Baum) 1856-1919

Hickory, Dickory, Dock!
The mouse ran up the clock.
The clock struck one,
The mouse ran down,
Hickory, Dickory, Dock!

Within the hollow wall of an old brick mansion, away up near the roof, there lived a family of mice. It was a snug little home, pleasant and quiet, and as dark as any mouse could desire. Mamma Mouse liked it because, as she said, the draught that came through the rafters made it cool in summer, and they were near enough to the chimney to keep warm in wintertime.

Besides the Mamma Mouse there were three children, named Hickory and Dickory and Dock. There had once been a Papa Mouse as well; but while he was hunting for food one night he saw a nice piece of cheese in a wire box, and attempted to get it. The minute he stuck his head into the box, however, it closed with a snap that nearly cut his head off; and when Mamma Mouse came down to look for him he was quite dead.

Mamma Mouse had to bear her bitter sorrow all alone, for the children were too young at that time to appreciate their loss. She felt that people were cruel to kill a poor mouse for wishing to get food for himself and his family. There is nothing else for a mouse to do but take what he can find, for mice can not earn money, as people do, and they must live in some way.

But Mamma Mouse was a brave mouse, and knew that it was now her duty to find food for her little ones; so she dried her eyes and went bravely to work gnawing through the baseboard that separated the pantry from the wall. It took her some time to do this, for she could only work at night. Mice like to sleep during the day and work at night, when there are no people around to interrupt them, and even the cat is fast asleep. Some mice run about in the daytime, but they are not very wise mice who do this.

At last Mamma Mouse gnawed a hole through the baseboard large enough for her to get through into the pantry, and then her disappointment was great to find the bread jar covered over with a tin pan.

"How thoughtless people are to put things where a hungry mouse cannot get at them," said Mamma Mouse to herself, with a sigh. But just then she espied a barrel of flour standing upon the floor; and that gave her new courage, for she knew she could easily gnaw through that, and the flour would do to eat just as well as the bread.

It was now nearly daylight, so she decided to leave the attack upon the flour barrel until the next night; and gathering up for the children a few crumbs that were scattered about, she ran back into the wall and scrambled up to her nest.

Hickory and Dickory and Dock were very glad to get the crumbs, for they were hungry; and when they had breakfasted they all curled up alongside their mother and slept soundly throughout the day.

"Be good children," said Mamma Mouse the next evening, as she prepared for her journey to the pantry, "and don't stir out of your nest till I come back. I am in hopes that after tonight we shall not be hungry for a long time, as I shall gnaw a hole at the back of the flour barrel, where it will not be discovered."

She kissed each one of them good-bye and ran down the wall on her errand.

When they were left alone Hickory wanted to go to sleep again, but little Dock was wide awake, and tumbled around so in the nest that his brothers were unable to sleep.

"I wish I could go with mother some night," said Dock, "it's no fun to stay here all the time."

"She will take us when we are big enough," replied Dickory.

"We are big enough now," declared Dock, "and if I knew my way I would go out into the world and see what it looks like."

"I know a way out," said Hickory, "but mamma wouldn't like it if we should go without her permission."

"She needn't know anything about it," declared the naughty Dock, "for she will be busy at the flour-barrel all the night. Take us out for a little walk, Hick, if you know the way."

"Yes, do," urged Dickory.

"Well," said Hickory, "I'd like a little stroll myself; so if you'll promise to be very careful, and not get into any mischief, I'll take you through the hole that I have discovered."

So the three little mice started off, with Hickory showing the way, and soon came to a crack in the wall. Hickory stuck his head through, and finding everything quiet, for the family of people that lived in the house were fast asleep, he squeezed through the crack, followed by his two brothers. Their little hearts beat very fast, for they knew if they were discovered they would have to run for their lives; but the house was so still they gained courage, and crept along over a thick carpet until they came to a stairway.

"What shall we do now?" whispered Hickory to his brothers.

"Let's go down," replied Dock.

So, very carefully, they descended the stairs and reached the hallway of the house, and here they were much surprised by all they saw.

There was a big rack for hats and coats, and an umbrella stand, and two quaintly carved chairs, and, most wonderful of all, a tall clock that stood upon the floor and ticked out the minutes in a grave and solemn voice.

When the little mice first heard the ticking of the clock they were inclined to be frightened, and huddled close together upon the bottom stair.

"What is it?" asked Dickory, in an awed whisper. "I don't know," replied Hickory, who was himself rather afraid.

"Is it alive?" asked Dock.

"I don't know," again answered Hickory.

Then, seeing that the clock paid no attention to them, but kept ticking steadily away and seemed to mind its own business, they plucked up courage and began running about.

Presently Dickory uttered a delighted squeal that brought his brothers to his side. There in a corner lay nearly the half of a bun which little May had dropped when nurse carried her upstairs to bed. It was a great discovery for the three mice, and they ate heartily until the last crumb had disappeared.

"This is better than a cupboard or a pantry," said Dock, when they had finished their supper, "and I shouldn't be surprised if there were plenty more good things around if we only hunt for them."

But they could find nothing more, for all the doors leading into the hall were closed, and at last Dock came to the clock and looked at it curiously.

"It doesn't seem to be alive," he thought, "although it does make so much noise. I 'm going behind it to see what I can find."

He found nothing except a hole that led to inside of the clock, and into this he stuck his head. He could hear the ticking plainer than ever now, but looking way up to the top of the clock he saw something shining brightly, and thought it must good to eat if he could only get at it. Without saying anything to his brothers, Dock ran up the sides of the clock until he came to the works, and he was just about to nibble at a glistening wheel, to see what it tasted like, when suddenly "Bang!" went the clock.

It was one o'clock, and the clock had only struck the hour; but the great gong was just beside Dock's ear and the noise nearly deafened the poor little mouse. He gave a scream of terror and ran down the clock as fast as he could go. When he reached the hall he heard his brothers scampering up the stairs, and after them he ran with all his might.

It was only when they were safe in their nest again that they stopped to breathe, and their little hearts beat fast for an hour afterward, so great had been their terror.

When Mamma Mouse came back in the morning, bringing a quantity of nice flour with her for breakfast, they told her of their adventure. She thought they had been punished enough already for their disobedience, so she did not scold them, but only said,

"You see, my dears, your mother knew best when she told you not to stir from the nest. Children sometimes think they know more than their parents, but this adventure should teach you always to obey your mother. The next time you run away you may fare worse than you did last night; remember your poor father's fate."

But Hickory and Dickory and Dock did not run away again.

Music: Review "He's Still Working On Me."

Multimedia Resources: This week, listen and sing along to selections from "The Amazing Book" CD.

Science/Arts & Crafts: Let the planets continue to dry. If students are old enough, you might add some rings to Saturn, or paint some rings. A big stick pin with a white head can symbolize the Earth's moon. It is up to you as to the amount of detail you add.

Arts & Crafts: Bring out the Earth, Sun, Moon, and stars saved from Lesson 79. Give the students construction paper, poster pens, and scissors. Let them draw and cut out their own version of comets, meteors, and asteroids. Arrange the Sun, Moon, Earth, stars, and other heavenly bodies around the room, keeping the Sun, Earth, and Moon in the correct relationship. If the students are able, let them walk around in orbits, holding their creations.

Physical Education: The planets are circles, as is the Earth. On concrete, place masking tape in the shape of a circle. Have students walk around the circle, stepping only on the tape. Now give them a ball. Standing on the outside of the circle, let the students bounce the ball to you with the ball bouncing inside the circle once. They may begin learning this skill by using two hands, then go to one hand. Can they make the ball bounce twice within the circle? Are they capable of catching the ball as it bounces back from you using two hands? Continue this type of exercise through this week. Count the consecutive times a student catches the ball and can properly throw the ball.

NOTES:

Lesson 88

Week 18: Day 3

Activities in this Lesson: Bible Lesson, Science/Arts & Crafts, Language Arts, Phonics, Reading, Writing, Memory Verse, Math, Shapes, Color, Story Time, Music, Physical Education

Bible Reference: Genesis 1:16-18.

Bible Concept to Present: When God made the planets on the fourth day of Creation, He made nine of them. The planets have names.

Bible Lesson: When God made the planets on the fourth day of Creation, God made eight planets. Let's count to eight. Very good! A planet is like a big ball. A planet moves in two ways. First, a planet will move around and around (rotate) on its own, much as when we spin the globe. Secondly, a planet moves around the Sun. So that you will understand how this works, I will be the Sun. You come and be a planet. First you are spinning (SLOWLY spin the child) but you are also moving around me (move child in circle around you). Planets move in both ways.

The planets have names. You will remember I told you there were eight planets. Well, all eight planets have names, just as you and I have a name. As I tell you the names of the planets, let's count them. Mercury (1), Venus (2), Mars (3), Jupiter (4), Saturn (5), Uranus (6), Neptune (7). Oh! Let's see. We only listed seven. But we said there were eight. Do you know the name of the eighth planet? It's Earth. Right where we live. Did you know that Earth was a planet, too? It is. I am happy God made the planets. I am very happy God made the planet Earth.

Science/Arts & Crafts: The planet balls will be dry today. We will now begin to label and hang the planets. You will need string, thumbtacks and small pieces of paper for labeling. If your students are writing, give them a list of planets written in manuscript, and let them copy the names onto the labels. If they are not writing, let them watch you write the names as you verbalize what name you are writing. Keep an active discussion going through this period together. After labeling the planets on the slips of paper, tie a string with a long tail around the balls. Now, using the following information, have your students place the labels on the balls.

> 10 inch ball - painted yellow - label it the Sun.
> 8 inch ball - is Jupiter
> 6 inch ball - is Saturn
> 3 inch balls - Uranus and Neptune
> 1 1/2 inch balls - Venus, Mars and Earth
> 7/8 inch ball - Mercury

As you are doing this project ask these questions:

1. Why is the Sun the biggest ball?
2. Why is Jupiter so big?
3. Find Earth. Did you know there were other planets that are bigger than ours?
4. Inform your students, that there is not life on any other planet. Earth alone has life on it.
5. We have sent machines to other planets and they have found the planets to be very cold or very hot and the planets do not have any water on them.
6. Some of the planets are easily distinguished from others. Saturn has rings around it. Jupiter has many moons and has a large red spot.

7. Take a straight pin, preferably one with a bright colored head. Put it on that ball that represents Earth. Tell your student that this represents where they live on Earth. Our planet is very small compared to the biggest ball, the Sun. Although the proportions are not exact, the child will get the general idea that the universe is a very big place and that he is very small in comparison.

Language Arts: Read the following action rhyme.

Reach for the Stars

Bend and stretch (bend low)
Reach for the stars (stretch high)
Here comes Jupiter (swing right arm to the left)
There goes Mars (swing left arm to the right)
Bend and stretch (bend low)
Reach for the sky (stretch high)
Stand on tiptoe (stand on toes)
Oh so high! (reach to ceiling)

Phonics: Review the initial sound of Bb. Review the initial sound of Aa. Review letter recognition Aa-Zz.

Do the Lesson 88 Phonics worksheet. The Sound of Bb. Review the letter sound with the picture and words on the worksheet. Ask the students for other words that begin with the same sound. Give them specific instructions for how the letter should be traced. Allow time for tracing the letters and observe their progress. If you have the students do one row at a time, the worksheet can be carried over to various parts of the day or another day.

Reading: Blend two parts of a compound word or two syllables. Represent "in written form," following an actual experience: directions for completing a recipe or craft, scientific observations of experiments, events.

Writing: For the remainder of the year the students should write their first name freehand. They should have their Name Plates to look at as they do this.

Writing Skill Builders: Keep these objectives in mind as you direct the class. Incorporate writing strokes wave, X, star, and zigzag line.

Memory Verse: Continue to work on Psalm 148:13. Take some time to review all the memory verses learned so far. Genesis 1:1, Genesis 1:3, Genesis 1:6, Genesis 1:10, I Peter 1:24-25, Genesis 8:22, Genesis 1:16, Psalm 90:12, Psalm 89:1, and Revelation 22:16. Give each student a piece of black construction paper. Have the students add stars to the top part of the paper and a big yellow circle to the center of the page. For each memory verse learned, cut a circle from another color of paper, and place it on the board. You are making a mini-mural of the planets. They do not need to be in order from the Sun, or in the correct size, but a comparison would be nice for continuation of what you are teaching.

Math: Review time to the hour. Review 1 + 1 = 2. Review 1 + 1 = 2 by writing the problem 1 + 1 = 2 on the board. Under each 1 draw one object with a + sign between them. Write the = sign and then draw 4 or 5 objects under the 2. Have a student come to the board and circle the correct number of objects under the 2 to make the addition problem correct. Erase the extra objects and orally say the problem with the class. Repeat several times drawing simple objects such as dots or various shapes.

Review the "I Am One" song learned earlier in the year to the tune of "Where is Thumbkin?"

I Am One
Tune of Where is Thumbkin?

I am one
I am one
We are two
We are two
One and one make two
One and one make two
Now we're through
Now we're through

Do the Lesson 88 Math worksheet. Count the number of objects in the box with the number 2. Trace the number 2. Count the objects in each box at the bottom of the page. Color the set that shows 2.

Sing the song "Hickory, Dickory, Dock" and move the hands of a clock to correspond to the verses.

Hickory Dickory Dock

Hickory Dickory Dock, tick, tock
The mouse ran up the clock, tick, tock
The clock struck one, the mouse ran down,
Hickory Dickory Dock! tick, tock

Hickory Dickory Dock, tick, tock
The bird looked at the clock, tick, tock
The clock struck two, and away she flew,
Hickory Dickory Dock!, tick, tock

Hickory Dickory Dock, tick, tock
The dog barked at the clock, tick, tock
The clock struck three, fiddle-de-dee,
Hickory Dickory Dock! tick, tock

Hickory Dickory Dock, tick, tock
The bear slept on the clock, tick, tock
The clock struck four, he ran out the door,
Hickory Dickory Dock! tick, tock

Hickory Dickory Dock, tick, tock
The bee buzzed round the clock, tick, tock
The clock struck five, she went to her hive,
Hickory Dickory Dock! tick, tock

Hickory Dickory Dock, tick, tock
The hen clucked at the clock, tick, tock
The clock struck six, fiddle-sticks,
Hickory Dickory Dock! tick, tock

Hickory Dickory Dock, tick, tock
The cat ran round the clock, tick, tock
The clock struck seven, she wanted to get 'em,
Hickory Dickory Dock! tick, tock

Hickory Dickory Dock, tick, tock
The horse jumped over the clock, tick, tock
The clock struck eight, he ate some cake,
Hickory Dickory Dock! tick, tock

Hickory Dickory Dock, tick, tock
The cow danced on the clock, tick, tock
The clock struck nine, she felt so fine,
Hickory Dickory Dock! tick, tock

Hickory Dickory Dock, tick, tock
The pig oinked at the clock, tick, tock
The clock struck ten, she did it again,
Hickory Dickory Dock! tick, tock

Hickory Dickory Dock, tick, tock
The worm squirmed out of the clock, tick, tock
The clock struck eleven, he said, "Let me get in",
Hickory Dickory Dock! tick, tock

Hickory Dickory Dock, tick, tock
The snail slimed up the clock, tick, tock
The clock struck twelve, what a sticky self,
Hickory Dickory Dock! tick, tock

Shapes: Teach the oval shape. Show the students the oval shape flashcard. Pass out plastic or hard boiled eggs and ping pong balls so that the students can feel the difference between the shapes.

Do the Lesson 88 Shapes worksheet. Have the students trace the oval and the letters in the word.

Color: Review the colors red, green, blue, black, white, yellow, brown, pink, purple, orange, and gray.

Story Time: Review the "Hickory, Dickory, Dock" story.

Music: Review "He's Still Working On Me."

Multimedia Resources: This week, listen and sing along to selections from "The Amazing Book" CD.

Physical Education: The planets are circles, as is the Earth. On concrete, place masking tape in the shape of a circle. Have students walk around the circle, stepping only on the tape. Now give them a ball. Standing on the outside of the circle, let the students bounce the ball to you with the ball bouncing inside the circle once. They may begin by using two hands, then go to one hand. Can they make the ball bounce twice within the circle? Are they capable of catching the ball as it bounces back from you using two hands? Continue this type of exercise through this week. Count the consecutive times a student catches the ball and can properly throw the ball.

NOTES:

Activities in this Lesson: Bible Lesson, Language Arts, Science/Language, Phonics, Reading, Writing, Memory Verse, Math, Shapes, Color, Story Time, Music, Science/Arts & Crafts, Physical Education

Bible Reference: Genesis 1:16-18.

Bible Concept to Present: God made meteors and every piece of rock and dust in space.

Bible Lesson: We have been studying the fourth day of Creation for many weeks now. God made everything in the sky, whether we can see it all or not. Have you ever watched the stars and seen a star fall to the Earth? Well, it looked like a star falling. They are called "shooting stars" but they aren't really stars. When God made the stars, He made them to stay right where they are. They don't "fall." Shooting stars are really small meteorites or pieces of space dust. As they fall, they burn up in our atmosphere, leaving a beautiful tail of light. Sometimes the Earth passes through a cloud of dust or meteors and we have a "meteor shower." Have you seen a shooting star?

There are a few things we see up in the sky that God didn't make. What could they be? They are pieces of spacecraft or rockets that are still up in the sky, orbiting the Earth. Sometimes, they fall to Earth and leave a bright trail of light as they burn up in the atmosphere.

Language Arts: In the western world, the planets are named after Roman gods. Mercury, Venus, Mars, Jupiter, and Saturn were all Roman Gods. When the ancients named the planets, they didn't know that Uranus and Neptune were there. Almost everything in the solar system, including the planets and their moons, was named from classical mythology or old myths and stories. Everything we know about in space is named. "Uranus is the only body in the Solar System with moons not named from classical mythology - its moons are named from works by Shakespeare and Alexander Pope."*

Science/Language Arts: Hand out Lesson 89 Science worksheet. Say, Scientists used to give every-thing in space a symbol. After time passed, they had to stop because they found too many things! Look at the symbols for the Sun, Moon and the planets. Read the words with the students. Instruct them to trace the symbols with their finger and to trace the dotted symbols with their pencil.

Review action rhyme "Reach for the Stars."

Phonics: Review the initial sound of Bb. Review the initial sound of Aa. Review letter recognition Aa-Zz.

Have the students brainstorm words that begin or include the letter Bb. Write these words on the board. Model the correct letter formation as you write the letters on the board. The students should practice forming the letter Bb on a blank sheet of paper. Students who are ready can practice copy-ing complete words from the board.

Do the Lesson 89 Phonics worksheet. The Sound of Bb. Review the letter sound with the picture and the word on the worksheet. Ask the students for other words that begin with the same sound. Trace the letters and say the sound of Bb. Observe the students as they trace the letters and help them with the letter strokes. If you have the students do one row at a time, the worksheet can be carried over to various parts of the day or another day.

Reading: Blend two parts of a compound word or two syllables. Represent "in written form," following an actual experience: directions for completing a recipe or craft, scientific observations of experiments, events.

Writing: For the remainder of the year the students should write their first name freehand. They should have their Name Plates to look at as they do this.

Writing Skill Builders: Keep these objectives in mind as you direct the class. Incorporate writing strokes wave, X, star, and zigzag line.

Memory Verse: Review Psalm 148:13. Review previous verses. Genesis 1:1, Genesis 1:3, Genesis 1:6, Genesis 1:10, I Peter 1:24-25, Genesis 8:22, Genesis 1:16, Psalm 90:12, Psalm 89:1 and Revelation 22:16. Before leaving the space scene started yesterday, review the memory verse several times. Talk about God's splendor and control being over ALL the heavens, everything in space.

Math: Review 1 + 1 = 2. Give each of the students 10 counters. Have them count the objects to make sure that they have 10 objects. Have them make 1 + 1 = 2 addition problems with the counters. Have them point to the counters and say, "one plus one equals two." The students should draw the plus and equal sign with their finger between the counters as they say the words. Can they make another problem with the counters that remain? How many counters are left after making the second problem?

Review the "I Am One" song.

Do the Lesson 89a Math worksheet. Addition 1 + 1 = 2. As the students trace the numbers have them say the addition problem.

Do the Lesson 89b Math worksheet. Match the analog clock to the o'clock time.

Sing the song "Hickory, Dickory, Dock" and move the hands of a clock to correspond to the verses. Clap instead of saying "tick, tock." Example: Hickory Dickory Dock, (clap) (clap)

Shapes: Review the oval shape. Make puzzles out of ovals made from construction paper by cutting them into pieces with jagged lines. Have the students put the puzzles together.

Do the Lesson 89 Shapes worksheet. The Sound of Bb Spiral maze.

Color: Review the colors red, green, blue, black, white, yellow, brown, pink, purple, orange, and gray.

Story Time: Read a story or stories of your choice.

Music: Review "He's Still Working On Me."

Multimedia Resources: This week, listen and sing along to selections from "The Amazing Book" CD.

Science/Arts & Crafts: Give the students black construction paper and white or silver glitter glue. Let the students draw with the glue, making a shooting star. After the glue is dry, let the students cut out around their shooting star. One more time, get out the Earth, Sun, Moon, stars and comets that you have made in past weeks. Lay them around the room, being sure the Earth, Sun and Moon are in correct relationship. Allow the students to be "shooting stars," zooming around "space." Have the students sit on the floor around the edge of their space map. Talk about each piece, reviewing all that has been learned in the past seven weeks. Talk about all that God made on the fourth day. Say, Tomorrow we will be hanging our crafted planets on the ceiling.

Physical Education: The planets are circles, as is the Earth. On concrete, place masking tape in the shape of a circle. Have students walk around the circle, stepping only on the tape. Now give them a ball. Standing on the outside of the circle, let the students bounce the ball to you with the ball bouncing inside the circle once. They may begin by using two hands, then go to one hand. Can they make the ball bounce twice within the circle? Are they capable of catching the ball as it bounces back from you using two hands? Continue this type of exercise through this week. Count the consecutive times a student catches the ball and can properly throw the ball.

NOTES:

*http://www.uwgb.edu/dutchs/planets/whatname.htm

Lesson 90

Week 18: Day 5

Activities in this Lesson: Bible Lesson, Science/Arts & Crafts, Phonics, Reading, Writing, Memory Verse, Math, Shapes, Color, Story Time, Music, Physical Education

Bible Reference: Genesis 1:16-18.

Bible Concept to Present: When God made the planets He placed them far, far, away from us. Our God is a VERY BIG God.

Bible Lesson: We have been studying about everything that God created on the fourth day of Creation. Can you tell me what God made on the fourth day of Creation? (Your goal is to have the students repeat the Sun, Moon, stars, comets, and planets.) I really like the way you have been listening and learning in school. Did you know that when God made the planets, He placed them very far away from each other? When we studied the Sun, we told you it would take very many years for you to get to the Sun. Some of the planets God made are even farther away from the Sun than the Earth is. The planets are in an order in the sky. Were we to pretend we were on the Sun, the planet that would be closest to us would be Mercury (Show the student's Lesson 90 Resource page, pointing to the planet you are referring to) next would be Venus, then Earth. Mars is beyond Earth, then Jupiter, Saturn, Uranus, and Neptune. Even though these planets are very far away from us and very far away from the Sun, God still was able to make all of them on one day. Our God is a great God. What is impossible for us, what we could never do, God does very easily. Could you have traveled that far in space to place a planet as far away as Neptune is? No, We couldn't, but God did. I'm glad I have such a wonderful, great God for my friend.

Science/Arts & Crafts: You should have your planets all ready to hang today. Review with the students the names of the planets and the size of each one. Using Lesson 90 Resource page as a guide, begin to hang the planets. Wrap the tip of the string around the thumbtack a couple of times so it will hold well. Then tack the string onto the ceiling. Begin in one corner with the Sun. Then place the balls at appropriate intervals from the Sun. Consider the type of ceiling you have beforehand. The balls should hang in the correct order for distance. Stress that this is a model of the planets. The planets are really much bigger, and much further between places. Refer to the pin which you placed into the Earth ball. Remind students that this tiny pin represents where we are. How big our universe is! Ask the following questions:

1. Find the Sun for me.
2. Find the largest planet. What is its name?
3. Find the planet Earth. How many planets are between us and the sun?
4. What is the name of the planet that has the ring around it?
5. What is the name of the planet that is the furthest away from us?
6. How many names of the planets can your student remember?

You will want to apply the knowledge that although God is so big, and He could make the planets to be so far away from us, He also loves us very much. Our God is worthy to be praised.

Phonics: Blend sounds of Bb and Aa. (ab, baa, bab) Review the initial sound of Bb. Review the initial sound of Aa. Review letter recognition Aa-Zz.

After a student learns to recognize some first letter sounds the next step is to begin to show the student that letter sounds can combine to make a word. Only two letter sounds have been covered but these two sounds can be combined to make words. Begin with *ba*. Say the sound of *b* then the sound of *a*, then combine the two to say *baa*. Make sure that you use a *short a* sound as in apple or alligator to say baa. Sing the song "Baa, Baa, Black Sheep" using the *short a* sound. Next add an ending *b* to the *ba* sound to say the word Bab. Repeat by pointing to the *ba* and saying the sound, then point to *baa* and say the word by combining the sounds.

Combine sounds to form words by following this procedure. Point under each letter and sound it out slowly – [B], then [a], then [b] – to make sure the students recognize each individual letter and know the sound. Then go back, point to each letter and read the sounds a little faster, giving each letter a longer sound than is normal, BBB-aaa-bbb. Finally, read the word without pausing between the sounds with yet a shorter sound for each letter. This should be quite close to the way the word should be read. Move your finger or pointer faster under the letters each time as you say the sounds faster.

To help with sounding individual letters write the words out twice as we have illustrated below. Words can be sorted into categories with common beginnings and endings to help illustrate the sounding out process. Explain that even though some words end in double letters we only say one sound.

b a	ba	a b	ab	
b a	baa	a b	ab	(like abs, stomach muscles)
B a b	Bab	B a b	Bab	(first name)

Do the Lesson 90a Phonics worksheet. Have the students put a circle around the Aa-Zz letters and an X on the numbers. Give them one direction at a time so they can focus on finding the correct shape.

Do the Lesson 90b Phonics worksheet. The Sound of Bb. Review the letter sound with the picture and words on the worksheet. Ask the students for other words that begin with the same sound. Trace the letters and say the sound of Bb. Observe the students as they trace the letters and help them with the letter strokes. If you have the students do one row at a time, the worksheet can be carried over to various parts of the day or another day.

Reading: Blend two parts of a compound word or two syllables. Represent "in written form," following an actual experience: directions for completing a recipe or craft, scientific observations of experiments, events.

Writing: For the remainder of the year the students should write their first name freehand. They should have their Name Plates to look at as they do this.

Do the Lesson 90 Writing worksheet, the loops worksheet. Demonstrate how to make the loops on the board by starting on the bottom left going across to the right, looping up and around in a big circle, and then moving across to the right. Have the students draw large loops in the air. Instruct the students to use a pencil and to follow the lines as closely as they can. Review pencil holding and writing techniques.

Writing Skill Builders: Keep these objectives in mind as you direct the class. Incorporate writing strokes wave, X, star, and zigzag line.

Memory Verse: Finish the verse for the week, Psalm 148:13. Congratulate students for all they have accomplished.

Math: Review 1 + 1 = 2. Use the Counting Beads to review 1 + 1 = 2. Have the students slide one bead to the end of the string. Say, "one bead plus one bead," have them slide another bead over, "equals," have them count the two beads slid over, "one, two, two beads." Do this on an abacus or with beads on a string or clothesline with them as you say the addition problem.

Do the Lesson 90a Math worksheet. Circle the correct number of objects to answer the addition problems. As the students trace the numbers have them say the addition problem.

Do the Lesson 90b Math worksheet. Count the number of objects in the box with the number 3. Trace the number 3. Count the number of diamonds in each tile. Circle the tile that has 3.

Review the "I Am One" song.

Sing the song "Hickory, Dickory, Dock" and move the hands of a clock to correspond to the verses.

Shapes: Teach the oval shape. Pass out plastic or hard boiled eggs and ping pong balls so that the students can feel the difference between the shapes.

Color: Review the colors red, green, blue, black, white, yellow, brown, pink, purple, orange, and gray.

Story Time: Read a story or stories of your student's choice or ones they have brought from home.

Music: Review "He's Still Working On Me."

Multimedia Resources: This week, listen and sing along to selections from "The Amazing Book" CD.

Physical Education: The planets are circles, as is the Earth. On concrete, place masking tape in the shape of a circle. Have students walk around the circle, stepping only on the tape. Now give them a ball. Standing on the outside of the circle, let the students bounce the ball to you with the ball bouncing inside the circle once. They may begin by using two hands, then go to one hand. Can they make the ball bounce twice within the circle? Are they capable of catching the ball as it bounces back from you using two hands? Continue this type of exercise through this week. Count the consecutive times a student catches the ball and can properly throw the ball.

NOTES:

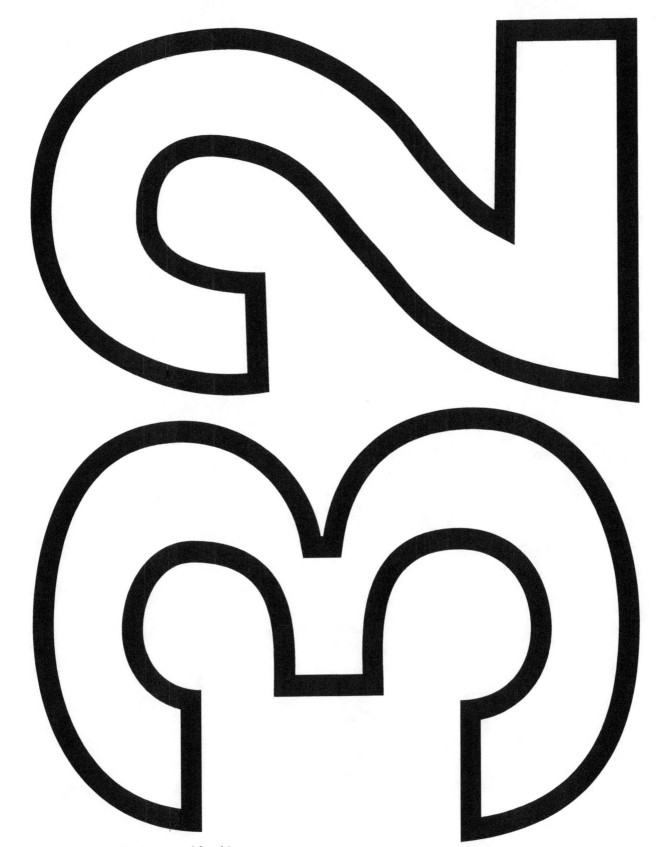

AOP's Commitment to Quality—Tell us how we are doing

As a publisher dedicated to providing high quality educational materials we invite you to tell us how we are doing. Please visit our website at www.aop.com to give us your comments, concerns, and/or compliments concerning Horizons Preschool. Contact information can be found in the support area for Horizons at the AOP website.

354